D1276751

Foundations of Special Education

CONTRIBUTORS

Louise H. Boothby, *University of South Florida*

Urie Bronfenbrenner, *Cornell University*

Jie-Qi Chen, *Erikson Institute for Advanced Study in Child Development*

Michael Churton, *University of South Florida*

Scot Danforth, *University of Missouri, St. Louis*

Albert J. Duchnowski, *University of South Florida*

Glen Dunlap, *University of South Florida*

Howard Gardner, *Harvard Graduate School of Education*

Steven R. Hooper, *University of North Carolina–Chapel Hill*

Kenneth R. Howe, *University of Colorado*

Lee Kern, *Children's Seahorse House*

Krista Kutash, *University of South Florida*

Carolyn Lavely, *University of South Florida*

Richard M. Lerner, *Boston College*

Kofi Marfo, *University of South Florida*

William C. Morse, *University of South Florida*

Sonia Nieto, *University of Massachusetts*

Nel Noddings, *Stanford University*

James L. Paul, *University of South Florida*

Hilda Rosselli-Kostoryz, *University of South Florida*

Lynda Stone, *University of North Carolina–Chapel Hill*

Daphne Thomas, *University of South Florida*

Julie Viens, *Harvard Graduate School of Education*

Edward Zigler, *Yale University*

Foundations of Special Education

BASIC KNOWLEDGE INFORMING RESEARCH AND PRACTICE IN SPECIAL EDUCATION

JAMES L. PAUL

MICHAEL CHURTON

HILDA ROSSELLI-KOSTORYZ

WILLIAM C. MORSE

KOFI MARFO

CAROLYN LAVELY

DAPHNE THOMAS

University of South Florida

Brooks/Cole Publishing Company

I(T)P® An International Thomson Publishing Company

Pacific Grove • Albany • Belmont • Bonn • Boston • Cincinnati • Detroit • Johannesburg • London
Madrid • Melbourne • Mexico City • New York • Paris • Singapore • Tokyo • Toronto • Washington

Sponsoring Editor: *Vicki Knight*
Marketing Team: *Jean Thompson and Deborah Petit*
Editorial Assistant: *Jana Garnett*
Production Coordinator: *Fiorella Ljunggren*
Production: *Scratchgravel Publishing Services*
Manuscript Editor: *Susan Pendleton*
Permissions: *Carline Haga*

Interior Design: *Anne and Greg Draus,*
    Scratchgravel Publishing Services
Cover Design: *Lisa Thompson*
Indexer: *James Minkin*
Typesetting: *Scratchgravel Publishing Services*
Cover Printing: *Lehigh Press*
Printing and Binding: *Quebecor Printing, Fairfield*

COPYRIGHT © 1997 by Brooks/Cole Publishing Company
A Division of International Thomson Publishing Inc.
I(T)P The ITP logo is a trademark under license.

For more information, contact:

BROOKS/COLE PUBLISHING COMPANY
511 Forest Lodge Road
Pacific Grove, CA 93950
USA

International Thomson Editores
Seneca 53
Col. Polanco
11560 México, D. F., México

International Thomson Publishing Europe
Berkshire House 168-173
High Holborn
London WC1V 7AA
England

International Thomson Publishing GmbH
Königswinterer Strasse 418
53227 Bonn
Germany

Thomas Nelson Australia
102 Dodds Street
South Melbourne, 3205
Victoria, Australia

International Thomson Publishing Asia
221 Henderson Road
#05-10 Henderson Building
Singapore 0315

Nelson Canada
1120 Birchmount Road
Scarborough, Ontario
Canada M1K 5G4

International Thomson Publishing Japan
Hirakawacho Kyowa Building, 3F
2-2-1 Hirakawacho
Chiyoda-ku, Tokyo 102
Japan

All rights reserved. No part of this work may be reproduced, stored in a retrieval system, or transcribed, in any form or by any means—electronic, mechanical, photocopying, recording, or otherwise—without the prior written permission of the publisher, Brooks/Cole Publishing Company, Pacific Grove, California 93950.

Printed in the United States of America

10 9 8 7 6 5 4 3 2 1

Library of Congress Cataloging-in-Publication Data
Foundations of special education : basic knowledge informing research
    and practice in special education / edited by James L. Paul . . . [et
    al.].
        p.   cm.
    Includes bibiliographical references and index.
    ISBN 0-534-34202-7 (alk. paper)
    1. Special education.   I. Paul, James L.
LC3965.F68   1997
371.9—dc21   96-39237
                                         CIP

BRIEF CONTENTS

FEB 27 1998

v

C O N T E N T S

PART II   **Learning, Development, and Intervention**   **85**

4 *Neuropsychology and Special Education:*
   Foundations, Applications, and
   Future Contributions   **92**
   Stephen R. Hooper

PART IV   **The Future of Special Education**   **229**

13   *Behavior Analysis and Its Relevance to Special Education*   279

Glen Dunlap and Lee Kern

PREFACE

This book was written as part of an intellectual experiment to define the knowledge foundations of special education in neuropsychology, cognitive psychology, developmental psychology, ecological psychology, philosophy, and ethics. In it, leading social scientists, neuroscientists, philosophers, and ethicists describe the current status of some of the knowledge considered relevant to understanding and providing services for children with disabilities and their families. The book also describes developmental, systems, and behavioral knowledge (drawn primarily from subdisciplines in psychology) that has shaped research, policy, and practice in the education of children with disabilities. The last chapter provides a postmodern critique of the essentially modern knowledge base of special education.

Foundations of Special Education is part of a project consisting of two volumes—one on foundational knowledge (this one) and the other on applied knowledge in special education. The goal of the present volume is to provide the knowledge foundation for the development of the applied-knowledge text, *Special Education Practice.* That text (1997, by Paul et al.), which is being published concurrently with this volume, integrates foundational knowledge with the practical input from policymakers, practitioners, parents, university faculty, and administrators in the field of special education.

The purpose of the project was to contribute to the integration of theory and practice across disciplinary lines, as well as to a substantive interdisciplinary discourse about special education. Among the basic assumptions on which this project rests, three are mentioned here. The first is that foundational knowledge can be distinguished from applied knowledge. Although this distinction is problematic in postmodern philosophy, as discussed in the last chapter of the book, it does seem appropriate in examining the knowledge base in special education, which is decidedly modern. The second assumption is that the applied research supporting special education policy and practice has become separated from the foundational discipline from which it grew—that is, psychology. There are various reasons for this separation, and they are discussed in the text. The third assumption is that special education research and practice, lacking the philosophical grounding of a discipline, will benefit from examining current perspectives and understandings of selected areas of knowledge in psychology and other relevant disciplines.

This project could not have been completed without an active and intensive collaboration involving several agencies and a large number of individuals who believed in our work. The leadership and staff of the Bureau of Student Services and Exceptional Education (BSSEE) in the Florida State Department of Education, which provided most of the funding, and the State Advisory Committee for Exceptional Student Education provided strong support for the project. Bettye Weir, Bureau Chief, believed in the value of the project and its potential contribution to the development of a more integrated knowledge base to support inclusion. She helped us shape the focus of the work and coordinate our efforts with policymakers and special education administrators in Florida. She also helped us relate our efforts to other states through state directors of special education. Doris Nabi, a senior staff member of the Bureau, and members of the Hillsborough County and Gulf Coast Florida Diagnostic and Learning Resources Systems provided invaluable assistance in planning and implementing the Vision 2000 Conference, which was instrumental in the development of this book and its companion volume.

Financial support for the Vision 2000 Conference was also provided by the Culverhouse Foundation at the Sarasota Campus of the University of South Florida. These funds were made available by Dean David Schenck, who supported the collaborative interdisciplinary agenda of the project and its goal of renewing the linkage of foundational and applied knowledge in special education. Faculty members, doctoral students, and support staff in the Department of Special Education at the University of South Florida made significant contributions to different phases of this project. Many of them served as facilitators of the dialogue sessions at the Vision Conference.

We are grateful for the strong support and patient guidance we received from all these individuals and agencies. From the very beginning it was clear that this project required the collective wisdom and energy of many people. We believed that the potential for making a substantial contribution to the field of special education depended on our ability to hear and learn from one another as we fashioned the plan for our work. The extent to which we have been able to identify and describe critical foundations of special education practice, policy, and research is a measure of our success in learning from all of our colleagues who participated in the project.

James L. Paul

INTRODUCTION

Foundational Knowledge and Special Education

JAMES L. PAUL AND KOFI MARFO
University of South Florida

The modern era of special education services dates back to approximately the middle of the 20th century. Since that time, many things have changed, including our understanding of children with disabilities, technical definitions of disabilities, classification systems, views of the role of families, curricula, assessment, professional standards, service delivery philosophy, the education of teachers, and the roles of professionals providing educational services. Children now have a right to a free appropriate education in the least restrictive alternative environment and benefit from other substantive and process provisions that were not established in law and public policy prior to 1975.

Our policies and educational approaches, which are based in part on available knowledge, have changed in response to the seismic shifts in culture, social and political philosophy, moral perspectives, and philosophy of care. These shifts have been accompanied and shaped by major changes in the economy and in the demographics of students attending school. All of these changes have profound effects on the field of special education and raise important questions about both the breadth and depth of the available knowledge that informs policy and practice in the field.

The development of this textbook represents a concerted effort not only to forge a better linkage between basic knowledge and applied research but also to stimulate dialogue about the implications of changing

Portions of the material presented in this book were developed by faculty in the Department of Special Education at the University of South Florida through a special project, Vision 2000, funded by the State of Florida, Department of Education, Division of Public Schools, Bureau of Student Services and Exceptional Education, through federal assistance under the Individuals with Disabilities Education Act (IDEA), Part B.

social and cultural dynamics of how we think about knowledge in general and foundational knowledge in particular. Special education practices and legislative mandates and policies are deeply entrenched in traditions and belief systems that are traceable to specific disciplinary and philosophical orientations. Consequently, no meaningful and lasting changes in special education practice can be effected without a corresponding quest to understand and rethink the philosophical, conceptual, and empirical foundations that inform the field.

As an applied field, special education draws its knowledge bases and research traditions from a variety of disciplines and subdisciplines. Reflections on these foundational sources of the special education knowledge base must necessarily be part of the dialogue about the future of the field. Such reflections are necessary for a variety of reasons. First, they help bring to the fore principal beliefs and assumptions that have informed the theoretical and empirical research literatures from which special education has drawn liberally for decades. Critical examination of such beliefs and assumptions should put us in a better position to assess their relevance, validity, and meaningfulness in the face of the indisputably complex challenges that the education of students with disabilities presents in contemporary society. Second, many disciplines are witnessing significant philosophical paradigm shifts, the net effect of which includes unprecedented pluralism in methodological approaches to inquiry. Being aware of and understanding these shifts are necessary to ensure that our approaches to inquiry stay abreast with current thinking in these disciplines. Indeed, it has been charged (rightly or wrongly) that one of the challenges facing educational research is its continued dependence on research paradigms, traditions, or analytic tools and assumptions that are no longer held sacred by the originating disciplines. In support of this criticism, developments in quantum mechanics are often cited to illustrate how paradigmatic shifts in one discipline (physics) have rendered almost obsolete significant aspects of a once-revered methodological tradition (namely, positivistic science) that remains the dominant paradigm in educational research today.

Perhaps, more important, to the extent that special education will continue to draw on other disciplines for basic knowledge about the mechanisms, processes, and contexts of children's development and learning, informed and reflective analyses of these knowledge bases are necessary. This must occur on an ongoing basis to ensure that our applications are based on the most current consensual understanding of the children who are at the heart of the special education enterprise. The chapters in this book offer students of special education a unique opportunity not only to acquaint themselves with some of the core foundational knowledge informing the field but also to appraise critically the assumptions and presuppositions undergirding this knowledge. The field will remain buoyant and relevant to the challenges of our times only to the extent that its practices and underlying knowledge bases continue to reflect a thorough appreciation of the changing dynamics of human society and the resultant diversification of values and cultural norms.

Reflections on Foundational Knowledge in Special Education

Foundational knowledge in special education is the knowledge that grounds and justifies public policy and practice. It includes empirical content as well as legal and moral perspectives, anthropologies of practices, and the multiple interpretations and reinterpretations of history. Social and political philosophies have been garnered in defense of special education as a publicly sanctioned professional practice. The field of special education was developed, and has been sustained, by foundational knowledge in the social, behavioral, and neurosciences. As it has grown, however, it has been guided by the applied research, beliefs, and interpretations of basic research by special educators. There has been no systematic link between the basic research of the social, behavioral, and neurosciences and the applied research of special educators. Furthermore, as the lines between the humanities and the social, behavioral, and neurosciences have blurred, there has been no mechanism to reflect the integration of science and areas of the humanities (such as art, history, literature, and ethics) that have relevance for contextualizing inquiry. This presents a particular challenge for special education because becoming a special education professional entails understanding the profound interaction of a disability and the professional and cultural contexts in which the disability is defined and addressed.

Additionally, efforts to develop foundational knowledge have focused more on empirical data than on broader humanistic and cultural foundations. This has created confusing and, at times, incoherent discourses. For example, professional practices (such as assessment) and policy perspectives (such as inclusion) have frequently been discussed as if they were technical issues that could be sufficiently addressed with adequate research. Much less attention has been given to ethical and contextual issues of professional practice and public policy development that require thoughtful and often highly contextualized deliberations. The uses of power in the complex politics of race, ethnicity, gender, disability, and social class, for example, may be obvious in the value-driven construction of public policy. But the use of power is less obvious, although no less real, in the construction of research and practice.

The incoherence of the discourse regarding special education practice and policy is not simply the creation of competing empirical, sociopolitical, and moral perspectives. Rather, the empirical arguments have become more complex as challenges to the assumptions of empiricism have become part of the discourse. Until slightly more than a decade ago, the question of the nature of knowledge in education and psychology was not perceived to be of major significance because the paradigm of positivism was so widely accepted. The consensus on positivism has changed. The traditional focus on generality and objectivity is now counterbalanced by a rapid growth of interest in local contexts, experience, and the practical value of understandings. This change has been increasingly reflected in education. For example, there has been a growing recognition of and respect for the knowledge that teachers use in the classroom, which has been increasingly recognized as a kind of local, special, or "craft" knowledge.

Today, fundamentally different paradigms of knowledge compete for primacy in educational arguments. The alternative perspectives of constructivist, critical, and postpositive paradigms of knowledge have strong implications for understanding the foundations of special education policy and practice. Although positivism continues to be the prevailing paradigm in fields such as educational psychology and special education, current research is now being grounded in alternative paradigms (Guba, 1990).

Certainly, the research base in special education has grown dramatically since mid-century. With that growth have come different perspectives on the nature of inquiry, producing a rich and diverse literature with important implications for policymakers and practitioners. The emerging literature in special education now reflects deep perspectival differences among educators. Policy disputes, such as the feasibility and desirability of full inclusion, are difficult to resolve because the quality of the available evidence is deemed to be disputable and conclusions reflecting "either-or" thinking are generally held to be inherently problematic. Another barrier to a consensus resolution of the policy debate stems from the multiple interpretations of data that rely heavily on paradigm-based assumptions and beliefs. Even the concept of "best practice," which seems so straightforward when viewed from a traditional perspective as validated knowledge, is disputed by those who, from a craft or social constructivist perspective, view knowledge as local.

One of the major challenges of special education, with regard to grounding research and reconciling major philosophical differences, is that it is not a discipline. Although it grew primarily out of the discipline of psychology and, to a less extent, out of medicine, special education has developed as a quasi-independent field of study and practice. There is a research base, however insufficient, for special education policy and practice. There is a codification of research and practice, and there is a cadre of educated and trained professionals who provide services, conduct and disseminate research, and educate and prepare other professionals. However, unlike disciplines such as psychology or sociology, special education research is not grounded in a philosophy of inquiry that is self-correcting.

Special education has relied extensively on the research methods of other disciplines. Until the last decade, the field had been driven primarily by the research methods of psychology. However, as the field has grown, researchers have, over time, referenced and built on the growing special education research base in an almost insular fashion. There has been very little connection between the research journals and professional activities (such as conferences) in special education with those of the foundational disciplines. The lamentable result of this is a progressive widening of the distance between the mostly applied research in special education and the basic and foundational knowledge of the primary disciplines. For example, although most of the research in special education is focused on the practical applications of developmental, systems, and behavioral knowledge, the research has not necessarily been guided by the changing philosophies and understandings in the related subdisciplines of psychology, such as developmental, ecological, and experimental psychology.

Ethics and Special Education as a Cultural Project

Although the field has a code of ethics and professional standards, it is not necessarily guided by the level of accountability established in many primary disciplines. This results in a lack of clarity about the ethical foundations of the field and a much wider band of tolerance for what constitutes "professional practice." As reflected in the literature, and in professional preparation programs, the ethics of teaching, policy making, and teacher education in special education have received relatively little attention. This is changing as indicated by a focus on ethics in a textbook on families and professionals (Turnbull & Turnbull, 1990), the recent publication of *Ethics and Special Education* by Howe and Miramontes (1992), and current research and training initiatives focusing on ethical policy making in local schools (Paul et al., 1997). All of these suggest a growing awareness of the need to develop a stronger ethical foundation for decision making in all aspects of special education policy and practice.

Special education is a cultural project with profound symbolic meaning and social functions. If the field has been found lacking in efficacy with respect to the achievement of students, it has been forgiven and thus maintained because of its presumed social good. The theories and rhetoric of the field reflect an innocence about the cultural role and the moral effects of the work of special educators. For example, special education professionals focus on the behavior, developmental characteristics, and dynamics of individual children, without real knowledge of the cultural traditions in which children live their lives. Pedagogy is rationalized with psychological principles, often without regard for variability in the values and ethnic traditions of students in the classroom. The school curriculum, for example, continues to reflect a primarily Euro-American content. Teacher preparation programs often relegate diversity to a special topic addressed in a course set apart from the rest of the curriculum. Teachers are trained in programs where the knowledge bases of positivism, the science of education, are equated with "real knowledge," and everything else is regarded as lesser folklore or practical wisdom. Teacher education curricula typically do not devote sufficient attention to the reality of racism, minimally challenge the values and beliefs of teachers, and include little or no content on ethical decision making.

Becoming a teacher involves internalizing the culture of teaching, societal constructions of learning, moral rules for behavior, and understandings of the roles of values, gender, and ethnic traditions of individuals in their learning. The reflective turn in teacher education clearly moves the point of focus closer to the person of the teacher as a believing, thinking, feeling, and moral person with a cultural history. However, neither the content provided for reflection in teacher education programs, nor the level of engagement with the sociocultural and moral perspectives of the student teacher, suggests that racism, sexism, ethnocentrism, classism, or linguicism will be abated in classrooms of the future (see Chapter 8 for the definition of linguicism and a discussion of these issues). Furthermore, in the internship, which is the most powerful preservice strategy for socializing teachers, local customs and practices are modeled and remembered. Neither a study of school culture nor ethical reflection on the dilemmas facing students, families, teachers, administrators, and pupil services personnel is necessarily a part of this important experience.

The cultural functions of special education in the context of general education and in the society must be acknowledged and addressed affirmatively with sensitivity to basic transcultural moral principles. In addition to reconnecting the knowledge base with the knowledge and research philosophies of primary disciplines, it is also essential to undergird special education policies and practices with moral principles that protect the integrity of all who are affected.

Perspective Informing This Text

Written in the context of deep changes in science and culture at the end of the 20th century (and important shifts in economic and political priorities over the past two decades), the chapters in this text focus on the knowledge and ethical foundations of special education policy and practice. Five general considerations guided the development of the material presented here. First, research guiding special education policy and practice has been generated and interpreted in a paradigm tradition, logical empiricism, that has changed substantially. Regardless, whether or not one considers the change to be a shift away from the empiricist or positivist tradition and an expansion of the boundaries of the traditional view of research, as Reid, Robinson, and Bunsen (1995) have suggested, it is difficult to set aside the epistemological debate in science as unimportant to our critical understanding of the knowledge base(s) of special education. An important assumption of this text is that research and practice in special education will be advanced by an informed and continuing dialogue in which alternative epistemological traditions are respected and the research potential of those traditions exploited in collaborative research communities (Kromery, Hines, Paul, & Rosselli, 1997).

Second, research in special education has developed to the point where it relies primarily on knowledge bases developed within the field by an established community of researchers. Although this research advances the field in important ways, much of it is not systematically grounded in, or necessarily informed by, established knowledge or emerging paradigm shifts in primary disciplines in the humanities and social sciences. Thus, another key assumption of the present text is that not only should the emergent knowledge base within special education build on the current knowledge bases of primary disciplines, but, perhaps more important, it should reflect and take better advantage of changing approaches to inquiry in other fields.

Third, special education practices—in which children are set apart for their differences from their age peers (whether or not they are removed from the general education classroom) and public resources are disproportionately allocated to meet their needs—raise fundamental ethical issues regarding the relative interests of all who are affected by those practices. Special education policies and instructional practices must be grounded in the most thoughtful formulation of basic moral principles that accord respect and care to the interests of all children, including the particular interests of children with disabilities and their families. Further, the interests of educators and other professionals who provide services and the missions of the institutions in which those services are provided must also be considered. Whereas there appears to be consensus that the field of special education is challenged by many unresolved ethical dilemmas, the study of ethics and the systematic application of ethical reasoning to clinical and policy problems continue to receive very little attention among researchers, teacher educators, and educational leaders. A key perspective informing this text, therefore, is that all aspects of professional practice in special education, whether in the classroom or in the boardroom, need to be infused with sensitivity to ethical considerations. Consequently, professional preparation at all levels must emphasize sensitivity to the ethical challenges of the field, while providing opportunities for professionals to develop competence in making ethically defensible decisions.

Fourth, contemporary special education has been developed as a professional area of practice in the social context of the last half of the 20th century. Unfortunately, even with positive values underlying public policy supporting special education (such as guaranteeing a free, appropriate public education for all children in the least restrictive environment), the tacit caretaking agenda of special education practice has acquired substantial negative cultural baggage over the years. Racism, sexism, classism, and other culture-based biases that shape the rules for participation in normative, or mainstream, activity have been, arguably, amplified in special education as a service delivery system dedicated to the education of children who, historically, have been understood to be deficient. The deficit model has guided the social construction of disability from the beginning of the field of special education. Fundamental ethical issues are associated with the construction of disability and with the unequal distribution of resources and power structures that serve either to include or to exclude children from the mainstream of school life. Special education services cannot be adequately understood apart from the political culture and moral philosophies in which they are embedded in schools. An assumption in this text is that a careful cultural analysis of the language, images, activities, and the moral and social ecologies of special education is essential to the integrity of the field.

Fifth, as a society we have focused on the individual and her or his merits or demerits. "Rugged" individualism is a part of the American tradition. A great deal of the rationale for a curriculum for children with disabilities, as well as others, concerns individual differences. Professional special educators have a checkered past in their views of parents and in their willingness to involve parents as partners in understanding and teaching their children. Since 1975 the law has guaranteed parents a role in making decisions about the education of their children. However, only recently have special educators begun to see children with disabilities as members of families who need to be involved in developing more systemic responses to improve the likelihood of success for the children. An assumption underlying this text is that the family systems context is an essential dimension of understanding and meeting the needs of children with disabilities.

These five considerations guided the selection of topics presented here. They reflect, we believe, both the highest values in the field at the present time and the areas in greatest need of attention. In some areas, such as the focus on families, the current literature seems to be clear and consistent. In other areas, such as interest in epistemology and ethics, the literature is less clear and certainly does not reflect a consensus of professional opinion. Most of the chapters that follow are prepared by leading social and neuroscientists, philosophers, and ethicists whose scholarship centers on one or more of these fundamental areas. By focusing on knowledge bases in primary disciplines, we emphasize a broad picture of the philosophical, ethical, and empirical foundations of special education. By inviting recognized scholars who are not in the field of special education to write most of the chapters, we hope to present cogent and valid accounts of the different foundational areas without the familiar voice of a special educator interpreting the knowledge within the traditional philosophical rubrics of special education. The last section, written by researchers in special education, provides an integrative and critical, if familiar, voice to the text.

The assumptions of this text are those of the editors who are the architects of this knowledge project. The individual chapter authors may or may not agree with all of these assumptions or with the general perspective within which the assumptions are embedded. However, these assumptions guided the selection of the topics and the authors and reflect the philosophical stance of the editors.

References

Guba, E. (Ed.). (1990). *The paradigm dialog.* Newbury Park, CA: Sage.

Howe, K., & Miramontes, O. (1992). *The ethics of special education.* New York: Teachers College Press.

Kromery, J., Hines, C., Paul, J., & Rosselli, H. (1997). Creating and using a knowledge base for restructuring teacher education in special education: Technical and philosophical issues. *Teacher Education in Special Education.*

Paul, J., Berger, N., Osnes, P., Martinez, Y., & Morse, W. (1997). *Ethical decision making in schools: Inclusion, policy, and reform.* Baltimore, MD: Paul Brooks Publishers.

Reid, D., Robinson, S., & Bunsen, T. (1995). Empiricism and beyond: Expanding the boundaries of special education. *Remedial and Special Education, 16,* 131–141.

Turnbull, A., & Turnbull, H. (1990). *Families, professionals, and exceptionality: A special partnership* (2nd ed.). New York: Macmillan.

CHAPTER 1

The Role of Basic Knowledge and the Future of Special Education

WILLIAM C. MORSE, JAMES L. PAUL, AND HILDA ROSSELLI-KOSTORYZ
University of South Florida

The field of special education is experiencing profound changes that will alter the nature of the work of special educators in the future. Although the field has always been dynamic and sensitive to shifts in political and economic environments, changes in the 1990s are likely to be the most substantial since those of the 1960s, when the modern era of special education began. Changes in special education are political and philosophical extensions of the broader reform of public education.

In addition to reflecting the economic realities and political *zeitgeist* of the last decade, the current reform of general and special education also reflects deeper changes in culture, philosophy, and science. These changes form the broad social, cultural, and political contexts for this text.

A Deeper Reform

Throughout the history of special education there have been reforms and advocates for needed changes, some perhaps more reasoned and better grounded than others. Regardless, these changes have reflected the values and understandings of the day, created out of contexts that change. For example, only thirty years ago there was a continuing debate about whether "trainable mentally retarded children" should receive an education since, by

definition, they were not educable. Perhaps thirty years from now the current debates about diversity, holism, care, constructivism, and the power of contexts may seem equally unfathomable.

During the 1980s there was, as there always seems to be, a great deal of discussion about definitions. Gross variability in prevalence estimates continued in large part as a result of imprecise definitions, and professionals continued to work hard to develop definitions that could be operationalized in research and practice. Labeling, always a necessary but objectionable reality for professionals, received renewed attention in spite of its lack of clinical or instructional utility. Professionals persevered in an effort to accommodate legitimate interests in developing the most appropriate and useful labels for generating revenue while attempting to minimize the social cost to students.

Since the inception of special education there have existed continuing differences among special educators with respect to philosophy of assessment, instructional methods, curriculum, discipline, teacher education, and other issues relevant to the education of children with disabilities. One of the most divisive issues, however, has been the development and implementation of an inclusion policy, which is special education's part of school reform.

During the 1990s, policy debates about inclusion have polarized both parents and the special education professional community. The current debates stand on the political and philosophical shoulders of earlier arguments about where and how to provide appropriate educational services for students with disabilities. During the 1960s, the focus was on the efficacy of special education; in the 1970s, reform shifted to mainstreaming; in the 1980s, the focus was on the regular education initiative; and in the 1990s, discussions have centered on the inclusion policy.

Now, as in the past, positions are passionately held. There are appeals to reason ("It is practical"), research ("The data support our position"), moral imperatives ("It is the right thing to do"), and law ("Children have a right"). The difficulty is that both sides of the policy argument appeal to the same principles. There are practical challenges for both positions: the research is neither consistent nor clear, there are legitimate moral claims supporting and opposing inclusion, and children have a right to a "free appropriate education in the least restrictive environment." However, interpreting that right in the context of the values and educational practices in a local school has proved to be rather difficult. Both those who support and those who resist the inclusion policy argue about the data, fairness, equality of opportunity, justice, and care. The debates are familiar. Many of the issues and arguments have appeared in the professional literature since the early 1960s. The political contexts and the advocates change, but many of the philosophical and moral dilemmas remain like old garments altered to embody new rhetorics.

Discussions of different policy perspectives are often acrimonious (Reid, Robinson, & Bunsen, 1995). This has been true for those participating in the inclusion debate who have so much at stake in the outcome. Whereas some arguments have the ring of political rhetoric, others are cast more as social science. Yet neither the moral argument nor the empirical argument appears sufficient to support either of the policy positions. As a result, special educators are left trying to advance the most thoughtful and most defensible positions they can as advocates and as professionals.

Policy arguments are typically considered well reasoned and empirically based or dismissed as political rhetoric. The same arguments can be viewed as "sound" by some and as empty rhetoric by others, depending on who places the "spin" or interpretation on the argument. This is not totally self-serving and it is not thought to be dishonest by those who place the spin. Rather, interpretations of data that appear to support the policy positions are predicated on assumptions about the nature of knowledge and rules of inference. Historically, there has been an innocence about "data" and the assumptions of the positivist epistemology that grounds the definition, analysis, and interpretation of data. That is, it has been regarded as amoral, as if reason transcended individual self-interests and objective data were collected and interpreted independent of the values of the researcher.

Analytic philosophy has dominated the philosophy of education in the United States since the 1950s, and logical empiricism has been the prevailing philosophy of research. Fundamental assumptions about reality as external to the observer, measurable, predictable, and generalizable, and the perception that the scientific lens through which that reality is viewed is value-free, have characterized the logical empiricist, or positivist, tradition. Positivist and functionalist assumptions have provided the context within which questions have been framed and addressed. Perhaps the reasons we have been unable to reach a consensus on definitions, labels, a system of identification, a philosophy of service delivery, or an approach to assessment are more basic than we have acknowledged. There are many who now argue that the difficulty is in the intellectual framework or paradigm within which we have been working; that is, in the closed and deterministic system that has framed the debates, structured the arguments, and provided the rules for evidence.

Although there have been debates about theory since the beginning of special education, alternative paradigms were not a part of the discussion until the early to mid-1980s. Since that time the conversation has become more interesting and complex. Now there is a growing number of special educators articulating constructive and critical alternatives to the traditional positivism that grounded research in education and shaped the discourse about professional issues (Danforth, 1995; Heshusius, 1982; Paul, Epanchin, Rosselli-Kostoryz, & Duchnowski, 1996). Alternative paradigms are providing various epistemological contexts within which to consider disability and difference, education and care, power and teaching, and learning and knowledge. Beginning with various assumptions and rhetorics for both reality and rationality, we will almost certainly end up with different understandings and conclusions.

As the paradigm dialogue continues within and between disciplines, a major challenge to researchers and policymakers is to avoid replacing one limiting view with another. The history of special education is replete with examples of extreme swings during which important content and perspectives were lost. This was illustrated during the late 1960s when the field shifted dramatically to behavioral philosophy and disregarded developmental knowledge. The current risk is that of exchanging the certainty hypothesis of one paradigm with an epistemological and ethical relativism that treats all knowledge as local and fails to develop standards to ensure accountability for both knowledge and moral claims.

Accompanying the ongoing discourse on knowledge is a more explicit interest in ethics and ethical reasoning associated with public policy and professional practice than in earlier periods. The research agenda is no longer advocated solely by those who simply want more data addressing a particular area of interest but also by those who seek support for different genres of inquiry to respond to the kinds of questions now being asked.

An increased focus on contexts is beginning to balance attention given to individual variability. The quantifiable differences between populations that have been so important in defending assessment, placement, and service delivery systems are now being examined from perspectives that focus more on the defining powers and moral features of contexts. The heterogeneity within groups identified for special education services, long acknowledged as a reality, may be evidence that neither the classification system nor the measurement philosophy is serving the intended purpose.

Diversity is being viewed more as a reality to be valued and appreciated for its contribution to an expanding universe of possible understandings rather than as a variable to be fit into models to describe and make predictions about a univariate reality. Complexity is being regarded more as the nature of things and as an appropriate focus for management rather than as a problem lacking imaginative solutions. Both diversity and complexity are finding a more substantial place in the consciousness of managers, practitioners, and researchers. This perspective is roughly analogous to Heisenberg's (1962) principle of complimentarity.

As illustrated, the current reform of special education is deeper and vastly different from reforms in the past. Even familiar words and concepts, such as inquiry and knowledge, have unfamiliar meanings. The sociology of knowledge has changed, the traditional hegemony of logical empiricism is loosening and giving way to alternative epistemologies, and moral perspectives used to articulate and defend practice are beginning to be more consciously and critically assessed. A primary assumption of this book is that the paradigm debate is important and vital to the future of special education.

An epistemological pluralism is essential in matching the increasingly complex needs for knowledge with the emerging philosophies of inquiry and care. The difficulty has rested in the political hegemony that has kept inquiry constrained to a single paradigm that lacks the ability to address many questions central to the understanding of how to provide a free and appropriate education for all children. The editors of this book believe that the renewal of both general and special education will occur, in part, as both reclaim the moral and artistic roots of care and accept alternative constructions of the scientific and technical foundations of child development, learning, and organizations.

Knowledge to Practice

Responding to these exciting and unsettling prospects for the future of special education, the Florida State Bureau of Exceptional Student Education and the University of South Florida Department of Special Education supported a philosophical project aimed at integrating knowledge, practice, and policy development. To that end, this book includes commissioned knowledge-based papers authored by nationally recognized scholars writing on topics of relevance to the future of education and particularly special education. These scholars developed seminal papers representing the current status of knowledge and wisdom in different disciplines in the social and neurosciences, philosophy, and ethics. These knowledge-based papers provide a context within which to critically assess current research on educational practice. These papers were later matched by a set of practitioner papers on critical issues in special education that were also commissioned from nationally recognized experts in special education.

The applied papers were read by a group of special educators, policymakers, parents, and teacher educators in special education who spent two days

at a dialogue conference reacting to the papers and sharing their ideas with the authors of the applied papers. The authors then used both the knowledge papers and the ideas from the dialogue conference to prepare the final draft of the applied papers. These revised papers on specific issues in special education have been published in a separate volume, *Special Education Practice: Applying the Knowledge, Affirming the Values, and Creating the Future* (Paul et al., 1997).

The present volume on knowledge in the social and neurosciences, ethics, and philosophy makes no pretense of covering all the areas that have implications for special education. Rather, the authors examine selected areas that have a direct bearing on the future of special education. For the special educator and general educator alike, many of the ideas challenge outmoded concepts, slogans, and generalized images that have shaped policies and practices in the past.

Embracing a Context of Change

Examination of the knowledge informing research and practice comes at a time of significant change in the United States, a time that has been characterized as the end of an epoch and a time of chaos. A primary motivation for the accelerated change is the competition for increasingly limited resources, especially among agencies dependent on public money for operation. The values that underlie educational policy decisions are being challenged and changed. On one hand, the inclination is to make schools more efficient and focused, with the job of teachers being limited to teaching knowledge and skills. On the other hand, from a needs perspective, the recognition is that many pupils require additional services from agencies attached to or even provided by comprehensive or full-service schools.

The shift of funding from the federal government to individual states and localities in block grants may move decision making to the local level but with reduced resources. Narrowing education's focus to only knowledge and skills appears to have considerable public support at the present time, as reflected in the deep cost-cutting measures being taken in education and social services at both the state and federal level. Special education, which emphasizes individualized needs-based instruction, is more expensive than general education and it, too, will lose resources in the budget reductions now underway.

In addition to the economic realities driving the reduction of funding for education and social service programs, there is also a widespread feeling that public institutions are not effective in doing what they are paid to do. This is reminiscent of the crisis of confidence in public institutions witnessed during the 1960s. The feeling is that government is failing, schools are failing, social service agencies are not serving their clients well, and so on. The "things are not working" slogan fuels the passion for change and budget reductions but it ignores those elements that *are* working. It also demoralizes professionals who are doing a good job and services that are working. Mistrust and criticism of social institutions produces a demand that those social institutions change. Changes are effected in a political process fueled by the values and *zeitgeist* of the day.

Values such as efficiency and cost savings appear to be dominant at the present time. Neither the social good nor the science supporting the practice is sufficient to drive public policy. The idea that values drive policy rather than research is not new. However, the values driving social policy at the present time, if one examines the nature of the cuts in spending, do not appear to include research. Although support for applied research in special education has always been meager, threats to funding raise a serious question of whether knowledge-based practice is valued at all.

When something appears not to be working well, questions are raised about the purpose and goals of the service itself. As we approach the end of the 20th century, there are conflicting views regarding the goals of public education as well as renewed interest in the relationship between schools and society in general. There is tension among policymakers, with some emphasizing the school's responsibility for meeting the increasingly complex needs of all children and families and others focusing more exclusively on the school's responsibility for teaching academic subjects and skills. Special education, with legal and policy mandated responsibility for meeting the needs of many of the children most in crisis, is in the center of this tension.

Another motivator for change at the present time comes from the widespread fear that there is an overall decline in public and private standards of behavior. The daily news could convince anyone that this decline is real. Social norms have declined to the level that the social contract that undergirds a democratic society seems endangered. Unethical behavior shows up in all strata and areas of society. Violence continues to curtail individual freedom and civil rights. Quick fixes are implemented but many fear there is no way to slow the apparent moral decline. Prisons are full and there is public support to build more. At the same time there does not appear to be comparable support to increase funding for education. Families and schools continue to be easy targets for scapegoating by social critics.

Given the destabilizing consequences of budget cuts, ethical issues, anxiety about the future, and the policy changes just discussed, a plethora of educational changes can be anticipated. The changes will be complex and will impact both general and special education. What follows is a discussion of the critical knowledge contained in the chapters of this book that will need to be considered by special educators as the field moves through the rapid transition that appears to characterize the 1990s. What is presented by the scholars in these chapters is not so much knowledge to support special education practice in the future; rather, it is the current formulation of selected foundational areas of knowledge in which applied research and practice in special education have been based. The following chapters also include some of the moral and technical features of the changes that are shaping the policy development process.

Challenges of New Philosophical and Ethical Understandings

We are facing drastically different parameters for "mind work" and "feeling work." Stone (Chapter 2) traces major philosophical movements and describes the radical changes stemming from the revolution in quantum physics. She indicates that paradigm shifts come slowly and multiple ways of thinking, even incompatible ones, are utilized during the process of change. Stone notes that the post modern paradigm is penetrating science and art as well as research and practice. It eschews the positivist search for certainty for a relativist frame of reference where multiple and diverse views are accepted and valued. Chaos is prevented by discourse leading to shared meanings with the overriding goal being a better life for all. Antiprivilege and member empowerment provide an ethical base for collaboration.

Danforth (Chapter 14) carries the postmodern argument further in challenging rationality and the foundations for modernist conceptions of knowledge. Postmodernism envisions a different type of education with teachers becoming constructors or co-constructors and interpreters of practice. Disability, as with gender, ethnicity, and social class, is understood to be constructed in contexts sensitive to "othering" and privileged status. Deficit-laden language and concepts are replaced by a positive value of diversity. The inclusion policy in a postmodern context emphasizes a different understanding of education rather than simply changing the educational placement of a child. Collaboration, shared responsibility, learning communities, and vision are among the central features of this view of education.

One of the most powerful and useful perspectives now being recognized in the social sciences is narrative, a familiar and ancient view of knowledge in the humanities. The storied nature of both general and special education becomes more evident as professional educators attempt to maintain the traditions that fit the stories they believe they are in and the roles they believe they are playing. Policymakers struggle to reconcile the story of education they know and learned in a different cultural, political, epistemological, and moral context with the apparent dysfunctionality and inefficacy of many traditional practices. Basic reform aimed at integrating general and special education will require a common story for educating all children that is sufficiently compelling to override the self-sustaining habits and traditions of both. A new story must account for the diversity of our experience of the world as well as new understandings of knowledge and the imaginative capacity of the postmodern mind. In the 21st century a new story must transcend and replace the traditional behavioral and technocratic picture of schooling with images that integrate child-rearing and education in the development of human potential with sustainable values. The narrative must reflect the diversity of human communities and individual differences, as well as make provision for alternative forms of knowledge and ways of knowing.

Increased attention to the philosophical and ethical aspects of special education has been stimulated by a scrutiny of the value of the proposed governmental changes and by the concern about the general state of ethical behavior in society. Howe (Chapter 10) presents the challenge of making ethical decisions in special education from various perspectives. He compares three currently dominant philosophical positions in American thinking: utilitarianism, which accords equal weight to everyone's benefit; libertarianism, in which individual freedom is the dominant premise; and liberal egalitarianism, committed equally to liberty and equality. Howe sees educational ethics as concerned with the kind of citizens schools should develop and the methods that would be appropriate. He argues that teachers and students should be able to engage as equals in the political processes that shape their lives.

These philosophical chapters challenge the imagination and stance of those who are responsible for and participate in the process of educational change. It is in this complex context of differences regarding the vision of the future that the story of special education for the 21st century is being created.

Recognizing the Implications of Fundamental Changes in Major Institutions

Today there are many different images of the American family that challenge the schools' assumptions and practices in collaboration. Similarly, the world of work has changed and schools must prepare youth for a world that is unfamiliar to many educators. Schools, families, and other social institutions are being simultaneously restructured by external events in our society. Acknowledging change is not enough. Examining the less obvious implications is part of how education will reinvent itself. Several of the chapters address the nature and complexity of the American family.

Of the three major institutions culturally designated to serve children (family, school, and church), the family is recognized as the most essential. Although school and home have a history of uneasy relationships, the necessity of close collaboration between the two is not debated. Bronfenbrenner (Chapter 3) makes a thorough ex-

amination of the current status of the family with implications for the lives of children. The traditional family function has been eroded by interactions of poverty, divorce, gender, and the new work world. From a concise review of the research in various areas, we confirm that one of our most essential child-rearing institutions is in serious trouble. When the family is in trouble, the trouble spreads to community agencies where the presented needs change, especially in schools. The consequences of various family policies are well documented. Bronfenbrenner notes that, although the research concentrates on family disarray, attention might best be turned to the study of ecologies that can strengthen the family.

In the policy arguments about who should do what to help children beyond the family, the obvious focus is on the schools and the traditional versus full-service schools debate mentioned earlier. Troubled families increase the likelihood of troubled children in the schools. Special education is at the vortex of the policy and moral debate on who is responsible. Children designated as "special," those with identifiable disabilities, are but a small part of the larger child population now deemed at risk, and school restructuring has to include attention to the welfare of all students. Gallagher (1997) points out that education by itself is a weak treatment, a "blunt instrument" for effecting the changes we seek to make. He estimates that school probably accounts for less than a quarter of whatever outcome we are after, be it academic or social behavior.

Duchnowski and Kutash (Chapter 11) present a current perspective on how to support families through service integration. The history of such efforts is reviewed before presenting the evidence for the best of current practice. These authors remind us that collaboration is not optional; collaboration is essential for survival. No one argues the rationality of collaboration, but the experiences of the authors emphasize the difficulties of actual accomplishment in a community. Realistically, fragmented support will not suffice for families and their children, as illustrated in later discussions of early intervention.

Zigler (Chapter 6) is a recognized authority on the promise of early intervention, especially for children in poverty. Political support and optimism have ebbed and flowed since the l960s with the birth of Head Start. The emphasis has changed from the early focus on cognitive and intellectual factors to the concept of attending to the stimulation of the whole child. Zigler reviews the successes and failures of early intervention efforts and argues that programs must be comprehensive, although few are. The suggested target is the whole family system, which requires the collaboration described by Duchnowski and Kutash (Chapter 11). Furthermore, Zigler offers considerable emphasis on the need for continuity from preschool to school in order to prevent any loss of gains made in the early years.

The holistic nature and interdependent complexities of our work are becoming increasingly evident. Education and special education succeed or fail, in part, as other agencies are effective in supporting families. Although it is easy enough to recognize this reality, it is more difficult to change familiar policies and practices to reflect that understanding.

Appreciating the Impact of Newly Emerging Ideological Concepts

There are currently many ideological challenges to common understandings about ourselves, our relationships, and our world. One of those challenges is coming to grips with the holistic nature and interdependence of our global world. What happens anywhere sends ripples or even waves throughout the world, but the decisions made in the United States have the greatest impact on the rest of the world. A common example used to il-

lustrate this point compares the world to a village of 1000 people in which only 70 are U.S. citizens. These 70 citizens, however, receive half of the village's income and control over half of the village's resources. The breadth and depth of our own power and its resulting responsibilities runs counter to our sense of individualism. This sense of individualism supports the belief that, within the limit of the law, individuals should have unlimited freedom to shape their own destinies without particular regard for larger contexts or consequences. In schools, students are taught about interrelatedness as a fact of life and a positive regard for differences is promoted as a value, but a real appreciation for the implications of this perspective comes from a different way of "seeing," which often is not modeled for students in their classrooms or communities.

Another challenge involves conflicting philosophies of individual differences and community. The presence of a diverse student population in a democratic society requires teachers, instructors, parents, and policymakers to establish an explicit moral agenda in a diverse democratic society. Schools are required to be equitable, excellent, and relevant to the needs of our society.

Another area now being rethought involves the enfranchisement of new groups and the accompanying changes in the power structure. Special education has undergone such a change in the distribution of power resulting from both legal and policy support for the participation of parents in decisions related to their children's education. Meanwhile, general education is attempting to assimilate a new organizational philosophy where authority previously held in state and district offices is shifted to local schools. These types of ideological changes require a transformation of thinking and patterns of behavior.

Several of the chapters in this book deal with aspects of individual differences and changes in attribution of given behaviors to biological or environmental factors over time. In addition to the chapters on basic knowledge in the social and neurosciences, ethics, and philosophy, the chapters on systems (Duchnowski and Kutash), behavioral (Dunlap and Kern), and developmental (Marfo and Boothby) knowledge foundations of special education clearly illustrate how attributional thinking has been divided in the literature that guides special education policy and practice.

Progress in the biological aspects of behavior has been spectacular, far beyond the scope of this book. Hooper (Chapter 4) focuses on the subspecialty of child neuropsychology. As Public Law 94-142 directs more attention to children with a variety of neurological disabilities and more and more children survive severe limitations as a result of advanced medical care, special education can expect additional enrollment of these students. The relationship to learning disabilities is clear and apparent in Hooper's account of the history of that field. At the present time attention is being paid to the ecological validity of assessment, matching test results with everyday functioning as well as providing initial guidance and monitoring techniques related to specific intervention strategies. As a result of the advances discussed, Hooper supports more thorough training of special educators in assessment and treatment approaches.

Yet another ideological revolution is presented in Viens, Chen, and Gardner's discussion of traditional and contemporary views of intelligence (Chapter 5). Our views of intelligence have had a tremendous impact on educational practice and policy. Also in this area, the sacredness of a pyschometric perspective has been substantially challenged. Important to professionals in special education is not simply the measurement and numerical ranking of a student's intellectual functioning but rather a clearer understanding of how intelligence develops and its applicability in the real world. The traditional view of intelligence as a single factor has limited the range of potential human abilities primarily to areas of accomplishment most valued by schools (namely, the mathematical, logical, and linguistic areas), thus ignoring many accomplishments valued in non-Western cultures.

Gardner (1983), in his own seminal theory of multiple intelligences, has clearly sought to accord merit to roles and abilities valued across cultures and environments. His view of intelligence holds promise for those students in special education who have been unfavorably labeled as a result of pychometric testing. Gardner's claim that traditional means of testing for intelligence are neither culture-fair nor intelligence-fair also uncovers rich and numerous implications for special education.

One of the most significant ideological changes that should be incorporated in restructuring in order to balance the traditional emphasis on achievement is the concept of caring, such as that developed in feminist psychology. The absence of an explicit ethic of care in schools and social service systems has been the focus of a great deal of literature in education, special education, philosophy, social work, nursing, and other related areas. During the past decade, caring has become a part of the new understanding of families and the role of schools and social service agencies. Yet, to make schools authentic caring communities where differences are valued will require a reassessment of many well-entrenched beliefs about the role of schools and how they should work.

An indicator of the lack of a culture of care in school is the increasing focus on alienation, a term that used to be relegated to a few adolescents. Now seen as rootlessness and the struggle to regain a sense of attachment in an increasingly diffuse social environment, alienation is part of the current struggle in the construction of self. For many persons the feeling of detachment, of not being a part of any group, prevents the development of a positive sense of self as one who belongs. To counteract this emptiness, there is a desire for affiliation through outgroups such as gangs for adolescents. The challenge for schools is to become the caring community being sought by youth.

Lerner (Chapter 7) documents this serious crisis in youth development from a slightly different perspective and argues that we will have to adopt new approaches because current methods are not working. Part of the failure is attributed to the lack of research on youth as a developmental period in the context of families, neighborhoods, society, and culture. Evaluative efforts should be collaborative and contextualized to reflect the changing relationships between individuals and their ecology; thus, youth are full participants in Lerner's research. His research, which indicates that high-risk behaviors are highly interrelated, reinforces the need for agency collaboration and a holistic thrust to change systems rather than concentrating energy on changing individuals.

Our increasing national diversity is easy to state but complex to appreciate in its many nuances. Nieto (Chapter 8) moves directly into implications for education and chides colleges of education for accepting the role of schools as agents of assimilation. Teacher education curricula need restructuring to accommodate diversity, by which she means the range of differences that stem from race, ethnicity, gender, social class, ability, and language. Elitist notions have prevented schools and teacher educators from addressing authentic diversity. The goal now is to produce better teachers for the diverse student populations we already have and to be prepared for the changes that will take place in many more schools where the majority-minority picture is being reversed. Nieto's insights are especially pertinent for special education, where minority overrepresentation has raised serious ethical and legal questions about special education policies and practices.

Another fundamental policy issue with clear ethical implications involves gender discrimination. Women have been denied equality and the potential of their special contributions to human welfare has been ignored the world over except for Native American and African American women who have held responsible and respected roles. Noddings (Chapter 9) presents a historical account of the discrimination before exposing how it plays out in the schools where differential gender treatment is rampant in classrooms. Boys receive more attention and are socialized in different ways than girls, who are expected to mute their aspirations. Noddings advocates counseling for both boys and girls, to understand the cultural constructions of gender roles. Substantial parts of the culture traditionally assigned to women, such as child-rearing and connected moral reasoning, should have a valued place in the curriculum.

Many of the chapters in this book reinforce the earlier statement that we are in a time of great changes, the end of an epoch. There are many changes that hold promise for addressing current problems, and many ideas for developing new school communities. Yet, perhaps most critical to the future of special education is discovering how we can bring about the informed changes we seek.

The Quest for New Methods of Resolving Differences

Special education is faced with considerable new knowledge. Although authors in this book provide information believed to be useful in informing clinical and policy decisions, deeper issues of differences in the social and moral constructions of care and education still must be addressed. There are multiple ways of understanding the knowledge presented here and interpreting the implications. Although we have better-informed differences, differences in fundamental perspectives remain. While increased diversity does not make resolution easier, it may make it richer. Changes in empowerment that move decision-making power from authoritarian leadership to social contracts necessitate new skills and competencies. Perhaps a deeper understanding and wider knowledge base on which to stand will increase the efficacy and validity, if not the certainty, of our decisions.

With the wide disparity of views concerning which changes best address basic problems, it becomes evident that resolution of conflict is a central task. It no longer suffices to rest just with the majority vote. Ignored losers join together in polarized, adamant subgroups making law by violence, or at the least withdrawing from the community effort to "make their own schools." Learning to work out differences without losing or sacrificing one's identity or compromising one's values has become an essential skill for citizens in a democracy.

This need to learn how to deal with significant differences without compromising one's integrity is being recognized in many ways. Schools have been teaching conflict resolution skills to reduce violent engagements. Training in collaboration has become the byword of change to help agencies work more effectively and underlies much of the restructuring taking place. Collaboration is proposed to replace confrontation between special education and regular education, schools and families, and neighborhood groups. Children are taught to avoid being victims by learning to collaborate with their peers.

Dialogue to stimulate thinking about new solutions rather than discussion of one solution was central to the design in the conference described earlier. The rational, consensus-oriented approach to solving problems, long valued in democratic societies, is being challenged in a world that has many valued ways of knowing and ethical approaches to differences.

Conclusion

Our understanding of knowledge has changed rather dramatically during the past thirty years. Those changes have impacted the approaches to research and the interpretation and application of knowledge in the social sciences and neuro-sciences. More recently, those changes have impacted areas of knowledge that have traditionally guided special education policy and practice.

These changes in science have influenced and have been influenced by concurrent changes in culture. They reflect the deep transition from a modern to a postmodern philosophy in the Western world that is impacting all aspects of society and human community.

In this chapter we have discussed the broad contexts within which these changes have been occurring and influencing the understanding of special education policy and practice. Some of the core knowledge, which historically has provided the foundation for special education, is presented in the chapters that follow.

References

Danforth, S. (1995). Toward a critical theory approach to lives considered emotionally disturbed. *Behavioral Disorders, 20*, 2.

Gallagher, J. J. (1997). The role of policy in special education reform. In J. L. Paul et al. (Eds.), *Special education practice: Applying the knowledge, affirming the values, and creating the future* (Ch. 2). Pacific Grove, CA: Brooks/Cole.

Gardner, H. (1983). *Frames of mind.* New York: Basic Books.

Heisenberg, W. (1962). *Physics and philosophy.* New York: Bantam Books.

Heshusius, L. (1982). At the heart of the advocacy dilemma: A mechanistic world view. *Exceptional Children, 49*(1), 6–13.

Paul, J., Epanchin, B., Rosselli-Kostoryz, H., & Duchnowski, A. (1996). The transformation of teacher education and special education: Work in progress. *Remedial and Special Education, 17*(5), 310–323.

Reid, D. K., Robinson, S. J., & Bunsen, T. D. (1995). Empiricism and beyond: Expanding the boundaries of special education. *Remedial and Special Education, 16*(3), 131–141.

Skrtic, T. (1995). *Disability and democracy: Reconstructing (special) education for postmodernity.* New York: Teachers College Press.

PART I

Intellectual and Social Contexts of Special Education Policy

WILLIAM C. MORSE AND HILDA ROSSELLI-KOSTORYZ
University of South Florida

A major restructuring is taking place or is pending in most of our institutions. In social policy, different values drive these changes. The restructuring movement in general and special education has generated a widespread search for a more appropriate educational community. Appearing in diverse and unexpected places are undercurrents such as the pursuit of more collegial affiliation in the workplace, the empowerment of the disenfranchised, a recognition of the growing interdependence of humankind and nature, and a challenge to restore the ethic of caring in our society.

The magnitude of current institutional restructuring in many components of society signifies the passing of an era. A pertinent issue for considering changes in special education is the knowledge base that will best inform our efforts to create new learning communities. Believing that change is inevitable is not the same as believing that every proposed change implies progress. The foundational knowledge useful and necessary to make astute decisions will not be found only within our own specialty field. To ensure that new policies will be well-grounded requires being conversant with knowledge from many of the disciplines supporting special education. The chapters in this section review basic knowledge in two contexts impacting special education: philosophy and family. These two chapters offer condensed but provocative probes in areas that hold promise for both policy and practice as we struggle to formulate a new vision of a special education learning community.

Lynda Stone (Chapter 2) discusses the history of philosophy as a context within which current debates about knowledge are occurring. Stone, a professor at the University of North Carolina at Chapel Hill, is a philosopher of education who has devoted a great deal of her scholarly work to feminist theory, pragmatism, and most recently to a postmodern explication of John Dewey's social theory.

Stone clearly illustrates how the postmodern paradigm shift is changing the way we make sense of our experiences. New assumptions and meanings are being incorporated into the sciences and the arts. While concentrating on the current century, Stone traces the connections to significant historical persons and movements. She finds a convoluted picture, as much diverse as unified, common to any era during which remnants of past ideologies persist with the new.

According to Stone, the central issue is found in the abandoning of the "search for certainty" as verified through the familiar methods of the positivist scientific tradition. This is replaced by the postmodern, relativistic frame of uncertainty, diversity, and constructed and socially negotiated knowledge. Objective, empirical evidence gives way to subjectivity or an intersubjective consensus where socially constructed meanings are bound together by uncertainty.

One of the consequences of this change is the increased alertness to the world as a source for deriving meaning. Multiple and diverse views are considered equal. Events become unpredictable and open to skepticism, experiences to be lived rather than overcome. As a result, we learn to live with ambiguity and chaos, facilitated by discourse through which we arrive at shared meaning. The goal is to facilitate change toward a more equal, just, happy, and prosperous life for more people, which, if translated to education, might read as a more equal, just, and prosperous education for all children.

What becomes evident from a closer look at postmodernism is that research outcomes and theories can offer only limited solutions to the continually changing context of teaching. The best we can do is to manipulate the tensions and commit to a deliberate exploration of new perspectives, new fields of knowledge, and new ideas.

The relationship between school and family has an uneasy history. Both institutions have undergone changes and both must overcome their ambivalent history and establish a fundamental collaboration in order to provide a continuity of experience for the next generation. Yet the family, impacted by many internal and external forces, continues to carry much of the blame for the problems of children. The challenges to families, such as the increasing number found at poverty levels and the proliferation of new and fluid family patterns, indicate the need for a new understanding of today's family.

In Chapter 3, Urie Bronfenbrenner, recently retired from the Department of Human Development and Family Studies at Cornell University, provides us with the necessary research knowledge base to support an understanding of the depth of the family dilemma needed to develop sound policies for families and children. A prolific writer and renowned researcher, Bronfenbrenner has produced seminal work applying ecological theory to child and family development.

Bronfenbrenner's work demonstrates that, as goes the family, so eventually, goes the nation. The United States rates at the top in many unfavorable indices, such as divorce, single-parent families, and poverty. In Chapter 3, Bronfenbrenner focuses not on the familiar ground of intrafamily processes but on the impact of external conditions on family, which, in turn, influence the developmental outcomes for children and adolescents. He reviews research designs used in studying families, noting the limits of the research design. The changing demography of family demands research models that are more complex in order to provide more valid accounts of the complexity of family life.

The topics in this review of family research read like the index of critical public concerns. What is the impact of adoptive families on IQ and on criminal behavior? How do families interact with the peer groups of youngsters? What impact does day care have on families? What is different in families with stepparents? How do parents and school best collaborate?

Bronfenbrenner reviews three environmental systems that help us understand the family as a more complex and socially impacted entity than we traditionally acknowledge. The first system, the mesosystem, acknowledges the family as only one of several contexts in which human development occurs. For example, studies within this perspective have reexamined earlier beliefs regarding the contribution of genetic endowment, often explored through studies of twins and adopted children, and expanded the ecology of the family to include hospital, day care, peer groups, and schools. The exosystem, defined as systems likely to affect the development of the child through their influence on family processes, includes parental employment, family support networks, and the community itself. The latter aspect of the exosystem has produced both positive and negative influences on child development that appear to vary with the child's age. Finally, Bronfenbrenner provides evidence supporting developmental studies that use a life-course perspective within the chronosystem.

According to Bronfenbrenner, directions for future research are varied. He proposes the need for studies that examine the nature of variation in persons of identical genetic backgrounds living in different contexts as well as more comparative studies of adoptive and biological families. Bronfenbrenner also suggests additional studies that explore a host of interactions occurring within successive transitions as well as studies of families in broader social contexts, including social class, occupational status, family income, family mobility, even families' television viewing patterns. Finally, and of particular interest in this textbook, Bronfenbrenner acknowledges the need to determine which policies and programs enable families to "make and keep human beings human" and reminds us that equal attention must also be paid to better understandings of ecologies that sustain and strengthen families.

This section on intellectual and social contexts of special education provides different perspectives on the nature and complexity of the *weltanschauung* within which current policies relevant to the education of children with disabilities are being developed. A primary social institution—the family—is changing in profound ways as the intellectual frameworks by which we define our world are undergoing radical transformation. The impact of relativism and pluralism, resulting from the loss of power in traditional hegemonies, is being experienced in all aspects of life. It is pervasive in the changing social and religious imagination, ethics, education, and all communities of learning and care. In this section, Stone and Bronfenbrenner provide illuminated accounts of the drama and complexity as well as the scholarship in understanding these changes.

CHAPTER 2
Philosophy: Traditional to Postmodern

LYNDA STONE
University of North Carolina at Chapel Hill

> Philosophy . . . is that discipline in which knowledge is sought . . . [and] only opinion . . . [but not just any opinion is] had.
>
> (Richard Rorty)

Introduction

These are changing times. Change is apparent in both material and mental life. This is a post-industrial society in which daily changes occur in economics, in communications, in politics, and elsewhere. Consider, for example, the global, inter-dependent nature of multinationals and the new trade accords and organizations. Consider the in-formation highways and MTV cultures. Consider the demise of the traditional nation-state and the emergence of new communities. Overall, consider the changing geocultural worldview: the decline of the hegemonic West, the north-south dialogue, the rise of formerly colonized powers. This is a post-enlightenment society in which change has taken place in conceptions of world and of persons who inhabit it. Although debate continues as to its name and status, modernity is giving way (or has given way) to postmodernity (see, for example, Wexler, 1987; Young, 1990).

Postmodernity, as a broad intellectual phenom-enon, is most easily defined with reference to the sciences and the arts, although they, too, change (Foster, 1983; Ross, 1988). According to French philosopher Jean-Francois Lyotard (1984), post-modern "designates the state of our culture follow-ing the transformations which, since the end of the nineteenth century, have altered the game rules for science, literature, and the arts" (p. xxiii). The transformations, he continues, relate to changing how "science" (broadly defined) is itself defined. In modernity, science legitimates itself

> with reference to a metadiscourse . . . [by] making an explicit appeal to some grand narrative, such as the dialectics of Spirit, the hermeneutics of meaning, the emancipation of the rational or working subject, or the creation of wealth. (p. xxiii)

Thus, "philosophical" or theoretical formula-tions are frameworks within which human dis-courses are understood—by grand narratives of the Enlightenment such as rationality, capitalism, or liberalism. In contrast, postmodernity, accord-ing to Lyotard (1984), is "incredulity toward grand narratives." The times have produced a crisis of le-gitimacy in which "the narrative function is losing its functors, its great hero, its great dangers, its great voyages, its great goal" (p. xxiv). The result is a dispersion of narrative elements into unstable language combinations and games, into what

Lyotard calls "a pragmatics of language particles" and a kind of "local determinism" (see also Calhoun, 1993; Fraser & Nicholson, 1990).

Postmodernity, defined with reference to science, has its most recognizable roots in the arts. The term was in fact first used in American literary criticism in the 1950s and 1960s and became known through innovations in architecture in the 1970s (Huyssen, 1990, p. 237). Because of diverse and widespread usage, there is a possibility of laying out postmodernity's complexity in the arts. At stake is not whether the "post" continues or breaks with its predecessor (whether there has actually been a paradigm shift) but rather what the newer condition entails. Two points are important: first, to define postmodernism is contradictory to the condition itself; second, to offer definition also obscures identifiable conservative and radical strands. There is no one postmodernism (Habermas, 1983, 1985; Shapiro, 1992).

Much more needs to be set out about postmodernism and its ramifications, especially for philosophy. This is returned to later in the chapter. Meanwhile, an overview of traditional philosophy and its connections to science is presented in order to understand the background to postmodernism and thus its connections to research today. In what follows, education does not figure explicitly, but there is an implicit connection: educational scholarship, significant for its own purposes, generally entails a development akin to that of both the epistemological elements and various traditions that constitute philosophy's story. The remainder of this chapter consists of the following sections: Traditional Philosophy, Science and Social Science, Postmodernism, and Conclusion.

Overall, this chapter undertakes a broad and complex task through what is a thematic rather than an encyclopedic approach (see Phillips, 1985; MacIntyre, 1990). The latter, although standard for the history of philosophy, is inappropriate for two reasons. First, the current state of philosophy is so diverse and complicated that a delineation of traditions and names is certain to leave out significant contributions and is also soon outdated. Second, educational researchers can better draw on themes for their own work rather than on more specific names and theories. What is potentially lost, however, is an exactness of contributors and their ideas; instead, a general picture is created.

Related to an introduction to philosophy is the present state of philosophy within educational research.[1] Currently, there are remnants of three "philosophic" traditions: pragmatism, analytic philosophy, and European neo-Marxism, as well as some emergent influences. Pragmatism exhibits a kind of slumbering progressivism with a renaissance of interest in Dewey (Stone, 1994b). This is found particularly in research in teaching and teacher education—in proposals for social reconstruction. Analytic philosophy manifests as a holdover of positivism—and some researchers hold on dearly. This is seen especially in the retention of "norms" of research, in opposing "relativism" with attempts to keep constructs of reliability and validity alive. European neo-Marxism, generally known as "critical theory," pervades much research today as a positivist alternative. Its most systematically developed forms fall under the rubric of "new sociology of knowledge." Its least enumerated forms combine Deweyan roots with radical contributions from Paolo Freire and others—as a kind of generic "critical" stance.

In addition to these traditions are several other philosophically based developments within educational research. The first development is the emergence of qualitative methodologies; here through the social sciences is the influence of hermeneutics

---

[1]An important tradition exists in "philosophy of education" in North America with a society and journal over fifty years old. The status of the field today reflects a general intellectual diversity common throughout the academy, with views that are sometimes contentious (see Kaminsky, 1993; Kohli 1995; Phillips 1985; and for related materials, see Bernstein, 1991).

(the ancient study of texts) and of Continental social theory in general. The second development, tied to the first, is the appearance of "narrative" in research (Stone, 1995), as personally voiced accounts that today extend beyond qualitative descriptions (for example, see Britzman, 1991). The third development, with some ties to philosophy, is actually from psychology—the constructivism movement, arising out of Piagetian roots. Its prevalence, its mention almost wherever one looks for theoretical basis, has assumed the hegemony—and the noncritical acceptance—once held by behaviorism. Constructivism functions as "philosophy" for much educational research today (see Popkewitz, 1991, for related material). Finally, there is a small but persistent tradition of feminist critique that deserves mention (Jaggar, 1983; Stone, 1994a).

What is interesting about these present traditions is their positioning relative to modernism/ postmodernism. Clearly modernist are positivist norms within research, some interpretations of Dewey, some Marxist theorizing that is highly structural, some interpretative work that seeks singular or unified meaning and some narratives of the same kind, and also some strong presentations of constructivism that privilege human agency and authorship. Not so clearly postmodernist are some neopragmatist and poststructuralist theorizings, some work in critical hermeneutics, and some radical constructivism. Also feminism is situated in both modernism and postmodernism. New "traditions" are turned to at the close of the chapter. It is significant to note that some but not many educational researchers write about postmodernism; excellent examples include Giroux (1988, 1991), Lather (1991), Popkewitz (1991), and Cherryholmes (1988). Many others mention postmodernism in passing; the latter are well-meaning progressives who long to hold onto the liberal project of educational and societal emancipation yet understand its modernist shortcomings. This is also of subsequent concern.

Traditional Philosophy

The discussion of postmodernism in the Introduction sets part of the intellectual context for understanding the "nature" of philosophy today. It does not, however, define the field, explore something of its history, or establish boundaries from which a postmodern perspective devolves. This is the task of the present section.

Perhaps a place to begin is with the assertion that "philosophy," as used here, refers to systematic study undertaken by professionals who inquire into major life questions. These professionals, like many other people, want to understand life and world, truth and beauty, science and art, but unlike others their ruminations are available publicly and over time. Philosophic study is, in the present rubric, "nonempirical" in asking questions, analyzing meaning, and raising objections. In these endeavors, as Max Rosenberg (1955) relates there are some initiating premises, among them that philosophic beliefs form "wholes" or systems (the -*isms*) (pp. 14–15). Today, philosophical unities or totalities are themselves called into question.

Philosophy has a normative as well as an intellectual history. It has been considered by many to be abstract and complex, esoteric and elitist, and something that most people can do without (Rosenberg, 1955). Although these criticisms are surely justified, especially during the recent analytic period (Bernstein, 1991), philosophy, as Mary Warnock (1992), reports has recently entered into the world (pp. 2–3). Since the 1960s, philosophy has been seen in several dimensions: first, in the development of applied fields and subspecialities such as philosophy of law, medicine, and, pertinent to this discussion, education; second, in the emerging emphasis of moral study (of everyday values); and third, in the "socializing" of philosophy as a result of the blurring of the Anglo-American/Continental distinction.

Finally, the internal organization of philosophy is changing. The "queen of the disciplines" has had a development of its own but has also had various connections with other fields. Initially, philosophy was connected to and then separated from mathematics—a connection revitalized in the 20th century. Then, its connection was to theology in medieval times and finally to science in the modern period. In this last there has been a recent separation. Moreover, within philosophy traditional subfields emerge over time: among them epistemology, ethics, and aesthetics. Most significantly, there is a general blurring of the disciplines across academia, as well as a dispersion in what traditional philosophy has meant. A newer, less perennial, dogmatic, and absolutist discipline lives on today in widely read texts (see Baynes, Bohman, & McCarthy, 1987; Rorty, 1982).

Traditional Themes

In the previous discussion, characterizing modernity were Lyotard's metanarratives, various epochal worldviews around which Western society has been and still is organized. These worldviews existed prior to modernity, but in this last epoch they have special significance because of their hegemony. Elements of these views are tied to theory, to disciplines concerned with social life. Throughout the history of philosophy, primarily as epistemology or theories of knowledge, three central themes (among others) appear. They are interrelated, are themselves metaphysically grounded (in prior and unquestioned assumptions), and focus on basic questions of men (*sic*) making sense of their worlds.[2] These central themes of philosophy include: (1) the appearance/reality distinction and

the question of representation, (2) the source and justification of sense making (knowing) and the question of foundation, and (3) the need for certainty and the question of truth. Their relationship is something like this: once a thematic distinction is assumed, a dualism of subject and object, person and world is established. Of the dualistic interaction, forms of explanation or foundation of the interaction are sought. Finally in the relationship, truth functions as "evidence" of absolute (or later contingent) certainty. These three themes, in some formulation or other, begin in the period of ancient philosophy, are altered during the medieval or Scholastic period, and, like metanarratives, are especially significant (and complex) during recent modernity. Given important distinctions between modernity and the two epochs of philosophic thought before it, it is easiest to divide thought into two larger periods: premodernity and modernity. Like postmodernity and modernity today, these two time periods are not discontinuous.

The earliest and perennial question of philosophy is this: What is the world made of? In other words, What is reality? What is person? What is the interaction of person and reality? According to philosophical historians Newton Stallknecht and Robert Brumbaugh (1950), this question "reveals a definite attitude toward the world on the part of the questioner." Premises are entailed in this attitude that set up the subject/object dualism just mentioned: persons are at the center of philosophic study; they think and reason; they desire to learn.

Premodernity

In the first era of premodernity, antiquity, this question is basic. Here are Stallknecht and Brumbaugh on the appearance/reality distinction:

> What we see and experience about us we recognize as being only an *appearance*. The true nature of

---

[2] *Sic* appears here as a placemarker for views of the world that historically have not been part of the tradition, the canon. These are from the "others"—minorities by gender, race, class, sexual preference, and so on.

things does not lie on the surface for all to see. The surface is a forever changing appearance that is open to the awareness of the most unreflective person. But we may correctly interpret this appearance and penetrate to its *reality*. (p. xiii)

Conducted by the Greeks and located especially in the writings of Plato and Aristotle, the first appearance/reality inquiries concern the composition of the world and the distinction between the physical and mental domains. Distinction itself is significant as an early process of sense making (Hamlyn, 1987, p. 19). Chief among oppositions, or dualisms, are perfection and imperfection and good and evil. Utilizing these, here is the basic view (with strong Platonic influence): innate ideas are perfect, true and real, and human thought is imperfect, not true and only appearance. Moreover, persons are imperfect but superior to animals (hierachy is established, too); and man is superior to woman (see Mahowald, 1983, pp. 264–274). Perfection as an innate idea or essence is itself a static ideal of objects and processes that may be dynamic. In premodernity, while man has a central place, it is less significant than the ideal reality that precedes and is external to him and that he desires to know (see Jay, 1994, p. 25).

As indicated, knowledge is "represented" in mental approximations of innate ideas. Idea or form has two formulations, one logical and the other metaphysical (see Russell, 1945, p. 121). Actually, a third formulation is mathematical. In philosophy, the first exists as a general word that stands for all forms (say, of "cat"). The second exists as goodness, an ideal of human perfection. Search for goodness is the highest calling of man, to gain wisdom as superior knowledge and with it the good life. Here, Plato's allegory of the cave, of seeking truth beneath appearance, initiates the representationalist tradition in Western philosophy, of a correspondence theory of truth.

Many of the questions of appearance/reality continue into the medieval period; among them the nature of the physical, mental, and now the spiritual worlds. God enters the epistemological equation with full force. Medieval scholarship, thus Scholasticism, is a renewal of interest in antiquity and especially a return to the writings of Plato and Aristotle. Given this base, there are principal studies about the existence of God, the place of man in the universe, and the relationship of reason and faith. Form or innate idea from antiquity is reinterpreted in this way:

> According to Christian Platonism, God is truly eternal, . . . but unlike the form he possesses actual concrete existence as well as intelligible subsistence, and . . . can speak out in the first person. He is the one ultimate condition of both intelligibility or order and of existence. (Stallknecht & Brumbaugh, 1950, p. 208)

According to the writings of the Platonic Augustine, appearance has special significance as the reflection by man of what God knows. Man's attempt, however, is always imperfect relative to God's absolute wisdom. The Aristotelian Aquinas adds to this view with an important mind/body distinction: The body houses in life the intellect and the soul, but the latter survives after death in a pure, nonbodily form (Hamlyn, 1987, pp. 108–109). This last contribution is a reinterpretation of Aristotle's hierarchy of mind over body. Moreover, Aquinas's attention to the body, undertaken through rational argument, is only one aspect of his interest in the physical world. Attempting to connect physical and spiritual reality, he explores the notion of "first cause": the world is motion, an actualization of potentialities, that themselves have initiation (Hamlyn, 1987, p. 107). The cause or mover is God.

Appearance in medieval Scholasticism is what men can know of God's truth, coming to him through meditation and revelation, and represented in texts. The study of these texts, hermeneutics, has Greek roots and significant biblical development. The term *hermeneutics* is derived from Hermes, the Greek god "associated with the function of transmuting what is beyond human understanding into a form that human understanding can grasp" (Palmer, 1969, p. 13), specifically through language and writing and the general process of interpretation. Representation is central here; important also is an understanding that interpretation is a historical process that is foundational to the humanities.

Also present in premodernity is appearance and representation that comes to be part of a "scientific" tradition. In this period, appearance/representation is often described through the metaphor of the mirror; incorporated are two interesting aspects. One is that purity in some formulations is a unity, an interplay of sameness and difference. Another is that appearance (mirror reflection) is imitation or craven image, never pure form; likeness is never truth (see Jay, 1994, pp. 32–33, 37–38). Variations within these themes antedate premodernity.

In addition, foundationalism has both continuing and changing forms. As defined here, foundationalism is a kind of essentialism; that is, an expression of totality, singularity, sameness, or oneness (Stone, 1992, p. 202). There are theoretical essentialisms, among them objectivism (the positing of an external epistemological standard) and universalism (the positing of something as the same for all people). Both objectivism and universalism, beginning in premodernity, retain special importance during modernity. Others, such as structuralism and formalism, develop in the later period.

In antiquity, rationalism and idealism are foundational. The former asserts man's reason as the process of knowing, the source of which is considered real. Recall that "the real" are innate ideas

knowable as ideal forms in contrast to unknowable matter. Incorporating idealism is somewhat misleading, however, because in antiquity, idealism/realism are one. Here, truth is a priori and inherent.

In the second epoch, during the time of medieval Christianity, foundationalism expands to include a realism/idealism distinction, or perhaps a realism/sensationalism distinction. An important Scholastic contribution is the possibility of earthly knowledge that "results from our being reminded by experience of eternal forms" (Stallknecht & Brumbaugh, 1950, p. 217). Within this definition are two interpretations. The realist insists that language (in theological text) corresponds to "real" universal forms and reflects them; the idealist insists that universals are instead instruments of the mind. The sensationalist understands that although truth is possible in the first two foundations (that is, of the mental and spiritual worlds), it exists but is not absolute in the physical world. Overall, to reasoning as a knowing process is introduced the idea of experience and observation as forming mental representations. But, in keeping with the medieval worldview, these representations are true only as they mirror the knowledge of God.

Modernity

In the modern period, as indicated earlier, the appearance/reality distinction becomes more complex and systematized. At bottom, important philosophical differences distinguish this epoch from previous epochs. If ancient philosophy is an endeavor to differentiate man from nature and medieval philosophy to differentiate man from God, then modern philosophy might be defined as differentiating man from himself. As Jurgen Habermas (1983) explains, this results in an epochal consciousness of seeing the present "as a transition from the old to the new" (p. 3). Such a view is both conservative and progressive, in revisioning tradition and in introducing novelty.

Locating modernity presents an initial problem. As used here, the term is distinguished from modernism (as in the arts) and from modernization (as in economics or general culture). Modernity has been variously defined—indeed Habermas traces the term to the 12th century (Habermas, 1983, p. 4; see also Nelson, Treichler, & Grossberg, 1992, pp. 15–16). A recent contribution from Stephen Toulmin (1990) questions the standard dating that starts with the rise of science—the work of Copernicus, Kepler, Galileo, and especially Newton—and with concomitant writings in philosophy beginning with Descartes (Stallknecht & Brumbaugh, 1950; Walsh, 1985). Toulmin proposes that modernity actually begins in the Renaissance as a first phase, in the 15th- and early 16th-century writings of Erasmus, Rabelais, Montaigne, and Shakespeare, and in the earlier science of Bacon. This is followed by the second and better-known phase of the 17th century, in which a kind of positivist rationalism replaces the earlier humanism (Toulmin, 1990, pp. 23–24). From Renaissance beginnings come important themes for later and postmodernity. These themes include an emphasis on the local, the particular, and the timely—in Toulmin's interpretation, an emphasis on intellectual "context." From the first phase to the second, beginning in 1630 nearly to the present day (around 1950 or so), rhetoric gives way to logic, cases to generalizations, and practical "philosophies" to theoretical abstractions (Toulmin, 1990, pp. 30–35).

Two traditions characterize modern philosophy, emerging from the premodern and influencing the postmodern as well. They are empiricism and rationalism, epitomized in the writings of Locke and Kant, respectively. Within these traditions are the by-then differentiated and well-established themes of representation, foundation, and truth.

Empiricism is based on the principle that internal or external "experience alone is the one and only source of all knowledge" (Walsh, 1985, p. 258). This principle, credited to Locke and other British empiricists of the 17th and 18th centuries, is basic to one branch of positivism in the 20th century as well. Its traditional roots are found in Aristotle and Aquinas. Seemingly a thoroughgoing "modern," Locke takes as real but not a priori the true existence of God and man (and sensation) and mathematics. Overall, there are no innate ideas, even founding beliefs are experienced.

For Locke, there are three kinds of knowledge, represented in three forms of thought—intuition, reflection, and sensation—and known through perception. Herein the earlier real/ideal distinction is transformed because all knowledge for Locke is real but exists as ideas—that is, the objects of what man thinks, incorporating thought and consciousness of it (Hamlyn, 1987, p. 169). Well known is the picture of mind basic to this epistemology, a precursor to today's philosophy of psychology: as a blank slate upon which is impressed the three forms of thought as particulars. This formulation initiates modern discussion of the formation of general ideas (Locke sees them as cumulative applications of particulars), and of sense data theory. Characteristic of this picture is the image of "sensa" coming from actual objects to strike the mind. Representation is central, because "knowledge is the perception of the agreement or disagreement of two ideas" (Russell, 1945, p. 611). Locke's empiricism entails that perception is experienced as ideas. Two aspects of this are paradoxical: one aspect is that their "causes," assumed to exist, are not experienced. Another aspect is that for an empiricist, "ideas" as representations are rationalist, of the mind, and not of the material world. This problem becomes acute in Locke's conceptualization of primary and secondary qualities of objects. The latter, which are qualities such as color and taste, are not "resembled" in the actual object, and the empiricist basis for modern science is left without philosophical foundation. This problem, as H. S. Thayer (1968) explains, is not Locke's alone but comes back to haunt the tradition itself (pp. 22–24).

Modern rationalism is actually initiated by Descartes in the 17th century, but its later, 18th-century, Kantian formulation is most pertinent for present purposes. Following on and responding to Locke, and especially Hume, Kant bases his philosophy on experience as well, but it is herein understood as presupposed, a necessary but not sufficient condition for knowledge. Foundational are his distinctions between the noumenal and phenomenal worlds, between "things-in-themselves" and appearances, as well as his general philosophical architectonic of three forms of thought. These are epistemology as basic and moral and aesthetics as derivative.

Kant's picture of mind has three central capacities—faculties of intuition, understanding, and sensation—that operate together to make judgments about the world. Knowledge is formed of objects that are "no more than what our sensible intuitions represent to us; they *are* representations subject to the *a priori* conditions that the forms of space and time determine" (Hamlyn, 1987, p. 220). These preconditions are an inherent universal set of relational categories wired, so to speak, in the mind. Kant names this rationalism "transcendental idealism" because although the noumenal world is presupposed, only the phenomenal world can be known.

The three forms of knowledge entail varying combinations of cognitive capacities but operate as a general process. First is apprehension in intuition, a coming together of elements of experience. Second, there is synthesis of the perceived unity in imagination. Third, there is another synthesis, one of recognition in a concept. Out of this process, two kinds of judgments are postulated: a priori and a posteriori. A priori operates in which verification or justification does not refer to experience, and it is presupposed as true. A posteriori is either presupposed to be true, as in mathematics and some

prior conditions for experience, or capable of experiential proof. This important distinction between analytic and synthetic knowledge continues down into 20th century philosophical debate. Finally, the three knowledge forms are varying utilizations of a priori and a posteriori formulations (see Russell, 1945; Stallknecht & Brumbaugh, 1950).

The rest of modern philosophy, at least in epistemology, might be termed as footnotes to Locke and especially Kant. In their formulations, the traditional themes assume characterizations that have present familiarity. What is systematized herein are basic tenets that dualistically separate rationalist/subjective formulations from empiricist/objective formulations. These play out in the history of philosophy of science and social science.

Science and Social Science

Science

Since antiquity, philosophers have been interested in science because it is constituted as knowledge, as justified true belief. Indeed, Aristotle's name is first identified with both the practice and philosophy of science (Oldroyd, 1986, p. 16), as is the empiricist tradition.

As in the preceding section, an encyclopedia discussion of subtraditions and principal contributors is not germane here; instead, these play out in several summing points. First, philosophic tenets of modern science encapsulate the epochal worldview. Second, of all human endeavors, science perpetuates the values not only of philosophical rationalism and empiricism but also of the method of experimentationalism of which they are a part. Third, in late modernity two movements of philosophy of science are especially significant: one is the advent of positivism and its aim of unified science, and the other is the Kuhnian "revolution" and its conceptions of normal science and paradigm shift.

As Toulmin (1990) recounts, in the late 17th century in the writings of Leibniz and Grotius and especially Descartes and in Newton's experiments, the modern or Cartesian view of science and the world is established. At its base, the traditional themes of representation, foundation, and truth are enacted through significant dualisms, of "matter from mind, causes from reasons, and nature from humanity" (Toulmin, 1990, p. 107). Summing Toulmin, here is the central dichotomy of nature/culture: On the one side, nature is governed by fixed causal laws set up at creation, composed of inert matter and incapable of thought. Here nature is set up as a hierarchical system of higher and lower things, whose motions follow their forms. On the other side, humanity and its creation, culture, is governed by rational thought and action with rules different from causality. Rationality establishes stable systems in society (like those of nature), but human life is both rational/spiritual and emotional, stable and unstable. Within humans the mind is still superior to and separate from the body (Toulmin, 1990 pp. 109–110).

Experimentalism, or scientific method, also has ancient roots and significant development during early modernity. As one historian put it, there are two principles underlying experimentation: ascending to first principles (induction favored by rationalists) or descending through explanation (deduction favored by empiricists) (Oldroyd, 1986, pp. 14, 29–30). The first utilizes logic and mathematics as primary scientific tools; the second utilizes "factual knowledge" and empirical testing. In the 18th and early 19th centuries, these two philosophic perspectives exhibited distinct development (see Hanson, 1958, for related materials).

Positivism enters in the late 19th century, a term earlier coined by Auguste Comte. Martin Jay (1994) calls this foundation a new name for sensationalism, the basis of empiricism (p. 84). There are many philosophies (both natural and social)

that can be called "positivist." Generally, they emphasize

> the importance of empirical evidence as the source of knowledge, and would wish to eliminate from science or philosophical discourse any kind of entities that lie beyond the reach of empirical investigation. (Oldroyd, 1986, p. 169)

In scientific empiricism, corresponding unities are premised, with the primary one being between logic/mathematics and reality (Stallknecht & Brumbaugh, 1950, p. 329), implying those of the real and ideal worlds and of philosophy with science. Moreover, whereas metaphysical essences are disabused, lawlike generalizations are avowed as the only philosophic/scientific aim (see Reichenbach, 1954, pp. 31, 5). These theoretical unities are incorporated in the programmatic movement of unified science. This proposal, coming from "logical positivists," creates a hierarchy of all science, with mathematical physics at the apex (Toulmin, 1990, pp. 154–155).

Finally, one important event generally undermining positivism, in addition to its own acknowledged "failure" to determine "certain" foundations, comes in Thomas Kuhn's description of how science functions (Kuhn, 1970). His "revolution" through a history of the scientific enterprise is to establish a sociology of science as typically a value-laden endeavor of communities of practitioners rather than the discoveries of single persons (Kuhn, 1980). Thus, science is nonobjectivist, working not from an ahistorical framework but relative to "paradigms." In addition, it is comprised of normal events, the kind of accretive inductive activity Toulmin names as "the tradition" as well as "revolutions" or paradigm shifts arising from accumulated anomalies. Significantly, one aspect of Kuhn's revolution maintains the positivist project of hierarchy but is itself later discounted (also see Lakatos & Musgrave, 1970). This is his definition of mature and nonmature sciences, with social sciences defined as immature, nonparadigmatic, and therefore hierarchically inferior to nature sciences (Rabinow & Sullivan, 1979, pp. 2–3).

Social Science

Two traditions of the development of social science are presently salient; one coming from the positivist movement of natural science, and the other arising from the interpretivist movement of history and literature. The first is historically prominent in Anglo-America and the second in Continental Europe.

The goal of the first tradition, what historian Dorothy Ross calls "distinctly American," is for an emulative social science to discover generalizations for the social and the natural worlds. In doing this, the methodology of experimentalism prevails, complete with theory formation based on testable empirical (now scientific) hypotheses (and empiricist premises). Begun from its own 18th-century European roots, positvism's development spans the post–Civil War period to the 1950s. The positivist hegemony includes such dimensions as the scientific orientation of behavioral sciences, quantitative modeling and systems analysis, and functionalism. The universalizing aspects of early structuralism are also positivistic. Underneath this tradition is a basic set of social beliefs that have an American flavor. Writes Ross, "Its liberal values . . . [of individualism], practical bent, shallow historical vision, and technocratic confidence are recognizable features of twentieth-century America" (1991, p. xiii). Such a view entails, of course, its own historical perspective. To summarize Ross: The character of American social science stems from "its involvement with the national ideology of . . . exceptionalism, the idea that America occupies an exceptional place in history"(p. xiv). This millennial vision, made up of republican institutions and economic processes to forestall the evils of immigrant-based industrialization, is based on fixed laws of historic change that perpetuate an existing social order and the sciences to study it. America is the "best" of modern society, a view, according to Ross, that is itself an ahistorical and scientistic distortion.

In contrast to positivism, the interpretivist tradition has what might be termed romanticist roots (also see Manicas, 1987). In the 20th century, interpretive social science undertakes what Paul Rabinow and William Sullivan (1979) describe as "the shattering of the triumphalist view of history bequeathed . . . by the nineteenth century . . . [that is, of Comte's] positive reason" (p. 1). One form of triumphalism is surely Ross' American exceptionalism.

Interestingly, both social sciences build from Kant: positivism from formalist categorization for a unified field, and interpretivism from postulates of a second type, those relating to rational man. The idea is that a person knows oneself and others through reflection not only on one's experience but also on one's intentional action; so "practical understanding . . . cannot be reduced to a system of categories defined only in terms of each other" (Rabinow & Sullivan, 1979, p. 3). Thus Kant is a precursor to a nonobjectivist tradition and more, important, the first "contextualist." With this interpretive turn, what Richard Bernstein (1983) identifies as the problem of modernity is transformed. Here he echoes Dewey (1929), who explains that man's quest for certainty has been to "escape from peril," in which a "distrust of himself caused him to desire to get beyond and above himself . . . [in a self-transcendence of] pure knowledge" (p. 7). Over the two centuries since Kant, much has happened.

From the impetus of the interpretive turn in the "human sciences," in extensions beyond traditional social science, gone is objectivism in some form of ahistorical foundation; also gone is relativism in its negative connotation. The point is to undermine a relativist nihilism, because in an interpretivist scheme, relativism means relative to context. In interpretive science this incorporates both content and method of inquiry: the language, institutions, and practices, as well as investigative tools. Moreover, contextualism also disabuses subjectivism, because not only is there no "essential" human opinion but also no privileged opinion. Meanings in context, according to Charles Taylor (1979), are always intersubjective and hermeneutic, that is, negotiated through encoded, common "languages of expression." In other words, they are textual in context (see also Nelson, Megill, & McCloskey, 1987).

As implied but evident, interpretive contextualism brings reformulation of traditional philosophic themes. Foundationalism as a grounding, as source, is given up, although forms of justification remain in the earliest interpretivist work. Here, intersubjective agreement or consensus often retains a kind of nonfallibilist flavor. Truth, in this tradition, assumes a late modern character—relative in the Tarskian idiom to a specific language, and always underdetermined. This means that without objectivist foundation language is always, to some theoretical degree, uncertain and noncorresponding. Most important, the appearance/reality distinction is transformed; however, a kind of representationalism remains in early interpretivism when text itself assumes a kind of "representation of true meaning." When a second turn occurs, representationalism departs. A double turn is indicated because language is first privileged and then deprivileged.

Finally, what results from this change is a blurring of the traditional separation of the sciences and humanities—a blurring that incorporates specific disciplines. This point has been made before (in another way) and has specific meaning for philosophy. John Rajchman (1985) describes three trends in "postanalytic" philosophy: (1) a continuation of the Kuhnian tradition in philosophy of science; (2) a melding of social and moral theory, particularly as a neo-Kantian tradition; and (3) a

developing intermarriage of philosophy with poststructuralist literary theory (see also Rorty, 1982, 1989). To understand these trends, further intellectual situating and explanation is required.

Postmodernism

The traditional discipline of philosophy continues through the 19th and early 20th centuries and finally results in a fixed division between Anglo-American and Continental scholarship. In England, empiricism evolves in the writings of Mill and the Utilitarians, and, prior to the "great divide," in an idealism with roots in Hegel. Two of idealism's 19th-century promoters are Thomas Hill Green and F. H. Bradley; two others in America and Italy are the philosophers of history and aesthetics, respectively, R. G. Collingwood and Benedetto Croce (see Hamlyn, 1987). German philosophy produces important post-Kantians in the 19th century, including Hegel, Schopenhauer, and Nietzsche. Then, with the writings of Marx, a general movement of "social theory" is delineated. In the 20th century, this continues in Germany and France (with distinct theoretical strands). At the same time, the analytic movement develops in England out of "the Vienna Circle" just prior to and during World War II; this group becomes the positivist philosophers. Finally, of particular importance is a new American philosophy—pragmatism—arising around the turn of the century. With roots that stem from the literary tradition of Emerson (West, 1989), it is dominant for half a century, declines for a similar period, and is currently undergoing an important renaissance. Within pragmatism and several other of the current trends, the divide between Anglo-American and Continental philosophies is disappearing.

The promise of pragmatism is one of the most significant trends of the present postmodernity. Other trends include a series of theoretical turns recently undergone, named the linguistic turn and the new historicism (they join the general interpretivist turn just described). In addition, other vital intellectual events are the development of "philosophical alternatives," one in feminism and the other in critical theory. Each of these is composed of complex and diverse viewpoints but all agree to what is understood as a larger "social frame," to the general contextualism just described. Further, all take place within a context of disciplinary blurring and the formation of new studies.

New Historicism

In the Anglo-American world, early 20th-century history changes from a 19th-century idealist and romanticist orientation to one strongly empiricist and positivist (Hutcheon, 1988) and is currently shifting again. It begins with the assumption that events of the past have relative meaning. The impetus for new historicism, with connections to hermeneutics and roots in Hegel, is less the idea that meaning is natural and static but instead relates to "a given group, society, or culture's conception of its present tasks and future prospects" (White, cited in Hutcheon, 1988, p. 97). This means, moreover, that history is more like literature than science. In his significant formulation, Hayden White proposes that historical narrative is a "purely verbal artifact purporting to be a model of structures and processes long past and therefore not subject to either experimental or observational controls" (White, 1986, p. 396). What the historian actually does, White continues, is configure a set of events to a "specific plot structure." The process is like creating a metaphor, a symbol that does not describe or imitate "the real," but instead "tells . . . what images to look for in . . . culturally encoded experience in order to determine how . . . [to] *feel* about the thing represented" (White, 1986, p. 402; see also White, 1978).

This position on history, developed by White, Quentin Skinner, and others is known as "new his-

toricism" and has great influence on present-day historians, literary critics, and other textualists. Understanding history as text means that objective history is an idea no longer salient. There are two results to this understanding. The first is to problematize text, especially as it reconstructs continuity from the past. Whatever is made of the past is always viewed with skepticism. The second is precisely to see history ironically; that is, in a playfulness of inevitable disparity. This is done by establishing "a representational ground" and then subverting it (Hutcheon, 1988, p. 92). The value of this playfulness makes irony the primary literary (and historical) trope of postmodernism.

The Linguistic Turn

New historicism with its interpretive, contextual frame is tied to textuality, and text to language. Of singular importance in 20th-century intellectual life is the linguistic turn, or "the double turn" of two phases. An epistemological movement away from reality to language changes irrevocably the nature of truth and of philosophy. In the linguistic turn there are two phases: The first is a privileging of language in traditional hermeneutics, literary theory, and analytic philosophy; the second is a retaining of linguistic emphasis but a deprivileging, this occurring in Wittgensteinian ordinary language philosophy (part of the analytic project), in poststructuralism and deconstructionism, and in neopragmatism.

The first linguistic turn is a philosophical revolution in assuming a new kind of nontraditional foundation based on the idea that philosophical problems are a matter of how words are used. Kantian theory is the root of this phase, in conceptualization of "formal essence" and "concept representation," and in the post-Kantian interest in meanings and sentences. The result, as A. J. Ayer put it in the mid-1940s, is that philosophy is transformed into expressions of "definitions, or the formal consequences of definitions" (Ayer, cited in

Rorty, 1992a, p. 5), and thus as a project to establish procedures for verification of these linguistic elements through positive utilization of mathematics, logic, and principles from empirical science. Two later developments are Wittgenstein's "socialization" of language through his insights that there is no direct correspondence between words and objects, and no private language but only contextualized language games, and Tarski's conception of semantic truth (see also Quine, 1961). The latter changes the traditional conception of truth in philosophy.

As noted, initially truth is said to correspond if some representation between a subjective belief and an objective state is asserted. More precisely in modern times when language is understood as a medium, this means correspondence between statements and states of affairs. The correspondence theory becomes one of coherence in a first transformation when a corpus of propositions are substituted for unreliable statements and "fragments of reality." Finally this again is transformed by Alfred Tarski and Donald Davidson in their important clarification that all there is are propositions with their truth underdetermined. Now truth is acknowledged for those statements in which there is agreed usage, and philosophy becomes nonabsolute since "there is nothing over and above what is said" (Rorty, 1992b, p. 365; Davidson, 1985). A kind of privileging remains in proposals for ideal languages and corresponding translations between languages but these projects are largely now gone.

The second linguistic turn works from a different tradition and ends up in a second phase of depriviledging. Its sources are traditional hermeneutics and linguistic structuralism. Its roots are synonymous with the analytic privileging of words, as the right meanings of texts. But, from Heidegger, this privilege is theoretically denied. The move is not all of a piece, and an important contribution from Hans-Georg Gadamer posits cultural limits to meaning, to confines of the literary tradition (see Eagleton, 1983, pp. 71–73). This phase develops as two aspects out of structuralism, that is, poststructuralism and deconstructionism (see Culler, 1982; DeGeorge & DeGeorge, 1972; Innis, 1985). Both begin with Ferdinand Saussure's important theory of signs (with connections to the pragmatist Peirce). The result of writings by Barthes, Foucault, and others led to a theory of discourse and its open meaning. The result of writings by Derrida, Lacan, and others led to a theory of language as always dispersed and deferred. In both, texts speak in voices other than the one presupposed, and truth is always indeterminate (see Cherryholmes, 1988). Of note is the influence of Freud in some of this theorizing. Also, significantly, truth in the second turn in some formulations is tied to power (see Foucault, 1980), as are two theoretical movements that since their inceptions have been alternatives to traditional philosophy. These are feminism and critical theory.

Feminism

Writings by women from a feminist stance date from antiquity but have had particular import in the "modern movement" of the last thirty years. The project has critiqued traditional philosophy on matters, among others, of epistemology, ethics, aesthetics, political theory, and philosophy of science. To name this tradition as "alternative," which is often done, misses the point of its own independent and rigorously developing scholarship (for related materials, see Lloyd, 1984).

Although diverse in theoretical and ideological orientation, feminist writing is initially and primarily undertaken by white women who, although themselves oppressed, gain access to academia and to political power far easier than women of color. Today, "feminisms" are named particularly to point out both the history of this bifurcation and especially the value of different rather than essentialist or the same viewpoints. Within feminisms' theory, four phases are historically identifiable (Jaggar, 1983; Stone, 1994a).

The first phase is universalist, connected to liberal feminism, posing that women and men are biologically equal and that the former are culturally denied equality. Equality comes as women take their place alongside men and are the "same." Central to this plane is philosophical attention to rationality, the basis of philosophy itself. The second phase is separatist, connected to radical feminism—the phase most often and still under conservative attack. In this strand, the pose is that females and males are equal and different but again denied equality. Herein equality comes in the creation of and valuation of different and separate arenas. Central to this phase is attention to public and private cultural spheres, but with a kind of sameness persisting as men and women are understood as different but each gender the same. The third phase is essentialist, connected to Marxist and other structuralist theorizing. Again, inequality is posed, solved in this case through reinterpretation and female solidarity. Central to this phase is critique out of the Continental tradition. This phase today is often conflated with the second. The fourth and present phase is particularist. Here, equality is advocated through specific attention to differences among women and the common struggle of earlier formulations deferred in light of the "uncommon" one among women (Stone, 1995). In this phase, all essentialisms are eliminated in work that is often poststructural (Weedon, 1987). Much of the most interesting writing is being done by African American and other feminists of color and those postcolonial in orientation (Collins, 1990; hooks, 1984; Spivak, 1990; Trinh, 1989).

At present, the poststructural position presents a particular problem for feminisms' theorizing, of giving up structures altogether, and especially that of gender (see Miller, 1991; and in general, Fraser, 1989). The contradiction is to retain attention to gender but deny its essentialist character—and two dangers result. One is to move away from the traditional reliance in feminist theory on women's experience, just at the time when all women are gaining power but especially those women whose experience has not formerly counted. The second is a potential reinscribing of oppressive conditions fought against and overcome as attention turns elsewhere. One suggestion to theoretically "resolve" this problem is for a general postmodern feminism (an umbrella for diverse extant views). Its basis, according to Nancy Fraser and Linda Nicholson (1990), is political practice, increasingly a matter of alliances across diversity. Such alliances recognize that inherent not only is difference but also conflict. As the authors conclude, such a view is "already implicitly postmodern" (p. 35).

Critical Theory and Cultural Studies

In the postmodern rapprochement between Anglo-American and Continental philosophy, new studies are emerging, among them cultural studies with roots in "Critical Theory." At the start of this chapter, a kind of generic body of critical scholarship was identified as present in education today; it has a connection to European social theory. Significantly, although postmodern philosophy permeates academia, it is a term that appears in some but not other new studies, in feminist studies as just described but not in multicultural or cultural studies. Cultural studies are connected to philosophy not only through their roots but also through the general trend to "deconstruct" traditional philosophy.

Critical Theory. A significant philosophical tradition of the 20th century is "Critical Theory," arising out of Marxist roots in Europe just prior to World War II. Significant as part of its foundation is the German Frankfurt School emigration to the United States and the establishment of the New

School of Social Research. Important philosophers of Critical Theory include Max Horkheimer, Theodor Adorno, and Herbert Marcuse; the present heir is Habermas (with ties to neopragmatism) (see Held, 1980; Seidman, 1983). In the years after its inception, various intellectual streams devolved into social philosophy across many disciplines, including education.[3]

For present purposes, critical theory is best understood as "criticism" of traditional but Continental philosophy of the 19th century (see also Bernstein, 1971). It is antipositivist in its critique of scientific rationality, but also essentialist, universalist, and in some formulations structuralist. Critical Theory is modernist in its initial intention to "redeem" the Enlightenment project (Horkheimer & Adorno, 1989; Huyssen, 1990).

Critical Theory's founding premise concerns the nature of philosophy itself. According to Horkheimer:

The real social function of philosophy lies in its criticism of what is prevalent. . . . [Given current society] philosophy exposes the contradiction in which man is entangled. (1972, pp. 364–365)

Such a contradiction denies the Enlightenment realization of justice, equality, and autonomy for all persons. This contradiction, at the base of Marxist accounts, is founded in the economic and societal structures of Western capitalism. Much of the early Marxist writings is a working through of key concepts, such as class, base and superstructure, ideology, and false consciousness.

For neo-Marxists, theory not only attends to economic and historical conditions (with roots in Hegel's historicism) but also to matters of the general culture. Initially these matters are about high

as opposed to low or popular culture, but this distinction subsequently blurs. The first studies, and even ones undertaken later, critique Kant's vision of the aesthetic (Bourdieu, 1984; see Horkheimer, 1972, p. 273).

Cultural studies. Beginning with studies of "culture" in the 1950s, a new movement of scholarship ultimately challenges Critical Theory for being teleological, essentialist, Eurocentric, and economistic. As a field of study in the postmodern condition, "cultural studies" lacks precise definition, although Stuart Hall's "study of culture's relations and effects" (1992, p. 284) is appropriate. Today, cultural studies draws on various sources, among them neo-Marxism, feminism, psychoanalysis, poststructuralism, and postmodernism (Grossberg, Nelson, & Treichler, 1992)—but in a move precisely antidisciplinary (During, 1993; Nelson, Treichler, & Grossberg, 1992). Two traditions have evolved within cultural studies: "culturalist" and "structuralist," with different but overlapping roots, interests, and methods of inquiry (During, 1993, p. 5).

As a critique or extension of critical theory, cultural studies attends to structures and poststructures beyond those that are economic and historical, to hegemony out of ideology, to all forms of social production, and to culture in everyday life (see McRobbie, 1992). Many of its studies focus on specific cultural forms (film, rock and roll, and so on), paradoxically one might say as nonrepresentational inquiry of cultural representations. Politically, cultural studies entails attention to the roles of intellectuals and their self-critique in specific historic situations, and its aim is intervention (see Hall, 1992). Within the field, varying national traditions have evolved out of roots in Great Britain, but in all settings—although not so much in the United States—work is conducted from the margins. One significant current interest is race theory, posed as "interruption"

---

[3] There are important contributions to critical theory in education; among them, movements in "the new sociology of knowledge," critical curriculum studies, and liberatory or "critical pedagogy."

to the study of culture, just as feminist theorizing has been (Hall, 1992, p. 282). Finally, philosophy appears to play a scant role in discussions of cultural studies, but much of its theory has philosophical connections.[4]

Pragmatism

"America's one original contribution to the world of philosophy" (Diggins, 1994, p. 2), pragmatism is applied to a diverse set of views originated just prior to the 20th century and, as indicated previously, dominant for up to three-quarters of a century thereafter. Initially, the logician Charles Sanders Peirce coins the term for a movement further developed by William James, John Dewey, George Herbert Mead, and several others. Among important contributions are the social psychologies of James and Mead, and Dewey writes in various fields, among them epistemology, ethics, and aesthetics. The roots of these contributors are diverse, from Socrates through Mill (Thayer, 1968, p. 5). Dewey is influenced by Hegel and Green, among others, and does a dissertation on Kant. Over the course of its development, pragmatism has come to mean

> one broad philosophic attitude toward . . . experience: theorizing over experience is . . . fundamentally motivated and justified by conditions of efficacy and utility . . . [in service to] various aims and needs. The ways in which experience is apprehended, systematized, and anticipated may be many. (Cherryholmes, 1994, p. 4)

Thus, pluralism characterizes pragmatism, as does a basic orientation toward useful consequences.

Often misunderstood as narrowly instrumental, the "pragmatist maxim" entails the idea that "knowledge is power" (Thayer, 1968, p. 6). This is because thought assumes credence, not essentially

for inherent meaning, but for what it portends. Pragmatists understand and begin from a significant logical point, one posited historically prior to the linguistic turn. This point is that thought is always more than "what it says." This move entails power because use or action logically follows from thought, and thus whose thought and in what circumstances (how contextualized) becomes salient. Moreover change is especially pertinent because action is embedded in interpretation itself—and new interpretations mean new "praxis" (see Gunn, 1992, p. 4). Because of this basis in "instrumentalism," pragmatism has always been a variety of active, practical doctrines (Thayer, 1968, p. 8). This is no less true for its first phase in the early part of this century as it is for its current second phase.

Various neopragmatisms are important today: they are what might be called the literary pragmatists, the social pragmatists, the language pragmatists, and the feminist pragmatists, among others (see Gunn, 1992; Murphy, 1990; Seigfried, 1991). These neopragmatists cross various traditional disciplines—philosophy (including ethics and aesthetics), political science, literary criticism, history, art history, and various social sciences. Intellectually, neopragmatism's most significant development is ties between American and European thought; now the "great divide" of the last century is seemingly irrevocably breached.

This development of a broad, pragmatist social theory has consequences for traditional philosophy and thus, this is "the promise of pragmatism," to borrow a phrase from historian John Patrick Diggins. Undercut, overall, is the appearance/reality distinction, the modern problem of representation. As Richard Rorty explains, pragmatism eschews any idea that "metaphysics, empirical science, or some other discipline might someday penetrate the veil of appearances and allow us to glimpse things as they are in themselves" (Rorty, 1990, p. 2). Thoughts, beliefs, assertions are simply true or false in themselves (a kind of irony), not as

---

[4]Thanks here to George Noblit and Joe Kretovics.

representations. Neopragmatism accepts the linguistic turn and a semantic conception of truth that accompanies it.

Finally, other tenets follow from the demise of representationalism. According to Richard Bernstein (1991), there are five tenets. First is antifoundationalism, the giving up of all searches for certainty. Second is fallibilism, "where we realize that although we must begin inquiry with prejudgments and can never call everything into question at once, nevertheless there is no belief or thesis . . . that is not open to further interpretation or criticism" (p. 327). Antifoundational, fallibilistic pragmatists are skeptical to theory. The third is related to the second, a skepticism toward one's own viewpoint and thus a nurturing of critical communities of inquirers; the self is always social. Fourth is "the awareness and sensitivity to radical contingency and chance that mark the universe, our inquiries, our lives" (p. 328). The "open universe" contains elements unforeseen and unpredictable. Fifth is pluralism, the idea that multiple visions of the world and multiple courses of action count. This plurality, contends Bernstein, characterizes what he calls a "decentering" of philosophy itself (others name the field dispersed, even dead). Today, philosophy is "a radical pluralization of different vocabularies, research programs, . . . [and] voices demanding to be heard" (Bernstein, 1991, p. 335), and neopragmatism is its most promising, currently developing tradition.

Conclusion

The quotation that begins this chapter—from America's best-known philosopher today, Richard Rorty (1992a, p. 2)—exemplifies the present state of philosophy, and intellectual life in general. It is playful and ironic, unstable and dispersed in meaning. Its content is precisely ambiguous and multiple: What is a discipline today? What is knowledge? How is it sought? What is the relation

of opinion? Which opinions matter? Philosophy has always been opinion, but always opinions of some folks and not others. Thus philosophy has always been about power but until recently this was denied or overlooked. The irony is that until very recently, philosophic opinions counted as certain knowledge, as truth. All this has changed. Today, philosophic inquiry is no longer traditional but postmodern, at least in the present interpretation. It is playful because other interpretations are surely possible: postmodern theory is humble and tentative (see also Hall, 1992). It is, as the introduction attests, part of a time of change. However, unlike previous times, change, uncertainty, and indeterminacy are characteristic and enduring, dimensions of personal and social life to be lived with, not controlled or overcome.

What has been presented here is one person's view and *I* am specifically contextualized: white, female, middle class, middle age, single/heterosexual, and even untenured as a professor, living as a fairly new emigre (with a cat) in the southeastern United States. All of this matters, as many feminists and others aware of new historicism know, in what I say and am able to say, in what kinds of power and limitations I have. As Stephen Toulmin writes, the local, particular, and timely were significant at the beginning of the Renaissance modernity and are again in postmodernity.

As the chapter attests, postmodern intellectual—and specifically philosophical—life is diverse, fluid and dynamic, unstable. Nonetheless, something—lessons one might posit—can be learned. I see these as intellectual, ethical, and programmatic. As intellectual lesson, one begins with context both in historicist and interpretivist terms, understanding that there is no neutral theory or idea; there are assumptions and they have histories and entailments, too. About this history, one sees that contrary to previous views, any era is comprised of conflict as well as consensus, of disruption as well as continuity. One knows also that the assumptions and worldviews of today are changing and will continue to change.

In general, the postmodern worldview is complex, and fixing a definition of the era is just untenable. Nonetheless, there are identifiable characteristics. One most significant feature is that person live with tentativeness and ambiguity toward which there are various ideological responses. Some persons long for tradition, stability, and home (Connolly, 1993), and some kind of standard or norm upon which to base their existence. Others, more adaptive perhaps, revel in the uncertainty, content to attempt some kind of meaningful life—and even create new meanings—without an initiating framework (see Rorty, 1989). Today, I and others see the first as moderns and the second as postmoderns. Interestingly, within both orientations are ideological responses that are conservative and progressive. What is ideological in this era of modern/postmodern tension is an understanding of and response to power.

Consideration of power is attending to relationships between persons and thus to ethics. One result of the movement from traditional to postmodern philosophy is a deprivileging of canon and thus of some groups of persons over others. No longer do the theoretical contributions of "dead, white males" (no matter how significant—and one notes their overwhelming dominance in this chapter) singly count; multiple views constitute philosophy and especially those from formerly marginalized peoples. This change in tradition bothers some persons, whereas it empowers others. A second result concerns the perceived failure of the Enlightenment project and the connection between human emancipation and philosophical theory. Currently, "the problem of poststructuralism," referred to in feminist theory, looms large and needs to be worked through. Finally, a result is to understand that philosophy itself is ethical. If one sees intellectual contributions and their connections to everyday life as inter-

twined vocabularies, then the postmodern prevails. But more is needed ethically. This is to accept or create and promote those vocabularies that avow liberalism—picking up the spirit of the Enlightenment but in a postmodern vein. As Rorty (1989) explains,

> human solidarity is not a matter of sharing a common truth or a common goal but of sharing a common selfish hope, the hope that one's world . . . [is free of humiliation, that is, that the little things woven into it are] not destroyed. (p. 92)

Finally, armed with a general intellectual understanding and an ethical commitment, there is a programmatic lesson. Each person, each educational researcher, each expert in special education has a responsibility to attend to the postmodern condition: we are in it, it isn't going away. The basic responsibility, I believe, is to read—a simple and straightforward beginning. First, reading must be about new perspectives, new fields of knowledge, new ideas. It is reading outside of a known literature. Such reading serves as an important catalyst to encourage new conceptions and new practices. Given the postmodern era, this is all that really can be proposed, and it just may be enough—that is, enough to facilitate educational change that genuinely builds in the hope for a more equal, just, happy, and prosperous life for more people within these changing times.[5]

References

Baynes, K., Bohman, J., & McCarthy, T. (Eds.). (1987). *After philosophy: End or transformation?* Cambridge: MIT Press.

Bernstein, R. (1971). *Praxis and action: Contemporary philosophies of human activity.* Philadelphia: University of Pennsylvania Press.

---

[5]A special thank-you to Jim Paul and Michael Churton for their invitation and patience. I am deeply humbled in this undertaking.

Bernstein, R. (1983). *Beyond objectivism and relativism: Science, hermeneutics, and praxis.* Philadelphia: University of Pennsylvania Press.

Bernstein, R. (1991). Appendix: Pragmatism, pluralism, and the healing of wounds. In *The new constellation: The ethical-political horizons of modernity/postmodernity* (pp. 323–340). Cambridge: MIT Press. (Original work published 1988)

Bourdieu, P. (1984). *Distinction: A social critique of the judgment of taste* (R. Nice, Trans.). Cambridge: Harvard University Press.

Britzman, D. (1991). *Practice makes practice: A critical study of learning to teach.* Albany: State University of New York Press.

Calhoun, C. (1993). Postmodernism as pseudohistory. *Theory, Culture & Society, 10*(1): 75–96.

Cherryholmes, C. (1988). *Power and criticism: Poststructural investigations in education.* New York: Teachers College Press.

Cherryholmes, C. (1994, April). *What pragmatism means: Different interpretations and views.* Paper presented at the annual meeting of the American Educational Research Association, New Orleans.

Collins, P. (1990). The social construction of black feminist thought. In M. Malson, E. Mudimbe-Boyi, J. O'Barr, & M. Wyer (Eds.), *Black women in America* (pp. 297–325). Chicago: The University of Chicago Press.

Connolly, W. (1993). *Political theory and modernity* (2nd ed.). Ithaca, NY: Cornell University Press. (Original work published 1988)

Culler, J. (1982). *On deconstruction: Theory and criticism after structuralism.* Ithaca, NY: Cornell University Press.

Davidson, D. (1985). On the very idea of a conceptual scheme. In J. Rajchman & C. West (Eds.), *Postanalytic philosophy* (pp. 129–144). New York: Columbia University Press. (Original work published 1973)

DeGeorge, R., & DeGeorge, F. (1972). *The structuralists: From Marx to Levi-Strauss.* Garden City, NY: Anchor.

Dewey, J. (1929). *The quest for certainty: A study of the relation of knowledge and action.* New York: Minton, Balch & Company.

Diggins, J. (1994). *The promise of pragmatism: Modernism and the crisis of knowledge and authority.* Chicago: The University of Chicago Press.

During, S. (Ed.). (1993). *The cultural studies reader.* London: Routledge.

Eagleton, T. (1983). *Literary theory: An introduction.* Minneapolis: University of Minnesota Press.

Foster, H. (1983). Postmodernism: A preface. In H. Foster (Ed.), *The anti-aesthetic: Essays of postmodern culture* (pp. ix–xvi). Port Townsend, WA: Bay Press.

Foucault, M. (1980). Truth and power. In C. Gordon (Ed.), *Power/knowledge: Selected interviews & other writings* (pp. 109–133). New York: Pantheon.

Fraser, N. (1989). *Unruly practices: Power, discourse and gender in contemporary social theory.* Minneapolis: University of Minnesota Press.

Fraser, N., & Nicholson, L. (1990). Social criticism without philosophy: An encounter between feminism and postmodernism. In L. Nicholson (Ed.), *Feminism/postmodernism* (pp. 19–38). New York: Routledge.

Giroux, H. (1988). Postmodernism and the discourse of educational criticism. *Journal of Education, 170*(3): 5–30.

Giroux, H. (Ed.). (1991). *Postmodernism, feminism, and cultural politics: Redrawing educational boundaries.* Albany: State University of New York Press.

Grossberg, L., Nelson, C., & Treichler, P. (Eds.). (1992). *Cultural studies.* New York: Routledge.

Gunn, G. (1992). *Thinking across the American grain: Ideology, intellect, and the new pragmatism.* Chicago: The University of Chicago Press.

Habermas, J. (1983). Modernity—An incomplete project. In H. Foster (Ed.), *The anti-aesthetic: Essays on postmodern culture* (pp. 3–15). Port Townsend, WA: Bay Press.

Habermas, J. (1985). Neoconservative culture criticism in the United States and West Germany: An intellectual movement in two political cultures. In R. Bernstein (Ed.), *Habermas and modernity* (pp. 78–94). Cambridge: MIT Press.

Hall, S. (1992). Cultural studies and its theoretical legacies. In L. Grossberg, C. Nelson, & P. Treichler (Eds.), *Cultural studies* (pp. 277–294). New York: Routledge.

Hamlyn, D. (1987). *A history of Western philosophy.* Middlesex, London: Viking Press.

Hanson, N. (1958). *Patterns of discovery.* Cambridge: Cambridge University Press.

Held, D. (1980). *Introduction to critical theory: Horkheimer to Habermas.* Berkeley: University of California Press.

hooks, b. (1984). *Feminist theory: From margin to center.* Boston: South End Press.

Horkheimer, M. (1972). *Critical theory: Selected essays.* New York: Herder and Herder. (Original work published 1968)

Horkheimer, M., & Adorno, T. (1989). *Dialectic of enlightenment* (J. Cumming, Trans.). New York: Continuum. (Original work published 1944)

Hutcheon, L. (1988). *A poetics of postmodernism: History, theory, fiction.* New York: Routledge.

Huyssen, A. (1990). Mapping the postmodern. In L. Nicholson (Ed.), *Feminism/postmodernism* (pp. 234–277). New York: Routledge. (Original work published 1984)

Innis, R. (Ed.). (1985). *Semiotics: An introductory anthology.* Bloomington: Indiana University Press.

Jaggar, A. (1983). *Feminist politics and human nature.* Totowa, NJ: Rowman & Allanheld.

Jay, M. (1994). *Downcast eyes: The denigration of vision in twentieth-century French thought.* Berkeley: University of California Press.

Kaminsky, J. (1993). *A new history of educational philosophy.* Westport, CT: Greenwood.

Kohli, W. (1995). *Critical conversations in philosophy of education.* New York: Routledge.

Kuhn, T. (1970). *The structure of scientific revolutions* (2nd ed.). Chicago: The University of Chicago Press.

Kuhn, T. (1980). Theory-choice. In E. Klemke, R. Hollinger, & A. D. Kline (Eds.), *Introductory readings in the philosophy of science* (pp. 207–209). Buffalo, NY: Prometheus. (Original work published 1970)

Lakatos, I., & Musgrave, A. (Eds.). (1970). *Criticism and the growth of knowledge.* Cambridge: Cambridge University Press.

Lather, P. (1991). *Getting smart: Feminist research and pedagogy with/in the postmodern.* New York: Routledge.

Lloyd, G. (1984). *The man of reason: "Male" and "female" in Western philosophy.* Minneapolis: University of Minnesota Press.

Lyotard, J. (1984). *The postmodern condition: A report on knowledge* (G. Bennington & B. Massumi, Trans.). Minneapolis: University of Minnesota Press.

MacIntyre, A. (1990). *Three rival versions of moral enquiry: Encyclopedia, genealogy, and tradition.* Notre Dame: University of Notre Dame Press.

Mahowald, M. (1983). *Philosophy of woman: An anthology of classic and current concepts* (2nd ed.). Indianapolis: Hackett.

Manicas, P. (1987). *A history & philosophy of the social sciences.* Oxford: Basil Blackwell.

McRobbie, A. (1992). Post-Marxism and cultural studies: A post-script. In L. Grossberg, C. Nelson, & P. Treichler (Eds.), *Cultural studies* (pp. 719–730). New York: Routledge.

Miller, N. (1991). *Getting personal: Feminist occasions and other autobiographical acts.* New York: Routledge.

Murphy, J. (1990). *Pragmatism: From Peirce to Davidson.* Boulder, CO: Westview.

Nelson, C., Treichler, P., & Grossberg, L. (1992). Cultural studies: An introduction. In L. Grossberg, C. Nelson, & P. Treichler (Eds.), *Cultural studies* (pp. 1–22). New York: Routledge.

Nelson, J., Megill, A., & McCloskey, D. (Eds.). (1987). *The rhetoric of the human sciences: Language and argument in scholarship and public affairs.* Madison: University of Wisconsin Press.

Oldroyd, D. (1986). *The arch of knowledge: An introductory study of the history and methodology of science.* New York: Methuen.

Palmer, R. (1969). *Hermeneutics: Interpretation theory in Schleiermacher, Dilthey, Heidegger, and Gadamer.* Evanston, IL: Northwestern University Press.

Phillips, D. (1985). Philosophy of education. In T. Husen & T. N. Postlethwaite (Eds.), *International encyclopedia of education: Research studies* (pp. 3859–3877). Oxford: Pergamon Press.

Popkewitz, T. (1991). *A political sociology of educational reform: Power/ knowledge in teaching, teacher education, and research.* New York: Teachers College Press.

Quine, W. (1961). Two dogmas of empiricism. In *From a logical point of view* (2nd ed.) (pp. 20–46). Cambridge: Harvard University Press.

Rabinow, P., & Sullivan, W. (1979). Introduction, the interpretive turn: Emergence of an approach. In P. Rabinow & W. Sullivan (Eds.), *Interpretive social science: A reader* (pp. 1–21). Berkeley: University of California Press.

Rajchman, J. (1985). Philosophy in America. In J. Rajchman & C. West (Eds.), *Post-analytic philosophy* (pp. ix–xxx). New York: Columbia University Press.

Reichenbach, H. (1954). *The rise of scientific philosophy.* Berkeley: University of California Press.

Rorty, R. (1982). *Consequences of pragmatism.* Minneapolis: University of Minnesota Press.

Rorty, R. (1989). *Contingency, irony, and solidarity.* Cambridge: Cambridge University Press.

Rorty, R. (1990). Introduction: Pragmatism as anti-representationalism. In J. Murphy, *Pragmatism: From Peirce to Davidson* (pp. 1–6). Boulder, CO: Westview.

Rorty, R. (1992a). Metaphysical difficulties of linguistic philosophy. In R. Rorty (Ed.), *The linguistic turn: Essays in philosophical method* (pp. 1–39). Chicago: University of Chicago Press. (Original work published in 1967)

Rorty, R. (1992b). Ten years after. In R. Rorty (Ed.), *The linguistic turn: Essays in philosophical method* (pp. 361–370). Chicago: University of Chicago Press. (Original work published 1977)

Rosenberg, M. (1955). *Introduction to philosophy.* New York: Philosophical Library.

Ross, A. (1988). *Universal abandon? A politics of postmodernism.* Minneapolis: University of Minnesota Press.

Ross, D. (1991). *The origins of American social science.* Cambridge: Cambridge University Press.

Russell, B. (1945). *A history of Western philosophy: And its connection with political and social circumstances from the earliest times to the present day.* New York: Simon & Schuster.

Seidman, S. (1983). *Liberalism and the origins of European social theory.* Berkeley: University of California Press.

Seigfried, C. (1991). Where are all the pragmatist feminists? *Hypatia, 6*(2): 1–20.

Shapiro, M. (1992). *Reading the postmodern polity: Political theory as textual practice.* Minneapolis: University of Minnesota Press.

Spivak, G. (1990). *The post-colonial critic: Interviews, strategies, dialogues.* New York: Routledge.

Stallknecht, N., & Brumbaugh, R. (1950). *The spirit of western philosophy: A historical interpretation including selections from the major European philosophers.* New York: Longmans, Green and Company.

Stone, L. (1992). The essentialist tension in reflective teacher education. In L. Valli (Ed.). *Reflective teacher education: Cases and critiques* (pp. 198–211, 258–261). Albany: State University of New York Press.

Stone, L. (1994a). Introducing education feminism. In L. Stone (Ed.), *The education feminism reader* (pp. 1–13). New York: Routledge.

Stone, L. (1994b, August). Misreading Dewey: A thesis and exemplar. In P. Smeyers (Ed.), *Identity, culture, and education* (pp. 317–331). Leuven, Belgium: Leuven University Press.

Stone, L. (1995). Narrative in philosophy of education: A feminist tale of "uncertain" knowledge. In W. Kohli (Ed.), *Critical conversations in philosophy of education* (pp. 173–189). New York: Routledge.

Taylor, C. (1979). Interpretation and the sciences of man. In P. Rabinow & W. Sullivan (Eds.), *Interpretive social science: A reader* (pp. 25–71). Berkeley: University of California Press. (Original work published 1971).

Thayer, H. (1968). *Meaning and action: A critical history of pragmatism.* Indianapolis, IN: Bobbs-Merrill.

Toulmin, S. (1990). *Cosmopolis: The hidden agenda of modernity.* New York: Free Press.

Trinh, T. (1989). *Woman, native, other: Writing postcoloniality and feminism.* Bloomington: Indiana University Press.

Walsh, M. (1985). *A history of philosophy.* London: Geoffrey Chapman.

Warnock, M. (1992). *The uses of philosophy.* Oxford: Blackwell.

Weedon, C. (1987). *Feminist practice and post-structural theory.* Oxford: Blackwell.

West, C. (1989). *The American evasion of philosophy: A genealogy of pragmatism.* Madison: University of Wisconsin Press.

Wexler, P. (1987). *Social analysis of education: After the new sociology.* London: Routledge & Kegan Paul.

White, H. (1978). *Topics of discourse: Essays in cultural criticism.* Baltimore: Johns Hopkins University Press.

White, H. (1986). The historical text as literary artifact. In H. Adams & L. Searle (Eds.), *Critical theory since 1965* (pp. 395–407). Tallahassee: Florida State University Press. (Original work published 1974)

Young, R. (1990). *A critical theory of education: Habermas and our children's future.* New York: Teachers College Press.

CHAPTER 3

Ecology of the Family as a Context for Human Development: Research Perspectives

URIE BRONFENBRENNER
Cornell University

The purpose of this article is to document and delineate promising lines of research on external influences that affect the capacity of families to foster the healthy development of their children. The focus differs from that of most studies of the family as a context of human development, because the majority have concentrated on intrafamilial processes of parent-child interaction, a fact that is reflected in Maccoby and Martin's (1983) recent authoritative review of research on family influences on development. By contrast, the focus of the present analysis can be described as "once removed." The research question becomes: How are intrafamilial processes affected by extrafamilial conditions?

This review is based on a longer background paper prepared at the request of the Human Learning and Behavior Branch of the National Institute of Child Health and Human Development in connnection with the development of their Five Year Plan for Research.

I am indebted to the following colleagues for their constructive criticism of the original document: Josephine Arastah, Mavis Hetherington, Richard Lerner, Jeylan T. Mortimer, Joseph H. Pleck, Lea Pulkinnen, Michael Rutter, Klaus Schneewind, and Diana Slaughter. Appreciation is also expressed to Gerri Jones for typing innumerable revisions of the manuscript.

Correspondence concerning this article should be sent to Urie Bronfenbrenner, Department of Human Development and Family Studies, Cornell University, Ithaca, NY 14853.

Copyright © 1986 by the American Psychological Association. Reprinted with permission.

Paradigm Parameters

In tracing the evolution of research models in developmental science, Bronfenbrenner and Crouter (1983) distinguished a series of progressively more sophisticated scientific paradigms for investigating the impact of environment on development. These paradigms provide a useful framework for ordering and analyzing studies bearing on the topic of this review. At the most general level, the research models vary simultaneously along two dimensions. As applied to the subject at hand, the first pertains to the structure of the external systems that affect the family and the manner in which they exert their influence. The second dimension relates to the degree of explicitness and differentiation accorded to intrafamilial processes that are influenced by the external environment.

External Systems Affecting the Family

Research paradigms can be distinguished in terms of three different environmental systems that can serve as sources of external influence on the family.

Mesosystem models. Although the family is the principal context in which human development takes place, it is but one of several settings in which developmental processes can and do occur.

Moreover, the processes operating in different settings are not independent of each other. To cite a common example, events at home can affect the child's progress in school, and vice versa. Despite the obviousness of this fact, it was not until relatively recently that students of development began to employ research designs that could identify the influences operating, in both directions, between the principal settings in which human development occurs. The term *mesosystem* has been used to characterize analytic models of this kind (Bronfenbrenner, 1979). The results of studies employing this type of paradigm in relation to the family are summarized in the section "Mesosystem Models."

Exosystem models. The psychological development of children in the family is affected not only by what happens in the other environments in which children spend their time but also by what occurs in the other settings in which their parents live their lives, especially in a place that children seldom enter—the parents' world of work. Another domain to which children tend to have limited access is the parents' circle of friends and acquaintances—their social network. Such environments "external" to the developing person are referred to as "exosystems." The findings of investigations employing exosystem designs are reviewed in the section "Exosystem Models."

Chronosystem models. Traditionally in developmental science, the passage of time has been treated as synonymous with chronological age; that is, as a frame of reference for studying psychological changes within individuals as they grow older. Especially during the past decade, however, research on human development has projected the factor of time along a new axis. Beginning in the mid 1970s, an increasing number of investigators have employed research designs that take into account changes over time not only within the person but also in the environment and—what is even more critical—that permit analyzing the dynamic relation between these two processes. To distinguish such investigations from more traditional longitudinal studies focusing exclusively on the individual, I have proposed the term *chronosystem* for designating a research model that makes possible examining the influence on the person's development of changes (and continuities) over time in the environments in which the person is living (Bronfenbrenner, 1986a).

The simplest form of chronosystem focuses around a life transition. Two types of transition are usefully distinguished: normative (school entry, puberty, entering the labor force, marriage, retirement) and nonnormative (a death or severe illness in the family, divorce, moving, winning the sweepstakes). Such transitions occur throughout the life span and often serve as a direct impetus for developmental change. Their relevance for the present review, however, lies in the fact that they can also influence development indirectly by affecting family processes.

A more advanced form of chronosystem examines the cumulative effects of an entire sequence of developmental transition over an extended period of the person's life—what Elder (1974, 1985) has referred to as the life course. During the past decade, studies of the impact of personal and historical life events on family processes and on their developmental outcomes have received increasing attention. Several of these investigations have yielded findings of considerable substantive and theoretical significance. These are described, along with other relevant searches employing a chronosystem design, below ("Chronosystem Models").

Family Processes in Context

With respect to explicitness and complexity, research paradigms can again be differentiated at three successive levels.

Social address model. At the first level, the family processes are not made explicit at all, because the paradigm is limited to the comparison of developmental outcomes for children or adults living in contrasting environments as defined by geography (e.g., rural vs. urban, Japan vs. the United States), or by social background (socioeconomic status, ethnicity, religion, etc.). Hence the name "social address" (Bronfenbrenner, 1979). Given their restricted scope, social address models have a number of important limitations summarized in the following passage:

> No explicit consideration is given . . . to intervening structures or processes through which the environment might affect the course of development. One looks only at the social address—that is, the environmental label—with no attention to what the environment is like, what people are living there, what they are doing, or how the activities taking place could affect the child. (Bronfenbrenner & Crouter, 1983, pp. 361–362)

Despite these shortcomings, social address models remain one of the most widely used paradigms in the study of environmental influences on development. Two reasons may account for their scientific popularity. The first is their comparative simplicity, both at a conceptual and an operational level. Indeed, they can be, and sometimes have been, employed without doing very much thinking in advance, a procedure, alas, that is reflected in the product. But social address models, when appropriately applied, can also serve as a helpful scientific tool. Precisely because of their simplicity, they can be implemented easily and quickly. Hence, they may often be the strategies of choice for exploring uncharted domains. Like the surveyor's grid, they provide a useful frame for describing at least the surface of the new terrain. A case in point is their application in identifying developmental outcomes associated with what Bronfenbrenner and Crouter (1983) have called the

"new demography"—single parents, day care, mothers in the labor force, remarriage, or (perhaps soon) fathers in the role of principal caregiver.

Process-context model. Paradigms at this second level explicitly provide for assessing the impact of the external environment on particular family processes. As documented in Bronfenbrenner and Crouter's analysis (1983), such paradigms represent a fairly recent scientific development, appearing in a reasonably full form only in the late 1960s and early 1970s. Because the corresponding research designs tend to be more complex than those employed in social address models, a concrete illustration may be helpful. For this purpose, I have selected one of the earliest examples of its kind, but one that still deserves to be emulated as a model for future research. In a series of researches growing out of his doctoral dissertation, Tulkin and his colleagues (Tulkin, 1973a, 1973b, 1977; Tulkin & Cohler, 1973; Tulkin & Covitz, 1975; Tulkin & Kagan, 1972) sought to go beyond the label of social class in order to discover its manifestations in family functioning. The first study focused on families with an infant under one year of age. To control for the child's sex and ordinal position, the sample was limited to firstborn girls, first studied when they were 10 months old. The initial publication (Tulkin & Kagan, 1972), based on home observations, reported that middle-class mothers engaged in more reciprocal interactions with their infants, especially in verbal behavior, and provided them with a greater variety of stimulation. The second study (Tulkin & Cohler, 1973) documented parallel differences in maternal attitudes; middle-class mothers were more likely to subscribe to statements stressing the importance of perceiving and meeting the infant's needs, the value of mother–child interaction, and the moderate control of aggressive impulses. Furthermore, the correlations between maternal behavior and attitudes were substantially greater in middle-class that in lower-class families. Next, in two experiments, Tulkin (1973a, 1973b) found that middle-class infants cried more when separated from their mothers, but were better able to discriminate the mother's voice from that of an unfamiliar female from the same social class. Finally, several years later, Tulkin and Covitz (1975) reassessed the same youngsters after they had entered school. The children's performance on tests of mental ability and language skill showed significant relationships to the prior measures of reciprocal mother–infant interaction, strength of maternal attachment, and voice recognition when the children had been 10 months old. Once again, the observed correlations were higher for middle-class families. Even more important from a developmental perspective, the relationships of maternal behavior at 10 months to the child's behavior at age 6 were considerably greater than the contemporaneous relationships between both types of variables in the first year of life. The investigators, however, were quick to reject the hypothesis of a delayed "sleeper effect." Rather, they argued that mothers who engage in adaptive reciprocal activity with their infants at early ages are likely to continue to do so as the child gets older, thus producing a cumulative trend.

Although a number of other investigators of socialization and social class have observed mother–child interaction, Tulkin's work remains unique in combining three critical features: (a) an emphasis on social class differences in *process* rather than merely in outcome; (b) demonstration of the key role played by child-rearing values and the higher correspondence between parental values and behavior among middle-class than working-class families; and (c) evidence of developmental effects over time.

Person-process-context model. As its name indicates, the next and last process paradigm adds a new, third element to the system. Although the process-context model represented a significant advance over its predecessors, it was based on an unstated assumption—namely, that the impact of a particular external environment on the family was the same irrespective of the personal characteristics of individual family members, including the developing child. The results of the comparatively few studies that have employed a triadic rather than solely dyadic research paradigm call this tacit assumption into question. Research by Crockenberg (1981) illustrates both the model and its message. Working with a middle-class sample, she found that the amount of social support received by mothers from their social network when their infants were 3 months old was positively related to the strength of the child's attachment to its mother at 1 year of age. The beneficial impact of social support varied systematically, however, as a function of the infant's temperament. It was strongest for mothers with the most irritable infants and minimal for those whose babies were emotionally calm. In addition, the author emphasizes that "the least irritable infants appear somewhat impervious to the low support environments which disrupt the development of their more irritable peers . . . the easy babies in this study were unlikely to develop insecure attachments even when potentially unfavorable social milieus existed" (p. 862).

As documented subsequently in this review, the personal characteristics of parents, especially of fathers, are of no less—and perhaps even greater—importance than those of the child in determining the positive or negative impact of the external environment on family processes and their developmental outcomes.

Although research paradigms in the study of development-in-context have become progressively more complex over time both with respect to the analysis of family processes and of environmental systems, this does not mean that the correlation applies at the level of individual studies. Indeed, the opposite is often the case. Thus one encounters chronosystem designs that still rely primarily on social address models for analyzing data, and, conversely, person-process-context designs that give no consideration to the length of time that a family has been exposed to a particular environmental context (for example, unemployment). Moreover, seldom in either instance is there recognition of the ambiguity of interpretation produced by the failure to use a more sophisticated design. Fortunately, a number of studies, reported below, do employ paradigms that are comparatively advanced on both dimensions and, thereby, produce a correspondingly rich scientific yield.

Mesosystem Models

Ecology of Family Genetics

Studies of twins have typically reported correlations between IQ scores of identical twins reared apart that are quite substantial and appreciably greater than those for fraternal twins reared in the same home. Thus Bouchard and McGue (1981), in their comprehensive review of studies of family resemblance in cognitive ability, report an average weighted correlation of .72 for the former group versus .60 for the latter. Such finding are typically interpreted as testifying to the primacy of genetic influences in the determination of intelligence (e.g., Burt, 1966; Jensen, 1969, 1980; Loehlin, Lindzey, & Spuhler, 1975). Underlying this interpretation is the assumption that twins reared apart are experiencing widely different environments, so that the substantial similarity between them must be attributable primarily to their common genetic endowment. A mesosystem model calls this assumption into question on the ground that, even thought they are not living in the same home, the twins may share common environments in other settings. To test this assumption, Bronfenbrenner

(1975) recalculated correlations based on subgroups of twins sharing common environments as follows:

1. Among 35 pairs of separated twins for whom information was available about the community in which they lived, the correlation in Binet IQ for those raised in the same town was .83, for those brought up in different towns, .67.
2. In another sample of 38 separated twins, the correlation for those attending the same school in the same town was .87, for those attending schools in different towns, .66.
3. When the communities in the preceding samples were classified as similar versus dissimilar on the basis of size and economic base (e.g., mining vs. agricultural), the correlation for twins living in similar communities was .86; for those residing in dissimilar localities, .26.

Subsequently, Taylor (1980) independently replicated the same pattern of findings in an analysis based on a reclassification of cases from the same studies as well as additional data from others.

Genetics–Environment Interaction in Family Processes

The pioneering investigation in this domain is one that has been much criticized on technical grounds by proponents of the hereditarian view (e.g., Jensen, 1973), but as a research paradigm it broke new ground. In the late 1930s, Skeels and his colleagues (Skeels & Dye, 1939; Skeels et al., 1938; Skodak & Skeels, 1949) published the first stage of what was to become a classical longitudinal study (Skeels, 1966). The investigators compared mental development of children brought up from an early age in adoptive families and in a control group of youngsters raised by their biological parents. Building on earlier work in this era (Burks, 1928; Leahy, 1935), the investigation is important in three respects. First, following

Burks, the researchers demonstrated, and took into account, the influence of selective placement (the tendency of children of more intelligent biological parents to be placed in more advantaged adoptive homes). Second, Skeels and his associates showed that, while parent–child correlations in intellectual performance were appreciably higher in biological families than in adoptive families, the mean IQ of the adopted children was 20 points higher than that of their natural parents. This phenomenon has since been replicated both in the United States (Scarr & Weinberg, 1976) and in Europe (Schiff et al., 1981, 1982). Third, and the most relevant for present purposes, Skeels and his colleagues gathered and analyzed critical data of a type never before examined in adoptive families—the nature of the home environments and parental behaviors that accounted for the more advanced development of children placed for adoption in middle-class families (Skodak & Skeels, 1949).

An even clearer example of the multiplicative effect of environmental and genetic forces are the Danish and American adoptive studies of the origins of criminal behavior. Taking advantage of the unusually complete multigenerational demographic and health statistics available in Denmark, Hutchings and Mednick (1977) compared the incidence of criminal offenses for males adopted early in life and for their biological and adoptive fathers. Among adopted men for whom neither father had a criminal record, 12% had a criminal record of their own. If either the biological or the adoptive father had a criminal record, the rate rose appreciably (21% and 19%, respectively). If both fathers had recorded offenses, the proportion jumped to 36%.

An American study (Crowe, 1974) reported a more precise multiplicative effect; among adult adoptees whose mothers had a criminal record, the only ones who had criminal records themselves were those who had spent considerable time in institutions or foster homes prior to adoption. This effect was independent of age of adoption, because children transferred at the same ages directly from the biological to the adoptive family did not have criminal records later in life. Crowe's research provides a telling example of how a rather complex mesosystem effect can be demonstrated by applying a fairly simple social address model.

The use of more advanced and differentiated research design for the study of genetics–environment interaction in development is still comparatively rare. A striking finding demonstrates by contradiction the paucity of our knowledge in this sphere. The modest but significant association between family background factors in childhood and subsequent educational and occupational achievement in adulthood has been documented many times. Yet . . . Scarr and McAvay (1984) reported an important qualification with respect to this often cited relationship. Exploiting the methodological leverage provided by a longitudinal study of brothers and sisters brought up in adoptive and biologically related families, the investigators demonstrated that, within biological families, such family background characteristics are much more predictive for sons than for daughters.

The Family and the Hospital

Given the critical importance that hospital care can play in the life and development of young children, it is surprising that so little attention has been paid to the relationship between the hospital and the home as a moderating influence on the child's recuperation. The importance of this relation is illustrated by the results of two studies. Scarr-Salapatek and Williams (1973) assessed the effects of an experimental program carried out with a sample of black mothers and their premature infants from extremely deprived socioeconomic backgrounds. In addition to providing special sensory stimulation procedures by hospital staff, the program involved home visits to the mothers in which they were given instruction, demonstration, and practice in observing, caring for, and carrying out a variety of activities with their infants. At one year of age, the latter showed an IQ score 10 points higher than that of randomly selected control groups, and achieved an average level of 95, thus bringing them to "nearly normal levels of development" (p. 99).

An earlier experiment with an older age group yielded equally impressive results. Prugh and his colleagues (1953) took advantage of a planned change in hospital practice to conduct a comparative study of the reaction of children and their parents to contrasting modes of ward operation. The control group consisted of children admitted and discharged over a 4-month period prior to the introduction of the contemplated change. They experienced "traditional practices of ward management" (p. 75) in which parents were restricted to weekly visiting periods of two hours each. The experimental group, admitted during the succeeding period, could receive visits from parents at any time. Parents were also encouraged to participate in ward care. Greater emotional distress was observed among the children in the control group, both before and as late as a year after discharge from the hospital.

The Family and Day Care

As pointed out by Belsky and his colleagues in a series of comprehensive reviews (Belsky, 1984; Belsky & Steinberg, 1978; Belsky, Steinberg, & Walker, 1982), researchers on day care have limited themselves almost exclusively to the direct effects on the child while neglecting possibly even more powerful influences on family processes. In his most recent review of the few studies that depart from this pattern, Belsky (1984) qualifies previous, more optimistic assessments regarding effects of infant day care on the formation of mother–infant

attachment. After analyzing several recent investigations, Belsky (1984) concludes as follows:

> These new data lead me to modify conclusions that have been arrived at in past reviews in order to underscore the potentially problematic nature of early entry into community-based, as opposed to university-based day care. . . . There seems to be cause for concern about early entry to the kind of day care that is available in most communities. (p. 11)

An additional study by Thompson, Lamb, and Estes (1982) lends support to Belsky's caveat. These investigators report data from a middle-class sample showing that stability of secure attachment between 12 and 19 months was lower among infants placed in day care or whose mothers had returned to work during the first year. The effect for day care was greater than that for maternal employment.

The Family and the Peer Group

In the middle 1960s and early 1970s, a series of studies, conducted both in the United States and other countries (Bronfenbrenner, 1967; Bronfenbrenner, Devereux, Suci, & Rodgers, 1965; Devereux, 1965, 1966; Devereux, Bronfenbrenner, & Rodgers, 1969; Rodgers, 1971), demonstrated powerful and often opposite effects of parental and peer influences on the development of children and youth. Especially instructive is the comparative investigation by Kandel and Lesser (1972), who found that Danish adolescents and youth, in contrast to American teenagers, paradoxically exhibited both greater independence from and closer and warmer relationships with their parents and other adults as opposed to peers, with a corresponding reduction in antisocial behavior. More recently, the developmental importance of the interface between family and peer group has been corroborated in studies focusing on the antecedents of antisocial behavior in adolescence and the entrapment of youth in juvenile delinquency, alcoholism, and substance use (Boehnke et al., 1983; Gold & Petronio, 1980; Jessor, 1986; Kandel, 1986; Pulkkinen, 1983a, 1983b).

Particularly revealing are three recent investigations that have used more sophisticated designs to reveal the interplay between family structure and functioning on the one hand, and indexes of peer group deviance on the other. Thus Dornbusch and his colleagues (1985) first show that, with effects of socioeconomic status held constant, adolescents from mother-only households are more likely than their age-mates from two-parent families to engage in adult disapproved activities (such as smoking, school misbehavior, and delinquency). They then demonstrate that a key process involved in this relationship is the contrasting pattern of decision making prevailing in the two types of family structure, with more unilateral decisions (parent alone, child alone) predominating in the single-parent setting. Substantial difference in antisocial behavior still remained after control for patterns of decision making. These differences were considerably reduced, however, by the presence of a second adult in the single-parent home, *except* in those cases in which the second adult was a stepparent, when the effect was reversed. In other words, having a stepparent increased the likelihood of socially deviant behavior. The effect of the child's own characteristics on the family process is reflected in the fact that all of the above relationships, especially the disruptive influence of a stepparent, were more pronounced for boys than for girls.

A subsequent study by Steinberg (1985) not only replicates the above pattern of findings but further illuminates the nature of the processes involved by using a measure not of the frequency of antisocial behavior per se but of susceptibility to peer group pressure for such activity. Finally, in his most recent report, Steinberg (1986) adds a caveat to conclusions drawn from prior studies of the growing phenomenon of the "latchkey child." Using a conventional "social address" model, these investigations had failed to detect any behavioral difference between such children and those who came home from school to a house in which the parent was present. By employing a person-process-context mesosystem model, Steinberg identified as a crucial variable the extent of parental monitoring and "remote control" of the child's activities in the parent's absence. For example, children whose parents knew their whereabouts were less susceptible to antisocial peer influence. Where such parental monitoring was weak, latchkey children were indeed at greater risk of becoming involved in socially deviant behavior. And once again, the importance of the characteristics of the child was reflected in the fact that males were more susceptible to antisocial influences than females and were less responsive to the moderating effect of increased parental control or monitoring.

Family and School

Research in this sphere has been heavily one-sided. Although there have been numerous investigations of the influence of the family on the child's performance and behavior in school, as yet no researchers have examined how school experiences affect the behavior of children and parents in the home. Several studies, however, have explored how the relation between these two settings might affect children's behavior and development in school environments (Becker & Epstein, 1982; Bronfenbrenner, 1974 a, b; Burns, 1982; Collins, Moles, & Cross, 1982; Epstein 1983a, 1984; Hayes & Grether, 1969; Henderson, 1981; Heyns, 1978; Lightfoot, 1978; Medrich et al., 1982; Smith, 1968; Tangri & Leitch, 1982). Smith's study (1968) is especially noteworthy. She carried out a planned experiment involving a series of ingenious strategies for increasing home–school linkages that brought about significant gains in academic achievement in a sample of approximately 1000 elementary pupils from low-income, predominantly black families.

Almost all of these investigations, however, including Smith's, have focused on techniques of parent involvement rather than on the associated processes taking place within family and classroom and their joint effects on children's learning and development. A notable exception is Epstein's research on "Longitudinal Effects of Family-School-Person Interactions on Student Outcomes" (1983a, 1983b). Working with a sample of almost 1000 eighth-graders, she examined the joint impact of family and classroom processes on change in pupils' attitudes and their academic achievement during the transition between the last year of middle school and the first year of high school. Children from homes or classrooms affording greater opportunities for communication and decision making not only exhibited greater initiative and independence after entering high school, but also received higher grades. Family processes were considerably more powerful in producing change than classroom procedures. School influences were nevertheless effective, especially for pupils from families who had not emphasized intergenerational communication in the home or the child's participation in decision making. The effects of family and school processes were greater than those attributable to socioeconomic status or race.

Exosystem Models

In modern, industrialized societies, there are three exosystems that are especially likely to affect the development of the child, primarily through their influences on family processes. The first of these is the parents' workplace; the second, parents' social networks; and the third, community influences on family functioning.

Family and Work

In their review of research on the effects of parental work on children, Bronfenbrenner and Crouter (1982) pointed out that, until very recently, researchers have treated the job situation of mothers and fathers as separate worlds having no relation to each other and, presumably, leading to rather different results. For mothers, it was the fact of being employed that was thought to be damaging to the child, whereas for fathers it was being unemployed that was seen as the destructive force. Because of this "division of labor," the principal research findings in each domain are most conveniently summarized under separate headings.

Parental Employment and Family Life

The first studies in this sphere appeared in the late 1930s and dealt with the impact on the family of the father's loss of a job during the Great Depression (Angell, 1936; Cavan & Ranck, 1938; Komarovsky, 1940; Morgan, 1939). The husband's unemployment resulted in a loss of status within the family, a marked increase in family tensions and disagreements, and a decrease in social life outside the home. At the same time, the father became increasingly unstable, moody, and depressed. In these early studies, no reference was made to any effects of these disruptive processes on the children; the latter were treated simply as participants playing secondary roles in the family drama. It was not until the 1970s that Elder (1974) began his exploitation of archival data to trace the life course of *Children of the Great Depression* (1974). Because he also employed a more powerful chronosystem paradigm for this purpose, Elder's findings will be presented in a later section, in which such models and their results are reviewed.

In 1958, Miller and Swanson called attention to another aspect of the father's work situation that appeared to affect parental child-rearing attitudes and practices. The investigators distinguished between two main types of work organization: bureaucratic and entrepreneurial. The first, represented by large-scale businesses, was characterized by relatively more secure conditions of work, manifested by such features as regular hours, stabilized wages, unemployment insurance, and retirement funds. The second, exemplified by small-scale, family-owned businesses, involved greater initiatives, competitiveness, risk taking, and insecurity regarding the future. Miller and Swanson reported that wives of men from bureaucratic backgrounds described styles of upbringing that were more permissive and laid greater stress on the development of interpersonal skills; by contrast, wives of husbands working in entrepreneurial settings were found to be more concerned with individual achievement and striving. A decade later, similar findings based on Miller and Swanson's occupational dichotomy were obtained by Caudill and Weinstein in Japan (1969).

The hypothesis that the structure and content of activities in the father's job can influence the family's child-rearing values has been investigated by Kohn and his colleagues. In his first study, Kohn (1969) demonstrated that working-class men whose jobs typically required compliance with authority tended to hold values that stressed obedience in their children; by contrast, middle-class fathers expected self-direction and independence, the qualities called for by the demands of their occupations. Occupational values were also reflected in both parents' child-rearing practices. Subsequently, Kohn and Schooler (1973, 1978, 1982, 1983) examined the nature of work in a more fine-grained analysis, focusing on the dimension of "occupational self-direction"—the extent to which a job requires complex skills, autonomy, and lack of routination—and its relation to worker's "intellectual flexibility" as measured in a series of standardized tests. Using causal modeling techniques with longitudinal data, the investigators demon-

strated that the occupational self-direction of a job could affect one's intellectual flexibility 10 years later. This finding was subsequently replicated in a comparative study including samples both from the United States and Poland (Slomezynski, Miller, & Kohn, 1981).

The key question left unresolved in the work of Kohn and his colleagues concerns the last step in the developmental sequence that he posits: Does the opportunity for self-direction in the parent's job, and the intellectual flexibility that it generates, influence the actual child-rearing behavior of the parents and thereby affect the development of the child? The one study I have been able to find that bears on this issue did not yield very powerful results. Using data from a sample of several hundred 12th-graders, Morgan, Alwin, and Griffin (1979) found the expected association between father's occupation and mother's child-rearing values. But when these value measures were related to various aspects of the adolescent's academic career, the findings presented a somewhat mixed picture. Neither the adolescents' school grades, academic self-esteem, expected educational occupational attainment, nor their generalized sense of personal control were affected. The mother's child-rearing values, however, did predict the child's curriculum placement (measured on a continuum from vocational-commercial courses to college preparation), as well as the young person's involvement in school activities. The latter finding, however, held only for white students, not for blacks. Note that even in this study, no data are available on the parents' behavior, which constitutes a critical link in the postulated causal chain.

A closer approximation of the processes involved appears in a longitudinal research conducted by Mortimer and her colleagues (Mortimer, 1974, 1975, 1976; Mortimer & Kumka, 1982; Mortimer & Lorence, 1979; Mortimer, Lorence, & Kumka, 1982). Applying Kohn's theoretical schema in a re-analysis of panel study data, the investigators were able to demonstrate a strong tendency for sons to chose an occupation similar to their fathers', as defined along dimensions of work autonomy and the function of work activities. The most effective transmission of occupational value and choice occurred under a combination of a prestigious parental role model and a close father–son relationship. Mortimer's most recent study (Mortimer, Lorence, & Kumka, 1986) establishes the mediating role of the family in adult development by documenting that, compared to men who remained single, men who married during the decade following graduation had greater career stability, income, and work autonomy and exhibited greater job satisfaction. There was substantial evidence that these findings were not attributable to selection processes. The special strength of Mortimer's work lies in the inclusion of family relationships as intervening links in her model.

A third line of investigation, emerging in the middle 1960s, reflects a significant elaboration in the latent structure of research designs in this sphere. The earliest studies in this domain focused on the effects of conflicting time schedules. For example, Mott, Mann, McLoughlin, and Warwick (1965) found that workers on the late afternoon shift rarely saw their school-age children during the work week. The job of discipline fell to the mother, and the shortage of time shared by both parents produced family conflicts over what to do with that time. A subsequent study (Landy, Rosenberg, and Sutton-Smith, 1969) examined the impact on daughters of the fathers' working on a night shift. The daughters of men so employed showed significantly lower scores in tests of academic achievement.[1]

Kanter (1977) introduced the concept of "work absorption" to describe the extent to which work made demands on one's physical and mental energy. In the same year, Heath (1977) studied the effects of this phenomenon and reported that it had a "narrowing effect" on men who had little time for nonwork activities, including spending time with their children. Work absorption tended to generate guilt and increased irritability and impatience in dealing with the child. Two studies have gone a step further to demonstrate the interaction between work and family as a two-way system, with "spillover," in both directions, of tension, satisfactions, and modes of interaction (Crouter, 1984; Piotrkowski, 1979).

Finally, Bohen and Viveros-Long (1981) exploited an experiment of nature to investigate the impact of flexible work hours (flextime) on family life. They compared two federal agencies engaged in similar work and staffed by similar personnel, but differing in arrangement of working hours. In one agency the employees worked a conventional schedule from 9:00 A.M. to 5:00 P.M.; in the other, they could choose to arrive within a 2-hour range in the morning and adjust their leaving time accordingly. The results of the experiment were somewhat ironic. Measures of family strain and participation in home activities showed a significant difference favoring flextime for only one group of families—those without children. One proposed explanation is that flextime arrangements did not go far enough to meet the complex scheduling problems experienced by today's parents. A second interpretation suggests that the flexible time may have been used for activities outside the home unrelated to child-rearing, such as recreation, socializing, or moonlighting. Unfortunately, no data were available to verify either hypothesis.

---

[1]A growing phenomenon in this regard that has received surprisingly little research attention is paternal employment requiring frequent and extending absence from the home. Results from one of the few studies of the developmental effects of this pattern, Tiller's (1958) investigation of Norwegian sailor and whaler families, suggests that the outcomes may be rather different from those observed for children of divorced, separated, or widowed parents.

Maternal Employment and the Family

As documented in three recent reviews (Bronfenbrenner & Crouter, 1982; Hoffman, 1980, 1983), an analysis of research in this sphere reveals a consistent contrast, summarized in the following passage:

> By 1980 there had accumulated an appreciable body of evidence indicating that the mother's work outside the home tends to have a salutary effect on girls, but may exert a negative influence on boys. . . . The results indicate that daughters from families in which the mother worked tended to admire their mothers more, had a more positive conception of the female role, and were more likely to be independent. . . . None of these trends was apparent for boys. Instead, the patterns of findings, especially in recent investigations, suggests that the mother's working outside the home is associated with a lower academic achievement for sons in middle-class but not in low-income families. . . . A similar tendency for maternal employment to have a negative influence on the development of boys was apparent in investigations conducted as far back as the 1930s. (Bronfenbrenner & Crouter, 1982, pp. 51–52)

The processes underlying this complex but consistent set of findings are illuminated in a study by Bronfenbrenner, Alvarez, and Henderson (1984). The basic data consisted of parents' free descriptions of their 3-year-old children. A systematic content analysis revealed that the most flattering portrait of a daughter was painted by mothers who were working full-time, but this was also the group that portrayed the son in the least favorable terms. A further breakdown by mother's education status indicated that the enthusiastic view of a daughter in the full-time group occurred only among those mothers who had some education beyond high school. In the light of both quantitative and qualitative findings, the authors make the following interpretative comment: "The pattern brings to mind the picture of an aspiring professional woman who already sees her three-year old daughter as an interesting and competent person potentially capable of following in her mother's footsteps" (p. 1366). The most salient feature of the findings for sons was the exceptionally positive description given by mothers working part-time, in contrast to the much lower evaluation offered by those fully employed. The advantages of part-time employment, so far as maternal perceptions are concerned, were appreciably greater for a son than for a daughter. The results of interviews with fathers (conducted separately) revealed the same highly differentiated profile, but in somewhat lower relief.[2]

Revealing as the foregoing studies are of the dynamics of the family-work exosystem, they fail to take account of what turns out to be a critical third dimension—that of continuity versus change in employment status over time. Research bearing on this issue is discussed below.

Parental Support Networks

Investigations in this domain first began to appear in the 1970s. In a study of child neglect among low-income families, Giovanni and Billingsley (1970) found that neglect was less frequent among families characterized by strong kinship networks and regular church attendance. The authors conclude that "among low-income people, neglect would seem to be a social problem that is as much

---

[2] Regarding the basis for the observed sex differences in the effects of maternal employment, the authors speculate as follows: "One possible explanation draws on the recurrent and generally accepted finding in research on early sex differences (Maccoby & Jacklin, 1974) that male infants tend to be more physically active from birth and hence require more control and supervision. Full-time work may limit opportunities for such necessary monitoring. Viewed from this perspective, the findings suggest that the reported sex difference in effects of maternal employment derive from the cumulative interaction of familial, organismic, and employment factors evolving in a larger socioeconomic context" (p. 1371).

a manifestation of social and community conditions as it is of any individual parent's pathology" (p. 204). Corroborative data come from a large-scale correctional analysis of child abuse reports and socioeconomic and demographic information for the 58 counties in New York State (Garbarino, 1976). In the investigator's words, "a substantial proportion of the variance in rates of child abuse/maltreatment among New York State counties . . . was found to be associated with the degree to which mothers do not possess adequate support systems for parents and are subjected to economic stress" (p. 185).

Subsequent research in this sphere has continued to focus almost exclusively on mothers of young children, particularly mothers in specially vulnerable groups such as teenage mothers, single-parent mothers, or families living in poverty. In general, these studies revealed that support was more likely to come from kin than nonkin, with the father being the principal source of help, even in single-parent households; the mother's mother was next in line, followed by other relatives, and then friends, neighbors, and professionals (Belle, 1981; Brown, Bhrolchin, & Harris, 1975; Crockenberg, 1987, 1988; Tietjen & Bradley, 1982). In the area of attitudes, Tietjen and Bradley (1982) found that mothers who had access to stronger social networks during their pregnancy reported lower levels of stress, anxiety, and depression, a better marital adjustment, and a more positive attitude toward their pregnancy. Support from the husband was more effective than that from friends, neighbors, or relatives outside the home. Studies conducted of families with young infants revealed that low family support evoked maternal attitudes of hostility, indifference, and rejection of the infant (Colletta, 1981), whereas mothers experiencing help and comfort, primarily from the immediate family and relatives, felt less stress and had more positive attitudes toward themselves and their babies

(Colletta, 1981, 1983; Colletta & Gregg, 1981; Colletta & Lee, 1983; Mercer, Hackley, & Bostrom, in press). In the realm of maternal behavior, mothers receiving higher levels of social support responded more quickly when their infants cried (Crockenberg, 1981, 1985) and provided more adequate caretaking behavior (Epstein, 1980; Wandersman & Unger, 1983).

With respect to behavior of the children themselves, Furstenberg and Crawford (1978) documented effects of family support on the child's social and emotional development. Working with a predominately black sample of teenage mothers, he found that children of mothers who continued to live with their families of origin experienced fewer behavior problems, showed less antisocial behavior, and scored higher on cognitive tests than did children of teenage mothers who lived alone with adult relatives.

A more differentiated picture of sources of external support, stress, and their interaction emerges from a study by Crnic and his colleagues (1983). These investigators devised separate indexes of stress and of support experienced by the mother from the beginning of her pregnancy until the infant had been home for 1 month. Moreover, the measure of support distinguished between help coming from three different sources: the mother's husband (or partner), friends, and other persons in the neighborhood or community. The analysis revealed that both environmental stress and environmental support had independent effects on the family. Maternal attitudes were influenced most; social support was associated with more positive orientations, stress with more negative ones. Effects on both the mother's and the infant's behavior, when observed after a 3-month interval, were less powerful, but still significant. Mothers who had received higher levels of support when the infants had been 1 month old were more responsive and positive interacting with the child 3 months later. Correspondingly, the babies acted more responsively and positively toward their mothers and gave clearer cues regarding their emotional state, needs, and desires. The infant's behavior was affected somewhat more than the mother's. The findings with respect to source of support were equally instructive. Whereas support from either spouse, friends, or community was about equally influential in increasing maternal levels of satisfaction, support from the father had an appreciably stronger and more general effect on the actual behavior of both mother and child than did help from friends or community. Finally, environmental stresses and supports interacted with each other, with support serving to buffer the disruptive effects of stress.

An analogous interaction effect appears in a study of the impact of environmental stress and social support in single- and two-parent families (Weinraub & Wolf, 1983); stress proved to be more debilitating and social support more effective when the mother was not married. Once again, it would appear that social support was most potent under conditions of stress.

This conclusion must be qualified, however, in the light of a subsequent study by Crockenberg (1987) with an extremely deprived sample—a group of teenage mothers who were also unmarried, uneducated, poor, and predominately black and Mexican American. Her findings indicate that, for mothers living under highly stressful conditions, social networks not only cease to exert a positive influence but can even become a source of stress.

A similar result is reported in a recent article by Riley and Eckenrode (1986). In a study of stresses and supports in mothers' lives, the investigators found that the influence of social networks on psychological well-being shifted in direction from positive to negative as a function of three kinds of factors: (a) reduced socioeconomic status, (b) the occurrence of misfortune in the lives of significant others (e.g., a close relative suffers an accident), or (c) low levels of belief either in one's capacity to influence one's own life (i.e., locus of control) or in the probable success versus failure of one's own help-seeking efforts.

Processes and outcomes of social support are set within a still broader social context in Crockenberg's study (1985) in which she compared English teenage mothers with a matched sample of their American counterparts. She found the "English mothers engaged in more smiling and eye contact, less frequent routine contact, and responded more quickly to their babies' crying than did American mothers" (p. 422). Control of possibly confounding variables through regression analysis pointed to the amount and type of social support as the factor accounting for the difference. Crockenberg elaborates as follows:

> In the United States most mothers rely on private doctors to serve their own and their children's health needs. . . . Public health nurses or social workers may be assigned to families in need of special assistance, but there is no comprehensive system designed to provide health-related and child care advice to parents. . . . In contrast, through the National Health Service, England incorporates community-based social support for parents in a comprehensive program of health care. This care begins before the child's birth and continues through his school years. . . . Midwives provide postnatal care for mothers and babies after they leave the hospital following delivery, and home health visitors see new mothers on a regular basis. . . . In England, mothers had only to be home and open their doors. (pp. 414–425)

Although this provocative cultural contrast clearly requires replication, in terms of research design it provides an excellent example of the power of a process-context model for analyzing external influences on family processes and their developmental effects.

The Family and the Community

The outstanding studies in this domain have been those conducted by Rutter and his colleagues, beginning with their classical comparison of rates of mental disorder in inner-London and the Isle of Wight (Rutter et al., 1975; Rutter & Quinton, 1977). In order to control for possible effects of migration, the investigators confined their samples to children of parents born and bred only in the given area. Their findings reveal that rates of psychiatric disorder were much more frequent in the metropolis. Nor could the observed effects be explained by any community differences with respect to ethnicity, social class, or demographic factors (Quinton, 1980; Rutter & Madge, 1976). Indeed, the same social class position appeared to have a different significance in urban versus rural environments, with low socioeconomic status being a much stronger predictor of mental illness in the city than in the country. In the light of this series of findings, Rutter concluded: "It seemed that there must be something about living in the city which predisposed to mental disorder" (1981, p. 612).

What is this "something"? Rutter's own efforts to answer this question have yielded results of particular relevance for child development. For example, taking advantage of the longitudinal design of the London–Isle of Wight study, Rutter (1981) analyzed community differences as a joint function of age of onset and type of disorder.

> The results were striking in showing that the biggest difference between London and the Isle of Wight applied to *chronic* disorders of *early* onset. . . . The least difference was found with psychiatric conditions beginning in adolescence for the first time. Moreover, the difference also mainly applied to disorders associated with serious family difficulties. In short, the problems most characteristic of city children were those beginning early, lasting a long time, and ac-

companied by many other problems in the family. (Rutter, 1981, p. 613, italics in original)

These findings raise the possibility that the observed community differences may simply reflect the aggregation of vulnerable families. To clarify this issue, Rutter and Quinton (1977) compared rates of psychiatric disorder in different neighborhoods controlling for such factors as the proportion of low-status, low-income families, and single-parent households. They found that families were affected irrespective of their background characteristics, so that, in general, persons living in a vulnerable area shared a higher risk of psychiatric disorder. In short, to use Rutter's words, the effect was to some extent ecological as well as individual.

Such an effect can operate in two ways. It can impinge on children directly, or indirectly through the child's family. To investigate these possibilities, Rutter and his colleagues (1975, 1977) developed an index of "family adversity" including such factors as marital discord and dissolution, mental disorder or criminality in the parents, large family size, and other conditions known to be associated with higher levels of psychiatric disturbance and social deviance. Again, the results were striking, but now in the opposite direction. With the degree of family adversity controlled, the difference between London and the Isle of Wight in rates of child psychiatric illness all but disappeared. The authors interpret this result as indicating that the main adverse effects of city life on children are indirect, resulting from the disruption of the families in which they live.

Similar evidence of indirect effects on the child via the family have also been found for juvenile delinquency. The relevant research has been summarized by Rutter and Giller (1983). For example, using a longitudinal design that permitted control for prior characteristics both of the child and of the family, West (1982) was able to demonstrate that delinquency rates for boys declined after the family moved out of London. As Rutter notes in a personal communication (1984), what is lacking in studies of this kind (including his own) is an identification of the particular features of an area that produce the given effect, and the process through which the effect takes place. "It is all very well to note the 'stresses' of inner-city life, but what is needed is to determine just what it is that makes inner-city life stressful for some families in some circumstances. Personally, I would see this as the most important needed direction for future research."

Finally, whereas the indirect effects of urban residence appear to be negative for social and emotional development, particularly in young children, there is evidence that the direct influence of the city environment may be beneficial for intellectual development among *older* children. The principal support for this conclusion comes from a two-stage investigation carried out in rural and urban areas of Switzerland. The first study (Meili & Steiner, 1965) was conducted with 11-year-old school children. The researchers found that performance in both intelligence and achievement tests increased as a direct function of the amount of industry and traffic present in the area. The relationship was still significant after controlling for social class, but the influence of the latter variable was more powerful than that of locality. Four years later, in a follow-up study, Vatter (1981) undertook to investigate the nature of the more immediate influences accounting for this result. Drawing on earlier work by Klineberg (1935, 1938) and Wheeler (1942), Vatter hypothesized that the superior cognitive functioning observed in city children was a product of exposure to richer and more differentiated cultural environment typifying the urban scene. To investigate his "stimulus hypothesis," Vatter obtained information from his subjects about their daily activities within the community, and about the nature of existing community facilities (for example, availability and use of libraries,

learning opportunities outside the home, etc.). In support of the author's hypothesis, there was a significant positive relation between indexes of the community environment and mental test scores. Moreover, community factors appeared to exert a stronger influence than intrafamilial variables (median r of .41 versus .26). Vatter acknowledges, however, that his design did not permit adequate control for migration effects, because his follow-up study did not include all of the original cases, and it was impossible to identify and reanalyze Time 1 data for the Time 2 sample.[3]

Chronosystem Models

The impact of a single life transition on family processes and the development of the child is well illustrated in the work of Hetherington and her colleagues (Hetherington, 1981; Hetherington, Cox, & Cox, 1978), which traced the progressive impact of divorce on the mother–child relationship and the child's behavior in school. The disruptive effects of separation reached their peak 1 year afterward and declined through the second year, although the divorced mothers never gained as much influence with the child as their married counterparts wielded. Two of Hetherington's findings illustrate the power of exosystem forces in influencing family processes. First, the mother's effectiveness in dealing with the child was directly related to the amount of support received from third parties such as friends, relatives, and especially her ex-husband. Second, the disruptive effects of divorce were exacerbated in those instances in which the separation was accompanied by the mother's entry into the workforce.

The potentially destabilizing impact of extrafamilial transitions on intrafamilial processes is el-

---

[3]Similar findings were reported in an earlier study by Clausen and Kohn (1959). The correlations between neighborhood characteristics and the development of psychiatric disorders were greater in large cities than in smaller ones.

egantly demonstrated in a doctoral dissertation by Moorehouse (1986). This researcher employed a two-stage model in order to investigate how stability versus change over time in the mother's work status during the child's preschool years affected patterns of mother–child communication, and how these patterns in turn influenced the child's achievement and social behavior in the first year of school. The complex nature of the feedback systems operating in the family–workplace–school interface is illustrated by the following seemingly paradoxical sequence of findings:

1. As reflected by grades and teacher ratings, the children experiencing the greatest difficulty in adapting to school were those whose mother was working full time. This relationship remained significant after control for mother's education.

2. As hypothesized, the generally positive relationship between mother's communicative activities at home and the child's performance at school varied systematically as a function of the mother's work status, and was strongest among the children of mothers working full time. In the author's words,

   > Rather than weakening the effectiveness of the mother–child system, a full-time job appears to increase the positive impact of this system on the child's school competence. . . . When high levels of communicative activities are maintained, these children are as competent, or more competent, than their peers with mothers who work fewer hours or not at all. Thus, mother–child activities seem to compensate or prevent detrimental consequences of maternal employment for children who are first entering school. (p. 129)

3. Moorehouse carried out a comparative analysis of mothers who had maintained the same employment status over the period of the study versus those who had changed in either direction; that is, working more hours, fewer hours,

or none at all. The results revealed that significant effects of work status were pronounced only in the latter group. Moreover, "instability, on the whole, is associated with less favorable school outcomes than stability" (p. 89).

Moorehouse cautions that her findings should be viewed as tentative, because her sample was comparatively small ($N = 112$), resulting in only minimally acceptable frequencies in some of the subgroups. Nevertheless her conclusion regarding the importance of stability in the family's environment finds independent confirmation in the results of a longitudinal study in Finland conducted by Pulkkinen (Pitkanen-Pulkkinen, 1980; Pulkkinen, 1982, 1983b, 1984). The investigator examined the influence of environmental stability and change on the development of children from 8 to 14 years of age. Specifically, the "steadiness" versus "unsteadiness" of family living conditions was measured by the occurrence of events such as the following: the number of family moves, changes in day care or school arrangements, parental absences, changes in family structure, and altered conditions of maternal employment. Greater instability in the family environment was associated with greater submissiveness, aggressiveness, and anxiety among children in later childhood and adolescence, and higher rates of criminality in adulthood. Moreover, the factor of stability of family living conditions appeared to be a stronger determinant of the child's development than the family's socioeconomic status. (The relation of socioeconomic status to family stability, however, was not examined.)

A similar finding was reported in a longitudinal study carried out in Hawaii (Werner & Smith, 1982). The investigators focused special attention on a subgroup of the sample whom they designated as "Vulnerable but Invincible." These were adolescents and youth who, over the course of their lives, had been "exposed to poverty, biological risks, and family instability, and reared by parents with little education or serious mental health problems—who remained *invincible* and developed into competent and autonomous young adults who worked well, played well, loved well, and expected well" (p. 3). A major environmental factor that distinguished this group from their socioeconomically matched "nonresilient" controls was a low number of chronic, stressful life events experienced in childhood and adolescence, and the presence of an informal multigenerational network of kin.

The Hawaiian research also validated in a longitudinal design a pattern of reversing sex differences previously detectable only in fragmented fashion from cross-sectional designs (Hetherington, 1972, 1981; Hetherington & Deur, 1971). Through the first decade of life, boys appeared to be substantially more vulnerable than girls both to biological and environmental insult; during the second decade of life, however, the pattern was reversed.

> Boys seemed now more prepared for the demands of school and work . . . girls were now confronted with social pressures and sexual expectations that produced a higher rate of mental health problems in later adolescence . . . often control of aggression appeared to be one of the major problems for the boys in childhood, dependency became a major problem for the girls in adolescence. . . . In spite of the biological and social pressures which in this culture appeared to make each sex more vulnerable at different times, more high-risk girls than high-risk boys grow into resilient young adults. (pp. 153–154)

The reader will have observed that the investigations just described are no longer confined to the developmental impact of a single event in a person's life. Rather they examine cumulative effects of a sequence of developmental transitions over time—what Elder has referred to as the *life course*. The scientific power of this paradigm is best illustrated by Elder's now classic study of

Children of the Great Depression (1974). To investigate the long-range effects of this experience on children's development, Elder reanalyzed archival data from two longitudinal studies that had been conducted in California with samples of children born in the early versus late 1920s (Elder, 1974, 1981, 1984). The basic design in these investigations involved the comparison of two otherwise comparable groups differentiated on the basis of whether the loss of income as a result of the Depression extended or fell short of 35%. The availability of longitudinal data made it possible to assess developmental outcomes through childhood, adolescence, and adulthood. Finally, the fact that children in one sample were born 8 years earlier than those in the other permitted a comparison of the effects of the Depression on youngsters who were adolescents when their families became economically deprived versus those who were still young children at that time.

The results for the two groups presented a dramatic contrast. Paradoxically, for youngsters who were teenagers during the Depression years, the families' economic deprivation appeared to have a salutary effect on their subsequent development, especially in the middle class. As compared with the nondeprived who were matched on pre-Depression socioeconomic status, deprived boys displayed greater desire to achieve and a firmer sense of career goals. Boys and girls from deprived homes attained greater satisfaction in life, both by their own and by societal standards. Though more pronounced for adolescents from middle-class backgrounds, these favorable outcomes were evident among their lower-class counterparts as well. Analysis of interview and observation protocols enabled Elder to identify what he regarded as a critical factor in investigating this favorable development trajectory: The loss of economic security forced the family to mobilize its own human resources, including its teenagers, who had to take on new roles and responsibilities both within and outside the home and to work together toward the common goal of getting and keeping the family on its feet. This experience provided effective training in initiative, responsibility, and cooperation. In the words of the banished Duke, "Sweet are the uses of adversity."

Alas, adversity was not so sweet for male children who were still preschoolers when their families suffered economic loss. The results were almost the opposite of those for boys in the earlier investigation. Compared with controls from non-deprived families, these youngsters subsequently did less well in school, showed less stable and successful work histories, and exhibited more emotional and social difficulties, some still apparent in middle adulthood. These negative outcomes were much more marked in boys than in girls and were accentuated in families from lower-class backgrounds.

Subsequently, Elder and his co-workers have emphasized the importance of mediating processes and conditions within the family as the vehicles through which economic hardship reaches into the child's life and shapes the course of subsequent development (Elder, Caspi, & Downey, 1986; Elder, Caspi, & Van Nguyen, 1986; Elder, Van Nguyen, & Caspi, 1985). Perhaps the most important factors in this regard were the personality characteristics of fathers and children. The presence in the family of an irritable father or an irritating child significantly increased the likelihood that unemployment would have long-range negative consequences for life course development. Also critical was the marital discord that often arose, or became exacerbated, following the father's loss of a job.

In an especially revealing analysis, Elder, Caspi, and Downey (1986) have traced the impact of life course experience across four generations, and shown the effects of unstable parents and family during the Depression on problem behavior of the children, who in turn are followed into their adult roles: work, marriage, and the raising of sons and daughters. Within a generation, it is the unstable personality of the parent, particularly the father, that gives rise to tension both in the marital relationship and the parent–child dyad. Across generations, it is disturbance in either of these family relationships that leads to the development of an unstable personality in the child as an adult.

In recent years, a number of developmental studies employing a life course perspective have yielded important research results. Some, like the researches of Scarr, Mortimer, and Pulkkinen, have already been mentioned. An additional example appears in the work of Furstenberg and Gunn (Furstenberg, 1976; Furstenberg & Brooks-Gunn, 1987). These investigators have shown that, contrary to conclusions drawn from previous research, teenage pregnancy does not necessarily lead to academic and personal failure in the rest of a woman's life. A special strength of the second volume is its emphasis on the feasibility of alternative pathways that could be provided through the development of appropriate policies and programs.

Although the advantages of a chronosystem model are best achieved within the framework of a longitudinal design, important benefits can also be gleaned from cross-sectional studies that gather key retrospective data and use appropriate analytic procedures, such as causal modeling. An example is the work of Schneewind and his colleagues (1983). Their sample consisted of 570 children (ages 9–14) from schools in six German states. Data were obtained independently from both children and their parents. The productivity of such a multigenerational path analytic model is best conveyed by some illustrative findings. For example, one of the analyses focused on the environmental antecedents of two contrasting clusters of children's maladaptive behavior: aggressiveness and antisocial behavior on the one hand and anxiety and helplessness on the other. Both patterns were influenced by factors outside the child's immediate family, but in each instance the causal path was indirect rather than direct, with the parental use of corporal punishment serving as a key intervening variable. Parents most likely to employ physical discipline were those who occupied a lower socioeconomic status or who themselves had experienced an unhappy childhood. But even here the influence on parental practices was not direct but operated principally through effects on parental personality structure, marital conflict, and child-rearing attitudes. Moreover, these findings, obtained from a cross-sectional sample in Germany, were strikingly similar to Elder's results from a longitudinal study in the United States.

Turning from the problematic to the constructive aspects of the child's behavior, Schneewind and his colleagues also examined the environmental and personality antecedents of children's creativity and social extravertedness as measured in psychometric tests. In both instances, a key intervening environmental variable was the family's social network. Moreover, in contrast to most American studies in which social networks are viewed as support systems influencing the family (e.g., Cochran & Brassard, 1979; Crnic et al., 1983; Crockenberg, 1981), Schneewind et al. (1983) interpreted social networks as a product of an expressive and stimulating climate within the family. This stimulating atmosphere also emerged as a major determinant both of the child's creativity (especially in girls) and social involvement (especially in boys), including establishment of the children's own social networks and their engagement in group and extracurricular activities.

Research Gaps and Opportunities

From the scientist's perspective, perhaps the most important functions of a review of existing knowledge in a particular area is to identify promising directions for future investigation. As in other spheres of exploration, there is uncharted terrain at all four points of the compass.

Ecological Variations in the Expression of Genotypes

Identification of discordant phenotypes. Studies of the role of family inheritance in human development have focused almost exclusively on concordant cases; that is, the fact that persons related by blood tend to exhibit similar psychological characteristics; almost no attention has been paid to discordant instances. For example, when one twin has been diagnosed as schizophrenic, or has a criminal record, or has failed to graduate from school, but the other twin has not, what patterns of behavior or life career does this other twin exhibit? In the absence of such comparative data, investigators are prone to draw conclusions about the existence of familial genetic dispositions that are highly specific; for example, one assumes a hereditarian proclivity for criminal behavior, or particular forms of mental disorder. The possibility exists, however, that the biological predisposition may be of a more general order. The issue could be resolved by examining the nature of variation and behavior patterns exhibited by persons of identical genetic constitution in different contexts. In reviewing the research literature, I have been able to find only one investigation that examines the career lines of discordant cases. In a study of psychiatric disorders among foster home-reared children of schizophrenic mothers, Heston (1966) reports that nonschizophrenic offspring tended to be persons of unusual creativity and competence. Unfortunately, there are a number of flaws in the study design. More rigorous investigations of this kind, encompassing positive as well as negative outcomes, would not only help define the scope of genetic predispositions but also elucidate the operation of both intra- and extrafamilial environments in shaping alternative courses of psychological development for persons of similar genetic endowment.

Child-rearing processes in adoptive families. In a series of publications, Scarr and her associates

(Scarr, 1981; Scarr & McCartney, 1983; Scarr & Weinberg, 1983) have argued that results of numerous studies purporting to demonstrate the environmental effect of parental behavior on children's development are in fact ambiguous because they are confounded by the genetic similarity between biological parents and their children. This similarity, Scarr contends, obtains both in the realm of perception and behavior, so that each party of the dyad is likely on genetic grounds to be especially responsive to the action (or passivity) of the other. In Scarr's view, such multiplicative effects account for most of the developmental variance within what she calls "the normal range"; that is, persons not severely damaged by organic or environmental insult. Implied in this provocative formulation is the assumption that patterns of parent–child interaction in adoptive families are quite different from those occurring among biological-related family members. Should such a difference in fact exist, it would have profound implications for the development of children raised by biological parents who possess psychological characteristics known to have a significant genetic basis. Microanalytic techniques for the analysis of parent–child interaction, such as those developed by Patterson (1982) would be particularly well-suited for the comparative study of adoptive and biological families as contrasting contexts of family functioning.

Relations Between the Family and Other Child Settings

Existing theory and research point to the importance for the child's development of the nature and strength of connections existing between the family and the various other settings that a young person enters during the first decades of life. Of particular significance in this regard are the successive transitions into (and within) day care, peer group, school, and work. In relation to each of these extrafamilial settings, three stages of transition deserve attention:

Preexisting intersetting relationships. How is the process of transition, and its developmental effects, influenced by the presence or absence of prior connections between the two settings. Such linkages may take the form of previous social interactions between participants in the two settings (e.g., parent and teacher are friends, the child has an older sibling at school) or of information, attitudes, and expectations existing in each setting about the other.

Transition feedback. Once the child has entered the new setting, this event can markedly alter attitudes, expectations, and patterns of interaction *within* the family, especially in relation to the child. Such reorganization of the family system following the child's transition into a new role in a new setting can have even more significance for the child's development than his or her experience within the new setting.

Posttransition changes in relations between settings. The child's development may be further affected by shifts over time in the nature and extent of linkages between the family and the other principal settings in which the child spends his or her time (for example, the parents encourage or discourage the child's contact with peers; there is a decline or increase of parental interest in the child's school experience).

A particularly effective research strategy for investigating the development of relations between the family and other settings is a controlled experiment designed to create or strengthen linkages between settings (for example, the experiment by Smith, 1968, cited previously).

The foregoing consideration is applicable to setting transitions and linkages in general. In addition, the relations between the family and specific settings in the child's life deserve further comment.

Family and day care. A major gap in research in this area is the absence of studies of how children's development is affected not directly but indirectly through the role of day care as a support system for parents, especially for mothers. Although a number of research reviews have emphasized the importance of such indirect influence (e.g., Belsky, 1984), no investigation has yet been specifically focused on this issue. A second and related omission is the failure to investigate the interrelation between day care and parental employment. It seems likely that the observed developmental effects in the latter sphere may be moderated by day care as a family support system.

Family and the peer group. As documented above, previous research in this sphere has focused primarily on the family's capacity to counteract pressures toward socially deviant behavior emanating from the peer group. Yet, a number of developmental theorists, most notably Piaget (1932), have emphasized the constructive role of experience with peers for both the child's moral and cognitive development. Subsequent investigations demonstrating the powerful interplay between parent and peer influences in the genesis of antisocial behavior by no means rule out the possibility of constructive processes emanating from the same parallelogram of forces. Of particular promise is the application of chronosystem designs in tracing alternative pathways from family to peer group and then, from both of these contexts, into adult roles in the areas of school, work, family formation, parenthood, and participation in the social and political life of the community.

Family and the school. The available research evidence suggests that a powerful factor affecting the capacity of a child to learn in the classroom is the relationship existing between the family and the school. Although, as previously noted, a number of investigations have addressed this interface, the majority are descriptive rather than analytic and are limited almost entirely to the role of parents as educators, with scholastic achievement serving as the principal psychological outcome. Lacking are process-oriented field studies or experiments that trace the emergence of a broader range of characteristics and employ research designs addressed to each of the three stages of interesting relationships set forth in the opening paragraph of this section. Of particular importance are investigations of feedback effects from school experience to family functioning.

Family and children's work experience. The developmental effects of this important life transition are only beginning to receive the attention they deserve. The gap in knowledge is all the more striking given the fact that, according to recent figures, about half of all American high school students engage in some form of paid employment. Moreover, a pioneering series of studies (Greenberger & Steinberg, 1986; Greenberger, Steinberg, & Vaux, 1981; Steinberg et al., 1982) has shown that, contrary to the expectations and recommendations of several blue ribbon panels (e.g., National Commission on Youth, 1980; President's Science Advisory Commission, 1973), such job involvement, rather than furthering the development of responsibility, diminishes the adolescent's involvement in the family and school, increases use of cigarettes and marijuana, generates cynical attitudes toward work, and encourages acceptance of unethical work practices. From this perspective, the role of the parents in influencing the timing, selection, and interpretation of the child's work experience, and the resulting feedback effect of such experience on the family's treatment of the child, may have considerable significance for the child's subsequent development in the adult roles of worker, spouse, parent, and citizen.

Relations Between Family Processes and Parental Participation in Other Settings of Adult Life

The directions for future research in this sphere are well indicated by the gaps in existing knowledge. These fall under two now-familiar headings.

Family and the conditions of parental work. Especially lacking in this sphere are studies examining the developmental impact of the *joint* employment patterns of father and mother. Of particular significance is conflict between the work schedules of the two parents, and the hecticness it may generate in their lives as these conditions affect the intensity and quality of parent–child interaction. A second omission is the failure to include within the same research design provision for investigating both links in the presumed causal chain: (a) the influence of parental employment on parental functioning and (b) the effect of the induced change in family processes on the behavior and development of the child. Finally, there is evidence to suggest that, as in other domains, both the sex and the age of the child may be critical in mediating the impact of parents' work. Specifically, conditions of employment may be more consequential, both positively and negatively, for younger children, although the full effect may not be observable until the children are older, and the outcome may be rather different for daughters and sons.

Family and parental social networks. Research in this sphere is plagued by the lack of clarity in the operationalization of concepts and causal processes. First, both agents and types of support need to be differentiated and related to the degree of environmental stress to which the family is subjected. Second, research designs must take into ac-

count the possibility that causal processes may actually be operating in the reverse direction, with supportive social networks being a creation rather than a condition of constructive family functioning. Finally, as in research on parents' working conditions, social network studies should be expanded to encompass the full, two-step causal sequence: first, from the network properties to family functioning (or vice versa) and second, from family functioning to the behavior and development of the child (or vice versa).

Families in Broader Social Contexts

Five topics are especially relevant here.

Unraveling social class. An essential task is to penetrate behind the label of socioeconomic status to identify the specific elements of social structure and substance that shape the course and content of human development. This unraveling process requires the decomposition of the typically composite measures of social class into their most common components (occupational status, parental education, and family income).

Family's occupational status. In their most recent work, Kohn and his followers (Kohn & Schooler, 1978, 1982, 1983; Miller & Kohn, 1983; Miller, Schooler, Kohn, & Miller, 1979) have used causal modeling techniques in order to demonstrate that the degree of occupational self-direction in the job promotes the development of the worker's intellectual flexibility. But, no evidence is available as yet on how the opportunity for self-direction at work, and the intellectual flexibility that it engenders, relate to parental patterns of child-rearing or how these, in turn, affect the behavior and development of the child. A related issue is whether and how parental experiences at work operate through the family to influence the selection, timing, and psychological content of the child's successive transitions into, and experience in, other settings such as school, peer group, and, especially, the world of work.

Parents' education. This variable takes on special significance in an ecological system model on several counts. First, it offers a unique advantage for the analysis of causal pathways, because, unlike either occupational status or income, it usually precedes both family formation and the birth of the child, and hence provides an index of social background, separately, for each parent, that is unlikely to be influenced by subsequent family processes, and therefore can be interpreted primarily as unidirectional in its effects. Second, as revealed in the work of Tulkin and others, education appears to be an important source for parents' conceptions of the nature and capacities both of the child and of the parent at successive stages of the child's life. A more complete understanding of the connection between parental schooling and family perceptions is clearly in the interest of both developmental science and of educational policy and practice.

Family income. As this author has pointed out elsewhere (Bronfenbrenner, 1982, 1984, 1986), income plays an especially telling role in American family life because, to a greater extent than in other modern industrialized societies, the resources and services required for sustaining the health and well-being of family members and furthering the development of the child are dependent on the family's financial resources. This issue becomes critical to families that are chronically poor or in which the principal breadwinner becomes unemployed. Because of the magnitude of the resultant effect on children, this issue is given separate consideration in the final section of this review.

Families in the community. It is a striking fact, and a provocative question for sociology of knowledge, that the overwhelming majority of systematic studies of community influences on families and children have been conducted in Europe. In addition to the British and Swiss studies reviewed above, a seminal line of investigation in France takes its impetus from the classic two-volume work by Chombart de Lauwe (1959–60), "Famille et habitation," and focuses primarily on neighborhood and housing as physical environments. In German-speaking Europe, a research tradition stimulated by the Muchows' (1935) classic study of the life-span of city children has led to investigations that are more diversified. For example, a recent compilation by Walter (1981–1982) fills two volumes with well-designed studies by more than a score of investigators representing a variety of theoretical orientations.

The European work is distinguished not only for its quantity, but also for the comparative sophistication of the research paradigms that have been employed. Whereas American studies have been confined almost exclusively to social address models documenting associated differences in the behavior of children (Barker & Schoggen, 1973; Garbarino, 1976; Hollingshead, 1949), European investigations have focused on variations in socialization processes arising in different types of communities or neighborhoods defined by their particular physical and social characteristics. For example, in the first volume of Walter's *Region and Socialization,* Bargel and his associates (1981) developed the concept of "Soziotope" for classifying types of residential areas. They then applied their taxonomy both to rural and urban districts in the West German state of Nordhessen in order to demonstrate that particular styles of child-rearing are associated with contrasting forms of Soziotope. The more differentiated taxonomies for describing communities developed by European researchers provide a point of departure for addressing what Rutter has designated as "the most important needed direction for future research" in the study of community influences on the family: identifying the particular features of community life that impair or enhance family functioning.

Family and geographic mobility. One key aspect of family ecology has been equally neglected by researchers in Europe and the United States—the impact on family functioning, and on children, of moving from place to place. The only research that has given at least partial attention to this problem is the previously mentioned longitudinal study by Pulkkinen (Pitkanen-Pulkkinen, 1980; Pulkkinen, 1982). Geographic mobility was one of the components in Pulkkinen's index of the instability of the family environment. This index, in turn, proved to be a major predictor of the child's subsequent development in adolescence and early adulthood. Although, to this writer's knowledge, no reliable figures exist for the United States on the frequency of moves among families with children, it seems likely that the incidence is quite high in certain occupations, for example, the military (McCubbin, Dahl, & Hunter, 1976). The much-needed studies in this area should take into account both the direct and indirect effects on the child of simultaneous disruption of established patterns of relations within the peer group, the school, and the family, as well as the subsequent processes of rebuilding linkages in the new location. Of special significance in this regard is the experience of newly immigrant families, particularly those who come from, and enter into, markedly contrasting environments with respect to values, customs, and socioeconomic conditions.

Television and the family. In terms of research, this area is truly a terra incognita. As this reviewer has written elsewhere (Bronfenbrenner, 1974a), the primary importance of television for child development may lie "not so much in the behavior it produces as the behavior it prevents," and the behavior that can be prevented is family interac-

tion—"the talks, the games, the family festivities, and arguments through which much of the child's learning takes place and his character is formed" (p. 170). The trouble with this seemingly authoritative conclusion is that it is based almost entirely on subjective opinion. To be sure, the opinion has subsequently been echoed in two necessarily brief reviews of research on television's role in family life (Garbarino, 1975; Dorr, 1981). But, insofar as I have been able to determine, the only empirical study that has examined the effect of television on patterns of family interaction is the pioneering research of Maccoby (1951). Her principal conclusion: "The nature of the family social life during a program could be described as 'parallel' rather than interactive, and the set does seem quite clearly to dominate family life when it is on" (p. 428). Given the massive expansion of the medium in the interim, it is clearly time to follow up on Maccoby's lead, employing research models that will be revealing not only of family processes but of the developmental outcomes that they may generate.

Family, poverty, and unemployment. Elder's follow-up studies of children of the Great Depression can carry special significance for the contemporary scene. As revealed in recent census data, the most rapid, and perhaps the most consequential, change taking place in American family life in the 1980s has been the widening gap between poor families and the rest of society. To quote an official census report (U.S. Bureau of the Census, 1981), recent data document "the largest decline in family income in the post–World War II period." As of March 1985 (U.S. Bureau of the Census, 1985), almost a fourth (24%) of the nation's children under 3 years of age, and between 3 and 6 as well, were living in families below the "poverty line," compared to 15% for the population as a whole, and 16% for those over 65 (Bronfenbrenner, 1986b, 1986c). The effects of the current economic trend are already being reflected in research findings (Farran & Margolis, 1983; Steinberg, Catalano, & Dooley, 1981). For example, Steinberg and his colleagues studied the impact of unemployment on 8000 families in California in a longitudinal design. Analyses of data over a 30-month period revealed that increases in child abuse were preceded by periods of high job loss, thus confirming the authors' hypothesis that "undesirable economic change *leads* to increased child maltreatment" (p. 975). More recently, Farran and Margolis (1983) have reported yet another more subtle but no less insidious impact of parental job loss. In families in which the father had been unemployed for several months, children exhibited a significant increase in susceptibility to contagious diseases. The authors offered two explanations for these effects: (a) reduced use of preventative health services because of income loss and (b) the greater vulnerability of children to contagious diseases in response to increased family stress.

As this author has written elsewhere:

It is the irony of our science that the greater the harm done to children, the more we stand to learn about the environmental conditions that are essential for making—and keeping—human beings human. As we enter the 1980s, there are indications that these essential conditions are being seriously undermined in broad segments of American society. It therefore becomes our professional obligation to employ the most advanced research designs at our disposal in order to forestall the tragic opportunity of significantly expanding our knowledge about the limits of the human condition for developing human beings. (Bronfenbrenner & Crouter, 1983, p. 412)

Research on the effects of child and family policy. Implied in the above statement is the responsibility of developmental science to go beyond the analysis of the status quo in order to design and evaluate the strategies that can sustain, enhance, and, where necessary, create environments that are conducive to healthy human growth. And indeed, in accord with this responsibility, during the 1960s and the 1970s a substantial number of investigators developed, carried out, and researched a variety of intervention programs that had both rehabilitation and prevention as their aims. Although some of the impressive initial gains appears to attenuate over time (Bronfenbrenner, 1974b), more recent analyses have revealed encouraging longer-term effects. For example, children who were enrolled as preschoolers more than two decades ago subsequently showed significantly higher rates of meeting school requirements than did controls as measured by lower frequency of placement in special education classes and of retention in grade (Berrueta-Clement, Schweinhart, Barnett, Epstein, & Weikart, 1984; Darlington et al., 1980). Today, preliminary reports of the most recent findings indicate that the same children, as they grew older, were better achievers in school and were more likely to graduate from high school. These experiences, in turn, predicted indexes of subsequent success as measured by such criteria as continuing one's education, being gainfully employed, or having income other than public assistance (Lazar, 1984).

Along the same line, follow-up studies of several guaranteed-income experiments conducted in the 1970s have revealed higher levels of school achievement by children of families in the randomly assigned experimental groups compared to their controls (Salkind, 1983). Also, a post hoc analysis of pregnant mothers participating in the WIC Program (Kotelchuck, 1983) showed that the treatment group had achieved the desired objective of increasing birth weight and reducing infant mortality as compared to findings for a carefully matched control group. That beneficial effects of community-based maternal care programs can extend into the realm of mother–child relations is indicated by the results of nurse home-visiting programs conducted with pregnant mothers at risk (Olds, 1983). Along with increased birth weight of babies born to teenage mothers, the experimental group, compared with carefully matched controls, showed a reduction in verified cases of child abuse, more positive maternal perceptions of the infant, and less restrictive and punitive behavior in the home.

In recent years, however, such studies of the consequences to children and parents of various forms of family policies and programs have become less frequent. Instead, the newly established field of family policy studies has shifted the focus of research attention to organizational issues. In the following passage, Bronfenbrenner and Weiss (1983) offer their assessment of the current trend as reflected in a recent collection of papers on child and family policy (Zigler, Kagan, & Klugman, 1983):

> Policy research is now a thriving enterprise encompassing such diverse and essential topics as legislation at national, state, and local levels; the evolution and nature of programs serving families and children; educational policies and practices; legal and judicial procedures; policies governing mass media; the role of advocacy in the policy process; the development of strategies for dealing with drugs, child abuse, and other social problems; the construction of childhood social indicators; and analyses of the policy process itself. Least salient in this newly evolving field is a concern that emerges as central in an ecological perspective on human development— namely, how do policies affect the experience of those whom they are intended to serve? To put the issue more succinctly: What is the nature of the interface between policies and people? (pp. 393–394)

At a time of financial retrenchment, when many children are being placed at greater risk as a result of parental unemployment, other income losses, and reduction of health and family services, it is essential to determine which policies and programs can do most to enable families to perform the magic feat of which they alone are capable: making and keeping human beings human.

The foregoing statement has yet another significance that is at once both broader and more concrete. Taken as a whole the body of research reviewed in these pages is curiously one-sided, for its predominant focus is on the ecologies of family disorganization and developmental disarray. Yet, for every study that documents the power of disruptive environments, there is a control group that testifies to the existence and unrealized potential of ecologies that sustain and strengthen constructive processes in society, the family, and the self. Nor is there reason to believe that the progressively more powerful paradigms that have illuminated our understanding of the roots of alienation cannot be turned about to shed light on the ecologies of social and psychological integration. Herein lies the challenge, and the opportunity, for the developmental science of the future.

References

Angell, R. C. (1936). *The family encounters the Depression.* New York: Scribner's.

Bargel, T. et al. (1981). Soziale und raumliche Bedingungen der Sozialisation von Kindern in verschiendenen Ergebnisse einer Befragung von Eltern in Landgemeinden und Stadtvierteln Nordhessens. In A. H. Walter (Ed.), *Region and Sozialisation: Volume 1* (pp. 186–261). Stuttgart: Frommann-Holzboog.

Barker, R. G., & Schoggen, P. (1973). *Qualities of community life: Methods of measuring environment and behavior applied to an American and an English town.* San Francisco: Jossey-Bass.

Becker, H. J., & Epstein, J. L. (1982). *Influences on teachers' use of parent involvement at home* (Report no. 324). Baltimore, MD: Johns Hopkins Center for Social Organization of Schools.

Belle, D. E. (1981, April). *The social network as a source of both stress and support to low-income mothers.* Paper presented at the biennial meeting of the Society for Research in Child Development, Boston.

Belsky, J. (1984). Two waves of day care research: Developmental effects and conditions of quality. In R. Ainslie (Ed.), *The child and the day care setting* (pp. 1–34). New York: Praeger.

Belsky, J., & Steinberg, L. D. (1978). The effects of day care: A critical review. *Child Development, 49,* 929–949.

Belsky, J., Steinberg, L. D., & Walker, A. (1982). The ecology of day care. In M. E. Lamb (Ed.), *Child rearing in nontraditional families* (pp. 71–115). Hillsdale, NJ: Erlbaum.

Berrueta-Clement, J. R., Schweinhart, L. J., Barnett, W. S., Epstein, A. S., & Weikart, D. P. (1984). *Changed lives: The effects of the Perry Preschool Program on youths through age 19.* Ypsilanti, MI: High/Scope Educational Research Foundation.

Boehnke, K., Eyferth, K., Kastner, P., Noack, P., Reitzle, M., Silbereisen, R. K., Walter, S., & Zank, S. (1983, July). *Youth development and substance use.* Paper presented at the seventh biennial meeting of the International Society for the Study of Behavioral Development, Munich, Germany.

Bohen, H., & Viveros-Long, A. (1981). *Balancing jobs and family life: Do flexible working schedules help?* Philadelphia, PA: Temple University Press.

Bouchard, T. J., & McGue, M. (1981). Familial studies of intelligence: A review. *Science, 29,* 1055–1059.

Bronfenbrenner, U. (1967). Response to pressure from peers versus adults among Soviet and American school children. *International Journal of Psychology, 2,* 199–208.

Bronfenbrenner, U. (1974a). Developmental research and public policy. In J. Romanshyn (Ed.), *Social science and social welfare* (pp. 159–182). New York: Council on Social Work Education.

Bronfenbrenner, U. (1974b). Is early intervention effective? *Teachers College Record, 76,* 279–303.

Bronfenbrenner, U. (1975). Nature with nurture: A reinterpretation of the evidence. In A. Montague (Ed.), *Race and IQ* (pp. 114–144). New York: Oxford University Press.

Bronfenbrenner, U. (1979). *The ecology of human development: Experiments by nature and design.* Cambridge, MA: Harvard University Press.

Bronfenbrenner, U. (1982, Winter). New images of children, families, and America. *Television & Children,* 1–15.

Bronfenbrenner, U. (1984). The changing family in a changing world: America first? In *The legacy of Nicholas Hobbs: Research on education and human development in the public interest, Part II. Peabody Journal of Education, 61,* 52–70.

Bronfenbrenner, U. (1986a). Recent advances in research on the ecology of human development. In R. K. Silbereisen, K. Eyferth, & G. Rudinger (Eds.). *Development as action in context: Problem behavior and normal youth development* (pp. 287–309). Heidelberg & New York: Springer-Verlag.

Bronfenbrenner, U. (1986b). Alienation and the four worlds of childhood. *Phi Delta Kappan, 67,* 430–436.

Bronfenbrenner, U. (1986c). The War of Poverty: Won or lost? America's children in poverty: 1959–1985. *Newsletter Division of Child, Youth, and Family Services, 9,* 2–3. Washington, DC: American Psychological Association.

Bronfenbrenner, U., Alvarez, W. F., & Henderson, C. R. (1984). Working and watching: Maternal employment status and parents' perceptions of their three-year-old children. *Child Development, 55,* 1362–1378.

Bronfenbrenner, U., & Crouter, A. C. (1982). Work and family through time and space. In S. B. Kamerman & C. D. Hayes (Eds.), *Families that work: Children in a changing world.* Washington, DC: National Academy Press.

Bronfenbrenner, U., & Crouter, A. C. (1983). The evolution of environmental models in developmental research. In W. Kessen (Ed.), *History, theory, and methods,* Vol. 1 of P. H. Mussen (Ed.), *Handbook of child psychology* (4th ed., pp. 357–414). New York: Wiley.

Bronfenbrenner, U., Devereux, E. C., Jr., Suci, G. J., & Rodgers, R. R. (1965, April). *Adults and peers as sources of conformity and autonomy.* Paper presented at the Conference on Socialization and Competence, sponsored by the Social Science Research Council, Puerto Rico.

Bronfenbrenner, U., & Weiss, H. B. (1983). Beyond policies without people. In E. Zigler, S. L. Kagan, & E.

Klugman (Eds.), *Children, families, and government: Perspectives on American social policy.* New York: Cambridge University Press.

Brown, D. W., Bhrolchin, M., & Harris, T. (1975). Social class and psychiatric disturbance among women in urban populations. *Sociology, 9,* 225–254.

Burks, B. S. (1928). The relative influence of nature and nurture upon mental development: A comparative study of foster parent–foster child resemblance and true parent–true child resemblance. *Yearbook of the National Society for the Study of Education, 27,* 219–316.

Burns, J. (1982). *The study of parental involvement in four federal education programs: Executive summary.* Washington, DC: Department of Education, Office of Planning Budget and Evaluation.

Burt, C. (1966). The genetic determination of differences in intelligence: A study of monozygotic twins reared apart and together. *British Journal of Psychology, 57,* 137–153.

Caudill, W., & Weinstein, H. (1969). Maternal care and infant behavior in Japan and America. *Psychiatry, 32,* 12–43.

Cavan, R. S., & Ranck, K. H. (1938). *The family and the Depression: A study of 100 Chicago families.* Chicago: University of Chicago Press.

Chombart de Lauwe, P. H. (1959–1960). *Famille et habitation* (2 volumes). Paris: Centre National de la Recherche Scientifique.

Clausen, J. A., & Kohn, M. (1959). The relation of schizophrenia to the social structure of a small city. In B. Pasamanick (Ed.), *Epidemiology of mental disorder* (pp. 69–74). Washington, DC: American Association for the Advancement of Science.

Cochran, M. M., & Brassard, J. (1979). Child development and personal social networks. *Child Development, 50,* 601–616.

Colletta, N. (1981). Social support and the risk of maternal rejection by adolescent mothers. *Journal of Psychology, 109,* 191–197.

Colletta, N. (1983). At risk for depression: A study of young mothers. *Journal of Genetic Psychology, 142,* 301–310.

Colletta, N. D., & Gregg, C. H. (1981). Adolescent mothers' vulnerability to stress. *Journal of Nervous and Mental Diseases, 169,* 50–54.

Colletta, N. D., & Lee, D. (1983). The impact of support for Black adolescent mothers. *Journal of Family Issues, 4,* 127–143.

Collins, C., Moles, O., & Cross, M. (1982). *The home-school connection: Selected partnership programs in large cities.* Boston, MA: Institute for Responsive Education.

Crnic, K. A., Greenberg, M. C., Ragozin, A. S., Robinson, N. M., & Basham, R. (1983). Effects of stress and social supports on mothers in premature and full term infants. *Child Development, 54,* 209–217.

Crockenberg, S. B. (1981). Infant irritability, other responsiveness, and social support influences on the security of infant–mother attachment. *Child Development, 52,* 857–865.

Crockenberg, S. B. (1985). Professional support and care of infants by adolescent mothers in England and the United States. *Journal of Pediatric Psychology, 10,* 413–428.

Crockenberg, S. B. (1987). Support for adolescent mothers during the postnatal period: Theory and research. In Z. Boukydis (Ed.), *Research on support for parents and infants in the postnatal period.* Norwood, NJ: Ablex.

Crockenberg, S. B. (1988). English teenage mothers: Attitudes, behavior, and social support. In E. J. Anthony (Ed.), *International yearbook series of the International Association for Child Psychiatry and Allied Professions.*

Crouter, A. C. (1984). Participative work as an influence on human development. *Journal of Applied Developmental Psychology, 5,* 71–90.

Crowe, R. R. (1974). An adoption study of antisocial personality. *Archives of General Psychiatry, 31,* 785–791.

Darlington, R., Royce, J. M., Snipper, A. S., Murray, H. W., & Lazar, I. (1980). Preschool programs and later school comparisons of children from low-income families. *Science, 208,* 202–204.

Devereux, E. C., Jr. (1965). *Socialization in cross-cultural perspective: A comparative study of England, Germany, and the United States.* Paper read at the Ninth

International Seminar on Family Research, Puerto Rico.

Devereux, E. C., Jr. (1966, May). *Authority, guilt, and conformity to adult standards among German school children: A pilot experimental study.* Paper presented to the Upstate New York Sociological Association. Rochester, New York.

Devereux, E. C., Bronfenbrenner, U., & Rodgers, R. R. (1969). Child rearing in England and the United States: A cross-national comparison. *Journal of Marriage and the Family, 31,* 257–270.

Dornbusch, S. M., Carlsmith, J. M., Bushwall, P. L., Ritter, P. L., Leiderman, H., Hastorf, A. H., & Gross, R. T. (1985). Single parents, extended households, and the control of adolescents. *Child Development, 56,* 326–341.

Dorr, A. (1981, August). *Television's role in family life.* Paper presented at the meetings of the American Psychological Association, Los Angeles.

Elder, G. H., Jr. (1974). *Children of the Great Depression.* Chicago: University of Chicago Press.

Elder, G. H., Jr. (1981). Scarcity and prosperity in postwar childbearing: Explorations from a life course perspective. *Journal of Family History, 5,* 410–431.

Elder, G. H., Jr. (1984). Families, kin, and the life course: A sociological perspective. In R. D. Parke (Ed.), *The family.* Chicago: University of Chicago Press.

Elder, G. H., Jr. (Ed.). (1985). *Life course dynamics: Trajectories and transitions, 1968–1980.* Ithaca, NY: Cornell University Press.

Elder, G. H., Jr., Caspi, A., & Downey, G. (1986). Problem behavior and family relationships: A multigenerational analysis. In A. Sorensen, F. Weinert, & L. Sherrod (Eds.), *Human development: Interdisciplinary perspectives.* Hillsdale, NJ: Erlbaum.

Elder, G. H., Jr., Caspi, A., & Van Nguyen, T., (1986). Resourceful and vulnerable children: Family influences in stressful times. In R. K. Silbereisen, K. Eyferth, & G. Rudinger (Eds.), *Development as action in context: Problem behavior and normal youth development* (pp. 169–186). Heidelberg & New York: Springer-Verlag.

Elder, G. H., Jr., Van Nguyen, T., & Caspi, A. (1985). Linking family hardship to children's lives. *Child Development, 56,* 361–375.

Epstein, A. (1980). *Assessing the child development information needed by adolescent parents with very young children.* Final report of Grant OCD-90-C-1341. Washington, DC: Office of Child Development, Department of Health, Education and Welfare (ERIC Document Reproduction Service No. ED 183286).

Epstein, J. L. (1983a). *Effects on parents of teacher practices of parent involvement.* Baltimore, MD: Center for Social Organization of Schools, Johns Hopkins University (Report no. 346).

Epstein, J. L. (1983b). Longitudinal effects of family–school–person interactions on student outcomes. *Research in Sociology of Education and Socialization, 4,* 101–127.

Epstein, J. L. (1984). *Single-parents and the schools. The effects of marital status on parent and teacher evaluations.* (Report No. 353). Baltimore, MD: Johns Hopkins University, Center for Social Organization of Schools.

Farran, D. C., & Margolis, L. H. (1983). *The impact of paternal job loss on the family.* Paper presented at the biennial meeting of the Society for Research in Child Development, Detroit, Michigan.

Furstenberg, F. F. (1976). *Unplanned parenthood: The social consequences of teenage child bearing.* New York: Free Press.

Furstenberg, F. F., & Brooks-Gunn. (1987). *Adolescent mothers in later life.* New York: Cambridge University Press.

Furstenberg, F., & Crawford, A. (1978). Family support: Helping teenage mothers to cope. *Family Planning Perspectives, 10,* 322–333.

Garbarino, J. (1975). A note on the effects of television viewing. In U. Bronfenbrenner & M. A. Mahoney (Eds.), *Influences on human development* (2nd ed., pp. 397–399). Hinsdale, IL: Dryden.

Garbarino, J. (1976). A preliminary study of some ecological correlates of child abuse: The impact of socioeconomic stress on mothers. *Child Development, 47,* 178–185.

Giovannoni, J., & Billingsley, A. (1970). Child neglect among the poor: A study of parental adequacy in families of their ethnic groups. *Child Welfare, 49,* 196–204.

Gold, M., & Petronio, R. J. (1980). Delinquent behavior in adolescence. In J. Adelson (Ed.), *Handbook of adolescent psychology.* New York: Wiley.

Greenberger, E., & Steinberg, L. D. (1986). *When teenagers work: The psychological and social costs of adolescent employment.* New York: Basic Books.

Greenberger, E., Steinberg, L. D., & Vaux, A. (1981). Adolescents who work: Health and behavioral consequences of job stress. *Developmental Psychology, 6,* 691–703.

Hayes, D., & Grether, J. (1969). *The school year and vacation: When do children learn?* Paper presented at the Eastern Sociological Convention, New York.

Heath, D. B. (1977). Some possible effects of occupation on the maturing of professional men. *Journal of Vocational Behavior, 11,* 263–281.

Henderson, A. (1981). *Parent participation—student achievement: The evidence grows.* Columbia, MO: National Committee for Citizen Education.

Heston, L. L. (1966). Psychiatric disorders in foster home-reared children of schizophrenic mothers. *British Journal of Psychiatry, 112,* 819–825.

Hetherington, E. M. (1972). Effects of father absence on personality development in adolescent daughters. *Developmental Psychology, 7,* 313–326.

Hetheringing, E. M. (1981). Children of divorce. In R. Henderson (Ed.), *Parent–child interaction.* New York: Academic Press.

Hetherington, E. M., Cox, M., & Cox, R. (1978). The aftermath of divorce. In J. H. Stevens, Jr. & M. Mathews (Eds.), *Mother–child, father–child relations.* Washington, DC: National Association for the Education of Young Children.

Hetherington, E. M., & Deur, J. (1971). The effects of father absence on child development in young children. *Young Children,* 233–248.

Heyns, B. (1978). *Summer learning and effects of schooling.* New York: Academic Press.

Hoffman, L. W. (1980). The effects of maternal employment on the academic attitudes and performance of school-age children. *School Psychology Review,* 319–335.

Hoffman, L. W. (1983). Work, family, and the socialization of the child. In R. D. Parke (Ed.), *Review of child development research: Vol. 7. The family.* Chicago: University of Chicago Press.

Hollingshead, A. B. (1949). *Elmtown's youth and Elmtown revisited.* New York: Wiley.

Hutchings, B., & Mednick, S. A. (1977). Criminality in adoptees and their adoptive and biological parents: A pilot study. In S. A. Mednick & K. O. Christensen (Eds.), *Biological bases of criminal behavior* (pp. 127–164). New York: Gardner Press.

Jensen, A. R. (1969, Winter). How much can we boost IQ and scholastic achievement? *Harvard Educational Review,* 1–123.

Jensen, A. R. (1973). Let's understand Skodak and Skeels, finally. *Educational Psychologist, 10,* 30–35.

Jensen, A. R. (1980). *Bias in mental testing.* New York: Free Press.

Jessor, R. (1986). *Adolescent problem drinking: Psychological aspects and development outcomes.* In R. K. Silbereisen, K. Eyferth, & G. Rudinger (Eds.), *Development as action in context: Problem behavior and normal youth development.* (pp. 241–264). Heidelberg & New York: Springer-Verlag.

Kandel, D. B. (1986). On processes of peer influence in adolescence. In R. Silbereisen, K. Eyferth, & G. Rudinger (Eds.), *Development as action in context: Problem behavior and normal youth development* (pp. 241–264). Heidelberg & New York: Springer-Verlag.

Kandel, D. B., & Lesser, G. S. (1972). *Youth in two worlds.* San Francisco: Jossey-Bass.

Kanter, R. N. (1977). *Work and family in the United States: A critical review and agenda for research and public policy.* New York: Russell Sage.

Klineberg, O. (1935). *Negro intelligence in selective migration.* New York: Columbia University Press.

Klineberg, O. (1938). The intelligence of migrants. *American Sociological Review, 3,* 218–224.

Kohn, M. L. (1969). *Class and conformity: A study in values.* Homewood, IL: Dorsey Press.

Kohn, M. L., & Schooler, C. (1973). Occupational experience and psychological functioning: An assessment of reciprocal effects. *American Sociological Review, 38,* 97–118.

Kohn, M. L., & Schooler, C. (1978). The reciprocal effects of substantive complexity of work and intellectual flexibility: A longitudinal assessment. *American Journal of Sociology, 84,* 24–52.

Kohn, M. L., & Schooler, C. (1982). Job conditions and personality: A longitudinal assessment of their reciprocal effects. *American Journal of Sociology, 87,* 1257–1258.

Kohn, M. L. & Schooler, C. (1983). *Work and personality: An inquiry into the impact of social stratification.* Norwood, NJ: Ablex Press.

Komarovsky, M. (1940). *The unemployed man and his family.* New York: Dryden Press.

Kotelchuck, M. (1983). Schwarts, J. B., Anderka, N. T., & Finison, K. F. *WIC participation and pregnancy outcomes.* Unpublished manuscript, Massachusetts Statewide Evaluation Project, Boston.

Lazar, I. (1984). Personal communication.

Leahy, A. M. (1935). Nature, nurture, and intelligence. *Genetic Psychology Monographs, 17,* 236–308.

Lightfoot, S. L. (1978). *Worlds apart: Relationships between families and school.* New York: Basic Books.

Loehlin, J. C., Lindzey, G., & Spuhler, J. N. (1975). *Race difference in intelligence.* San Francisco: W. H. Freeman.

Maccoby, E. E. (1951). Television: Its impact on school children. *Public Opinion Quarterly, 15,* 421–444.

Maccoby, E. E., & Jacklin, C. N. (1974). *The psychology of sex differences.* Stanford, CA: Stanford University Press.

McCubbin, H. I., Dahl, B. B., & Hunter, E. J. (Eds.). (1976). *Families in the military system.* New York: Sage.

Medrich, E. A., Roizen, J., Rubin, V., & Buckley, S. (1982). *The serious business of growing up: A study of children's lives outside school.* Berkeley: University of California Press.

Meili, R., & Steiner, H. (1965). Eine untersuchung zum intelligenzniveau elfjahriger der deutschen schweitz. *Schweizerishe Zeitschrift für Psychologie und ihre Anwendungen, 24,* 23–32.

Mercer, R. T., Hackley, K. C., & Bostrom, A. (in press). Social support of teenage mothers. *Birth Defects: Irugubak Article Series.*

Miller, D. R., & Swanson, G. E. (1958). *The changing American parent: A study in the Detroit areas.* New York: Wiley.

Miller, K. A., & Kohn, M. L. (1983). The reciprocal effects of job conditions and the intellectuality of leisure-time activity. In M. L. Kohn & C. Schooler, *Work and personality: An inquiry into the impact of social stratification.* Norwood, NJ: Ablex Press.

Miller, K. A., Schooler, C., Kohn, M. L., & Miller, K. A. (1979). Women and work: The psychological effects of occupational conditions. *American Journal of Sociology, 85,* 66–94.

Moorehouse, M. (1986). *The relationship among continuity in maternal employment, parent–child communicative activities, and the child's school competence.* Unpublished doctoral dissertation. Cornell University, Ithaca, NY.

Morgan, W. L. (1939). *The family meets the Depression.* Minneapolis: University of Minnesota Press.

Morgan, W. R., Alwin, D. F., & Griffin, L. J. (1979). Social origins, parental values, and the transmission of inequality. *American Journal of Sociology, 85,* 156–166.

Mortimer, J. T. (1974). Patterns of intergenerational occupational movements: A smallest-space analysis. *American Journal of Sociology, 79,* 1278–1299.

Mortimer, J. T. (1975). Occupational and value socialization in business and professional families. *Sociology of Work and Occupations, 2,* 29–53.

Mortimer, J. T. (1976, May). Social class, work, and the family: Some implications of the father's career for familial relationships and son's career decisions. *Journal of Marriage and the Family,* 241–256.

Mortimer, J. T., & Kumka, D. (1982). A further examination of the "occupational link hypothesis." *Sociological Quarterly, 23,* 3–16.

Mortimer, J. T., & Lorence, J. (1979). Work experience and occupational value socialization: A longitudinal study. *American Journal of Sociology, 84,* 1361–1385.

Mortimer, J. T., Lorence, J., & Kumka, D. (1982). Work and family linkages in the transition to adulthood: A panel study of highly-educated men. *Western Psychological Review, 13,* 50–68.

Mortimer, J. T., Lorence, J., & Kumka, D. (1986). *Work, family, and personality: Transition to adulthood.* Norwood, NJ: Ablex Press.

Mott, P. E., Mann, F. C., McLoughlin, Q., & Warwick, D. P. (1965). *Shift work: The social, psychological and physical consequences.* Ann Arbor: University of Michigan Press.

Muchow, M., & Muchow, H. H. (1935). *Der Lebenstraum des Grosstadkindes.* Hamburg, Germany: Riegel.

National Commission on Youth. (1980). *The transition of youth to adulthood: A bridge too long.* Boulder, CO: Westview Press.

Olds, D. L. (1983). An intervention program for high-risk families. In R. A. Hockelman (Ed.), *Minimizing high-risk parenting* (pp. 249–268). Media, PA: Harwal.

Patterson, G. R. (1982). *Coercive family processes.* Eugene, OR: Castalia.

Piaget, J. (1932). *The moral judgment of the child.* New York: Harcourt-Brace.

Piotrkowski, C. S. (1979). *Work and the family system: A naturalistic study of working-class and lower-middle class families.* New York: Free Press.

Pitkanen-Pulkkinen, L. (1980). The child in the family. *Nirdisk Psykologi, 32,* 147–157.

President's Science Advisory Committee. (1973). *Youth: Transition to adulthood.* Chicago: University of Chicago Press.

Prugh, D. G., Staub, E. M., Sands, H. H., Kirschbaum, R. M., & Lenihan, E. A. (1953). A study of the emotional reactions of children in families to hospitalization and illness. *American Journal of Orthopsychiatry, 23,* 70–106.

Pulkkinen, L. (1982). Self-control and continuity in childhood delayed adolescence. In P. Baltes & O. Brim (Eds.), *Life span development and behavior* (Vol. 4, pp. 64–102). New York: Academic Press.

Pulkkinen, L. (1983a). Finland: Search of alternatives to aggression. In A. Goldstein & M. Segall (Eds.), *Aggression in global perspective.* New York: Pergamon Press.

Pulkkinen, L. (1983b). Youthful smoking and drinking in a longitudinal perspective. *Journal of Youth and Adolescence, 12*(4), 253–283.

Pulkkinen, L. (1984). *Nuoret ja kotikasvatus [Youth and home ecology].* Helsinki: Otava.

Quinton, D. (1980). Family life in the inner city: Myth and reality. In M. Marland (Ed.), *Education for the inner city* (pp. 45–67). London: Heinemann.

Riley, D., & Eckenrode, J. (1986). Social ties: Costs and benefits within differing groups. *Journal of Personality and Social Psychology, 51,* 770–778.

Rodgers, R. R. (1971). Changes in parental behavior reported by children in West Germany and the United States. *Human Development, 14,* 208–224.

Rutter, M. (1981). The city and the child. *American Journal of Orthopsychiatry, 51,* 610–625.

Rutter, M., & Giller, H. J. (1983). *Juvenile delinquency: Trends and perspectives.* New York: Penguin.

Rutter, M., Cox, A., Tupling, C., Berger, M., & Youle, W. (1975). Attainment and adjustment in two geographical areas: 1. The prevalence of psychiatric disorder. *British Journal of Psychiatry, 126,* 493–509.

Rutter, M., & Madge, N. (1976). *Cycles of disadvantage.* London: Heinemann.

Rutter, M., & Quinton, D. (1977). Psychiatric disorder—Ecological factors and concepts of causation. In H. McGurk (Ed.), *Ecological factors in human development* (pp. 173–187). Amsterdam: North-Holland.

Salkind, N. J. (1983). *Impact of a guaranteed income on children.* Paper presented at the biennial meeting of the Society for Research in Child Development, Detroit, Michigan.

Scarr, S. (1981). *Race, social class, and individual differences in IQ: New studies of old issues.* Hillsdale, NJ: Erlbaum.

Scarr, S., & McAvay, G. (1984). *Predicting the occupational status of young adults: A longitudinal study of brothers and sisters in adoptive and biologically-related families.* Unpublished manuscript, Department of Psychology, University of Virginia.

Scarr, S., & McCartney, K. (1983). How people make their own environment: The theory of genotype–environment effect. *Child Development, 54,* 424–436.

Scarr, S., Weinberg, R. A. (1976). IQ test performance of black children adopted by white families. *American Psychologist, 31,* 726–739.

Scarr, S., & Weinberg, R. A. (1983). The Minnesota adoption studies: Genetic differences and malability. *Child Development, 54,* 260–267.

Scarr-Salapatek, S., & Williams, M. L.(1973). The effects of early stimulation on low-birth weight infants. *Child Development, 44,* 94–101.

Schiff, M., Duyme, M., Dumaret, A., & Tomkiewicz, S. (1981). Enfants de travailleurs manuels adoptes par des cadres: Effet d'un changement de classe sociale sur le cursus scolaire et les notes de QI. *Travaux et Documents, 93.*

Schiff, M., Duyme, M., Dumaret, A., & Tomkiewicz, S. (1982). How much *could* we boost scholastic achievement and IQ scores? A direct answer from a French adoption study. *Cognition, 12,* 155–196.

Schneewind, K. A., Beckman, M., & Engfer, A. (1983). *Eltern und kinder.* Stuttgart: Kohlhammer.

Skeels, H. M. (1966). Adult status of children with contrasting early life experiences: A follow-up study. *Monographs of the Society for Research in Child Development, 31*(105), 1–65.

Skeels, H. M., & Dye, H. B. (1939). A study of the effects of differential stimulation on mentally retarded children. *Proceedings and addresses of the American Association on Mental Deficiency, 44,* 114–136.

Skeels, H. M., Updegraff, R., Wellman, B. L., & Williams, H. M. (1938). A study of environmental stimulation: An orphanage preschool project. *University of Iowa Studies in Child Welfare, 15*(4).

Skodak, M., & Skeels, H. M. (1949). A final follow-up study of one hundred adopted children. *Journal of Genetic Psychology, 75,* 85–125.

Slomezynski, K. M., Miller, J., & Kohn, M. (1981). Stratification, work, and values: A Polish-United States comparison. *American Sociological Review, 46,* 720–744.

Smith, M. B. (1968). School and home: Focus on achievement. In A. H. Passow (Ed.), *Developing programs for the educationally disadvantaged.* New York: Teachers College Press.

Steinberg, L. (1985). *Single parents, stepparents, and the susceptibility of adolescents to antisocial peer pressure: When two parents are not enough.* Unpublished manuscript. University of Wisconsin, Department of Child and Family Studies.

Steinberg, L. (1986). *Latchkey children and susceptibility to peer pressure: An ecological analysis.* Unpublished manuscript. University of Wisconsin, Department of Child and Family Studies.

Steinberg, L. D., Catalano, R., & Dooley, D. (1981). Economic antecedents of child abuse and neglect. *Child Development, 52,* 975–985.

Steinberg, L. D., Greenberger, E., Garduque, L., Ruggiero, M., & Vaux, A. (1982). The effects of working on adolescent development. *Developmental Psychology, 18,* 385–395.

Tangri, S. S., & Leitch, M. L. (1982). *Barriers to home–school collaboration: Two case studies in junior high school.* Final Report submitted to the National Institute of Education. Washington, DC: The Urban Institute.

Taylor, H. F. (1980). *The IQ game.* New Brunswick, NJ: Rutgers University Press.

Thompson, R. A., Lamb, M. E., & Estes, D. (1982). Stability of infant–mother attachment and its relationship to changing life circumstances. *Child Development, 53,* 144–148.

Tietjen, A. M., & Bradley, C. F. (1982). *Social networks, social support and transition to parenthood.* Unpublished paper. University of British Columbia, Vancouver, Division of Family Studies.

Tiller, P. O. (1958). Father absence and personality development of children in sailor families: A preliminary research report. In N. Anderson (Ed.), *Studies of the family.* Göttingen: Vandenhoeck and Ruprecht.

Tulkin, S. R. (1973a). Social class differences in infants' reactions to mother's and stranger's voices. *Developmental Psychology, 8,* 137.

Tulkin, S. R. (1973b). Social class differences in attachment behaviors of ten-month-old infants. *Child Development, 44,* 171–174.

Tulkin, S. R. (1977). Social class differences in maternal and infant behavior. In P. H. Leiderman, A. Rosenfeld, & S. R. Tulkin (Eds.). *Culture and infancy* (pp. 495–557). New York: Academic Press.

Tulkin, S. R., & Cohler, B. J. (1973). Child-rearing attitudes and mother–child interaction in the first year of life. *Merrill-Palmer Quarterly, 19,* 95–106.

Tulkin, S. R., & Covitz, F. E. (1975). *Mother–infant interaction and intellectual functioning at age six.* Paper presented at the meeting of the Society for Research in Child Development, Denver, CO.

Tulkin, S. R., & Kagan, J. (1972). Mother–child interaction in the first year of life. *Child Development, 43,* 31–41.

U.S. Bureau of the Census. (1981). Current Population Reports, Series P-60, No. 127. *Money income and poverty status of families and persons in the United*

States, 1980. Washington, DC: U.S. Government Printing Office.

U.S. Bureau of the Census. (1985). Current Population Reports, Series P-60, No. 149. *Money income and poverty status of families and persons in the United States, 1984.* Washington, DC: U.S. Government Printing Office.

Vatter, M. (1981). Intelligenz und regionale Herkunft. Eine Langsschnittstudie im Kanton Bern. In A. H. Walter (Ed.), *Region und sozialisation* (Vol. 1, pp. 56–91). Stuttgart: Frommann-Holzboog.

Walter, H. (Ed.) (1981–1982). *Region und sozialisation* (Vol. I and II). Stuttgart: Frommann-Holzboog.

Wandersman, L. P., & Unger, D. G. (1983). *Interaction of infant difficulty and social support in adolescent moth-ers.* Paper presented at the biennial meeting of the Society for Research in Child Development, Detroit, MI.

Weinraub, M., & Wolf, B. M. (1983). Effects of stress and social supports on mother–child interactions in single-and two-parent families, *Child Development, 54,* 1294–1311.

Werner, E. E., & Smith, R. S. (1982). *Vulnerable but invincible.* New York: McGraw-Hill.

Wheeler, L. R. (1942). A comparative study of the intelligence of East Tennessee mountain children. *Journal of Educational Psychology, 33,* 321–334.

Zigler, E., Kagan, S. L., & Klugman, E. (1983). *Children, families, and government: Perspectives on American social policy.* New York: Cambridge University Press.

PART II

Learning, Development, and Intervention

KOFI MARFO AND HILDA ROSSELLI-KOSTORYZ
University of South Florida

With so much cynicism around the subject of educational change, it may be risky, and perhaps even futile, to assert that we are witnessing a new era of change. But there is a sense in which it is no mere cliché to characterize the past decade as having ushered the field of special education, in particular, into a new epoch of change. Reform, restructuring, and reengineering are key concepts that have engulfed the continuing dialogue on the education of children with special needs. The imperative to forge new directions for the field emanates largely from the practical realities of a nation and an educational system struggling to come to terms with acknowledged failure to respond adequately and prudently to individual differences in an increasingly diverse society. What is different about this current era of change is the clear evidence that we seem to be going beyond the practice arena, both in our diagnosis of the problem and in our search for new directions. Some past change efforts can safely be characterized as "policy and practice tinkering," but the current change effort shows significant evidence of a commitment to go to the very radicle of the problem—to the assumptions, belief systems, and knowledge bases that inform educational practice.

The chapters in this section present contributions to the knowledge base on children's development and learning from the fields of neuropsychology (Chapter 4), cognitive science (Chapter 5), and applied developmental psychology (Chapters 6 and 7). The authors were given the following mandates: outline what we currently know about the topic by presenting an overview of trends in the development of the knowledge base; identify key issues and challenges or lines of inquiry that have produced or shaped what we currently know about the topic; highlight newer insights, emerging themes, and potential future developments within the knowledge base; and draw implications for practice and intervention.

In Chapter 4, Steven R. Hooper, director of Child and Adolescent Neuropsychology at the Clinical Center at the University of North Carolina at Chapel Hill, focuses on the emerging field of child neuropsychology, emphasizing particularly the manifest as well as potential contributions of advances in this field to special education practice. The chapter begins with an overview of basic research on brain-behavior relations, much of which is anchored in the seminal work of Soviet neuropsychologist A. R. Luria, linking structures and processes in different parts of the human brain with specific cognitive functions. This is followed by an insightful historical account of the development of child neuropsychology as an independent field of inquiry. Hooper shows how the nature, goals, and tools of neuropsychological assessment have changed from the field's primordial beginnings in the mid-1940s, when global and static differentiation of damaged versus normal brains was the central concern, to its present-day emphasis on ecologically valid assessment and descriptive analysis of the behavioral effects of special cerebral lesions. According to Hooper, ecological validity has become a primary concern in neuropsychological assessment in response to practitioners' and parents' needs to know the precise implications of diagnoses and prescribed interventions for a child's everyday functioning and future potential.

Various approaches to neuropsychological assessment (along with examples of specific test or test batteries utilized within the approach) are delineated and evaluated prior to assessing the educational and clinical contributions of contemporary child neuropsychology. Hooper points to advances in research on reading as presenting one of the clearest indications of the educational contributions of child neuropsychology. Not only are specific components of the reading process being linked to specific brain structures and functions or dysfunctions, but more important, significant advances have been made in the subtyping of reading problems. For example, differentiation of development surface dyslexia and developmental phonological dyslexia as two separate subtypes of reading disability has been made possible by the identification of distinct underlying neuroanatomic dysfunctions.

Beyond the high-incidence category of learning disabilities, Hooper shows how research in the cognitive neurosciences is improving our understanding of other children whose need for special education may stem from (1) known neurological disorders (such as traumatic head injury, seizure disorders, and structural abnormalities of the brain, such as hydrocephalus), (2) systemic illnesses that may impact neurological function by the very nature of the illness (that is, pediatric acute lymphocytic leukemia), and (3) psychiatric disorders.

Hooper concludes the chapter by drawing implications and identifying future directions in the areas of assessment, the linkage between assessment and treatment, the preparation and continuing education of teachers and other educational professionals, and public policy. Hooper expects research in child neuropsychology to impact the learning disabilities field in particular as special education moves into the 21st century—especially in light of his observation that research in the cognitive neurosciences has produced insights that are already challenging both the use of IQ and the reliance on discrepancy formula in the definition of learning disabilities.

Theories of intellectual development have been debated for over a century and the discussion is still heated as evidenced by the media's response to recent publications regarding intelligence. Unable to reach agreement on the respective contributions of heredity and environment, researchers have left the practitioner with an array of theory-based explanations from which to draw. Indeed, a thorough discussion of these theories constitutes more than a chapter can adequately handle. Viens, Chen, and Gardner, authors of Chapter 5, examine the views most representative of the major shifts in intelligence theory; namely, psychometric models, Piagetian theory, information-processing models, neo-Piagetian theories, and more recent integrative models of intelligence. Best known for their involvement in Project Zero at the Harvard Graduate School of Education, both Julie Viens and Jie-Qi Chen (now at the Erikson Institute) have researched the application of multiple intelligences theory in young and elementary-aged children. Howard Gardner is a professor of education at the Harvard Graduate School of Education where he also co-directs Project Zero with David Perkins. Best known for his book *Frames of Mind*, which introduced his theory of multiple intelligences, Gardner has also written about the lives of creative individuals, the Chinese system of education, as well as the implications of children's thinking on school reform.

Vien and her coauthors have traced the landscape of this important field and noted the ethical implications for policy and educational practice from the atrocities committed at Ellis Island to the common practices of labeling and segregating students on the basis of IQ. Readers will certainly recognize the familiar recountings and critiques offered by Vien and her coauthors but will also resonate to the uncomfortable tension that has undergirded many of the practices of special education. Clearly, as special educators seek to revision their future relationship with general education, they will repeatedly challenge the existing structures and assumptions that have evolved over time as society has attempted to explain differences in human ability. Chapter 5 also offers a hopeful perspective on the current views of intelligence that seek to draw from a wider range of disciplines and to view human intelligence from both macro and microperspectives. The authors' quest for a theory of intelligence that helps individuals improve their capacity to adapt, craft, and construct their surrounding environment suggests new avenues through which the extensive interest in this field might be harnessed for the benefit of improving the quality of life and education for America's children.

Addressing the remarkable interface between developmental science on the one hand, and education and social policy on the other, Chapter 6 by Edward Zigler examines the challenges and promises of early intervention services for children growing up in poverty. Director of the Bush Center in Child Development and Social Policy at Yale University, Zigler has served as a special consultant to several presidents, cabinet officers, and private foundations on issues related to child development. Taking Head Start as his point of departure, he provides an overview of the historical context that gave birth to the early intervention movement and appraises the assumptions and expectations responsible for or associated with early intervention's alternating waning and waxing image over the years.

Against the backdrop of the unusually high expectation in the 1960s and 1970s—that early intervention would somehow undo the unfortunate impact of poverty and social disadvantage—Zigler undertakes a critical appraisal of some of the core developmental principles and beliefs predicating this high expectation. He argues, for example, that not only was the hope of raising intelligence through early intervention overrated, but the emphasis on gains in intelligence and achievement test scores as the primary (and in some cases the sole) indicator of successful intervention outcomes were misplaced. Similarly, he blames the political vulnerability of the intervention movement for the myopic view that brief periods of intervention occurring in the critical period of early childhood could somehow inoculate children against lifelong exposure to poverty and other disadvantaging conditions.

As he has done so consistently in his advocacy for early intervention services throughout his distinguished career, Zigler presents a broader perspective on the goals and outcomes of intervention. He underscores the fact that Head Start was intended to be, and has always been, a much more comprehensive program than its evaluators and critics portrayed it to be in the past. For example, beyond the enhancement of intellectual and academic skills, goals relating to health, nutrition, and socioemotional development have always been part of the Head Start tradition. It is from this perspective that Zigler laments the manner in which first-generation evaluations of Head

Start concentrated almost exclusively on IQ gains as the basis for judging the program's efficacy and, ultimately, its potential role in the national policy designed to address the challenges of poverty and social inequity.

Having addressed the variety of problems that troubled the early intervention movement and the research it spawned in the early years, Zigler proceeds to review relatively more recent research on Head Start and non–Head Start types of early intervention programs. This research confirms that early intervention has positive short- and long-term impact on indicators of school adjustment and placement and on prosocial behavior. Indeed, some of this newer evidence sheds some light on the beneficial effects of various forms of intervention, not only on parents but on the family environment as a whole. While this newer generation of research may be doing better justice to the broader goals and scope of early intervention services for poor and disadvantaged children, Zigler's cautionary note about the status of research in this field is one that requires our attention. We may have come a long way, but his observation that "the potential benefits of intervention are documented by theory and scattered evidence rather than by cohesive research" may be as valid today as it was a decade ago.

Zigler ends the chapter with some directions for reconceptualizing the early intervention enterprise as it relates to poor and disadvantaged children. To provide for continuity and to maximize the benefits of intervention, Zigler proposes the transformation of the Title I program to become the school-age version of Head Start, and calls for the age of entry to include children from birth to 3 years of age. In addition, he makes a number of specific recommendations for program design and delivery. Zigler argues that unless programs are comprehensive in their coverage of most childhood developmental needs and of high quality in terms of developmental appropriateness and adequacy of resources, it would be unrealistic to expect any sustained desirable outcomes. Echoing the ecological theme that also runs through Chapter 7, Zigler predicts that "programs that address the broad ecology in which the child develops will be the most effective." Perhaps even more to the heart of the ecological view is the position reflected in his statement that, "Early intervention can help prepare children for school and enhance some aspects of their families' functioning, *but it alone cannot end poverty and crime and guarantee successful schooling.*"

In Chapter 7, Richard M. Lerner makes a strong passioned plea for increasing the practical relevance of theory and research in child and adolescent development. After painting a rather somber picture of a wide range of preventable but nevertheless intractable problems that are placing millions of youth at health, educational, and economic risk in society today, Lerner laments developmental psychology's dismal record in addressing real-world problems in real-world settings. Among the poignant criticisms of developmental psychology raised by Lerner are the following: (1) that the large majority of developmental theory and research has little to do with the most pervasive problems of childhood and adolescence—namely, violence, drug abuse, unsafe sex, adolescent parenting, and poverty, and (2) that there is a wide gap between the worlds of those charged with policy and program development and the developmental scientists whose work should be providing the intellectual base for policies and programs. To increase the practical relevance of developmental research and bridge the gap between scientists and policymakers, Lerner proposes *outreach scholarship* as an alternative model of science in which researchers work collaboratively with communities to generate, transmit, and apply knowledge for the direct benefit of children, families, neighborhoods, and communities.

Lerner's own theory of *developmental contextualism* —a theory that "embeds the study of children in the actual families, neighborhoods, and communities within which they live"—is presented as a framework for a new applied developmental science characterized by increased outreach, multiprofessional collaboration, and full partnerships between scientists and the communities that stand to benefit from developmental research. Examining the study of human development from a historical standpoint, Lerner notes that the field has evolved in at least three significant directions: increased recognition of the human organism's contributions to its own development; the emergence of a life-span perspective about human development; and the growing prominence of the role of context or ecology in development. Thus, developmental contextualism represents state-of-the-art thinking within a discipline that has undergone significant transitions during the course of the last two decades.

After spelling out the core features of developmental contextualism, Lerner shows how the theory can be used as a framework for designing comprehensive intervention programs to address the problems of childhood and adolescence. A core maxim of interventions that are founded on developmental contextualism is that "interventions should be aimed at changing individuals" per se. Other principles of intervention articulated in this chapter underscore Lerner's strong systems perspective and life-span orientation. Finally, Lerner not only presents a developmental contextual model for evaluating applied programs, he also enumerates specific suggestions and strategies for forging collaborative networks within communities to both implement and evaluate community-based programs.

Lerner's work has implications beyond the specific social and developmental problems of adolescence discussed in Chapter 7. The plea to view the systemic contexts of children's problems as primary targets of intervention is one that the field of special education should do well to heed. Too many of our interventions are directed toward children as individuals even when the problems they manifest are conceptualized as being systemic. A case in point is intervention programming for children considered to be at risk for educational failure. Although most of the children in programs for at-risk students are classified because of factors associated with their developmental, learning, and socioeconomic environments, the interventions offered in such programs typically *treat* the children as if the problem resides in them rather than in their environments. To borrow an Akan proverb (from Ghana, West Africa), "You do not beat the sides of a drum when the surface is there." Regrettably, many of our interventions, especially those for environmentally at-risk children, do exactly what this West African proverb admonishes us not to do. Chapter 7 offers both a conceptual and a practical guide for considering interventions aimed at changing the very contexts that trigger and nurture the problems of childhood and adolescence.

CHAPTER 4

Neuropsychology and Special Education: Foundations, Applications, and Future Contributions

STEPHEN R. HOOPER
University of North Carolina at Chapel Hill

Introduction

There has been a tremendous growth of interest in child neuropsychology as a distinct subspecialty within the broader field of clinical neuropsychology. Whereas it was not too long ago that one could find only selected chapters dealing with children in some of the major texts within the field (for example, Filskov & Boll, 1981; Reitan & Davison, 1974), there are now entire volumes (such as Gaddes & Edgell, 1994; Hynd & Willis, 1988; Rourke, Fisk, & Strang, 1986; Rutter, 1983; Tramontana & Hooper, 1988a) as well as journals (such as *Child Neuropsychology*) devoted exclusively to the topic. Similarly, there has been a proliferation of symposia, workshops, and journal articles covering various aspects of neuropsychological research and practice with children. All of this certainly attests to the emergence of child neuropsychology as a focus of vigorous interest and inquiry. This growth has been predicated on many factors, with three of the more recent factors being highlighted here (Hooper & Hynd, 1993).

First, although child neuropsychology is a strongly emergent specialty area, its foundations are significantly associated with developmental psychology, pediatric neurology, the psychology of individual differences, cognitive neurosciences,

and adult neuropsychology. The knowledge gained from these disciplines, and other related disciplines such as neonatology, has contributed to forming and refining some of the core theoretical notions that child and developmental neuropsychologists hold (for example, children are not simply scaled-down versions of adults).

Second, with the passage of the Education for All Handicapped Children Act (Public Law 94-142) (U.S. Office of Education, 1977), specific attention has been directed to studying children with a variety of neurodevelopmental and acquired handicaps. For example, the area of learning disabilities has received an enormous amount of attention from the field of child neuropsychology, particularly with respect to clinical differentiation and issues related to subtyping (Feagans, Short, & Meltzer, 1991; Hooper & Willis, 1989; Rourke, 1991). In general, child neuropsychologists have not only been instrumental in refining our knowledge about specific neurodevelopmental disorders, including more severe and pervasive disorders such as autism (Hooper, Boyd, Hynd, & Rubin, 1993), but they have also contributed to the development of more detailed educational plans for these children (Hooper, Willis, & Stone, 1996).

A third related contribution to the growth of child neuropsychology involves the application of neuropsychology knowledge and assessment techniques to children with pediatric, neurologic, and psychiatric disorders. For example, advances in medical care have brought about a dramatic increase in the survival of children whose conditions (or their treatments) have a potentially adverse impact on the developing brain (for example, very low birth weight associated with prematurity, and iatrogenic effects of childhood cancer treatment). Thus, although mortality has decreased, there has been a relative increase in morbidity. These conditions, along with the emergence of devastating diseases such as human immunodeficiency virus (HIV), have created a greater need for the careful assessment of the extent, pattern, and developmental significance of possible neuropsychological sequelae in these children. It has also created an increased need for knowledge of these conditions to be communicated to education and special education personnel who will be working directly with these children.

Taken together, these three factors have contributed to significant advances in the field of child neuropsychology, particularly over the past decade or two. In fact, these factors and related efforts have contributed to advancing the field beyond its infancy and into what some would consider to be its adolescence (Spreen, 1988). Despite this growth in our understanding of brain-behavior relationships and the outcomes of children experiencing acquired and neurodevelopmental insults, the relationship between child neuropsychology and special education remains somewhat circumscribed, if not suspect.

This chapter is devoted to underscoring important issues in child neuropsychology, particularly as these issues may contribute to the special education setting. This chapter presents a brief discussion of basic knowledge relevant to brain-behavior relationships, a general review of historical trends within the field, a brief description of typical assessment approaches in child neuropsychology, a

discussion of specific clinical applications (including proposed models of brain functioning as applied to core academic skills), and selected findings for many populations of children in the school setting. The chapter concludes with a discussion of the future implications of professionals utilizing a child neuropsychological perspective in special educational settings.

Basic Brain-Behavior Relationships

The basic knowledge base with respect to brain-behavior relationships is still evolving, particularly with respect to overarching neurodevelopmental issues and corresponding behavioral changes that can be observed in a child, adolescent, or even an adult. Further, it is likely that brain-behavior relationships change throughout the life span, and that functional brain organization covaries with ontogeny. The focus of this section is on the principles of neuropsychology that are germane for a beginning understanding of the field and its potential impact on education and special education. A specific theoretical orientation and associated functional brain-behavior relationships are presented. Recent advances in our understanding of brain-behavior relationships are also highlighted.

Theoretical Foundations

Perhaps one of the most widely applied theories of brain-behavior relationships throughout the life span has come from Luria (1970). He proposed that there are three basic functional units of the brain: subcortical, posterior cortical, and anterior cortical. Each of these units incorporates distinctive functions that are mutually interdependent. Thus, there are extensive interconnections within and among these units. All three units of the brain are involved in the performance of any given behavior—covert as well as overt—and each unit influences and is influenced by the other units.

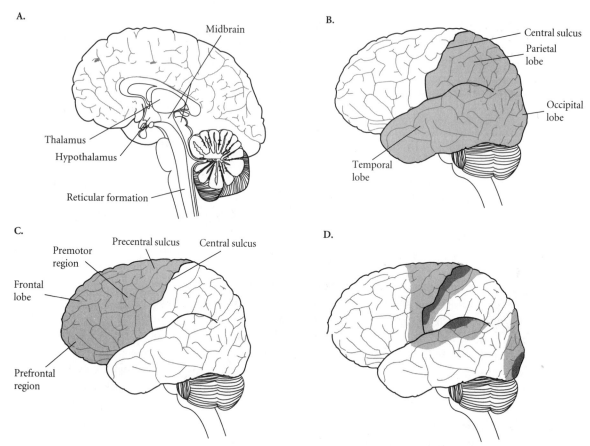

Figure 4-1   Luria's three functional units of the brain: (A) subcortical unit, (B) posterior cortical unit, (C) anterior cortical unit, (D) hierarchical organization within the cortical units. Primary zones are shaded heavily; secondary zones are shaded lightly; tertiary zones are unshaded cortical regions. (Based on G. W. Hynd, & W. G. Willis, 1988. *Pediatric neuropsychology,* p. 107. Orlando, FL: Grune & Stratton.)

Figure 4-1 shows the regions of the brain included in each of these cortical units and the hierarchical nature of the zones within these units.

Subcortical unit. The subcortical unit of the brain is associated with the brain stem reticular formation and is illustrated in Figure 4-1A. The reticular formation is a concept based on brain morphology that includes groups of neurons from the regions of the medulla oblongata, pons, and midbrain. Through a system of projection fibers, the reticular formation influences and is influenced by neuroanatomical structures located more anteriorly and posteriorly along the craniocaudal axis. Luria (1973) suggested that conscious activity always involves this unit as well as the other two units of the brain. Brodal (1981) emphasized the role of this unit in autonomic activity as well. The morphological features of the reticular formation support the notion that this group of neurons is involved in the activation, inhibition, and regulation of central nervous system (CNS) activities.

Brodal (1981) proposed the functional concept of the "activating system" to correspond to the structural concept of the reticular formation. This is descriptive of the characteristic electrophysiological response of the brain stem reticular formation to stimulation that signals attention or alertness. Similarly, Luria (1973) described the functional significance of this unit of the brain for the "maintenance of . . . [an] optimal level of cortical tone . . . essential for the organized course of mental activity" (p. 45).

Sources of activation to the subcortical unit of the brain may be metabolic, environmental, or cortical regulatory. The latter influence, in particular, emphasizes the interdependent relationship of the three units of the brain. Although the subcortical unit normally mediates a degree of cortical activation that is proportional to the intensity of the source of stimulation, that relationship can become distorted in the presence of dysfunction of the subcortical unit. This is consistent, for example, with the notion advanced by some theorists that the attention deficits and hyperactivity that accompany some learning disabilities may be associated with dysfunctions affecting this unit of the brain or those regions with which it has extensive interconnections (Halperin, McKay, Matier, & Sharma, 1994; Zametkin & Rapoport, 1987).

Cortical units. The cerebral cortex occupies the surfaces of the cerebral hemispheres. It is a highly differentiated structure that comprises six layers of cells of varying morphology. Particular cell layers may be well developed or indistinct, depending on the region in which they are located. These cytoarchitectonic differences provide the structural basis for the differentiation and hierarchical organization within the two cortical functional units of the brain. At about two weeks following conception, a major sulcus, the lateral fissure, develops that divides the telencephalon into two hemispheres. Between fourteen and twenty weeks after conception, other major sulci develop (Dooling, Chi, & Gilles, 1983) that divide each cerebral hemisphere into four lobes: frontal, temporal, parietal, and occipital.

Hemispheric lateralization. Functional asymmetries associated with the cortex of the cerebral hemispheres have been a major source of interest to neuropsychologists for many years. These asymmetries, or cerebral hemispheric lateralizations, refer to the relative (as opposed to exclusive) specialization of one cerebral hemisphere for a particular function. It was once thought that only higher-order cognitive functions were subject to lateralization (Luria, 1973); however, it seems equally likely that some sensory functions may also be lateralized, albeit perhaps less strongly (Davidoff, 1982).

Through the clinical and scientific interests in cerebral lateralization, several well-documented findings have emerged that are relevant to a developmental perspective on this topic. For example, it was once believed that the cerebral hemispheres were equipotential for function at birth and that they became progressively more lateralized for function with postnatal development (Lenneberg, 1967). However, this notion is no longer supported. Research conducted at anatomical, physiological, and behavioral levels of analysis strongly supports the notion that the cerebral hemispheres are specialized, at least for some functions, at a very early age (Molfese & Segalowitz, 1988). Speech-related cognitive functions, in particular, appear to be functionally lateralized to the left cerebral hemisphere for most individuals by birth or shortly thereafter. This does not suggest that interactions among various cerebral regions are constant throughout development, but it does indicate that particular aspects of cerebral hemispheric lateralization appear independent of developmental influences.

Posterior cortical unit. According to Luria's (1973) functional organization of the brain, the cortical units are not considered in terms of the sagittal axis of cerebral hemispheric lateralization (that is, left versus right) but instead are considered in terms of the coronal axis that demarcates posterior from anterior divisions. The cortex of the parietal, occipital, and temporal lobes comprises the posterior cortical unit, as shown in Figure 4-1B. Within this unit there is a hierarchical arrangement of primary, secondary, and tertiary zones. These zones are depicted in Figure 4-1D. There is one primary zone within each of the three lobes, and each primary zone is essentially surrounded by a secondary zone. A major tertiary zone of the posterior cortical unit is demarcated by the parieto-occipito-temporal region of overlap, which roughly corresponds to a neuroanatomical structure known as the angular gyrus.

The common function of the posterior cortical unit is the reception, analysis, and storage of information. The primary and secondary zones within this unit are modality specific for function. Thus, primary and secondary zones within the parietal, occipital, and temporal lobes are functionally specialized for the processing of kinesthetic/somatosensory, visual, and auditory stimuli, respectively. Olfactory and gustatory sense modalities are also represented in this functional unit of the brain, but they assume relatively minor emphasis in humans.

The primary (that is, projection) zones essentially function in an afferent fashion to discriminate among various stimuli in a highly specific manner. They also function in an efferent fashion, influencing sensory receptors (for example, retina and cochlea) to ensure optimal perceptual capabilities. In contrast, the secondary (association or gnostic) zones are adapted especially for relaying afferent impulses to the tertiary zones for further analysis. Although also modality specific, the functions of the secondary zones are more integrative

than the primary zones. Thus, although lesions to the primary zones are usually associated with sensory deficits of the corresponding modality, lesions to the secondary zones are likely to disrupt higher-order cognitive processes because of a disorganization in the perception of complex groups of stimuli and the relationship among them (Luria, 1970). Disruption of the primary and/or secondary zones may also have an influence on the subsequent development of other associated regions and, consequently, on behavior.

The tertiary zones of the posterior cortical unit are functionally specialized for the multimodal integration of stimuli. Luria (1973) suggested that this integrative function may be associated with the process of abstract thinking and memorization (that is, storage) of organized experience, involving the conversion of successive stimuli into simultaneously processed groups. In this sense, developmental anomalies or acquired injuries to this zone are likely to impair the simultaneous synthesis of information (Luria, 1980), a cognitive process clearly related to a variety of higher-order academic functions such as arithmetic and reading (Das, Kirby, & Jarman, 1979).

Anterior cortical unit. Within the anterior cortical unit, presented in Figure 4-1C, there is also a hierarchical arrangement and development of primary, secondary, and tertiary zones. The primary zones are concerned with the most basic elements of motor movement, whereas the secondary zones are functionally specialized for the preparation of motor programs and organized movements. These motor programs are executed by neurons of the primary zones of the anterior cortical division. In contrast to the progression of function from primary to secondary to tertiary zones in the posterior cortical unit, the process is reversed in the anterior cortical unit. The functions associated with the secondary and primary zones of the cortical division are guided by tertiary influences.

The tertiary zones, located in the prefrontal regions of the frontal lobes, receive significant afferent input from the posterior cortical unit and are believed to be essential for the performance of goal-directed, selective behavior. Luria (1973) suggested that these zones "play a decisive role in the formation of intentions and programs, and in the regulation and verification of the most complex forms of human behaviour" (p. 84). Such behavior, for example, includes motor, speech, and intellectual acts (such as problem solving). The tertiary zones have also been implicated in the mediating of consciousness, affective states, and memory functions (Luria, 1980). There are extensive interconnections between this unit and the subcortical unit of the brain. Also, the regulatory role of the anterior cortical unit has been implicated in attentional problems and overactivity (Lou, Henriksen, & Bruhn, 1984). Many of these behaviors may be characterized by the successive synthesis of information, and a clear developmental progression has begun to be uncovered (Welsh, Pennington, & Groisser, 1991).

Functional system. From an educational perspective, one of Luria's fundamental concepts deserves additional mention; namely, the concept of a functional system (Luria, 1980). The human central nervous system is highly specialized for function. This fact is often misconstrued, however, to suggest that particular regions of the brain operate independently. Currently, for example, there is an abundance of popular press literature that dichotomously characterizes the two cerebral hemispheres and suggests that individuals primarily may be "left-brained" or "right-brained." Such literature renders a disservice to the discipline of neuropsychology by its oversimplification, and it is especially problematic when applied to treatments for children with learning differences. In addition to impeding progress in understanding brain-behavior relationships, this kind of misconstruction is inconsistent with the concept of a neurological functional system that provides the substrates for behavior.

Thus, although even the neonatal brain is highly differentiated for function, the neural substrates for these functions correspond to systems of components rather than to discrete regions. These components operate interdependently toward a unified result. One approach to neuropsychological evaluation is to investigate the integrity of functional systems of behavior according to these individual components. Additionally, it is useful to know the neuroanatomical bases for those components. This is a difficult task because there is less than an optimal research base. This is particularly true for child and adolescent populations. Moreover, especially for higher-order cognitive processes such as reading, writing, and arithmetic, relationships among components of functional systems may change developmentally (Valsiner, 1983).

For example, during the early stages of postnatal development, relatively direct and associative processes are dominant. During later stages, however, more complex integration related to speech and higher-order cognitive processes become more pronounced. On the basis of this cognitive developmental progression, Vygotsky (1960) was among the first to speculate that cerebral lesions that are associated with relatively basic sensory processes and that occur during early childhood may adversely affect higher-order cognitive functioning. This is because the foundation for the higher-order cognitive functioning is disrupted. Similar lesions that occur during adulthood, however, are expected to have a much more limited effect because the functional systems that subserve the higher-order cognitive functions are already formed. Consequently, Vygotsky proposed that during early stages of development, cerebral lesions primarily disrupt hierarchically higher components of functional systems subserved by the affected region, whereas during later stages of development, cerebral lesions primarily disrupt hierarchically lower components that may be regulated by the affected region. The application of this concept to selected educational functions is discussed later in this chapter.

Selected Advances in Brain-Behavior Relationships

In conjunction with these theoretical foundations, there have been a number of recent advances in our understanding of basic brain-behavior relationships over the past decade. In particular, a number of specific neurodevelopmental models have evolved with respect to attention (Halperin et al., 1994), learning disabilities (Mayeux & Kandel, 1985; Roeltgen, 1993; Rourke, 1989), and child psychopathology (Rourke, 1989). Further, studies examining early predictors of learning problems have proliferated (Molfese, 1995; Torgeson, Wagner, Bryant, & Pearson, 1992; Tramontana, Hooper, & Selzer, 1988). From a brain-behavior perspective, a number of studies have also begun to describe the potential neurological mechanisms in selected neurodevelopmental disorders. (The interested reader should consult Filipek (1995) for a more detailed overview of these neurobiological correlates.)

For example, using postmortem and neuroimaging techniques, a number of irregularities have begun to be described in individuals with dyslexia. In most individuals, the planum temporale in the left hemisphere tends to be larger than in the right hemisphere (Geschwind & Levitsky, 1968), even in fetuses (Witelson & Pallie, 1973). However, this asymmetry typically is not found in individuals with dyslexia. These individuals tend to show symmetrical plana, or reversed asymmetry with the right side being larger than the left (Hynd et al., 1990; Jernigan, Hesselink, Stowell, & Tallal, 1991; Leonard et al., 1993). These findings have been correlated with linguistic deficits (Semrud-Clikeman, Hynd, Lorus-Vernon, Novey, & Eliopulos, 1991) and, more specifically, with phonological processing deficiencies (Larsen, Hoien, Lundberg, & Odegaard, 1990). Most recently, using state-of-the-art functional magnetic resonance imaging, Shaywitz and associates (1995) found gender differences in the functional correlates of these brain regions. These investigators found that males and females develop phonological processing abilities via different regions of the brain. While males were found to show the expected left temporal lobe activity, females were found to show increased activity in the right hemisphere as well.

In addition, neuroimaging studies have also shown that individuals with dyslexia have symmetrical or reversed asymmetry in the parietal-occipital regions (Haslam, Dalby, Johns, & Rademaker, 1981; Jernigan et al., 1991) as well as in prefrontal regions (Jernigan et al., 1991). Further, Galaburda and Livingstone (1993) have demonstrated on postmortem examination that cellular layers sensitive to the processing of visual information (the ventral magnocelluar layers in the lateral geniculate) tend to be disorganized and smaller in shape. The corpus callosum also has begun to be examined in individuals with dyslexia. Using magnetic resonance imaging, initial findings suggest that the anterior region of the corpus callosum is smaller in children with dyslexia, and that this region of interest is significantly correlated with reading achievement (Hynd et al., 1995).

Historical Trends in Child Neuropsychology

Clinical neuropsychology is an applied science concerned with issues pertinent to known or hypothesized brain-behavior relationships. Although its early roots lie in clinical neurology dating back to the 19th century, the history of child neuropsychology is of recent origin. In general, the history of child neuropsychology can be divided into four distinct but overlapping stages of development. These are similar to, but generally have lagged behind, the stages of development that have characterized adult neuropsychology. In general, these stages have focused on specific conceptual models for neuropsychological assessment and the specific techniques available at designated time periods.

The First Stage in the Development of Child Neuropsychology

The first stage, the single-test approach, dominated the field from about the mid-1940s to the mid-1960s. It was characterized by the use of general, all-purpose measures for diagnosing brain damage or "organicity." The approach was guided by the belief that brain damage, regardless of its extent, location, or pathological process, manifested itself in a unitary fashion—whether it was in terms of a loss of abstraction abilities, perceptual-motor skills, or other functions. The goal was to differentiate brain-damaged children from normals. It was thought that a single, well-chosen measure could achieve that mission. The issue of how brain dysfunction was being manifested did not really matter because the interest was more in the global differentiation of cases. Examples of tests used in this fashion (although not necessarily with the encouragement of their authors) included the Bender Visual Motor Gestalt Test (Bender, 1938; Koppitz, 1964), the Visual Retention Test (Benton, 1963), and the Memory for Designs Test (Graham & Kendall, 1960).

The problems with the single-test approach have been well documented. For example, over thirty years ago Herbert (1964) conducted a thorough review of the tests in use up to the early 1960s and concluded that none achieved a sufficient differentiation of brain-damaged and normal children to justify its clinical use with individual cases.

Even if there were such a justification, there would still remain the issue of whether anything is really gained by simply being able to classify a child as brain-damaged or not. The single-test approach did have the historical significance of introducing psychologists into the role of making inferences regarding brain dysfunction. By today's standards, however, most neuropsychologists would regard the continued reliance on this approach as constituting malpractice, largely because of the advances in more sophisticated neuroimaging techniques (e.g., Bigler, 1995).

The Second Stage in the Development of Child Neuropsychology

Next came the test battery/lesion-specification stage of neuropsychological assessment. Ernhart and colleagues are credited as being among the first to apply a battery of psychological tests in assessing the developmental outcomes of a heterogeneous group of children with documented brain damage (Ernhart, Graham, Eichman, Marshall, & Thurston, 1963; Graham, Ernhart, Craft, & Berman, 1963). These investigators found that brain-damaged children manifested deficits on verbal and conceptual measures as well as on perceptual-motor tasks. Also, whereas no single measure yielded a satisfactory discrimination of brain-damaged children, use of the entire test battery did achieve this goal. This underscored the variability of brain damage and the need for a test battery covering a broad range of functions to capture the effects and behavioral manifestations of brain impairment. Shortly thereafter, Reitan and his colleagues (Reed, Reitan, & Klove, 1965) reported on the successful discrimination of brain-damaged children and normals using the Halstead-Reitan Neuropsychological Battery (HRNB). This battery (and its variants) quickly came to be the predominant assessment approach of this period—at least in North America.

There was another significant aspect to this stage of development in neuropsychology. The work with adults had shown that test batteries, such as the HRNB, not only provided a valid discrimination of brain-damaged and normal adults, but they were also reasonably accurate in distinguishing among brain-damaged patients who differed in terms of the extent, location, and other characteristics of their lesions (see Reitan & Davison, 1974). Indeed, neuropsychological test batteries achieved an equal, if not superior, discrimination of lesion characteristics in comparison with many of the other neurodiagnostic methods available at the time (Filskov & Goldstein, 1974). Inspired by this success with adults, similar efforts were made with children, albeit with unimpressive results. In the absence of significant hemimotor signs, even attempts to lateralize early cerebral lesions on the basis of neuropsychological test performance remains a controversial and poorly validated enterprise at best (Chadwick & Rutter, 1983).

Both of the stages just described constituted what Rourke (1982) has referred to as the static phase of development in clinical neuropsychology. The emphasis was on the detection and localization of brain lesions. The approach (either with single tests or with test batteries) was empirical, atheoretical, and geared heavily toward establishing cutoff scores and rules of inference for the purpose of maximizing hit-rates in categorical diagnoses. These applications were quite appealing at the time because of the void that existed in noninvasive neurodiagnostic technology until about the mid-1970s.

The Third Stage in the Development of Child Neuropsychology

The test battery/lesion-specification stage gave way to the functional profile stage, or what Rourke (1982) has referred to as the cognitive phase of neuropsychological assessment. Controversy over the validity of neuropsychological batteries to localize brain lesions in children, coupled with the rapid development of other noninvasive neurodiagnostic methods, resulted in a gradual deemphasis on using neuropsychological tests for making inferences regarding brain lesions. The emphasis shifted more to the role of neuropsychological assessment in specifying the behavioral effects of cerebral lesions. The goal was to differentiate between spared and impaired abilities; that is, functional strengths and weaknesses. The concern was not only on the extent of impairment but also on the pattern of deficit and the underlying components of impaired performance. It represented the "re-psychologizing" of neuropsychology, in that the emphasis was on assessing the psychological aspects of neurological insults and anomalies. Of all the available neurodiagnostic methods, neuropsychological assessment had a unique and complementary role to play in determining the mental and behavioral effects of brain injury, in identifying functional assets and deficits for the purpose of treatment planning, and in evaluating subsequent change.

A particularly important aspect of this period involved the neuropsychological study of children with learning disabilities. Just as the field of neuropsychology in general had moved away from unitary concepts and single-test measures of brain dysfunction, so, too, the study of learning disabilities progressed from single-factor research to multivariate research and the identification of subtypes of learners with disabilities (see Hooper & Willis, 1989, for a review). Neuropsychological test profiles, along with statistical clustering techniques, were used in identifying more homogeneous groupings of children having distinguishable patterns of disability. The work was not exclusively descriptive and empirical but also entailed theory building and model testing. This was important not only because it involved the extension of neuropsychological assessment into syndrome definition, particularly in the educational realm, but also because it represented a major line of neuropsychological research focused on children. Furthermore, it promoted a closer link between assessment and treatment, in that the differentiation of learning disabilities into subtypes provided at least a theoretical basis for the specification of differential approaches to treatment.

Although this stage of development represented a shift in the goals of neuropsychological assessment, there were no dramatic changes or innovations in the types of tests and measures being used. Basically, many of the same measures that originally had been validated on their ability to discriminate brain damage were being used now for the purpose of neuropsychological description and functional analysis. The existing methods usually allowed for the assessment of a broad range of brain function, but many of the measures were never designed to achieve a detailed analysis of the underlying components of complex deficits. This limited the specificity of neuropsychological description, and quite possibly the degree of meaningful differentiation that could be achieved in empirical studies of subtypes of neuropsychological disability.

The Fourth Stage in the Development of Child Neuropsychology

The field has now entered yet another stage of development, with its chief characteristic being an emphasis on ecological validity. Issues identified in the third stage continue to be addressed, but now there is an added demand to relate assessment findings to an individual's everyday functioning (Chelune & Edwards, 1981). Parents of children with brain impairments, special educators, and other consumers of neuropsychological services want to be provided with more than just a delineation of the child's deficits. They want to know pre-

cisely what these will mean in terms of the child's everyday functioning and future potential. The emphasis is not only on obtaining detailed descriptions but also on making prescriptive statements regarding the types of treatments and environments that will maximize adaptive functioning.

Rourke (1982) has referred to this as the dynamic phase of development in neuropsychological assessment, with the goal being to evaluate the individual's current neuropsychological functioning in relation to the specific environmental demands and developmental tasks that must be faced. Rourke and associates (1986) have incorporated this thinking in their model of a treatment-oriented approach to the neuropsychological assessment of children. According to this model, behavioral predictions and treatment plans should be based on a careful consideration of "the interaction that obtains between brain lesion(s) and the child's ability structure as this impacts on adaptive behavior" (p. 251). This entails not only assessing brain-behavior relationships within the child but also relating these to the unfolding developmental demands of the child's immediate and long-range environments. However, a potential limitation has to do with the actual power of existing neuropsychological measures to reflect important aspects of everyday functioning. As Rourke and associates have pointed out, the use of brief, homogeneous, narrow-band tests—although internally consistent and stable—may be of little use in assessing the child's capacity to meet complex environmental demands.

Summary of the Historical Trends in Child Neuropsychology

The foregoing overview highlighted some of the major historical trends in child neuropsychology, with a particular emphasis being placed on assessment and assessment-related issues. We have seen the goals of assessment shift from a static emphasis on diagnosing brain lesions to more of a focus on neuropsychological description and the analysis of functional deficits as well as strengths, and more recently, to an emphasis on neuropsychological prescription that is relevant to everyday functioning. Neuropsychologists will continue to make important contributions to diagnosing brain damage and brain dysfunction, and delineating its effects, but in a fashion that operates more from a biopsychosocial framework. The emphasis now is on ecological validity, and the relationship between assessment results and the individual's capacity to deal with important tasks of daily life. This is one area in which the current status of neuropsychological assessment with children actually appears to be somewhat ahead of work with adults. That is, the major attention given to the neuropsychological assessment of learning disabilities certainly has dealt with the child's adaptive capacity (and future potential) in an important real-life context; namely, school. This clearly accents the utility of a child neuropsychological perspective in the schools.

Neuropsychological Assessment Approaches

Fixed-Battery Approaches

A fixed-battery approach in neuropsychological assessment is one that aims to provide a comprehensive assessment of brain function using an invariant set of validated test procedures. The composition of the battery is not tailored to the presenting characteristics of the individual patient being assessed nor to the specific clinical hypotheses to be addressed. Rather, the emphasis is on administering as many of the designated procedures as the patient's condition will permit. Individual variability is thought to be captured reasonably well as long as the battery has been designed to tap a broad range of human capabilities. Moreover, the use of a fixed battery across patients pro-

vides a standard database on which different clinical groups can be compared.

To date, fixed batteries such as the Halstead-Reitan Neuropsychological Battery (HRNB) and the Luria-Nebraska Neuropsychological Battery (LNNB), have represented the most commonly used approaches in neuropsychological assessment (Hynd, Snow, & Becker, 1986). A detailed review of these batteries is beyond the scope of this chapter, and the reader may wish to refer to other available sources for a more thorough description of the composition and validation of the HRNB (Boll, 1981; Reitan & Davison, 1974) and the children's revision of the LNNB (Golden, 1981, 1987). Also, Hynd and colleagues (1986) and Tramontana and Hooper (1988b) have provided thorough critical reviews of the validity and utility of both of these batteries in child neuropsychological assessment. Suffice it to say that both batteries obtain similar hit-rates in identifying children with brain impairment, and they have been used successfully to identify children with learning disabilities. However, neither battery has been very successful in localizing brain lesions, although some efforts have been made to utilize these batteries for subtyping efforts in the learning disability domain (see Tramontana & Hooper, 1988b, for a review). On the horizon are other child neuropsychological batteries, such as the NEPSY (Korkman, 1995), and the field eagerly awaits these new initiatives, particularly given their potential for increased applicability in the educational setting.

Eclectic Test Batteries

This approach strives to preserve the quantitative nature of neuropsychological assessment by selecting standardized tests that, when taken together, cover a broad range of neuropsychological functions. There generally is at least an implicit outline of the relevant functions and abilities that should be assessed routinely (see Mattis, 1992). However, any of a variety of available tests may be selected to quantify the extent of deficit in each of the functional areas of interest. The psychometric properties of individual tests (such as adequacy of norms) as well as their complementarity when embedded in a battery are usually important factors guiding specific test selection.

For example, Mattis (1992) provided a decision tree for performing neuropsychological assessment. Once a decision is reached to conduct this extensive evaluation, a battery of measures is selected for assessing a child's functioning in each of the following areas: intelligence, attention, perception across modalities, memory and learning, language, motor, constructional abilities, academic, achievement, and affect/personality. A similar construct-driven battery has also been proposed for preschoolers (Hooper, 1991). Many other examples of eclectic batteries for children could be cited, but the foregoing should give some idea of the possibilities that exist.

Qualitative Approaches

Rather than an emphasis on quantifying the extent of a deficit, qualitative approaches are concerned more with determining how the individual passes or fails a particular task. For example, although a child may recall a memory item accurately, it is extremely important from a qualitative perspective to understand what strategies the child used to remember, and how efficiently that strategy was implemented. Did the child utilize cues based on the verbal, visual, or multimodal aspects of the task? Were contextual cues employed (such as main themes or key words)? Perhaps rehearsal, chunking, verbal labeling, or other mnemonic strategies were utilized to some degree. These kinds of data are extremely important not only in distinguishing the precise nature of underlying neuropsychological dysfunction but also in identifying possible treatment strategies that can be used in helping the child to compensate for deficits in particular outcomes of concern.

Qualitative approaches are less concerned with test standardization or in comparing an individual's performance against general norms than with conducting a careful idiographic analysis of performance for each case. Almost any task can be used or modified in such a way as to facilitate an in-depth analysis of where and how a particular individual's performance breaks down. Typically, informal testing procedures are used, but even standardized tests can be utilized from a qualitative perspective as long as the emphasis is on observing how the individual performs instead of focusing only on the test scores that are obtained.

Probably the most recognized approach to qualitative assessment is exemplified in the work of Luria (1966, 1973) as described by Christensen (1975). There are three major parts to Luria's neuropsychological investigation. The first part consists of an initial evaluation of the individual's functioning using a hypothesis testing approach. Based on the patient's initial performance, the second part employs a more individualized set of tasks to explore suspected deficits more fully. Finally, once the qualitative information is obtained, the results are formulated according to Luria's theory of functional systems. Christensen organized the various examination tasks used by Luria into eleven major areas of function. Golden, Hammeke, and Purisch (1980) later used these as the original pool of items from which the summary scales of the LNNB were developed.

Process-Oriented Approaches

These approaches represent a hybrid of quantitative and qualitative methods in neuropsychological assessment. For example, in the Boston Process Approach (Milberg, Hebben, & Kaplan, 1986) the emphasis is on understanding the qualitative nature of the behavior assessed by psychometric tests. It draws selectively from a core set of standardized tests for the purpose of gaining a quantified overview of the patient's general pattern of spared and impaired functions. Depending on the initial results, the examination thereafter is guided by clinical hypothesis testing aimed at pinpointing the precise nature of the individual's deficits. This is achieved through the use of various "satellite tests," which may consist of standardized tests, the addition of new components to published tests, or a set of tasks designed specifically for each patient. The possibilities are limited only by the examiner's knowledge of available tests and his or her creativity in designing new tasks for assessing particular deficit areas.

Using a similar logic, Wilson (1986) has presented a branching hypothesis testing model of neuropsychological assessment designed specifically for preschool-aged children. An initial selection of measures is used for a general assessment of complex cognitive functions. On the basis of these results, additional measures are selected for further assessment of specific functional areas. These are organized according to a scheme of neuropsychological constructs that include language (auditory integration, auditory cognition, short-term auditory memory, semantic retrieval), visual functions (visual-spatial, visual cognition, short-term visual memory), and motor functions (fine-motor, graphomotor). Wilson provides an extensive list of tests currently available for use with preschool-aged children that can be drawn upon in assessing these various aspects of neuropsychological functioning.

Summary of Neuropsychological Assessment Approaches

The differences among the various approaches to neuropsychological assessment seem to have gotten overstated, sometimes for the sake of academic argument. In practice, there probably are relatively few neuropsychologists who are purists with respect to one approach or another, and a melding of approaches probably is quite common. This

makes good sense because the different perspectives can be combined in a complementary fashion in an effort to maximize both breadth and depth of assessment. A fixed or eclectic battery of procedures that is brief, but nonetheless spans a broad range of abilities, helps to ensure a consistently comprehensive assessment that can produce comparable results across times, patient groups, and different research settings. It provides a horizontal analysis of general functioning that, along with qualitative observation, can be used in tailoring an in-depth or vertical analysis of specific functional areas based on a more flexible selection of tests. Qualitative and process-oriented approaches achieve this to some extent, but the validity of initial screening decisions may be compromised by the absence of a fixed set of procedures that could ensure a consistently broad-based assessment for all cases. Further, the fixed and eclectic approaches appear to be much more fruitful in the school setting because they are more directly applicable to the skills of educationally trained professionals.

Regardless of the approach, it is clear that the typically psychoeducational approach to assessment, especially the dependence on intelligence test scores (Gardner, 1987), does not capture the wide array of normal or abnormal variability that can be present in the school-age child. Further, this approach provides little toward increasing our understanding of basic learning strengths, weaknesses, or basic differences in learning and, ultimately, aids us in an inadequate manner with respect to educational treatment and program planning initiatives.

Educational Contributions and Clinical Applications

As was apparent in the discussion of historical trends in child neuropsychology, the field has continued to evolve such that it now maintains a number of major functions. In general, these functions include: (1) aiding in the detection of brain dysfunction for the purpose of differential diagnosis, (2) providing a precise specification of the behavioral effects of known brain injury, (3) helping to identify the specific underlying dimensions of dysfunction in particular disabilities, (4) using assessment data to help formulate effective treatment strategies, (5) helping to assess the child's prognosis and risk for certain developmental outcomes, and (6) conducting ongoing assessments of functional change over the course of development and in response to particular interventions. The precise form and relative importance of these different functions in child neuropsychology depend, to some extent, on the particular clinical population under consideration. Further, in the process of evolving these functions, the field has also asserted many contributions to the fields of education and learning.

In this section, several of the key contributions to education and learning will be discussed, with particular emphasis being placed on the neuropsychological basis of reading. In addition, given the rapidly changing population of school-age children and adolescents (that is, increased morbidity), the application of child neuropsychology to four different but overlapping clinical populations will be described.

Neuropsychological Contributions to Education

In addition to the recent advances noted in brain-behavior relationships described earlier in this chapter, evidence is accumulating that suggests a dependent relationship between development and interactions among components of functional systems. For example, in conjunction with Luria's (1980) theory, functional systems for reading (Mayeux & Kandel, 1985), spelling (Frith, 1983), writing (Roeltgen, 1993), and arithmetic (Gianni-

trapani, 1982; Hooper & Willis, 1989) have been proposed. A proposed functional system for reading has been pursued with the greatest vigor to date, and this will be described briefly.

Luria (1980) considered reading as well as writing to be special forms of speech activity. According to this conception, the reading process begins with the visual perception and analysis of a grapheme. The grapheme is recoded to its phonemic structure that is subsequently comprehended. The automaticity of this process varies as a function of development. Thus, during initial stages of reading, all of the operations noted are incorporated in a clear serial fashion. However, during later stages, graphemes may come to elicit direct comprehension of written words or even entire phrases, essentially eliminating intermediate phonemic analysis and synthesis.

When the process of reading is considered in this fashion, a number of components of a substrate functional system are implicated. For example, Hynd and Hynd (1984) suggested that graphemes are registered in the occipital lobes, where they are associated with known letters or words. This information is then shared with input from other sensory modalities in the region of the left angular gyrus. Linguistic semantic comprehension of this multimodal integration of information may be subserved in the region of the planum temporale (that is, region on the floor of the lateral sulcus) and Wernicke's area of the temporal lobe. Finally, the comprehended information potentially is communicated to Broca's area by way of the arcuate fasciculus, an intrahemispheric band of connecting fibers. This putative functional system for reading is sometimes referred to as the Wernicke-Geschwind model (Mayeux & Kandel, 1985) and is illustrated in Figure 4-2.

Based on this proposed functional system for reading, Hynd and Hynd (1984) hypothesized that particular subtypes of dyslexia, based on a neurolinguistic subtype model (Marshall, 1984),

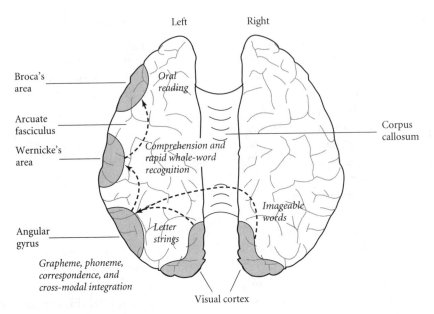

Left   Right

Broca's area

Oral reading

Arcuate fasciculus

Corpus callosum

Wernicke's area

Comprehension and rapid whole-word recognition

Angular gyrus

Imageable words

Letter strings

Grapheme, phoneme, correspondence, and cross-modal integration

Visual cortex

Figure 4-2   A proposed functional system for reading. (From G. W. Hynd & C. R. Hynd, 1984. Dyslexia: Neuroanatomical/neurolinguistic perspectives. *Reading Research Quarterly, 19,* 482–498.)

may follow from dysfunction involving particular components and interconnections. For example, developmental surface dyslexia, which is characterized by an overreliance on phonological rules such that reading of irregular words is affected, may be due to an impaired process in semantic access to what is read. Neuroanatomically, this may be related to a disruption of pathways associated with Wernicke's area. Developmental phonological dyslexia, which is characterized by an inability to apply phonological rules, may be due to an impaired process in grapheme-phoneme conversions. Neuroanatomically, this may be related to a disruption of pathways associated with the angular gyrus. Other reading disability subtypes have been proposed based on this functional system, and specific treatment interventions have been suggested (Hynd, 1986; Newby, Recht, & Caldwell, 1994). As noted earlier, some support has also arisen from neuroimaging (Hynd & Semrud-Clikeman, 1989), electrophysiological (Languis &

Wittrock, 1986), and postmortem studies (Galaburda, Sherman, Rosen, Aboitiz, & Geschwind, 1985), and much remains to be learned about the composition and evolution of these functional systems.

Clinical Applications

Neurological disorders. There are literally dozens of neurological disorders in childhood that may require a careful neuropsychological assessment. These include genetic disorders (such as Turner's syndrome); structural abnormalities of the brain (for example, agenesis of the corpus callosum, hydrocephalus); traumatic injuries; and a variety of neuropathological processes, including anoxic episodes, viral and bacterial encephalitis, toxicity (such as carbon monoxide poisoning, lead poisoning), metabolic disorders, demyelinating diseases (such as multiple sclerosis), neuromuscular disorders (such as muscular dystrophy), tumors (for example, medulloblastomas, craniopharyngioma, cerebellar astrocytomas), and cerebral vascular accidents. Given the rapid improvements in medical care over the past decade, it is likely that teachers will be faced with teaching children with some kind of neurological disorder.

Although studies have appeared in the literature depicting neuropsychological findings for selected childhood neurological disorders (see Snow & Hooper, 1994, for a review on pediatric head trauma), the effects of most insults to the immature nervous system are only beginning to be understood. Suffice it to say that the precise effects depend on a complex interplay involving the type of injury, age at the time of injury, specific organism variables, and environmental factors.

One area in which neuropsychological methods have been used extensively is in children with seizure disorders. This is an important group of disorders to assess, not only because they are among the most prevalent neurological disorders of childhood (Meighan, Queener, & Weitman, 1976) but also because their frequent chronicity carries the potential for continued impact throughout a child's life. There is no such thing as a "typical" neuropsychological profile for children with seizure disorders (Boll & Barth, 1981), although, as a group, their overall cognitive abilities tend to fall toward the lower end of the normal range (Bolter, 1984), they tend to be at greater risk for learning difficulties (Stores, 1981), and there is some debate as to whether they show a higher incidence of psychopathology than the general population (Curley, 1992; Dreisbach, Ballard, Russo, & Schain, 1982; Rutter, Graham, & Yule, 1970). The variability among children with seizure disorders certainly underscores the importance of careful individual assessment and thoughtful consideration to treatment planning in the education setting.

Childhood head injury is another example of a relatively prevalent group of neurological disorders and, given the relatively recent Individuals with Disabilities Education Act (IDEA) (U.S. Office of Education, 1992), an important area for special education as well. There are many factors to consider in evaluating the child with a head injury, including the specific nature of the injury and its resultant process (shearing, contre coup), age at onset, premorbid cognitive and emotional functioning, duration of impaired consciousness, and the rate of posttraumatic recovery. The effects of a closed head injury tend to be less localized than in the case of brain tumors or cerebral vascular accidents, with deficits spanning a wide variety of functions (Chadwick, Rutter, Brown, Shaffer, & Traub, 1981; Snow & Hooper, 1994). As with adults, the first six months of postinjury seems to be the time when neuropsychological deficits are most prominent in children (Levin & Eisenberg, 1979), with the bulk of recovery occurring in twelve to twenty-four months (Brink, Garrett, Hale, Woo Sam, & Nickel, 1970). However, neuropsychological changes have been observed to occur over a much longer period, which may sometimes extend up to five years (Klonoff, Low, & Clark, 1977). Besides the child's general adjustment, educational functioning is one of the most important areas to be monitored. The child's social-emotional adjustment also appears to be a critical dimension to assess because children with accidental head injuries appear to be at higher risk for developing psychiatric difficulties (Brown, Chadwick, Shaffer, Rutter, & Traub, 1981).

Some neurological disorders may require neurosurgical intervention, as in the case of partial lobectomies or complete hemispherectomies for the treatment of severe seizures. Probably the most common neurosurgical intervention in childhood involves the insertion of a shunt for the treatment of hydrocephalus. Children successfully treated by shunt insertion have been reported to show difficulties in attention (Hurley, Laatsch, & Dorman, 1983), memory (Cull & Wyke, 1984), and visual-motor functions (Soare & Raimondi, 1977). One study also found academic lags and poor impulse control but a relative sparing of verbal fluency, motor coordination, and verbal naming abilities (Fennell et al., 1987). Difficulties may result from the actual insertion of the shunt, and secondary complications may sometimes contribute to severe impairment in cognitive and adaptive functioning. Further, the neuropathology of hydrocephalus, which may include fiber stretching, delays in myelination, and interference with thalamocortical connections as well as limbic structures (Spreen et al., 1984), can result in a rather varied neuropsychological picture in these children. It is important that the effects of this disorder as well as its treatment be assessed individually, with careful follow-up assessment of functions associated with so-called "silent" brain regions that normally would not emerge until later developmental periods (for example, metacognitive processes).

Systemic illness. Recently, interest in the neuropsychological functioning of children with systemic illness has grown (for example, Hynd & Willis, 1988). A variety of pediatric illnesses can impact negatively on the developing nervous system, including defects in specific organ systems (pulmonary disease, congenital heart disease, renal dysfunction), metabolic disorders (elevated blood phenylalanine, defects in amino acid metabolism, lipid storage diseases, and mucopolysaccharidosis), autoimmune disorders (HIV), and infections (meningitis, cytomegalovirus, Reye's syndrome). Evidence regarding the neuropsychological sequelae of such childhood illnesses has begun to emerge.

For example, Holmes and Richman (1985) examined the cognitive profiles of children with insulin-dependent diabetes and found that children with early disease onset (7 years of age or younger) and a chronic course (five years or more) were more likely to show reading and memory difficulties. They also tended to have a lower performance IQ on the Wechsler Intelligence Scale for Children-Revised (WISC-R), but this appeared to be due largely to slow response time rather than to a specific deficit in visual-spatial abilities. Similar findings have been obtained by other researchers (Ryan, Vega, & Drash, 1985; Ryan, Vega, Longstreet, & Drash, 1984). However, interacting factors must be considered as well. For example, Rovet, Gore, and Ehrlich (1983) found that whereas females with diabetes onset prior to 3 years of age tended to experience deficits in visual-motor functioning, their male counterparts did not. More recently, Rovet and colleagues found a trend for children with diabetes to be somewhat more likely to show reading or arithmetic disabilities, with a greater percentage of these children coming from the early-onset group (Rovet, Ehrlich, Czuchta, & Akler, 1993); however, these findings were not conclusive.

A major area in which neuropsychological assessment can play a crucial role is in pediatric oncology (Stehbens & Cool, 1994). For example, acute lymphocytic leukemia (ALL) accounts for 35% of all childhood malignancies, with approximately 40% of these cases becoming disease-free survivors (George, Aur, Mauer, & Simone, 1979). An important question concerns the possible iatrogenic effects of the various treatments required to stabilize these children medically. The evidence is inconclusive, but there is some indication that children with ALL who receive intracranial radiation and chemotherapy may suffer a variety of post-treatment neuropsychological deficits (Goff, 1982; Waber, Sollee, Wills, & Fischer, 1986) and are more likely to be diagnosed later as having learning disabilities (Elbert, Culbertson, Gerrity, Guthrie, & Bayles, 1985).

As was noted, advances in medical care have resulted in a dramatic increase in the survival of children with serious illnesses. This has created a greater need for the careful assessment of possible neuropsychological sequelae associated with these diseases and their treatment. Ongoing neuropsychological assessment may contribute effectively to monitoring improvement, stability, or deterioration in the child's functioning, and may indicate the need for other kinds of intervention (such as special education). Its utility in assessing children with various pediatric illnesses is only beginning to be realized, and it may provide an effective bridge between medicine and education for these children.

Psychiatric disorders. There is strong evidence that brain dysfunction in childhood is associated with an increased risk for psychiatric disorders (Hynd & Hooper, 1992). The risk is much greater than for children with other types of physical disabilities (Seidel, Chadwick, & Rutter, 1975), and the relationship appears to hold both for children with documented brain damage (Brown et al., 1981; Rutter et al., 1970) and for those with so-called soft neurological signs (Shaffer et al., 1985). Among children with accidental head injuries, the risk is compounded by such factors as psychosocial adversity and any preexisting tendencies toward behavioral or emotional disturbance (Brown et al., 1981). The relationship is not trivial, given that the effects appear to persist and influence the child's long-range behavioral adjustment (Breslau & Marshall, 1985; Shaffer et al., 1985).

Conversely, there is a relatively high rate of neuropsychological dysfunction among children with psychiatric disorders, even when cases with known brain damage are excluded (Tramontana, Sherrets, & Golden, 1980). Tramontana and Sherrets (1985) found that neuropsychological abnormality in such cases actually corresponded to differences on various indices of brain density as revealed by cat scan results, which was a remarkable finding in view of the exclusion of cases having documented neurological involvement. Moreover, the presence of neuropsychological deficits has been found to be associated with more extensive behavior problems among younger boys with psychiatric disor-

ders, regardless of factors such as IQ, socioeconomic status, and whether the deficits could be linked specifically with a history of brain injury (Tramontana, Hooper, & Nardolillo, 1988). Thus, the presence of neuropsychological deficits in childhood appears to constitute an important index of increased psychiatric risk, and consequently, increased special education needs for children with behavioral and emotional disturbance.

A number of studies have examined whether there are distinguishing neuropsychological features associated with specific forms of child psychopathology, including autism (Fein, Waterhouse, Lucci, & Snyder, 1985; Hooper, Boyd, Hynd, & Rubin, 1993), attention deficit disorder (Chelune, Ferguson, Koon, & Dickey, 1986; Hooper, Tramontana, Linz, & Stein, 1995; Passler, Isaac, & Hynd, 1986), conduct disorder (Hooper & Brown, 1995; Tramontana & Hooper, 1987), and depression (Tramontana & Hooper, 1987; Wilson & Staton, 1984).

In a comprehensive review of this research, Tramontana and Hooper (in press) concluded that there was little evidence of specificity with respect to the type or pattern of brain dysfunction associated with different forms of child psychopathology. Although there were some promising leads, the greater weight of evidence suggested a largely nonspecific, indirect relationship between brain dysfunction and psychopathology in childhood. There is absolutely no evidence to support earlier thinking (for example, Wender, 1971) regarding the existence of a behavioral stereotype among children with brain dysfunction, consisting of symptoms such as hyperactivity, inattention, and impulsivity. Symptoms such as these do not distinguish children with either documented brain damage (Brown et al., 1981; Rutter et al., 1970) or soft neurological signs (Shaffer et al., 1985) because they appear to be common features of psychiatric disorders in general, regardless of whether neurological abnormality is present (Rutter, 1977).

If anything, it appears that internalizing rather than externalizing symptoms are more distinctively tied to brain dysfunction in childhood, with symptoms such as anxiety, withdrawal, and depression being among the more common outcomes associated with a history of chronic disability (Breslau & Marshall, 1985; Shaffer et al., 1985). Child neuropsychologists and/or a child neuropsychology perspective may play an important role in determining more precisely how this process unfolds so that it might be redirected more positively, if not prevented. This information and service provision should be welcomed activities for educators who must work with these children on a regular basis.

Learning disabilities. The study of learning disabilities has been one of the most intensive areas of investigation in child neuropsychology. The explicit presumption of central nervous system dysfunction in current definitions of learning disability (Interagency Committee on Learning Disabilities, 1987) has served to underscore the important role of a neuropsychological perspective in this field. Neuropsychological assessment can contribute effectively both in the identification of specific underlying dimensions of dysfunction in particular learning disabilities, and in the formulation and evaluation of specific educational plans. The work in learning disabilities—which has dealt with the child's adaptive capacity (and future potential) in the real-life context of school—has taken an exemplary lead in relating neuropsychological assessment to questions of ecological validity. Much remains to be learned, but major advances have been achieved in the area of syndrome definition and subtype analysis (Feagans et al., 1991; Hooper & Willis, 1989; Rourke, 1985) and in the identification of developmental precursors of learning disabilities (Torgeson et al., 1992; Tramontana, Hooper, & Selzer, 1988), possible neuroanatomical (Semrud-Clikeman et al., 1996) and

neurophysiological (Duffy, Denckla, Bartels, & Sandini, 1980) factors, as well as relevant treatment issues (Lyon, Moats, & Flynn, 1988; Newby et al., 1994).

Perhaps one of the key contributions of the cognitive neurosciences to date has been the identification of one of the core deficits in reading disabilities. In this regard, a number of studies have underscored phonological processing deficits as key underpinnings for reading proficiency and reading deficiencies (Stanovich & Siegel, 1994). Another major contribution is clarification of the definition of learning disabilities (Fletcher et al., 1992; Fletcher et al., 1994), wherein significant scientifically based challenges have been asserted against the use of discrepancy formulae as well as against the use of IQ in such definitions (Francis et al., 1991; Siegel, 1989). Clearly, these findings will impact on the field of special education as it moves into the next century.

Implications and Directions

As the field of child neuropsychology progresses into the next century, there are a number of implications and directions for which there could be direct application in special education. Several key areas of impact include assessment technology and general assessment goals, assessment-treatment linkages, training of special education professionals, and policy issues, particularly with respect to conceptualizations of different kinds of learning problems and how these problems should be assessed, treated, and generally monitored in an educational setting.

Assessment

As we move into the next decade, it is essential that alternative assessment models be developed aggressively and implemented in the educational setting. It is clear that the traditional psychoeduca-

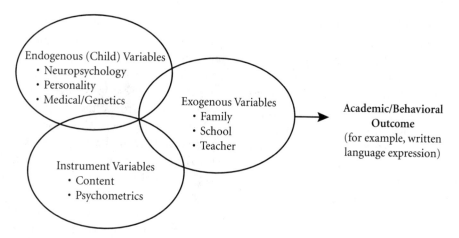

Figure 4-3   Endogenous, exogenous, and instrument variables in assessing behavioral outcomes. (From Hooper et al., 1994. Measurement of written language. In G. R. Lyon (Ed.), *Frames of reference for the assessment of learning disabilities: New views on measurement issues*, p. 385. Baltimore: Paul H. Brookes Publishing Co.)

tional model, which typically includes intelligence testing, achievement testing, and perhaps a visual-motor drawing task, does not capture all of the specific nuances of an individual's learning style, needs, and capacities, nor are these models necessarily developmentally sensitive. Although it would be naive to think that a neuropsychological assessment paradigm could begin to address all of these questions in and of itself, it is clear that the neuropsychological perspective would contribute to expanding the range of abilities tapped via an individual assessment. Further, such an assessment would complement a variety of educational assessment models, such as curriculum-based assessment strategies, in describing an individual's learning profile in an accurate yet detailed manner. In addition to the individual's unique learning attributes, such a model should encapsulate test variables (such as reliability and validity), environmental variables (home and school), and their interaction with the individual attributes in the evaluation process as well (Lerner, 1991). With this

perspective, the assessment of individual students, when necessary, would address more potential learning strengths and weaknesses than the typical psychoeducational assessment, and it would help to ensure greater ecological validity in the assessment process. A model illustrating these endogenous and exogenous variables is depicted in Figure 4-3.

In a related vein, a neuropsychological perspective could also be useful in facilitating neurodevelopmental screenings, particularly in a preschool population. In a review of the preschool prediction literature, Tramontana, Hooper, and Selzer (1988) found the predictive aspects of learning problems to be dependent on a number of factors. These factors included what academic function was trying to be predicted, at what age, and what tools might be most useful in this regard. In structuring screening batteries, these variables should be taken into consideration. Another clear example involves the employment of phonological processing strategies in the assessment process.

These assessment strategies are quick, relatively inexpensive, and yield a large amount of diagnostic information and treatment suggestions. They should be employed in any assessment for a child referred for special services, but especially in cases referred for reading problems. Further, it is important to note that a neuropsychological perspective has also been applied to infants (Aylward, 1994; D. L. Molfese, 1992; V. Molfese, 1992), which is another population that has received increased attention from the schools in recent years.

Assessment-Treatment Linkages

If any assessment strategy is to prove useful, then it should lend itself to relevant suggestions for intervention. Despite the current practice of using IQ in identifying children for many of our special education categories, this construct has provided little in the way of intervention suggestions. By using a neuropsychological perspective in an assessment model, the detailed information gained from such assessments should lend itself to identifying underlying information-processing strengths and weaknesses that should provide guidance for instructional strategies, behavioral management, and selection of vehicles for psychological therapy. When coupled with the environmental and educational assessments, this should provide a rich backdrop for developing specific interventions that can be tested in the classroom situation. A number of such linkages have been discussed (Berninger & Abbott, 1994; Fleischner, 1995; Hooper, Willis, & Stone, 1996; Lyon et al., 1988; Rourke et al., 1986), and a number of neuropsychological intervention attempts have been asserted (for example, Bakker, Licht, & Kappers, 1995; Korkman & Peltomaa, 1993; Newby et al., 1994).

A neuropsychological assessment and/or perspective can also play a key role in helping to monitor treatment progress and to adjust the program as needed. Rourke and colleagues (1986) have provided a general framework for integrating neuropsychological assessment in the treatment planning process. To date, however, little is known regarding the prescriptive significance of different patterns of neuropsychological data in the actual selection of treatments. Treatment options tend to be selected on the basis of theory (Luria, 1966, 1973), personal experience, or practical issues such as the availability of particular therapeutic resources. There has been little research that could serve to link neuropsychological assessment and treatment more directly, although several important initiatives have been put forth (for example, Bakker et al., 1995; Korkman & Peltomaa, 1993; Newby et al., 1994). This is a critical new frontier for child neuropsychology and one that holds great promise with respect to its contributions to special education, but it is in great need of systematic inquiry.

Training in Special Education

Perhaps the place to start for the assessment and assessment-treatment initiatives is with the training of special education professionals. This training should be occurring not only with seasoned professionals via continuing education models but also within the confines of our university training programs. From a neuropsychological perspective, it would seem imperative that teachers, school psychologists, guidance counselors, school social workers, and other school-based professionals become more attuned to the issues inherent in learning, learning problems, and their possible linkages to brain-based functions. Further, this learning should be extended to the field of medicine, especially primary care providers (such as pediatricians), because many parents may initially take their concerns about their child's learning to the family doctor. Such training for primary care providers will also improve the communication between professionals and, hopefully, improve the continuum of care provided to these children.

The intent here is not to turn educators or any other professional into neuropsychologists but rather to increase the knowledge around such issues as the neurological basis of learning. While some may argue that this information is not applicable to an educational setting (Sandoval & Haapanen, 1981), or at least question its relevance in the daily activities of teaching, it would seem that having some knowledge that a particular task requires extensive language and memory abilities, and that a specific student may have particular difficulties with these underlying functions, would merit some instructional modification in order to facilitate this student's learning. Indeed, these issues come to life in children with frank neurological impairment (such as traumatic brain injury) and they are manifested in children with neurodevelopmental disorders (such as learning disabilities) as well. Further, having some basic understanding that these functions are subserved by neurological mechanisms may permit greater flexibility in how a teacher approaches a selected student as opposed to immediately assuming that a student is uninterested in the topical material or unmotivated or attributing the problem solely to family problems.

In general, it seems that increasing our training initiatives in this vein at all educational levels has the potential to increase our understanding of a wide variety of learning and behavioral difficulties, or at least provide another alternative for explanation. Further, this perspective may also encourage greater modifications of instructional materials to selected students. This could prove vital to increased policy changes with respect to inclusion and other alternative models of service delivery (such as consultation models).

Technology

Although the technology of neuropsychology will probably contribute little to the field of special education over the next decade, outside of perhaps new assessment procedures for use in the schools, new technological advances in the fields of neurology and neuroimaging will likely provide greater glimpses into the functioning of the brain. For example, as noted earlier in this chapter, using state-of-the-art functional magnetic resonance imaging, Shaywitz and associates (1995) found that males and females develop phonological processing abilities via different regions of the brain, and a number of studies have uncovered a variety of subtle neuroanatomical differences in the brains of individuals with dyslexia. These findings are important not only because they contribute to our knowledge of the neurological underpinnings in many different types of learning problems but they also begin to shed light on such issues as individual learning differences, gender differences in learning, and possibly treatment issues. These findings hold great potential for understanding children who may have suffered a brain trauma and/or neurodevelopmental deficits, and what might be expected from them at a specific developmental stage.

Public Policy

The neuropsychological aspects of many learning problems have been asserted in legislative mandates, such as Public Law 94-142, as well as in the recent amendments to this legislation via the Individuals with Disabilities Education Act (U.S. Office of Education, 1992) wherein traumatic brain injury was introduced as a designated handicapping condition. This latter classification hopefully will spur educators to address children who have experienced an acute traumatic brain injury with greater assessment rigor, more tight-knit monitoring of their functioning, particularly as it may apply to recovery of function and well-timed treatment modifications, and increased knowledge of brain-behavior relationships, particularly with respect to behavioral manifestations.

Another example lies with the most recently proposed definition for learning disabilities by the Interagency Committee on Learning Disabilities (1987), which suggested a "presumed neurological dysfunction" as the underlying mechanism for a specific learning disability. Current research initiatives under the auspices of the National Institute of Health (Lyon, 1995) have also been set in motion to examine neurological underpinnings, possible nosologies for learning disorders, and well-validated treatments for these disorders. Findings from these studies undoubtedly will have a significant impact on how special education will evolve over the next decade, particularly with respect to the utility of inclusion as well as specific designated classifications, and hopefully it will impact the training models for teachers and other professionals involved with the field of special education, assessment paradigms, and assessment-treatment linkages.

Conclusions

This chapter has addressed a number of key issues for consideration in special education as the field advances into the next century. Basic knowledge on brain-behavior relationships, including recent advances in this area, was presented. An overview of the historical foundations was also presented, with particular emphasis being placed on assessment issues and assessment approaches typically used in the field. Although many of these approaches may not be immediately applicable in a school setting, a neuropsychological perspective would certainly advocate for a more expanded approach to many of the learning and behavioral problems encountered by school-based personnel. Educational applications of this knowledge base

were discussed, with a focus being placed on the domain of reading. The application of neuropsychological techniques to specific populations of children was also outlined. Outcome studies and various research-based characteristics of these heterogeneous populations were highlighted, and it was noted that the presence of these children in regular and special education settings will likely become more prevalent in the near future.

A major portion of this chapter was related to implications and directions for the field of special education to consider with respect to the knowledge base represented by the field of child neuropsychology. The field of special education could truly benefit from a neuropsychological perspective when considering assessment strategies and assessment-treatment linkages. The field of special education has begun to question the traditional psychoeducational assessment model and, while efforts to shorten the assessment process (for example, via curriculum-based assessment) might be warranted from an educational perspective, neither the traditional psychoeducational assessment nor abbreviated methods provide a thorough description of an individual's learning strategies, abilities, or deficiencies. Such information is also the basis for formulating a wide variety of interventions that could be used for instructional as well as therapeutic treatments. For such a perspective to be understood and utilized, it is essential for university training programs and continuing education models to place more emphasis on the biological bases of learning, and attempt to link these bases to daily assessment and instructional practices.

Finally, it is clear that many rich research findings have been generated in the fields of child neuropsychology and related cognitive neurosciences, and their applications to learning and individual differences have only begun. Some of this information may have an impact on the policies of our special education legislation, such as in the reshaping of definitions for special education classifications, assessment procedures to be considered in evaluation, and perhaps even in the implementation of alternative service delivery models. It is hoped that this chapter has provided some food for thought in this regard, and that the relationship between child neuropsychology and special education will continue to mature as we move into the 21st century.

References

Aylward, G. P. (1994). Update on early developmental neuropsychological assessment: The Early Neuropsychological Optimality Rating Scales. In M. G. Tramontana & S. R. Hooper (Eds.), *Advances in child neuropsychology* (Vol. 2, pp. 172–200). New York: Springer-Verlag.

Bakker, D. J., Licht, R., & Kappers, E. J. (1995). Hemispheric stimulation techniques in children with dyslexia. In M. G. Tramontana & S. R. Hooper (Eds.), *Advances in child neuropsychology* (Vol. 3, pp. 144–177). New York: Springer-Verlag.

Bender, L. (1938). *A visual motor gestalt test and its clinical use* (Research Monograph No. 3). New York: American Orthopsychiatric Association.

Benton, A. L. (1963). *The Revised Visual Retention Test: Clinical and experimental applications.* New York: Psychological Corporation.

Berninger, V. W., & Abbott, R. D. (1994). Redefining learning disabilities: Moving beyond aptitude-achievement discrepancies to failure to respond to validated treatment protocols. In G. R. Lyon (Ed.), *Frames of reference for the assessment of learning disabilities. New views on measurement issues* (pp. 163–183). Baltimore: Paul H. Brookes Publishing Company.

Bigler, E. D. (1995). Advances in brain imaging with children and adolescents. In M. G. Tramontana & S. R. Hooper (Eds.), *Advances in child neuropsychology* (Vol. 3, pp. 48–83). New York: Springer-Verlag.

Boll, T. J. (1981). The Halstead-Reitan Neuropsychology Battery. In S. B. Filskov & T. J. Boll (Eds.), *Handbook of clinical neuropsychology* (pp. 577–607). New York: Wiley.

Boll, T. J., & Barth, J. T. (1981). Neuropsychology of brain damage in children. In S. B. Filskov & T. J. Boll (Eds.), *Handbook of clinical neuropsychology* (pp. 418–452). New York: Wiley.

Bolter, J. F. (1984). *Neuropsychological impairment and behavioral dysfunction in children with chronic epilepsy.* Unpublished doctoral dissertation, Memphis State University.

Breslau, N., & Marshall, I. A. (1985). Psychological disturbance in children with physical disabilities: Continuity and change in a 5-year follow-up. *Journal of Abnormal Child Psychology, 13,* 199–216.

Brink, J., Garrett, A., Hale, W., Woo Sam, J., & Nickel, V. (1970). Recovery of motor and intellectual function in children sustaining severe head injuries. *Developmental Medicine and Child Neurology, 12,* 565–571.

Brodal, A. (1981). *Neurological anatomy in relation to clinical medicine* (3rd ed.). New York: Oxford University Press.

Brown, G., Chadwick, O., Shaffer, D., Rutter, M., & Traub, M. (1981). A prospective study of children with head injuries: III. Psychiatric sequelae. *Psychological Medicine, 11,* 63–78.

Chadwick, O., & Rutter, M. (1983). Neuropsychological assessment. In M. Rutter (Ed.), *Developmental neuropsychiatry* (pp. 181–212). New York: Guilford.

Chadwick, O., Rutter, M., Brown, G., Shaffer, D., & Traub, M. (1981). A prospective study of children with head injuries: II. Cognitive sequelae. *Psychological Medicine, 11,* 49–61.

Chelune, G., & Edwards, P. (1981). Early brain lesions: Ontogenetic-environmental considerations. *Journal of Consulting and Clinical Psychology, 49,* 777–790.

Chelune, G., Ferguson, W., Koon, R., & Dickey, T. (1986). Frontal lobe dysinhibition in attention deficit disorder. *Child Psychiatry and Human Development, 16,* 221–234.

Christensen, A. L. (1975). *Luria's neuropsychological investigation.* New York: Spectrum.

Cull, C., & Wyke, M. A. (1984). Memory function of children with spina bifida and shunted hydrocephalus. *Developmental Medicine and Child Neurology, 26,* 177–183.

Curley, A. D. (1992). Behavioral disturbance in children with seizures. In M. G. Tramontana & S. R. Hooper,

(Eds.), *Advances in child neuropsychology* (Vol. 1, pp. 109–136). New York: Springer-Verlag.

Das, J. P., Kirby, J. R., & Jarman, R. F. (1979). *Simultaneous and successive processes.* New York: Academic Press.

Davidoff, J. B. (1982). Studies with non-verbal stimuli. In J. G. Beaumont (Ed.), *Divided visual field studies of cerebral organization* (pp. 30–55). New York: Academic Press.

Dooling, E. C., Chi, J. G., & Gilles, F. H. (1983). Telencephalic development: Changing gyral patterns. In F. H. Gilles, A. Leviton, & E. C. Dooling (Eds.), *The developing human brain: Growth and epidemiologic neuropathology* (pp. 94–104). Boston: John Wright.

Dreisbach, M., Ballard, M., Russo, D. C., & Schain, R. J. (1982). Educational intervention for children with epilepsy: A challenge for collaborative service delivery. *Journal of Special Education, 16,* 111–121.

Duffy, F. H., Denckla, M. B., Bartels, P. H., & Sandini, G. (1980). Dyslexia: Regional differences in brain electrical activity by topographic mapping. *Annals of Neurology, 7,* 412–420.

Elbert, J. C., Culbertson, J. L., Gerrity, K. M., Guthrie, L. J., & Bayles, R. (1985, February). *Neuropsychological and electrophysiologic follow-up of children surviving acute lymphocytic leukemia.* Paper presented at the annual meeting of the International Neuropsychology Society, San Diego.

Ernhart, C. B., Graham, F. K., Eichman, P. L., Marshall, J. M., & Thurston, D. (1963). Brain injury in the preschool child: Some developmental considerations. II. Comparison of brain-injured and normal children. *Psychological Monographs, 77*(Whole No. 574), 1733.

Feagans, L. V., Short, E. J., & Meltzer, L. J. (Eds.). (1991). *Subtypes of learning disabilities. Theoretical perspectives and research.* Hillsdale, NJ: Erlbaum.

Fein, D., Waterhouse, L., Lucci, D., & Snyder, D. (1985). Cognitive subtypes in developmentally disabled children: A pilot study. *Journal of Autism and Developmental Disorders, 15,* 77–95.

Fennell, E. B., Eisenstadt, T., Bodiford, C., Rediess, S., de Bijl, M., & Mickle, J. (1987, February). *The assessment of neuropsychological dysfunction in children shunted for hydrocephalus.* Paper presented at the fifteenth annual meeting of the International Neuropsychological Society, Washington, DC.

Filipek, P. A. (1995). Neurobiologic correlates of developmental dyslexia: How do dyslexics' brains differ from those of normal readers? *Journal of Child Neurology, 10,* S62–S69.

Filskov, S. B., & Boll, T. J. (Eds.). (1981). *Handbook of clinical neuropsychology.* New York: Wiley.

Filskov, S. B., & Goldstein, S. G. (1974). Diagnostic validity of the Halstead-Reitan Neuropsychological Battery. *Journal of Consulting and Clinical Psychology, 42,* 383–388.

Fleischner, J. E. (1995). Educational management of students with learning disabilities. *Journal of Child Neurology, 10,* S81–S85.

Fletcher, J. M., Francis, D. J., Rourke, B. P., Shaywitz, S. E., & Shaywitz, B. A. (1992). Validity of discrepancy-based definitions of reading disabilities. *Journal of Learning Disabilities, 25,* 555–561.

Fletcher, J. M., Shaywitz, S. E., Shankweiler, D. P., Katz, L., Liberman, I. Y., Stuebing, K. K., Francis, D. J., Fowler, A. E., & Shaywitz, B. A. (1994). Cognitive profiles of reading disability: Comparisons of discrepancy and low achievement definitions. *Journal of Educational Psychology, 86,* 6–23.

Francis, D. J., Espy, K. A., Rourke, B. P., & Fletcher, J. M. (1991). Validity of intelligence test scores in the definition of learning disability: A critical analysis. In B. P. Rourke (Ed.), *Neuropsychological validation of learning disability subtypes* (pp. 12–40). New York: Guilford Press.

Frith, U. (1983). The similarities and differences between reading and spelling problems. In M. Rutter (Ed.), *Developmental neuropsychiatry* (pp. 453–472). New York: Guilford Press.

Gaddes, W. H., & Edgell, D. (1994). *Learning disabilities and brain function: A neuropsychological approach* (3rd ed.). New York: Springer-Verlag.

Galaburda, A. M., & Livingstone, M. (1993). Evidence for a magnocellular defect in developmental dyslexia. *Annals of the New York Academy of Science, 682,* 70–82.

Galaburda, A. M., Sherman, G. F., Rosen, G. D., Aboitiz, F., & Geschwind, N. (1985). Developmental dyslexia: Four consecutive patients with cortical anomalies. *Annals of Neurology, 18,* 222–233.

Gardner, H. (1987). Beyond the IQ: Education and human development. *Harvard Educational Review, 57,* 187–193.

George, S. L., Aur, R. J. A., Mauer, A. M., & Simone, J. V. (1979). A reappraisal of the results of stopping therapy in childhood leukemia. *New England Journal of Medicine, 300,* 269–273 .

Geschwind, N., & Levitsky, W. (1968). Human brain: Left-right asymmetries in temporal speech region. *Science, 161,* 186–187.

Giannitrapani, D. (1982). Localization of language and arithmetic functions via EEG factor analysis. *Research Communications in Psychology, Psychiatry, and Behavior, 7,* 39–55.

Goff, J. R. (1982, August). *Memory deficits and distractibility in survivors of childhood leukemia.* Paper presented at the annual meeting of the American Psychological Association, Washington DC.

Golden, C. J. (1981). The Luria-Nebraska Children's Battery: Theory and formulation. In G. W. Hynd & J. E. Obrzut (Eds.), *Neuropsychological assessment and the school-age child: Issues and perspectives* (pp. 277–302). New York: Grune & Stratton.

Golden, C. J. (1987). Manual for the Luria-Nebraska Neuropsychological Battery–Children's Revision. Los Angeles: Western Psychological Services.

Golden, C. J., Hammeke, T. A., & Purisch, A. D. (1980). *Manual for the Luria-Nebraska Neuropsychological Battery.* Los Angeles: Western Psychological Services.

Graham, F. K., Ernhart, C. B., Craft, M., & Berman, P. W. (1963). Brain injury in the preschool child: Some developmental considerations: I. Performance of normal children. *Psychological Monographs, 77*(Whole No. 573), 1–16.

Graham, F. K., & Kendall, B. S. (1960). Memory-for-Designs Test: Revised general manual. *Perceptual and Motor Skills Monograph* (Supp. No. 2-VII), *11,* 147–188.

Halperin, J. M., McKay, K. E., Matier, K., & Sharma, V. (1994). Attention, response inhibition, and activity level in children: Developmental neuropsychological perspectives. In M. G. Tramontana, & S. R. Hooper (Eds.), *Advances in child neuropsychology* (Vol. 2, pp. 1–54). New York: Springer-Verlag.

Haslam, R. H. A., Dalby, J. T., Johns, R. D., & Rademaker, A. W. (1981). Cerebral asymmetry in developmental dyslexia. *Archives of Neurology, 38,* 679–682.

Herbert, M. (1964). The concept and testing of brain damage in children: A review. *Journal of Child Psychology and Psychiatry, 5,* 197–216.

Holmes, C. S., & Richman, L. C. (1985). Cognitive profiles of children with insulin-dependent diabetes. *Journal of Developmental and Behavioral Pediatrics, 6,* 323–326.

Hooper, S. R. (1991). Neuropsychological assessment of the preschool-age child. In B. Bracken (Ed.), *The psychoeducational assessment of preschool children* (2nd ed.) (pp. 465–485). San Antonio, TX: Grune & Stratton.

Hooper, S. R., Boyd, T. A., Hynd, G. W., & Rubin, J. (1993). Definitional issues and neurobiological foundations of selected severe neurodevelopmental disorders. *Archives of Clinical Neuropsychology, 8,* 279–307.

Hooper, S. R., & Brown, T. T. (1995). *Neuropsychological functioning of children and adolescents with conduct disorder and aggressive-assaultive features.* Manuscript submitted for review.

Hooper, S. R., & Hynd, G. W. (1993). The neuropsychological basis of disorders affecting children and adolescents: An introduction. *Journal of Clinical Child Psychology, 22,* 138–140.

Hooper, S. R., Tramontana, M. G., Linz, T. D., & Stein, M. B. (1995). *Short-term memory abilities in children with differential patterns of inattention and impulsivity.* Manuscript submitted for review.

Hooper, S. R., & Willis, W. G. (1989). *Learning disability subtyping. Neuropsychological foundations, conceptual models, and issues in clinical differentiation.* New York: Springer-Verlag.

Hooper, S. R., Willis, W. G., & Stone, B. (1996). The treatment of learning disabilities: A neuropsychological perspective. In R. S. Dean & E. S. Batchelor (Eds.), *Pediatric neuropsychology: Interfacing assessment and treatment in the rehabilitation of neuropsychological disorders* (pp. 211–247). Boston: Allyn & Bacon.

Hurley, A. D., Laatsch, L. K., & Dorman, C. (1983). Comparison of spina bifida, hydrocephalic patients, and matched controls on neuropsychological tests. *Zeitschrift for Kinderchir, 17,* 65–70.

Hynd, C. R. (1986). Educational intervention in children with developmental learning disorders. In J. E.

Obrzut & G. W. Hynd (Eds.), *Child neuropsychology: Vol. 2. Clinical practice* (pp. 265–297). Orlando, FL: Academic Press.

Hynd, G. W., Hall, J., Novey, E. S., Eliopulos, D., Black, K., Gonzalez, J. J., Edmonds, J. E., Riccio, C., & Cohen, M. (1995). Dyslexia and corpus callosum morphology. *Archives of Neurology, 52,* 32–38.

Hynd, G. W., & Hooper, S. R. (1992). *The neurological basis of child psychopathology.* Newbury Park, CA: Sage Publications.

Hynd, G. W., & Hynd, C. R. (1984). Dyslexia: Neuroanatomical/neurolinguistic perspectives. *Reading Research Quarterly, 19,* 482–498.

Hynd, G. W., & Semrud-Clikeman, M. (1989). Dyslexia and brain morphology. *Psychological Bulletin, 106,* 447–482.

Hynd, G. W., Semrud-Clikeman, M., Lorys, A. R., Novey, E. S., & Eliopulos, D. (1990). Brain morphology in developmental dyslexia and attention deficit disorder/hyperactivity. *Archives of Neurology, 47,* 919–926.

Hynd, G. W., Snow, J., & Becker, M. G. (1986). Neuropsychological assessment in clinical child psychology. In B. Lahey, & A. Kazdin (Eds.), *Advances in clinical child psychology* (Vol. 9, pp. 35–86). New York: Plenum.

Hynd, G. W., & Willis, W. G. (1988). *Pediatric neuropsychology.* New York: Grune & Stratton.

Interagency Committee on Learning Disabilities. (1987). *Learning disabilities: A report to the U.S. Congress.* Washington, DC: Author.

Jernigan, T. L., Hesselink, J. R., Stowell, E., & Tallal, P. A. (1991). Cerebral structure on magnetic resonance imaging in language- and learning-impaired children. *Archives of Neurology, 48,* 539–545.

Klonoff, H., Low, M. D., & Clark, C. (1977). Head injuries in children with a prospective 5-year follow-up. *Journal of Neurology, Neurosurgery, and Psychiatry, 40,* 1211–1219.

Koppitz, E. M. (1964). *The Bender Gestalt Test for Young Children.* New York: Grune & Stratton.

Korkman, M. (1995). A test-profile approach in analyzing cognitive disorders in children: Experiences of the NEPSY. In M. G. Tramontana & S. R. Hooper (Eds.), *Advances in child neuropsychology* (Vol. 3, pp. 84–116). New York: Springer-Verlag.

Korkman, M., & Peltomaa, A. K. (1993). Preventive treatment of dyslexia by a preschool training program for children with language impairments. *Journal of Clinical Child Psychology, 22,* 277–287.

Languis, M., & Wittrock, M. C. (1986). Integrating neuropsychological and cognitive research: A perspective for bridging brain-behavior relationships. In J. E. Obrzut & G. W. Hynd (Eds.), *Child neuropsychology: Vol. 1. Theory and research* (pp. 209–239). Orlando, FL: Academic Press.

Larsen, J. P., Hoien, T., Lundberg, I., & Odegaard, H. (1990). MRI evaluation of the size and symmetry of the planum temporale in adolescents with developmental dyslexia. *Brain and Language, 39,* 289–301.

Lenneberg, E. H. (1967). *Biological foundations of language.* New York: Wiley.

Leonard, C. M., Voeller, K. K. S., Lombardino, L. J., Morris, M. K., Hynd, G. W., Alexander, A. W., Andersen, H. G., Garofalakis, M., Honeyman, J. C., Mao, J., Agee, F., & Staab, E. V. (1993). Anomalous cerebral structure in dyslexia revealed with magnetic resonance imaging. *Archives of Neurology, 50,* 461–469.

Lerner, R. M. (1991). Changing organism-context relations as the basic process of development: A developmental contextual perspective. *Developmental Psychology, 27,* 27–32.

Levin, H. S., & Eisenberg, H. M. (1979). Neuropsychological impairment after closed head injury in children and adolescents. *Journal of Pediatric Psychology, 4,* 389–402.

Lou, H. C., Henriksen, L., & Bruhn, D. (1984). Focal cerebral hypoperfusion in children with dysphasia and/or attention deficit disorder. *Archives of Neurology, 41,* 825–829.

Luria, A. R. (1966). *Human brain and psychological process.* New York: Harper & Row.

Luria, A. R. (1970). Functional organization of the brain. *Scientific American, 222,* 66–78.

Luria, A. R. (1973). *The working brain: An introduction to neuropsychology.* New York: Basic Books.

Luria, A. R. (1980). *Higher cortical functions in man.* New York: Basic Books.

Lyon, G. R. (1995). Research initiatives in learning disabilities: Contributions from scientists supported by the National Institute of Child Health and Human

Development. *Journal of Child Neurology, 10,* S120–S126.

Lyon, G. R., Moats, L., & Flynn, J. M. (1988). From assessment to treatment: Linkage to interventions with children. In M. G. Tramontana & S. R. Hooper (Eds.), *Assessment issues in child neuropsychology* (pp. 113–142). New York: Plenum Press.

Marshall, J. C. (1984). Toward a rational taxonomy of the developmental dyslexias. In R. M. Malatesha & H. A. Whitaker (Eds.), *Dyslexia: A global issue* (pp. 45–58). The Hague: Nijhoff.

Mattis, S. (1992). Neuropsychological assessment of school-aged children. In I. Rapin & S. J. Segalowitz (Vol. Eds.), *Handbook of neuropsychology* (Vol. 6, pp. 395–415). New York: Elsevier Science Publishers.

Mayeux, R., & Kandel, E. R. (1985). Natural language, disorders of language, and other localizable disorders of cognitive functioning. In E. R. Kandel & J. H. Schwartz (Eds.), *Principles of neural science* (2nd ed., pp. 688–703). New York: Elsevier Science Publishers.

Meighan, S. S., Queener, L., & Weitman, M. (1976). Prevalence of epilepsy in children of Multnomah County, Oregon. *Epilepsia, 17,* 245–256.

Milberg, W. P., Hebben, N., & Kaplan, E. (1986). The Boston process approach to neuropsychological assessment. In I. Grant & K. M. Adams (Eds.), *Neuropsychological assessment of neuropsychiatric disorders* (pp. 65–86). New York: Oxford University Press.

Molfese, D. L. (1992). The use of auditory evoked responses recorded from newborn infants to predict language skills. In M. G. Tramontana & S. R. Hooper (Eds.), *Advances in child neuropsychology* (Vol. 1, pp. 1–23). New York: Springer-Verlag.

Molfese, D. L. (1995). Electrophysiological responses obtained during infancy and their relation to later language development: Further findings. In M. G. Tramontana & S. R. Hooper (Eds.), *Advances in child neuropsychology* (Vol. 3, pp. 1–11). New York: Springer-Verlag.

Molfese, D. L., & Segalowitz, S. J. (1988). *Brain lateralization in children: Developmental implications.* New York: Guilford Press.

Molfese, V. (1992). Infant neuropsychology. In I. Rapin & S. J. Segalowitz (Vol. Eds.), *Handbook of neuropsychology* (Vol. 6, pp. 353–376). New York: Elsevier Science Publishers.

Newby, R. F., Recht, D., & Caldwell, J. (1994). Empirically tested interventions for subtypes of reading disabilities. In M. G. Tramontana & S. R. Hooper (Eds.), *Advances in child neuropsychology* (Vol. 2, pp. 201–232). New York: Springer-Verlag.

Passler, M., Isaac, W., & Hynd, G. W. (1986). Neuropsychological development of behavior attributed to frontal lobe functioning in children. *Developmental Neuropsychology, 1,* 349–370.

Reed, H. B. C., Reitan, R. M., & Klove, H. (1965). Influence of cerebral lesions on psychological test performance of older children. *Journal of Consulting Psychology, 29,* 247–251.

Reitan, R. M., & Davison, L. A. (Eds.). (1974). *Clinical neuropsychology: Current status and applications.* New York: Wiley.

Roeltgen, D. P. (1993). Agraphia. In K. M. Heilman & E. Valenstein (Eds.), *Clinical neuropsychology* (3rd ed., pp. 63–89). New York: Oxford University Press.

Rourke, B. P. (1982). Central processing deficiencies in children: Toward a developmental neuropsychological model. *Journal of Clinical Neuropsychology, 4,* 1–18.

Rourke, B. P. (1985). *Neuropsychology of learning disabilities: Essentials of subtype analysis.* New York: Guilford Press.

Rourke, B. P. (1989). *Nonverbal learning disabilities: The syndrome and the model.* New York: Guilford Press.

Rourke, B. P. (Ed.). (1991). *Neuropsychological validation of learning disability subtypes.* New York: Guilford Press.

Rourke, B. P., Fisk, J. L., & Strang, J. D. (1986). *Neuropsychological assessment of children: A treatment-oriented approach.* New York: Guilford Press.

Rovet, J., Gore, M., & Ehrlich, R. (1983). Intellectual and behavioral deficits associated with early onset diabetes mellitus. *Diabetes, 32* (Supp. 1), 17.

Rovet, J. F., Ehrlich, R. M., Czuchta, D., & Akler, M. (1993). Psychoeducational characteristics of children and adolescents with insulin-dependent diabetes mellitus. *Journal of Learning Disabilities, 26,* 7–22.

Rutter, M. (1977). Brain damage syndromes in childhood: Concepts and findings. *Journal of Child Psychology and Psychiatry, 18,* 1–21.

Rutter, M. (Ed.). (1983). *Developmental neuropsychiatry.* New York: Guilford Press.

Rutter M., Graham, P., & Yule, W. (1970). A neuropsychiatric study in childhood. *Clinics in Developmental Medicine* (Nos. 35–36). London: Spastics International Medical Publications/Heinemann Medical Books.

Ryan, C., Vega, A., & Drash, A. (1985). Cognitive deficits in adolescents who developed diabetes early in life. *Pediatrics, 75,* 921–927.

Ryan, C., Vega, A., Longstreet, C., & Drash, A. (1984). Neuropsychological changes in adolescents with insulin-dependent diabetes. *Journal of Consulting and Clinical Psychology, 52,* 335–342.

Sandoval, J., & Haapanen, R. M. (1981). A critical commentary on neuropsychology in the schools: Are we ready? *School Psychology Review, 10,* 381–388.

Satz, P., & Fletcher, J. M. (1982). *Florida Kindergarten Screening Battery.* Odessa, FL: Psychological Assessment Resources.

Seidel, U. P., Chadwick, O., & Rutter, M. (1975). Psychological disorders in crippled children: A comparative study of children with and without brain damage. *Developmental Medicine and Child Neurology, 17,* 563–573.

Semrud-Clikeman, M., Hooper, S. R., Hynd, G. W., Hern, K., Presley, R., & Watson, T. (1996). Prediction of group membership in developmental dyslexia, attention deficit-hyperactivity disorder, and normal controls using brain morphometric analysis of magnetic resonance imaging. *Archives of Clinical Neuropsychology.*

Semrud-Clikeman, M., Hynd, G. W., Lorus-Vernon, A. R., Novey, E. S., & Eliopulos, D. (1991). Dyslexia and brain morphology: Relationships between neuroanatomical variation and neurolinguistic tasks. *Learning and Individual Differences, 3,* 225–242.

Shaffer, D., Schonfeld, I., O'Connor, P. A., Stokman, C., Trautman, P., Shafer. S., & Ng, S. (1985). Neurological soft signs. *Archives of General Psychiatry, 42,* 342–351.

Shaywitz, B. A., Shaywitz, S. E., Pugh, K. R., Constable, R. T., Skudlarski, P., Fulbright, R. K., Bronen, R. A., Fletcher, J. M., Shankweiler, D. P., Katz, L., & Gore, J. C. (1995). Sex differences in the functional organization of the brain for language. *Nature, 373,* 607–609.

Siegel, L. S. (1989). IQ is irrelevant to the definition of learning disabilities. *Journal of Learning Disabilities, 22,* 469–479.

Snow, J. H., & Hooper, S. R. (1994). *Pediatric traumatic brain injury.* Newbury Park, CA: Sage Publications.

Soare, P. L., & Raimondi, A. J. (1977). Intellectual and perceptual-motor characteristics of treated myelomeningocele children. *American Journal of Diseases of Children, 131,* 199–204.

Spreen, O. J. (1988). Foreword. In M. G. Tramontana & S. R. Hooper (Eds.), *Assessment issues in child neuropsychology* (pp. ix–xii). New York: Plenum.

Spreen, O. J., Tupper, D., Risser, A., Tuokko, H., & Edgell, D. (1984). *Human developmental neuropsychology.* New York: Oxford University Press.

Stanovich, K. E., & Siegel, L. S. (1994). Phenotypic performance profile of children with reading disabilities: A regression-based test of the phonological-core variable-difference model. *Journal of Educational Psychology, 86,* 24–53.

Stehbens, J. A., & Cool, V. A. (1994). Neuropsychological sequelae of childhood cancers. In M. G. Tramontana & S. R. Hooper (Eds.), *Advances in child neuropsychology* (Vol. 2, pp. 55–84). New York: Springer-Verlag.

Stores, G. (1981). Problems of learning and behavior in children with epilepsy. In E. H. Reynolds & M. R. Trimble (Eds.), *Epilepsy and psychiatry* (pp. 34–48). London: Churchill Livingstone.

Torgeson, J. K., Wagner, R. K., Bryant, B. R., & Pearson, N. (1992). Toward development of a kindergarten group test for phonological awareness. *Journal of Research Development in Education, 25,* 113–120.

Tramontana, M. G., & Hooper, S. R. (1987). Discriminating the presence and pattern of neuropsychological impairment in child psychiatric disorders. *International Journal of Clinical Neuropsychology, 9,* 111–119.

Tramontana, M. G., & Hooper, S. R. (Eds.). (1988a). *Assessment issues in child neuropsychology.* New York: Plenum.

Tramontana, M. G., & Hooper, S. R. (1988b). Overview of current status of child neuropsychological assessment. In M. G. Tramontana & S. R. Hooper (Eds.), *Assessment issues in child neuropsychology* (pp. 3–38). New York: Plenum.

Tramontana, M. G., & Hooper, S. R. (in press). Neuropsychology of child psychopathology. In C. R. Reynolds (Ed.), *Handbook of child clinical neuropsychology* (2nd ed.). New York: Plenum.

Tramontana, M. G., Hooper, S. R., & Nardolillo, E. M. (1988). Behavioral manifestations of neuropsychological impairment in children with psychiatric disorders. *Archives of Clinical Neuropsychology, 3,* 369–374.

Tramontana, M. G., Hooper, S. R., & Selzer, S. C. (1988). Research on the preschool prediction of later academic achievement. *Developmental Review, 8,* 89–146.

Tramontana, M. G., & Sherrets, S. D. (1985). Brain impairment in child psychiatric disorders: Correspondences between neuropsychological and CT scan results. *Journal of the American Academy of Child Psychiatry, 24,* 590–596

Tramontana, M. G., Sherrets, S. D., & Golden, C. J. (1980). Brain dysfunction in youngsters with psychiatric disorders: Application of Selz-Reitan rules for neuropsychological diagnosis. *Clinical Neuropsychology, 2,* 118–123.

U.S. Office of Education. (1977). Assistance to states for education of handicapped children: Procedures for evaluating specific learning disabilities. *Federal Register, 42*(250), 65082–65085.

U.S. Office of Education. (1992). Individuals with Disabilities Education Act (IDEA). *Federal Register, 57*(189), 44842–44843.

Valsiner, J. (1983). Hemispheric specialization and integration in child development. In S. J. Segalowitz (Ed.), *Language functions and brain organization* (pp. 321–343). New York: Academic Press.

Vygotsky, L. S. (1960). *Development of the higher mental functions.* Moscow: IZD. AKAD. Ped. Nauk ASFSR.

Waber, D., Sollee, N., Wills, K., & Fischer, R. (1986, February). *Neuropsychological effects of two levels of cranial radiation in children with acute lymphoblastic leukemia (ALL).* Paper presented at the fourteenth annual meeting of the International Neuropsychological Society, Denver, CO.

Welsh, M. C., Pennington, B. F., & Groisser, D. B. (1991). A normative developmental study of executive function: A window on prefrontal function in children. *Developmental Neuropsychology, 7,* 131–149.

Wender, P. (1971). *Minimal brain dysfunction in children.* New York: Wiley.

Wilson, B. C. (1986). An approach to the neuropsychological assessment of the preschool child with developmental deficits. In S. B. Filskov & T. J. Boll (Eds.), *Handbook of clinical neuropsychology* (Vol. 2, pp. 121–171). New York: Wiley.

Wilson, H., & Staton, R. D. (1984). Neuropsychological changes in children associated with tricyclic antidepressant therapy. *International Journal of Neuroscience, 24,* 307–312.

Witelson, S. F., & Pallie, W. (1973). Left hemisphere specialization for language in the newborn: Neuroanatomical evidence of asymmetry. *Brain, 96,* 641–646.

Zametkin, A. J., & Rapoport, J. L. (1987). Neurobiology of attention deficit disorder with hyperactivity: Where have we come in 50 years? *Journal of the American Academy of Child and Adolescent Psychiatry, 26,* 676–686.

CHAPTER 5

Theories of Intelligence and Critiques

JULIE VIENS
Harvard University

JIE-QI CHEN
Erikson Institute

HOWARD GARDNER
Harvard University

Introduction

The construct of intelligence is essential to our understanding of what it means to be human. How intelligence is described, however, has been a point of contention since its introduction. Were it only an issue of scholarly debate, the discourse about intelligence would rage on in spirited, academic circles. But the debate on intelligence is not an isolated academic quarrel, as its recent reemergence in the popular press, in the discussion of *The Bell Curve,* forcefully reiterates (Herrnstein & Murray, 1994; see also Fraser, 1995). Constructs of intelligence can and have had tremendous social impact and educational implications.

In this chapter, we present several models of intelligence and intellectual development. We chose not to bring to the table an exhaustive review of theories of intelligence, but offer a representative sampling essential to this particular discussion. We begin with a discussion of *psychometric intelligence,* the first formal scientific approach to intelligence. Developed at the turn of the century, psychometric intelligence is couched in that era's evolutionary mind-set, emphasizing heritability of intelligence and applying mathematical tools to measure individual differences. Since the turn of the century, psychometric intelligence has been

defended and disputed; it is the theory upon which some have built and against which others have reacted, and it continues to play a significant role in the intelligence discourse.

Next, we discuss *Piaget's theory of intellectual development,* initially introduced in the United States during the 1930s but not widely known until the 1960s. Piaget's theory represented a distinct theoretical departure from psychometric intelligence, and in many quarters supplanted the vogue of intelligence testing. Piagetian theory emphasizes children's *developing* structures of reasoning. Piaget himself was interested in the qualitatively different stages of intellectual development through which *all* individuals pass; that is, he was concerned with universals rather than individual differences. With an emphasis on developing reasoning, Piaget moved the study of intelligence from measurement and ranking of test performance to the close scrutiny of children's reasoning. The implications of Piagetian theory yielded distinct educational "suggestions" as well.

We follow the discussion of Piagetian theory with two approaches to intelligence in the post-Piagetian era: *information-processing models* and *neo-Piagetian theories.* Building on and moving beyond the psychometric and Piagetian models, these two approaches illustrate the growing complexity of intelligence theories. Whereas information-processing models emphasize the microprocesses of thinking and problem solving, neo-Piagetian theories bring to bear distinctions among intellectual domains and the role of the environment in intellectual development.

The final section introduces three recent theories of intelligence: *Sternberg's triarchic theory, Ceci's bioecological framework,* and *Gardner's theory of multiple intelligences.* Each of these theories moves beyond previous conceptualizations, considering and synthesizing evidence from a wide range of perspectives, among them cognitive and developmental psychology, anthropology, neuropsychology, and education. In the discussion, we draw more attention to the theory of multiple intelligences, which indicates our preferences regarding appropriate and useful lenses into intelligence. Our main purpose for this chapter, however, is to make a useful contribution to the understanding of intelligence theories and their implications for education.

Psychometric Intelligence

Background

In the late 1800s, Sir Francis Galton introduced *intelligence* as an object of scientific study. Galton, who was Darwin's half cousin and the first eugenicist, spent much of his life trying to prove that intelligence was also an inherited trait. Galton posited that because information was transmitted to the mind through senses, those with greater sensory perception had greater mental abilities. Based on his assumption, Galton developed tests of sensory skills (for example, discriminating colors), physical characteristics (such as height), and psychophysical characteristics (such as reaction time) to study innate, individual differences in mental abilities (Galton, 1869, 1973a, 1973b).

At the turn of the century, French psychologist Alfred Binet, after investigating the work of Galton

and others, concluded that tests of mental ability had to include tests of "higher mental processes" (Binet & Simon, 1916; Pollack & Brenner, 1969). Binet believed that comprehension, reasoning, judgment, and invention were at the core of human mental abilities. In 1904, the French educational authorities solicited Binet to devise a test that would predict those children who would require special assistance in school.

Between 1904 and 1911, Binet and his colleague Theodore Simon developed and administered these tests, which consisted of a variety of practical tests, such as counting coins and naming body parts. Binet chose items he felt reflected information familiar to the children, because he did not believe that intelligence was independent of environmental input. Binet and Simon sampled their test, gauging which tasks were passed successfully by average groups of children at a given age, and devised the breakthrough concept of "mental age" to score children's performances. Although the performances were assigned a single number, Binet did not believe that this number represented a single, underlying general ability (Pollack & Brenner, 1969; Varon, 1936).

Binet's test became the basis for intelligence tests across many countries and languages. Indeed, Carroll (1982) notes that most of the content of today's Stanford-Binet scale can be traced to Binet's original scale. German psychologist William Stern felt that disparities between mental and chronological age had different implications for children of different chronological ages. Therefore, he devised a ratio measurement, the intelligence quotient (IQ), which is the child's mental age (MA) divided by the chronological age (CA), multiplied by 100 to get rid of decimal points (Carroll, 1982).

At this point on the American scene, Lewis Terman adapted Binet's tests for American children and developed the Stanford-Binet IQ scale. Like his colleagues, Terman wedded Binet's test approach and items with the notion of intelligence as significantly innate, inherited, and thus largely immutable. After World War I, Terman and Yerkes developed the National Intelligence Test, an intelligence test for schoolchildren that could be administered on a wide scale (Gould, 1981).

At the time, the United States was in the midst of the industrial revolution, with concomitant huge increases in population (primarily due to immigration) and the advent of mass public education. Intelligence testing held out the promise of a fair, systematic means by which to assess ability and rank, select, and place individuals in industry and schools. Because these tests were efficient—they could be administered on a wide scale—and purportedly scientific, they became extremely popular and widely used. The popularity of the tests in the United States led to intelligence being equated with performance on short-answer exams, with no grounding in any particular areas of expertise. In short, IQ *was* intelligence.

What Is "Mental Ability"?

The early American psychologists studying intelligence were psychometricians. They explored individual differences in intelligence by developing tests of mental ability and statistically analyzing the results. To these psychologists, intelligence tests help us understand the nature or "structure" of intelligence. But how do they define "mental ability"? *What* do intelligence tests measure?

In the early 1900s, Charles Spearman carried out a number of studies in Hampshire, England, testing children in different disciplines, ranging from mathematics to music to perceptual ability. Using a matrix of correlations based on Galton's work, Spearman found that the variables—academic and nonacademic test scores, teacher rankings, and sensory discrimination scores—could be analyzed to demonstrate positive correlations. Spearman concluded that whereas each individual test measured specific abilities, or *s,* all of the tests measured one underlying attribute, or *g* (for general intelligence). Spearman believed that *g* represented one underlying force or mental energy upon which all mental activities draw to varying degrees (Spearman, 1927).

Spearman's conclusion was also based on the results of factor analysis, a statistical technique he developed. Factor analysis mathematically extracts the common factor among intercorrelated tests, identifying the latent sources of underlying variation in the test scores, called "factors." Factor analysts such as Spearman propose that individual differences in test performance can be decomposed into individual differences within these factors. Each factor represents a distinct, underlying ability. For Spearman, the common factor his study yielded was a general intelligence, or *g.* He used the notion of specific skills, or *s,* needed for particular tests to explain why the correlations were not perfect (Spearman, 1927).

Most testing done before 1935 was based on the notion of intelligence as a general ability. However, given that more than one factor could be extracted from a correlation matrix of several tests, other psychologists disagreed with Spearman, as well as with each other, regarding the *number* of factors representing intelligence. Louis L. Thurstone developed multiple factor analysis, demonstrating that "intelligence" was not necessarily a single entity. Thurstone (1938) claimed that intelligence was multidimensional and reflected in several factors. He posited seven "primary mental abilities": verbal comprehension, verbal fluency, number, memory, perceptual speed, spatial visualization, and inductive reasoning.

J. P. Guilford (1950) claimed 120 separate factors in his "structure of intelligence" model. He organized the factors across three categories: 4 types of content categories, 5 types of operation categories, and 6 types of product categories. The dimensions are typically represented by a cube, and when multiplied together, they equal the 120 abilities.

Later in his life, Guilford posited 150 separate factors (Guilford, 1967).

Most factor analysts, up to recent times, have stood the middle ground, positing hierarchical patterns of group factors, although *g* still explains part of the variance in all tests. For example, Philip E. Vernon (1971) claims four levels of intellectual structure. At the top is a general factor, followed by two major group factors (verbal-educational ability and spatial-mechanical ability) at the second level. While minor group factors are at the third level, specific factors are at the fourth level. Cattell and Horn also put forth two broad factors—fluid ability and crystallized ability. The former is more representative of *g*; the latter of more accumulated knowledge. Furthermore, this model includes three "second-order" factors (Horn, 1986). Recently, John Carroll (1993) proposed a "three-stratum" theory: Stratum III is *g*, the highest ability; Stratum II includes eight broad abilities, such as fluid and crystallized intelligence; and Stratum I factors represent many narrow abilities.

Critique of Psychometric Theories

Although there are internal distinctions among psychometric theories, primarily regarding the number and arrangement of factors, for the most part they are more alike than different. All assume that factors and individual differences are at the heart of understanding intelligence. Therefore, the central course of study from the psychometric viewpoint is the administration of intelligence tests and analysis of individual differences. Thus, *g* is not a direct measure of ability but an implied measure of relative ability. As Gould (1981) notes, factor analysis has allowed a highly manipulable mathematical artifact to become reified as intelligence, as "a thing with a locus in the brain and a definite degree of heritability" (p. 239).

Having emphasized measurement technology, the psychometric view of intelligence does not help us understand the processes or development of intelligence. It leaves out cognitive and developmental psychology altogether. Even current researchers such as Eysenck and Jensen, who look to biological correlates of intelligence, have not incorporated neuroscientific understandings of the brain into their models (Andrist et al., 1992). In general, the psychometric model has extended from intelligence tests to some limited correlational research in the laboratory. Thus it is greatly limited in its applicability to the operation of intelligence in the real world. Although empirical, the psychometric model is based only marginally on a theory of how the mind works (Gardner, 1993a).

Intelligence tests include only a small range of human abilities, primarily language and mathematical abilities (Bornstein & Sigman, 1986; Gardner, 1993a; Sternberg, 1985, 1995). Moreover, this narrow band of abilities is tested in a narrow manner: decontextualized test items, paper-and-pencil tests, usually in a timed situation. It is not surprising, then, that test scores are not strongly related to performance in the real world (Snyderman & Rothman, 1988; Sternberg, 1985) nor to occupational success (Settler, 1990). Short-answer test questions cannot capture the complexity of life situations. Thus, individuals with high IQs may have difficulty dealing with everyday problems, and individuals who lead productive lives may not earn high scores on intelligence tests. In terms of being predictive of school success, the importance placed on these tests has often led to curriculum that is thinly disguised test preparation. Therefore, findings that correlate test scores with classroom performance should be examined carefully.

Gardner (1987a, 1993a) and Sternberg (1985, 1995) point out that intelligence tests do not measure a number of basic capacities, such as the abilities to assimilate new information and to formulate new ideas. Apparently, many experts in the field share this concern. Based on their survey of psychologists and educators with expertise in areas related to intelligence testing, Snyderman and Rothman (1988) report that 96% of the respondents identified the capacity to acquire knowledge as an important element of intelligence. Yet only 42.2% felt that this capacity was adequately measured by most intelligence tests.

Since Terman's time, intelligence and intelligence-like tests have been used as a gating mechanism, shifting people into particular programs and closing them out of others. It is, as Sternberg (1995) notes, ". . . a cultural artifact that we forget we have created and that we later try to explain as a natural phenomenon" (p. 3). Although intelligence testing is not nearly as widespread as it was early in the century, it still has a central place on the U.S. educational scene. The SAT test, which is similar to IQ tests, is required for college admissions. Standardized measures, such as readiness tests and achievement tests, are used for districtwide accountability, school readiness criterion, and placement in programs for the "gifted and talented" to the "educable mentally retarded." On average, an individual will take dozens of standardized tests through his or her school career (Gardner & Hatch, 1989).

General tracking—placing students into homogeneous groups based on test performance—has been the most significant use of intelligence tests since their inception (Carroll, 1982; Oakes, 1985). General tracking assumes that student performance on intelligence and other standardized tests suggests their placement in *any* academic context. That is, students are seen generally as "low track" or "high track" students, with no regard to specific areas of ability. General tracking is thus reflective of the concept of general intelligence.

Many studies show that those labeled "low" ability are negatively affected by tracking, while "high" ability children typically show no benefit.

Low ability tracks usually entail a "dumbed down" curriculum, both in terms of content and the intellectual processes it requires (Oakes, 1985). "Low ability" students tend to do worse academically when tracked (Findlay & Bryan, 1975; Slavin, Karweit, & Madden, 1989). Studies reflect a general pattern: low-track students are at a consistent disadvantage.

Given what we know about which populations do and do not do well on intelligence and related ability tests, it is easy to predict the consequences: disproportionate numbers of poor, minority children are subject to low-ability and remedial classes. Tracking has been dubbed "in-school desegregation" given the disproportionate numbers of African Americans, Latinos, and recent immigrants that fill the ranks of the low-ability classrooms (Oakes, 1985; FairTest, 1993). It seems that the social Darwinian agenda perpetuated by the original IQ tests finds a life in its product, tracking. "[T]hose at the bottom of the social and economic ladder climb up through twelve years of the great equalizer' . . . and end up still on the bottom rung" (Oakes, 1985 p. 4).

In criticizing intelligence tests, we are not implying that all standardized testing is inappropriate. For example, a standardized test can be a good gauge of particular academic strengths and deficits, if used with other assessments. Low test scores have had the effect of drawing attention to low quality schools for low-income and minority students. If used in combination with other assessments and in random or matrix samples (not used in every grade, with every student), standardized testing can provide accountability information without harming the individual students taking the tests (FairTest, 1993). Overall, however, psychometric intelligence and its various associated tests are limited in what they tell us, how they can help us understand human intelligence, and the positive impact on school practices.

Piaget's Theory of Intellectual Development

Swiss psychologist Jean Piaget introduced his theory of intellectual development in the 1920s, and it made its way to the United States in the 1930s. However, Piaget's overall work received scant attention in this country until the Sputnik generation of the 1960s. As a student of Theodore Simon (Binet's former associate), Piaget was trained in the psychometric tradition. While working in Simon's laboratory in the early 1920s, Piaget was asked to standardize intelligence tests by recording the ages by which children were able to answer certain test items correctly. But Piaget found himself far more interested in children's wrong answers, and in the reasoning underlying those errors. This early work led Piaget to a lifelong study of the development of children's conceptual understandings (DeVries & Kohlberg, 1987).

Intellectual Development

Piaget posited that children develop cognitive structures of reasoning through a sequence of qualitatively different stages of development. Each stage has particular structural characteristics that make possible as well as limit particular forms of reasoning. With increasing age and experience, these structures change from being bound by motor actions in infancy, to being dominated by perceptual and intuitive processes in the preschool years, and finally, to being concrete and then formal operational processes during middle childhood and adolescence. These stages are invariant: all children must pass through the preceding stage before going on to the next. The reorganization of structures developed during each preceding stage produces the qualitative shifts in children's thought that constitute intellectual development. This conceptualization of intelligence was a dramatic shift from the psychometric perspective, which assumed that the structures of intelligence were largely inherited and static, and significantly fixed by the age of 5 (DeVries & Kohlberg, 1987; Piaget, 1970).

Central to Piaget's conceptualization of the intellect is the child's active construction of his or her understanding. In Piagetian terms, physical and logical mathematical knowledge is constructed by children through the interaction between their mental structures and their environment. Children do not passively absorb knowledge. Rather, they develop intelligence while acting on, or later, *thinking about,* their physical actions on objects (DeVries & Kohlberg, 1987; Labinowicz, 1980).

For aspects of his view of intellectual development, Piaget borrowed vocabulary from his work in biology. In particular, he termed two processes central to his model: *assimilation* and *accommodation.* In assimilation, the individual fits external actions on objects to an already existing organized pattern of behavior, what Piaget labeled a *scheme.* In accommodation, the individual fits his or her own behavior to the external world. Assimilation and accommodation are two simultaneous and complementary aspects of adaptational processes in the child's cognitive development. Piaget held that intellectual progress occurs when there is "disequilibration," when schemes do not match or when assimilation and accommodation are in disorder. Disequilibrium provokes a child to revise his or her scheme, thereby advancing intellectual development (DeVries & Kohlberg, 1987; Piaget, 1972).

What motivates most psychometricians are the differences in intellectual strength among individuals, groups, and species. Therefore, the use of IQ and intelligence-like tests supports and promotes ranking and ultimately sorting of individuals. Piaget's goal was to uncover the laws that guide children's development across all domains and problems. Thus, in another contrast to the psychometric perspective's differential psychology, Piaget sought to understand the principles of cognitive development common to all human beings (Feldman, 1986; Ginsburg & Opper, 1979; Siegler & Richards, 1982).

Critique of Piaget's Theory

Piaget proffered a generative theory, one that explores the course of intellectual development. This theory, however, has been challenged on nearly every front. Despite the ambitious scope of Piaget's efforts, many scholars find Piaget's theory limited (Feldman, 1993; Flavell, Miller, & Miller, 1993; Gardner, 1993a). For example, Gardner (1993a) finds Piaget's work incomplete in that it describes only the development of logical-mathematical thought. According to Gardner, Piaget was mistaken in his assumption that logical-mathematical thought provides the basis for all intellectual activity.

Another serious challenge is the criticism of Piaget's stage theory. Many studies (Gelman & Baillargeon, 1983; Lempers, Flavell, & Flavell, 1977; Shantz, 1975; Gelman, 1972) report that the preoperational child frequently proves to be more competent than stage theory predicts. The concrete operational child's development is often domain-specific rather than an integrated whole required by Piaget's general stage theory. Adult reasoning about certain problems appears to reflect the same underlying structures that characterize the reasoning of preschoolers and older children. These studies provide little evidence to support the existence of the major stages in cognitive development that Piaget described.

In application, Piaget's stages are useful in that they provide educators with a general understanding of children's abilities at given ages. However, because the behavior of students in the classroom does not show the consistency predicted by the stage theory, the teacher is hard pressed to categorize students according to Piaget's stage in order to program developmentally appropriate education and to devise curricula to meet specific instructional needs (Ginsburg, 1981). Furthermore, the stages often have been used in a manner that underestimates children's ability, rather than as a springboard to challenge children's thinking and to encourage their "wonderful ideas" for further development (Bredekamp 1987; Duckworth, 1972; Pitcher, Feinburg, & Alexander, 1989).

Although his stage theory acknowledges children's varying rates of attainment of the various cognitive structures, Piaget had little interest in studying individual differences. His lack of interest perhaps significantly limited the relevance of his theory to education. As Ginsburg (1981) states, "To a large degree, education is or should be concerned with developing meaningful forms of learning for individuals who differ in important ways" (p. 326). Although Piaget gets away from the ranking and sorting of psychometrics, any differences among children on which to base their learning is ignored.

Piaget is credited with acknowledging the environment in development; however, for the most part Piaget disregarded environment as a significant variable for cognitive development. Piagetian theory gives scant attention to the role of adults and adult instruction in the child's learning process. In fact, one of Piaget's most famous assertions is, "Every time we teach a child something, we keep him from inventing it himself" (Piaget, 1972). No doubt, some aspects of children's learning (for example language development), can take place with minimal adult input and no instruction. However, development is not an isolated biological event within the child. Adults have a distinct responsibility in a child's intellectual development. As we have learned from the work of Vygotsky (1978), adults' scaffolding and guidance are critical to move a child through developmental junctures, or "zones of proximal development."

Unfortunately, Piagetian theory has been translated as a "hands off" policy toward adult mediation of learning activities.

After Piaget

Piaget's work led to new conceptualizations of intelligence drawn from two distinct sources: information-processing models of cognition and neo-Piagetian theories of development. Rather than posit broad stages of development, as Piaget did, the information-processing approach attempts to explain the cognitive processes that occur during task performance. Building on Piaget's general progression, neo-Piagetian theories attempt to address some of the problems in Piaget's work to provide a more comprehensive view of cognitive development.

Information-Processing Theories

Information-processing theories surfaced in the 1960s and the 1970s and were in great part a reaction to behaviorist views of human learning as a passive stimulus-response process. Information-processing theories focus on the ways in which incoming information is actively received, interpreted, and responded to.

Information-processing theories conceive the human mind as a complex cognitive system, analogous in some ways to a digital computer. The basic assumption underlying this approach is that task performances can be broken down into microprocessing components that occur in particular sequences. The goal of information-processing models is to identify and describe the set of processes that constitutes problem-solving or intelligent behavior (Flavell, Miller, & Miller, 1993).

Information-processing theories vary in terms of the level of processing they emphasize. Some theorists, harkening back to Galton's psychophysical tests, focus on speed of information-processing, (such as reaction time), choice-reaction time, and speed of lexical access studies (for example, Jensen, 1982; Mathews & Dorn, 1989). Other researchers (for example, Klahr & Wallace, 1976; Siegler, 1978, 1983) have emphasized higher-order processes such as reasoning and problem solving. These psychologists typically use Piaget-style tasks to provide a picture of the mental steps involved as an individual solves a problem. Still other researchers, such as Robert Sternberg (1977), attempt to identify operations involved in the solution of standard intelligence test items.

The detailed focus on processing and describing the microstructure of performing tasks is a useful conceptualization that in some ways is an advance over previous theories. Instead of attempting to identify the broad dimensions of human abilities, the information-processing approach focuses on the thought processes or components underlying those abilities, and views intelligence as a set of interacting processes operating on a variety of knowledge structures, and provides a more dynamic view of the process of problem solving. Using a computer flowchart metaphor, information-processing models describe basic mechanisms for task performance, such as short- and long-term memory, as well as higher-level control mechanisms, such as metacomponents (Sternberg, 1977, 1985).

Information-processing models, however, suffer from the lack of an articulated theory through which to compare and contrast different forms of cognition. The models are equally at home with a modular or with a general problem-solving perspective. There seem to be many different processors or components that apparently are not connected. Another criticism of information processing is that it is always dependent on the most recent computer model; thus, when one computer model replaces another, the whole model of the child's cognition changes as well. Thus one must ask, "Where is the grounding?" The information-processing school provides no means by which to judge among its principal debates. Is there a central mechanism or "executor"? Which elements change with development? Storage-area capacity? Available strategies? Overall efficiency (Gardner, 1993a)?

Similar to Piagetian and psychometric models of intelligence, information-processing approaches are nonbiological, virtually ignoring what we know about the nervous system (Gardner, 1993a; Martin & Weingartner, 1992). There is no grounding basis to evaluate which component is a central component of intelligence and which is not. Component scores (the product of componential analysis) are at best valid performance parameters. They have proved not to have construct or any other kind of validity (Flavell, Miller, & Miller, 1993).

Neo-Piagetians

The *term neo-Piagetian* refers to a group of researcher-theorists who generally share Piaget's view of development, yet at the same time attempt to address some of the critiques of the theory. We briefly describe two neo-Piagetian approaches, those of Robbie Case and David Feldman, that modify and extend Piaget's stage theory and challenge his notion of universal development.

Like Piaget's theory, Case's (1985, 1986) theory proposes four general stages of children's cognitive development between the ages of 4 months and 19 years: sensorimotor, relational, dimensional, and vectorial stages. Within each major stage, Case also identifies a universal sequence of three substages: unifocal, bifocal, and elaborated coordination. What differentiates these substages is the number of elements they represent and the way in which these elements are organized. Assuming normal conditions, children progress through each stage and substage of development over a characteristic length of time and across a broad range of content domains. Through a process of differentiation and coordination, the structures of one stage or substage build on those of the previous stage or substage.

Unlike Piaget's theory, Case's theory attempts to model the process of children's thinking at each stage and substage of their development in a relatively detailed fashion, partially building on the information-processing approach. According to Flavell and associates (1993), Case's model of cognitive development "is a sequence of increasingly powerful procedures for solving problems, along with an increasingly powerful set of conceptual knowledge structures" (p. 13). Children express a concept through processes such as attention, memory, and strategies in a particular environment, and children's limited short-term memory capacity constrains this expression. Although practice increases children's short-term storage, which in turn increases their operating efficiency, there are biological limits: myelinization of the neural tissue in the system of the brain controls the particular set of operations involved in the operating task (Case, 1986; Flavell, Miller, & Miller, 1993).

In Case's theory of cognitive change, the child is seen as a problem solver (Flavell, Miller, & Miller, 1993). As children develop, their capacity for problem solving—encompassing more components, differentiation, coordination, setting subgoals, and the like—increases. Among their peers, the child with more capacity is more likely to benefit from instruction on a new concept. Activities such as exploring objects, observing and imitating other people, and cooperating with others in problem solving spur on cognitive change. Instruction plays an increasingly significant role in children's thinking at each successive stage of their development (Case, 1985, 1986).

David Feldman is a key player in taking intellectual development beyond Piaget's universal notion. His research with prodigies (children who perform at an adult level in a domain) has provided a strong line of evidence that supports nonuniversal development (Feldman with Goldsmith, 1986). Specifically, Feldman and his colleague Lynn Goldsmith demonstrate that although these children stand out markedly within their domain—be it music composition at the age of 6 or writing novels at the age of 5—they appear undistinguished from their peers when studied in other domains or when given standard tests of operational thinking.

In contrast to universal development, Feldman's nonuniversal development is neither spontaneous nor fully achieved by all individuals. Feldman suggests a continuum of domains ranging from universal to cultural to discipline-based to idiosyncratic to unique. The number of individuals who master the higher levels of domains decreases from universal to unique; that is, all human beings master the universal domains, whereas only very few master a unique domain (Feldman, 1974, 1993).

Feldman claims that cognitive structures must be built gradually in each cognitive domain. There are no general structures applied to every domain. Rather, what exists in the mind of the child at a moment in time is a variety of skills in a variety of domains. Given that the source of individual differences in nonuniversal development ties in the potential for mastery of various domains, and in the variety of domains made available and accessible to the individual, individual differences in cognition describe how individuals are advancing in one or several domains.

Finally, development in nonuniversal domains is the result of joint efforts of the child and those around him or her to construct and share ever-more sophisticated understanding. For progressive and productive change to occur in nonuniversal developmental domains, quite specific environmental conditions—in the form of culturally evolved technologies and techniques for catalyzing, facilitating, and enabling progress—must be systematically presented and sustained over time. The teachers, peers, materials, competitions, and incentives of a domain must be well orchestrated for development to occur in optimal fashion. The more

that the various environmental conditions of development are in optimal coordination, the more likely they are to lead to optimal states of developed potential in the child (Feldman, 1993; Feldman with Goldsmith, 1986).

Recent Integrative Theories of Intelligence

In the last few decades, theories of intelligence and intellectual development have become more complex, acknowledging that previous theories have really just looked at particular aspects of intelligence. This growing complexity of theories is evident from the work of neo-Piagetians such as Robbie Case. The final section of this chapter introduces three theories that draw most comprehensively on a range of theoretical sources, including psychology, anthropology, sociology, and education. Because of limited space, we review only three theories: Sternberg's triarchic theory, Ceci's bioecological approach, and Gardner's theory of multiple intelligences.

Sternberg's Triarchic Theory

In his triarchic theory of human intelligence, Sternberg proposes three subtheories: componential, experiential, and contextual. The componential subtheory refers to the information-processing mechanisms through which individuals carry out intelligent behavior. Sternberg posits three central processes: knowledge-acquisition components, which come to the fore when learning how to perform tasks; performance components, utilized in the act of performing tasks; and metacomponents, which are engaged to plan, monitor, and evaluate task performance. The componential subtheory tries to identify underlying processes of behaviors in which individuals engage to fit with the environment (Sternberg, 1983, 1985, 1988).

The experiential subtheory, as the name implies, deals with the role of experience in intelligence. It identifies points of a person's interaction with a task that are most germane to understanding the role of intelligence in the task experience. These points are on a continuum, and for each experience they fall somewhere between novel and automatized. Therefore, intelligence is related to an individual's ability to work through novel tasks and situations and to automatize information processing (Gardner, Kornhaber, & Wake, 1996; Sternberg, 1985). Novelty and automatization interact, with increased automatization freeing up mental resources for processing novelty.

An important implication of the experiential subtheory is in careful task selection for measuring intelligence. Completely novel tasks and tasks requiring automatized skills do not impart a great deal of information about an individual's intelligence because neither taps problem-solving. In novel tasks an individual has no frame of reference, and in completely automated tasks an individual does not partake in problem-solving behavior. Sternberg claims that it is experiential intelligence that explains why simple speed tasks (such as reaction time) correlate with intelligence test performances: they measure automatized skills (Steinberg, 1985, 1988).

The contextual subtheory deals with intelligent activity necessary for particular environmental contexts. Sternberg views intelligence as mental processes that are directed toward "purposive adaptation to, and selection and shaping of, real-world environments relevant to one's life" (Sternberg, 1985, p.45). That is, contextual theory refers to intelligent behavior involved in achieving a fit with the context. An individual adapts to the environment by attempting to find the best fit between oneself and the environment. When a good fit is not possible, an individual may try to select another environment where he or she might find a better fit. Where alternative selection is not feasible, environmental shaping comes to the fore. At this point, an individual tries to reshape the environment toward a better fit.

The contextual subtheory has interesting implications. Because what is needed for adaptation—selection and shaping—is likely to differ among individuals and groups and across environments, intelligence is different across individuals, groups, and environments and at different points in the life span (Sternberg, 1985). Thus, whereas the components of information processing are fixed, the contextual aspects are relative. Sternberg has used measures of tacit or "practical" intelligence to research the contextual subtheory. For example, Sternberg found a positive correlation between scores on questionnaires that tapped individuals' understanding of the "hidden agenda" of their fields and measures of professional success. Sternberg concludes that practical intelligence is an important aspect of intelligence related to success in the real world (Gardner, Kornhaber, & Wake, 1996; Sternberg, 1985).

Sternberg's triarchic theory brings together many aspects of intelligence for a more comprehensive theory of intelligence. For example, the basic processing components, the role of experience, and high-level views of intelligence are brought together with the componential, experiential, and contextual subtheories. However, the theory leaves a gap in terms of biological aspects of intelligence. Although Sternberg's practical intelligence correlates to real-world performance, it does not give insight into how context affects problem solving.

Ceci's Bioecological Approach

Even more than Sternberg, Steven Ceci, representing a contextualist approach, focuses on dimensions outside the individual as critical to intelligence. Contextualists emphasize how intelligence is affected by the environment, such as school, other individuals, technology, culture, and historical era, to name a few (for example, Ceci, 1990; Sternberg, 1983; Vygotsky, 1978). Like Sternberg, Ceci's approach includes information-processing components, experience, and context, with the greatest emphasis on the latter. Ceci also claims that low-level mental processing is affected by knowledge and experience. Ceci argues against general intelligence, g, and posits biologically based multiple cognitive potentials (Ceci, 1990; Ceci & Liker, 1986).

Key aspects of Ceci's bioecological approach include cognitive processes, knowledge, domain, cognitive complexity, and IQ. Briefly, cognitive processes are mental processing mechanisms that constrain an individual's intelligence. Knowledge refers to rules, information, and the like that are garnered through cognitive processes. A domain is a set of organized knowledge (juggling, computer programming, and carpentry are domains of knowledge). Domains organize "bits" of knowledge, which can be part of different domains. Cognitive complexity refers to an individual's ability to engage cognitive processes efficiently within knowledge structures. IQ is a score derived from an intelligence test. According to Ceci, IQ is a measure of only one type of intelligence (Ceci, 1990)

Ceci argues that intelligences are biologically based yet completely tied to the environment in which they develop. Ceci describes the relationship between the biologically based intelligences and the environmental constraints and opportunities as "a state of constant symbiosis" (Ceci, 1990). Whereas Gardner argues that neuropsychology provides strong evidence for multiple intelligences, Ceci claims that the evidence is not unequivocal, and in fact could be used to argue the case for a general intelligence.

Ceci holds that psychometrics provides strong evidence for multiple cognitive potentials by way of group factors extracted from intelligence tests, such as linguistic, spatial, or logical abilities. Ceci draws on a range of sources to make his argument for multiple cognitive potentials, including neuropsychology, cognitive experiments, and psychometric research. Ceci also uses cognitive studies that demonstrate individuals' use of high-level

thought in some contexts but not in others to argue that different domains rely on different cognitive potentials (Ceci, 1990).

Context is broadly defined in the bioecological approach, encompassing mental, social, and physical contexts of problem solving. It includes domains of knowledge, materials, motivation, personality, and schooling, as well as a historical era within which individuals live. Ceci has criticized past studies (such as Terman's famous study connecting high IQ with high achievement), to demonstrate the contextual factors that may have come into play. For example, he showed that the rich "Termites" (the subjects in Terman's study) were far more likely to succeed than the poor ones (Gardner, Kornhaber, & Wake, 1996). Ceci also conducts his own research to draw out the inextricable role of context in assessing intellectual abilities. By using *problem isomorphs*—problems that use different materials but require the same problem-solving processes—Ceci has been able to demonstrate that children's abilities improve dramatically when a task is made meaningful and relevant to them; specifically, when generic geometric shapes become butterflies and bees, for example, and the activity is given gamelike qualities (Ceci, 1990).

According to the bioecological framework, knowledge is central to intelligence as well. Ceci argues that the capacity to think in complex ways within a domain is based on one's knowledge in that domain. The interaction between multiple cognitive potentials and rich knowledge bases is where success in the real world is placed.

Gardner's Theory of Multiple Intelligences

Howard Gardner formulated the theory of multiple intelligences by trying to "erase from his mind" the traditional psychometric perspective of intelligence, intelligence tests, and correlations of intelligence tests. He began by considering what people can do, examining the range of "end states" that are valued in diverse human cultures: hunters, farmers, military leaders, civil authorities, artists, musicians, religious leaders, shamans, parents, athletes, to name but a few. Gardner saw the challenge of defining intelligence as one of formulating a view of cognition that fully accounts for this range of roles and abilities that are valued across diverse societies and human history (Gardner, 1986, 1993a).

A theory of intelligence that asks "What are the basic cognitive abilities responsible for what people can do?" is in stark contrast to one that assumes intelligence is a single, measurable unit. Whereas the definition of intelligence according to the psychometric view is "general intelligence," at best implied through a test made up primarily of language and math problems, multiple intelligences (MI) theory defines intelligence as "the ability to solve a problem or fashion a product that is valued in at least one culture or community" (Gardner 1993a).

Like other recent theories, some described earlier, Gardner's is a synthesis of evidence from diverse sources, and similarly, an attempt to better explain the complexity of intelligence. Gardner and his colleagues studied cognition as it is manifested in the human nervous system and examined how cognitive abilities have been garnered toward a range of intellectual ends. Starting with this definition of intelligence, couched in genuine problem solving, Gardner surveyed a set of criteria, drawn from diverse sources, with which to review abilities as candidate intelligences (Gardner, 1993a). In his original presentation of multiple intelligences theory, Gardner identified seven relatively autonomous intelligences: linguistic, logical-mathematical, bodily-kinesthetic, musical, spatial, interpersonal, and intrapersonal (Gardner, 1993a).

Multiple intelligences theory. In identifying a group of representative intelligences, Gardner identified and applied eight key criteria for an in-

telligence. The first, *potential isolation by brain damage*, suggests that to the extent that a particular ability can be destroyed or spared in isolation, its relative autonomy from other faculties seems likely. Second, the *existence of savants, prodigies, and other exceptional individuals* evidences highly uneven "profiles of intelligence." For example, prodigies are extremely precocious in one area (sometimes more) while not exceptional in others. Savants, such as autistic children, exhibit one specific strength among mediocre or highly retarded performances in other areas. Again, these exceptional individuals demonstrate the relative autonomy of intelligences.

Third, and central to the consideration of an ability as an intelligence, is that it exhibits an *identifiable core operation or set of operations*—that is, the existence of one or more basic information-processing operations that can deal with specific kinds of input. For example, sensitivity to pitch is a core operation of musical intelligence. Fourth, an intelligence should have an *identifiable, distinctive developmental history* with a definable set of expert "end-state" performances through which normal and gifted individuals pass. Because intelligences do not develop in isolation, the focus is on the roles or contexts where the relevant intelligence occupies a central place.

Fifth, the plausibility of an intelligence is greatly increased when an *evolutionary history and evolutionary plausibility* can be identified. The existence of birdsong and evidence of music in prehistory are two such examples from musical intelligence. The sixth criteria, *support from experimental psychological tasks*, proposes studies of tasks that interfere with each other, or that transfer across contexts, and other experimental tests that can help demonstrate how particular abilities do and do not interact in the execution of complex tasks.

To the extent that psychometric tasks correlate highly with one another, and less so with those that purportedly assess other intelligences, it enhances the MI formulation. Thus, *support from psychometric findings* is identified as the seventh criterion. Factor analysis, carefully interpreted, provides another piece of evidence toward the autonomy of particular functions. *Susceptibility to encoding in a symbol system* is the eighth and final criterion. Language, picturing, and mathematics are three examples of symbol systems that are central to human survival and productivity. MI theory considers a natural gravitation toward embodiment in a symbolic system as an important criterion for an intelligence (Gardner, 1993a).

Checking candidate intelligences against this list of criteria—dubbed a "subjective" factor analysis by Gardner (1993a)—resulted in the identification of seven distinct intelligences. These seven core intelligences are described briefly as: *logical-mathematical* (sensitivity to patterns, orderliness, and systematicity and the ability to handle long chains of reasoning); *linguistic* (sensitivity to the sounds, rhymes, and meanings of words and sensitivity to the different functions of language); *musical* (abilities to produce and appreciate rhythm, pitch, and timbre and appreciation of the forms of musical expressiveness); *spatial* (capacities to perceive the spatial world accurately, to perform transformations on one's initial perceptions, and to recreate aspects of one's visual experience); *bodily-kinesthetic* (abilities to control one's bodily movements and to handle objects skillfully); *interpersonal* (capacities to discern and respond appropriately to the moods, temperaments, motivations, and desires of other people); and *intrapersonal* (access to one's own feelings, the ability to discriminate among them and draw on them to guide behavior) (Gardner, 1993a).

It is important to note that Gardner makes no claims "about the sacrosanctity of the particular intelligences identified, the levels of analyses featured, or the number of intelligences nominated" (1986, p. 74). In 1983, this present list originally was posited as a reasonable accounting for the end

states valued in different cultures. In a recent paper, Gardner (1995b) considers evidence for two "new" candidate intelligences: a naturalist intelligence and a spiritual intelligence. Judged against the eight criteria, the naturalist intelligence proved robust. A naturalist is an individual who demonstrates expertise in the recognition and classification of the numerous species of his or her environment. In cultures without science, the naturalist is the individual most skilled in the application of the current "folk taxonomies"; in cultures with science, the naturalist is a biologist, an individual with outstanding knowledge of the living world; or those individuals who study organisms for more theoretically oriented purposes. John James Audubon, Charles Darwin, and E. O. Wilson all fit this category, as would a hunter, fisherman, farmer, gardener, or cook.

Briefly, in terms of the eight criteria, several core capacities can be identified in the naturalist intelligence. It has a well-established evolutionary history (survival of an organism has been dependent on its ability to discriminate among quite similar species), and a scale ranging from novice to expert can be stipulated for a budding naturalist. Moreover, entire formal fields of study, such as botany, have been constructed as a means of aiding the development and deployment of the naturalist. Because the naturalist similarly checks out against all eight criteria, Gardner (1995b) has added it to the original list of seven intelligences unceremoniously.

Multiple intelligences theory does not claim the intelligences as physical entities but rather as constructs useful to think about the workings of intelligence (Gardner, 1993b). According to MI theory, intelligence is not a thing, but rather a potential whose presence allows access to types of thinking appropriate to specific types of content (Kornhaber & Gardner, 1991). That is, we are at promise for seven, now eight, distinctive forms of thinking that, when combined in different manners, result in the range of abilities exhibited among human beings.

Multiple intelligences theory counters the psychometric model's unitary view of intelligence, *g*. Similarly, it also goes beyond Piaget's attempts to establish the unitary and universal structures he believed underlies intelligent behavior. In these respects, MI theory aligns itself with more recent conceptualizations, such as those described earlier, that acknowledge the multidimensional nature of intelligence and the domain-specificity, or nonuniversal character, of the intellectual and its development.

Educational implications. As a developmental psychologist and neuropsychologist, Gardner developed multiple intelligences theory as an account of intelligence that can be empirically tested. He expected an audience primarily of psychologists, debating whether MI theory was an appropriate and sensible representation of intelligence. Although the book that introduced MI theory generated discussion and controversy within psychological circles, it has in fact been more widely read and discussed by educators (Gardner, 1993b; Krechevsky, Gardner, & Hoerr, 1995).

As a theory of intelligence, multiple intelligences posits little regarding the "how to's" of application (Kornhaber & Krechevsky, 1995). Nonetheless, it does harbor several educational implications worthy of discussion (Gardner, 1993b; Walters & Gardner, 1985). Moreover, within six years of Gardner's presentation of his theory, several schools were formed or reorganized around multiple intelligences theory. Although there are a range of applications of MI theory, MI schools, as we'll call them, converge on certain key implications: giving children substantive experience in each of the intelligences; providing children with opportunities in their own areas of strength (and interest); and attempting to help children develop and learn by drawing on their strengths and

unique profiles of intelligences (Kornhaber & Krechevsky, 1995; Chen, Feldman, Gardner, Krechevsky, & Viens, in press).

In sharp contrast to the psychometric perspective, MI theory is also affecting "intelligence-fair" assessment in schools (Gray & Viens, 1994; Krechevsky, 1991). Intelligence-fair assessments allow children to demonstrate their abilities using media and contexts that are authentic and appropriate to that intelligence or domain. Project Zero's Spectrum Project includes a set of preschool assessment activities based on multiple intelligences and integrated into the regular classroom context. For example, spatial and logical-mathematical abilities are brought to bear as children disassemble and reassemble mechanical objects; oral language ability is assessed as children tell stories using a storyboard; and interpersonal understanding is demonstrated through the use of a scaled-down model of the classroom containing miniatures of class members. The development of intelligences needed for these activities are regularly observed by teachers and researchers (Gray & Viens, 1994; Krechevsky, 1991; Krechevsky & Gardner, 1990). Rather than an "implied" intelligence drawn from a paper-and-pencil test score, these assessments allow for an authentic appraisal of children's abilities within particular intelligence areas.

MI theory claims that intelligence is significantly determined by the environment; that is, by culture, family, teachers, materials, nature of activities, choices that are made, and so on. As such, it implies the importance of a carefully structured classroom environment (including instruction,) responsive to students' unique profiles of intelligence. The theory also emphasizes the importance of providing children opportunities to engage with the tools, materials, technologies, and experts of their own areas of strength and interest (Hoerr, 1994; Kornhaber & Krechevsky, 1995; Krechevsky, Gardner , & Hoerr, 1995; Chen et al., in press).

Critique of Multiple Intelligences Theory

Multiple intelligences theory has been criticized on both theoretical and educational grounds. Some scholars (Sattler, 1990) argue that MI theory is simply labeling talents or skills and that such labeling does not advance understanding of intelligence. Gardner counters that regarding only skills in language and logic mathematic intelligence reflects the Western tradition heavily influenced by intelligence testing. To step away from the Western bias, it is reasonable, and probably important, to call the diverse faculties Gardner has posited the same term, be it *intelligences* or *talents* or *skills* (Gardner, 1993a, 1993b).

MI theory has been criticized for taking the position that differences in intellectual profiles are due to genetic factors. As human beings, we are shaped by genetics. Gardner (1987b, 1994, 1995a) argues, for example, that Mozart and Einstein were born with different intellectual proclivities, and their respective genetic legacies influenced their options and their ultimate achievements. However, it does not follow that Gardner and MI theory minimize the central role of environmental or motivational factors. Indeed, Gardner notes that both nature *and* nurture are far more important than scientists had previously acknowledged. More to the point, and to which we have previously referred, a great deal of research has demonstrated that contextual features are central to the development of individuals' intellectual strengths and weaknesses.

Gardner's claim that the intelligences are autonomous has also been criticized. Decades of psychometric research has demonstrated that abilities are positively correlated. Gardner counters that positive correlations are obtained because psychometric measures detect aptitude within a particular intelligence, such as linguistic or logical-mathematical intelligence. Positive correlations are also due to the fact that many psychometric tests measure paper-and-pencil, short-answer test-taking ability and one's ability to maintain composure under timed situations. To know whether the intelligences are autonomous, intelligence-fair assessments must be utilized.

MI theory has been criticized for not providing an empirical test of the theory of multiple intelligences (Gardner, 1994). Robert Sternberg warns of the dangers to educational reform in embracing such an untested theory. When labeling multiple intelligences a theory, Gardner took care to note that it is less a set of hypotheses and predictions than it is an organized framework for configuring an ensemble of data about human cognition in different cultures. MI theory is not the kind of theory that is going to be proved correct or incorrect by a single study or set of studies. It represents Gardner's best effort to organize a large amount of data in a way that is sensible to psychologists and educators. In that sense, it resembles Sternberg's own triarchic theory of intelligence.

This does not mean that multiple intelligences theory is not empirical. In fact, it is based on empirical findings. Upon continued reflection on and reorganization of the same and new bodies of data, MI theory will endure or be dismissed. Gardner continues to monitor the tenability of the theory of multiple intelligences and to collect data relevant to its principal assertions, and even to carry out studies that bear on particular claims. For example, Gardner and Hatch (1989) show that among a sample of preschool children, there is reasonable evidence for the disaggregation of intellectual factors. And as described earlier, Gardner recently modified the theory of multiple intelligences, adding the naturalist intelligence.

In terms of application, MI theory resonates with people, particularly practitioners, as an appropriate representation of intelligence, and a ready way to capture individuals' differences and strengths. Therefore, it has proved a positive and useful framework for organizing school changes, as described earlier. However, MI theory is still simply a theory of intelligence, with few explicit educational implications. As such, MI theory often functions as a Rorschach test: individuals interpret in different ways, and perhaps even try to implement it in ways that are self-contradictory (Krechevsky, Gardner, & Hoerr, 1995).

"There are many more theories that are propounded than have influence; and there are many more theories that have influence than theories that can push practice in a positive direction" (Gardner, 1994, p. 5) Our view is that MI theory has proved to be a catalyst in schools across the country because it allows individuals to look more carefully at children in a nonthreatening way, to examine their own assumptions about students' potential and achievement, to consider a variety of teaching approaches, and to try out alternative forms of assessment. In short, MI theory has been central to many individuals and schools that are initiating a fundamental kind of self-transformation necessary if schooling is to improve significantly (Gardner, 1994).

Conclusion

In this chapter we have presented an overview of several theories of intelligence and intellectual development. Rather than present a comprehensive review of past and current theories, we chose to present an overview of the landscape of the field of intelligence over the past century. Therefore, we emphasized those perspectives most representative of the state of the intelligence field and of its major shifts.

We began our discussion with the psychometric perspective, as the first and most influential scientific theory of intelligence in the field and in society. We critiqued the psychometric view's hold on the field of intelligence, given its roots in an era of biological determinism, with negative consequences still apparent in today's schools. Piaget's theory represents the first distinctive move away

from the psychometric tradition, with its emphases on universal cognitive structures and representation of intelligence from a qualitative, developmental lens. In contrast to psychometric psychology and Piaget's theory, information-processing approaches of the 1960s and 1970s focus on the microprocesses involved in intelligent activities. Information-processing theorists utilize computer flowchart models in their effort to illustrate the active processes that come to the fore in intelligent behavior. Such models give rise to a major critique of information processing because they are vulnerable to change with each new conceptualization of computing.

Although information-processing models were a distinct reaction to identified lackings in Piagetian theory, neo-Piagetians maintain central aspects of Piaget's theory. While preserving the general developmental, stagelike approach to intellectual development, this group of researchers also modify the theory, in part given new understandings of children's abilities. Neo-Piagetians emphasize the process of change, domain knowledge, and the environmental impact on children's development.

Finally, we described three recent integrative theories of intelligence: Sternberg's triarchic theory, Ceci's bioecological approach, and Gardner's theory of multiple intelligences. While maintaining different emphases, each of these theories goes beyond previous approaches by drawing on a wide range of sources to develop and test theories of intelligence that more adequately represent the intellect's complexity and workings in the real world. By providing a global view of human intelligence on the one hand and detailed conceptualizations underlying mechanisms on the other, these more recent theories enable a better, comprehensive view of human intelligence from both macro- and microperspectives. Moreover, recent theories are more integrated, or synthesizing, going beyond narrow disciplinary confines and drawing on fields such as anthropology, neurology, education, and cross-cultural studies.

Contemporary theories of intelligence are more relevant to the real world. More theorists and practitioners see intelligence—and its description—as grounded in the environment, and that it must be assessed in real-world contexts. The purpose of a theory of intelligence should be to help people adapt, craft, and construct their surrounding environment. Thus, these theories should be appropriate and necessarily complex representations. In that sense, our most recent theories of intelligence—and the trends they represent in the field—hold great promise.

References

Andrist, C., Kahana, M., Spry, K., Knevel, C., Persanyi, M., Evans, S., Luo, D., & Detterman, D. (1992). Individual differences in the biological correlates of intelligence: A selected overview. In D. Detterman (Ed.), *Current topics in human intelligence: Vol 2. Is mind modular or unitary?* (pp. 1–59). Norwood, NJ: Ablex.

Binet, A., & Simon, T. (1916). *The development of intelligence in children (the Binet-Simon Scale)* (E. S. Kite, Trans.). Baltimore, MD: Williams & Wilkins.

Bornstein, M. H., & Sigman, M. D. (1986). Continuity in mental development from infancy. *Child Development, 57,* 251–274.

Bredekamp, S. (Ed.). (1987). *Developmentally appropriate practice in early childhood programs serving children from birth through age 8* (expanded edition). Washington, DC: National Association for the Education of Young Children.

Carroll, J. (1982). The measurement of intelligence. In R. Sternberg (Ed.), *Handbook of human intelligence* (pp. 29–120). Cambridge, England: Cambridge University Press.

Carroll, J. (1993). *Human cognitive abilities: A survey of factor-analytic studies.* Cambridge, England: Cambridge University Press.

Case, R. (1985). *Intellectual development: Birth to adulthood.* New York: Academic Press.

Case, R. (1986). The new stage theories in intellectual development: Why we need them, what they assert. In M. Perlmutter (Ed.), *Minnesota symposia on child psychology: Vol. 19. Perspective on intellectual development.* Hillsdale, NJ: Erlbaum.

Ceci, S. (1990). *On intelligence . . . More or less.* Englewood Cliffs, NJ: Prentice-Hall.

Ceci, S. J., & Liker, J. (1986). A day at the races: A study of IQ, expertise, and cognitive complexity. *Journal of Experimental Psychology: General, 115,* 255–266.

Chen, J., Feldman, D., Gardner, H., Krechevsky, M., & Viens, J. (in press). *Building on children's strengths: The experience of Project Spectrum.* New York: Teachers College Press.

DeVries, R., & Kohlberg, L. (1987). *Constructivist early education: Overview and comparison with other programs.* Washington, DC: National Association for Education of Young Children.

Duckworth, E. (1972). The having of wonderful ideas. *Harvard Educational Review, 42,* 217–231.

FairTest. (1993). *Standardized tests and our children: A guide to testing reform.* Cambridge, MA: Author.

Feldman, D. H. (1974). Universal to unique: A developmental view of creativity and education. In S. Rosner & L. Abt (Eds.), *Essays in creativity* (pp. 4–16). Croton-on-Hudson, NY: North River Press.

Feldman, D. H. (1986). How development works. In I. Levin (Ed.), *Stage and structure: Reopening the debate* (pp. 284–306). Norwood, NJ: Ablex.

Feldman, D. H. (1993). *Beyond universals in cognitive development.* Norwood, NJ: Ablex.

Feldman, D. H., with Goldsmith, L. (1986). *Nature's gambit: Child prodigies and the development of human potential.* New York: Basic Books.

Findlay, W. G., & Bryan, M. M. (1975). *The pros and cons of ability grouping.* Bloomington, IN: Phi Delta Kappa.

Flavell, J. H., Miller, P. H., & Miller, S. A. (1993). *Cognitive development* (3rd ed.). Englewood Cliffs, NJ: Prentice-Hall.

Fraser, S. (Ed.). (1995). *The bell curve wars: Race, intelligence and the future of America.* New York: Basic Books.

Galton, F. (1869). *Hereditary genius.* London: Macmillan.

Galton, F. (1973a). *Inquiries into human faculty and its development.* New York: AMS Press.

Galton, F. (1973b). *Natural inheritance.* New York: AMS Press.

Gardner, H. (1986). The waning of intelligence tests. In R. Sternberg & D. Detterman (Eds.), *What is intelligence?* (pp. 73–76). Hillsdale, NJ: Erlbaum.

Gardner, H. (1987a). Beyond the IQ: Education and human development. *Harvard Educational Review, 57,* 187–193.

Gardner, H. (1987b). The theory of multiple intelligences. *Annals of Dyslexia, 37,* 19–35.

Gardner, H. (1993a). *Frames of mind: The theory of multiple intelligences.* New York: Basic Books.

Gardner, H. (Ed.). (1993b). *Multiple intelligences: The theory in practice.* New York: Basic Books.

Gardner, H. (1994). Intelligences in theory and practice: A response to Elliot W. Eisner, Robert J. Sternberg, and Henry M. Levin. *Teachers College Record, 95*(4), 576–583.

Gardner, H. (1995a). Cracking open the IQ box. In S. Fraser (Ed.), *The bell curve wars* (pp. 23–35). New York: Basic Books.

Gardner, H. (1995b). Reflections on multiple intelligences: Myths and messages. *Phi Delta Kappan, 11,* 200–209.

Gardner, H., & Hatch, T. (1989). Multiple intelligences goes to school. *Educational Researcher, 18,* 4–7.

Gardner, H., Kornhaber, M., & Wake, W. (1996). *Intelligence: Multiple perspectives.* Fort Worth, TX: Harcourt Brace.

Gelman, R. (1972). Logical capacity of very young children: Number invariance rules. *Child Development, 43,* 75–90.

Gelman, R., & Baillargeon, R. (1983). A review of some Piagetian concepts. In J. H. Flavell & E. M. Markman (Eds.), *Handbook of child psychology: Volume 3. Cognitive development* (4th ed., pp. 167–230). New York: Wiley.

Ginsburg, H. (1981). Piaget and education: The contributions and limits of genetic epistemology. In I. E. Sigel, D. M. Brodzinsky, & R. M. Golinkoff (Eds.), *New directions in Piagetian theory and practice* (pp. 315–332). Hillsdale, NJ: Erlbaum.

Ginsburg, H., & Opper, S. (1979). *Piaget's theory of intellectual development* (2nd ed.). Englewood Cliffs, NJ: Prentice-Hall.

Gould, S. J. (1981). *The mismeasure of man.* New York: Norton.

Gray, J., & Viens, J. (1994). The theory of multiple intelligences: Understanding cognitive diversity in school. *National Forum, LXXIV*(1), 22–25.

Guilford, J. P. (1950). Creativity. *American Psychologist, 5,* 444–454.

Guilford, J. P. (1967). *The nature of human intelligence.* New York: McGraw-Hill.

Herrnstein, R. J., & Murray, C. (1994). *The bell curve: Intelligence and class structure in American life.* New York: Free Press.

Hoerr, T. (1994, January). The theory of multiple intelligences (MI) at New City School. Unpublished manuscript.

Horn, J. (1986). Some thoughts about intelligence. In R. Sternberg & D. Detterman (Eds.), *What is intelligence?* (pp. 91–96). Norwood, NJ: Ablex.

Jensen, A. R. (1982). Reaction time and psychometric *g.* In H. J. Eysenck (Ed.), *A model for intelligence.* New York: Springer-Verlag.

Klahr, D., & Wallace, J. G. (1976). *Cognitive development: An information-processing view.* Hillsdale, NJ: Erlbaum.

Kornhaber, M., & Gardner, H. (1991). Critical thinking across multiple intelligences. In S. Maclure & P. Davies (Eds.), *Learning to think, thinking to learn.* Oxford: Pergamon Press.

Kornhaber, M., & Krechevsky, M. (1995). Expanding definitions of learning and teaching: Notes from the MI underground. In P. Cookson & B. Schneider (Eds.), *Transforming schools* (pp. 181–208). New York: Garland.

Krechevsky, M. (1991). Project Spectrum: An innovative assessment alternative. *Educational Leadership, 48*(5), 43–49.

Krechevsky, M., & Gardner, H. (1990). The emergence and nurturance of multiple intelligences: The Project Spectrum approach. In M. J. A. Howe (Ed.), *Encouraging the development of exceptional skills and talents* (pp. 222–245). Leicester, England: British Psychological Society.

Krechevsky, M., Gardner, H., & Hoerr, T. (1995). Complementary energies: Implementing MI theory from the laboratory and from the field. In J. Oakes & K. H. Quartz (Eds.), *Creating new educational communities: Schools and classrooms where all children can be smart* (94th Yearbook of the National Society for the Study of Education, Part 1). Chicago: University of Chicago Press.

Labinowicz, E. (1980). *The Piaget primer: Thinking, learning, teaching.* Reading, MA: Addison-Wesley Publishing Co.

Lempers, J. D., Flavell, E. R., & Flavell, J. H. (1977). The development in very young children of tacit knowledge concerning visual perception. *Journal of Genetic Psychology, 95,* 3–53.

Martin, A., & Weingartner, H. (1992). Modules, domains, and frames: Towards a neuropsychology of intelligence. In D. Detterman (Ed.), *Current topics in human intelligence: Is mind modular or unitary?* (pp. 117–139). Norwood, NJ: Ablex.

Mathews, G., & Dorn, L. (1989). IQ and choice reaction time: An information processing analysis. *Intelligence, 13*(4), 299–317.

Oakes, J. (1985). *Keeping track: How school structures inequality.* New Haven, CT: Yale University Press.

Piaget, J. (1970). Piaget's theory. In P. H. Mussen (Ed.), *Carmichael's manual of child psychology* (Vol. 1, 3rd ed., pp. 703–732). New York: Wiley.

Piaget, J. (1972). Some aspects of operations. In M. W. Piers (Ed.), *Play and development* (pp. 15–27). New York: Norton.

Pitcher, E. G., Feinburg, S. G., & Alexander, D. A. (1989). Helping young children learn (5th ed.). Columbus, OH: Charles E. Merrill.

Pollack, R. H., & Brenner, M. W. (Eds.). (1969). *The experimental psychology of Alfred Binet: Selected papers.* New York: Springer.

Sattler, J. M. (1990). *Assessment of children* (3rd ed.). San Diego: Sattler.

Shantz, C. U. (1975). *The development of social cognition.* Chicago: University of Chicago Press.

Siegler, R. S. (1978). The origins of scientific reasoning. In R. S. Siegler (Ed.), *Children's thinking: What develops?* (pp. 109–150). Hillsdale, NJ: Erlbaum.

Siegler, R. S. (1983). Information processing approaches to cognitive development. In P. H. Mussen (Ed.), *Handbook of child psychology: Vol. 1. History, theory, and methods.* New York: Wiley.

Siegler, R. S., & Richards, D. D. (1982). The development of intelligence. In R. J. Sternberg (Ed.), *Handbook of human intelligence* (pp. 897–971). New York: Cambridge University Press.

Slavin, R., Karweit, N. L., & Madden, N. A. (Eds.). (1989). *Effective programs for students at risk.* Boston: Allyn & Bacon.

Snyderman, M., & Rothman, S. (1988). *The IQ controversy.* New Brunswick, NJ: Transaction.

Spearman, C. (1927). *The abilities of man.* New York: Macmillan.

Sternberg, R. J. (1977). *Intelligence, information processing, and analogical reasoning: The componential analysis of human abilities.* Hillsdale, NJ: Erlbaum.

Sternberg, R. J. (1983). Components of human intelligence. *Cognition, 15,* 1–48

Sternberg, R. J. (1985). Cognitive approaches to intelligence. In B. B. Wolman (Ed.), *Handbook of intelligence: Theories, measurements, and application* (pp. 59–118). New York: Wiley.

Sternberg, R. J. (1988) *The triarchic mind: A new theory of human intelligence.* New York: Viking Press.

Sternberg, R. J. (1995). For whom the bell curve tolls? A review of the bell curve. *Psychological Science, 6,* 257–261.

Thurstone, L. L. (1938). *Primary mental abilities.* Chicago: University of Chicago Press.

Varon, E. J. (1936). Alfred Binet's concept of intelligence. *Psychological Review, 43,* 32–58.

Vernon, P. E. (1971). *The structure of human abilities.* London: Methuen.

Vygotsky, L. S. (1978). *Mind in society: The development of higher psychological processes.* Cambridge, MA: Harvard University Press.

Walters, J., & Gardner, H. (1985). The development and education of intelligences. In F. Link (Ed.), *Essays on the intellect* (pp. 1–21). Washington, DC: Curriculum Development Associates.

CHAPTER 6

The Promise of Early Intervention to Enhance the Life Outcomes of Children in Poverty

EDWARD ZIGLER
Yale University

Programs to improve school performance of young children raised in poverty fill a relatively recent page in the history of education in the United States. Early childhood intervention did not begin to form a circumscribed discipline until after the birth of the antipoverty program, Head Start, in the mid-1960s. The first years of the emerging field were characterized by overoptimism, theoretical excesses, and heated controversy within the behavioral sciences. The most contentious issue was whether intervention programs could make poor children smarter. It appeared that they could, but only temporarily. The disappointment over their perceived failure was tempered by later reports of long-term benefits in other behavioral areas. Today there is a consensus among developmental scientists and teaching professionals that quality preschool education programs are an effective way to prepare impoverished children for school. Programs that offer more expansive services might also enable them to be more competent in later life pursuits.

Political support for early intervention has undergone its own ebb and flow somewhat independent of the opinions formed in the scientific community. Preschool programs were first championed primarily by liberal policymakers. Head Start, for example, was initiated under President Lyndon Johnson's War on Poverty—an effort to eradicate socioeconomic class differences and move the nation toward a "Great Society." Interest in preschool programs waned under the more conservative administration of Ronald Reagan, although he did spare Head Start the budget cuts he imposed on most social welfare programs. In the mid-1980s, the traditionally conservative business sector embraced preschool training as a first step in enhancing the education—and educability—of the future labor force. This tack encouraged Republican President George Bush to promote the largest expansion in Head Start's history and governors across the nation to support public prekindergartens. By the 1992 national elections, early intervention was enjoying strong bipartisan support.

The advancement of the preschool movement seemed assured with the election of the first Democratic president in more than a decade, Bill Clinton. He considered preschool services to be an investment in the future social and economic health of the nation and presented plans to hasten Head Start's expansion. Soon, however, lawmakers' approval of early childhood programs in general and Head Start in particular came to a near halt. Growth of the federal Head Start effort was slowed not only by budgetary constraints but also by sudden attention to lapses in program quality and supportive research. In a more general sense, there was a growing conservative backlash against government sponsorship of social programming. The Republican sweep of Congress and state governorships in 1994 promised a reduction in "big government," giving families more responsibility for their economic plight and the care and education of their children. Once again, advocates of preschool services for at-risk children were put on the defensive.

How can the concept of early intervention have swung so rapidly between opinions of universal support and popular skepticism? And how can a practice so widely endorsed within the behavioral science and education fields be assailed by once-supportive policymakers? One reason is that the potential benefits of intervention are documented by theory and scattered evidence rather than by cohesive research. Another is that expectations of preschool programs continue to be unrealistically high, assuring their falling short. Finally, political ideologies have swayed judgments of the usefulness of intervention for young children raised in poverty.

This chapter examines the hopes placed in early intervention programs over the years and the evidence regarding their power to enhance two areas of current interest to policymakers: school performance and prosocial behavior. The purpose is to define the contributions such programs can and cannot make toward solving social problems, to give them an objective rather than a political justification, and to suggest how they can be strengthened to have a greater impact on the developmental outcomes of at-risk children.

Factors That Shaped the Expectations Placed on Early Intervention

Over the past three decades, several academic and popular fads have influenced the field of early intervention and the degree of support accorded it. These perspectives have changed with the spirit of the times and with added knowledge, but remnants of them still color judgments of current programs. In very general terms, the intervention efforts of the 1960s were based on a deficit model to explain the learning problems of poor children. There was a preoccupation with intelligence, to the exclusion of other aspects of human development. The times were also characterized by a naive belief in the malleability of intelligence, a belief that IQ scores could be raised easily and quickly through environmental intervention. The concept of critical periods of development was in vogue, and the preschool years were seen as the most critical—as the time when the entire course of the child's development could be shaped by the proper experiences. By examining these points of view, we can understand how they affected and still affect perceptions of the efficacy of early intervention. The discussion will center on the Head Start program because it is the nation's largest and oldest continuing intervention effort. As such, the political and scientific debates surrounding it are commonly generalized to all other preschool programs.

Deficit Model

In the mid-1960s, President Lyndon Johnson initiated a massive attempt to eradicate social class inequities in the United States. One facet of this "War on Poverty" was the preschool intervention program, mounted in the hope of enabling young children reared in poverty to do better in school. Compared to children of middle socioeconomic status (SES), lower SES children generally were poorer students and achieved lower scores on IQ tests. A program of early environmental enrichment was envisioned as a way to give lower SES children the "head start" they needed to perform on a par with their wealthier peers. The hope was that class differences in performance would be eliminated by the time of school entry. Carrying this goal a step further, many expected that the brief preschool experience would be so potent a counteraction to the deficits in poor children's lives that they would continue to do well in school and eventually secure good jobs, ending the cycle of welfare and poverty.

The deficit model embodied some paternalistic ideas that have had a long life in civilized societies. The notion of "social" or "cultural" deprivation was a blatant assumption that the culture of the lower classes was inferior to that of the middle class. Because the child-rearing practices of middle-class parents apparently worked, intervention programs were intended to provide poor children with the rich experiences supposedly lacking in their rearing environments.

The planners of Head Start were the first to design a program that avoided the deficit model, but they did so partly out of necessity. As a Community Action Program, funded by the 1964 Economic Opportunity Act, Head Start was mandated to allow "maximum feasible participation" of the economically disadvantaged population it was designed to serve. One way Head Start's planners accomplished this was by emphasizing parental involvement. Not only were parents to participate in the daily activities of the program, but they were also given real decision-making power in all planning and administrative aspects of their local centers. This was a major break from past practices in which educated and paid professionals dictated the operation of poverty programs to passive recipients. Today, it is widely recognized that parents, regardless of their material wealth, are the primary educators and socializers of their children. Parental involvement is thus imperative to the success of early intervention and later education.

The inferiority-superiority tenet of the deficit model has now generally been disregarded in favor of approaches emphasizing differences among groups rather than deficiencies. Ethnic pride and the import accorded cultural diversity are reflections of more recent attitudes that place value on social and individual differences. In education

programs, the goal is no longer to inculcate middle-class values but to build on the unique strengths that each child brings to the classroom. Yet despite this more equalitarian view, preschool programs are still judged by how well graduates fare according to middle-class norms. Indeed, the "failure" of preschool education to turn poor children into middle-class ones has premised a recent resurrection of the deficit model (Herrnstein & Murray, 1994).

Focus on Raising Intelligence

During the formative years of early intervention programs, there was an infatuation with cognitive development among behavioral scientists, who spread their excitement among the public. American psychologists, long bogged down in studies of observable behavior and the role of conditioning and external reinforcements in learning, had suddenly discovered the sizable body of work on cognition by prominent European scholars, particularly Jean Piaget. They became so captivated with his classic efforts in charting the sequence of cognitive development that they began to focus on intelligence to the exclusion of other human behaviors. And not only was IQ the favored topic of interest, but the expectation formed that the environment had enormous power to promote cognitive growth. This was a major break from earlier views that physical and cognitive development were predetermined processes governed by hereditary and maturational factors. Instead of building new theories on the wisdom of old ones, scientists quickly abandoned predeterminism in favor of environmentalism, and development came to be viewed as wide open to the manipulation of experts.

The excitement with raising intelligence was fed by the writings of some respected theorists whose ideas were exactly what newly "enlightened" scientists wanted to hear. For example, Hunt (1961) argued against the notion of genetically fixed intelligence by taking the opposite stance—that intelligence is essentially a product of the environment. He theorized that it is possible to promote a faster rate of intellectual development and higher level of adult intelligence by "governing the encounters that children have with their environments, especially during the early years of their development" (p. 363). Hunt (1971) continued into the 1970s to argue that IQ changes of 50 to 70 points could be obtained through appropriate intervention. The notion of dramatically raising intelligence was augmented by another concept popular at the time—that of critical or "magical" periods in development. The preschool years came to be viewed as the most formative stage in the life cycle, the time when intervention would have the most potent impact.

The mass media were eagerly responsive to the idea of easy IQ changes through environmental manipulations. Reporters were quick to publicize the early and often tentative results of various enrichment programs. For example, Deutsch and Deutsch's (1963) preliminary report of a 10-point IQ increase after their ten-month program was published in New York newspapers under the headline, "Program Raises Children's IQ Scores a Point a Month." Books and articles in the popular press poured forth informing parents how to give their children superior minds and how to teach them to read at the age of 2. Crib mobiles and "educational" toys flooded the market.

Given that much of the social science community had embraced both a simplistic environmentalism and the idea of magical periods, it is not surprising that early research focused almost exclusively on how much intervention programs could raise children's intelligence and achievement test scores. Numerous studies showed that children made immediate IQ increases averaging about 10 points after most programs (Datta, 1979). The excitement diminished after the release of a study on Head Start by the Westinghouse Learning Corporation (Cicirelli, 1969). The findings, which showed that the achievement gains made in pre-

school purportedly faded away in the early grades of school, called into question the efficacy of early intervention.

Experts in statistics and evaluation eventually discredited the Westinghouse report after uncovering problems with sampling procedures, data analysis, and appropriateness of the outcome measures (for example, Campbell & Erlebacher, 1970; Smith & Bissel, 1970). Nonetheless, subsequent studies of Head Start and almost every other early intervention program reached the same conclusion: preschool graduates generally do not continue to do better on cognitive tests or school quizzes. These reports dashed hopes that brief preschool experiences could guarantee higher IQs or academic success for poor children.

As will be discussed in the next section, other worthwhile benefits of early intervention have since been revealed. Nonetheless, preschool programs continue to be judged largely on the basis of sustained increases in IQ (Herrnstein & Murray, 1994). The fact is that with very few exceptions (Garber, 1988; Ramey & Campbell, 1991), intervention programs do not permanently boost measured intelligence. The initial gains following intervention have been traced to such factors as better familiarity with the test content, improved motivation, and comfort and self-confidence in the testing situation (Seitz, Abelson, Levine, & Zigler, 1975; Zigler, Abelson, Trickett, & Seitz, 1982; Zigler & Butterfield, 1968). These changes are not as exciting as the possibility of turning children into geniuses, but they have a bearing on school performance and are certainly worthwhile outcomes.

The difficulty of effecting true increases in IQ has been noted by several scholars (for example, Spitz, 1986; Zigler, 1988). Looking at why various programs have failed at raising IQ scores but have succeeded on other measures tells us much about the degree of malleability of different human systems. The developing child is a complex combination of socioemotional, physical, and cognitive subsystems, each differentially sensitive to environmental input. The brain appears to be the most buffered against external events and stressors, making intelligence a highly stable trait. This does not mean that it is predetermined, but scholars now suggest that the practical reaction range for IQ is about 25 points; this is a defensible expectation of what intervention can in fact accomplish (see Zigler & Seitz, 1982). The physical and socioemotional aspects of development are more strongly controlled by the environment and therefore more effectively targeted by intervention. There is no doubt that the child who enjoys good health and has the motivation and self-confidence to learn will do better in school regardless of whether his or her IQ is measurably higher.

Judging early intervention programs by the sole criteria of elevated IQ scores not only short-changes the scope of their potential impact but also gives the trait of intelligence unwarranted import. IQ tests were designed to predict school performance, and this they do quite well. IQ scores are much less robust predictions of success outside of school, however, and the school years are a relatively short space in a person's life span. Behaving competently in social and employment settings is far more important to life success than doing well on an IQ test. Expecting intervention to raise IQs is therefore a narrow, relatively insignificant goal. Broader and richer outcomes are desired and, as we will discuss next, may in fact be effected by quality intervention.

What Can Early Intervention Accomplish?

Hopes that preschool enrichment can make children smarter have never been extinguished but have been joined by further promises. Recent popular and political support of early intervention has assumed that it will improve high school graduation rates, stop teenage pregnancy and juvenile delinquency, end welfare usage, and save a great deal of taxpayers' money. There is only a smattering of evidence that these outcomes might be possible, so such conclusions are vastly premature. They also overshadow the less idolized but hardly trivial benefits of intervention that have been substantiated by over thirty years of research in the field. Positive effects in the areas of academic and prosocial behavior are among them.

School Adjustment

In a welcome break from the narrow focus on IQ that characterized early research, the Consortium for Longitudinal Studies (1983) brought to light some of the noncognitive benefits of early intervention. The Consortium consisted of researchers who had evaluated eleven preschool programs during the 1960s and early 1970s. The researchers located original program participants and collected a uniform set of information about their current status. The findings confirmed that children who attend quality preschool programs do gain an initial boost in IQ and achievement scores that lasts for some years but eventually fades. However, lasting effects were found in other areas: participants were less likely to be assigned to special education classes and were somewhat less likely to be held back a grade in school. The rigor of the Consortium methodology, and the findings of benefits that persisted until many children had reached 12 or more years of age, did much to restore public and scientific faith in the value of early intervention.

More recent studies and research reviews have yielded similarly encouraging results. Among the most comprehensive analyses of the literature are reviews by Haskins (1989) and Woodhead (1988). Both were careful to separate experimental preschools (typically small and university based; carefully designed, implemented, and evaluated; and of high quality) from Head Start (which serves some

750,000 children and families each year in programs across the nation that range from excellent to poor quality). The reviewers noted that Head Start and the smaller programs produced immediate gains in intelligence and achievement that generally dissipated within a few years. Haskins (1989) concluded that after that, there was very strong evidence that the models improved school performance (including less grade retention and special education class placement) but that the evidence for Head Start was only modest. Life success indices (avoidance of delinquency, teenage pregnancy, and welfare, for example) produced modest evidence for the models but "virtually no evidence for Head Start" (p. 278). This does not mean that Head Start has no such benefits but that little or no data have been collected about them (Zigler & Styfco, 1994). On the other hand, the Head Start synthesis (McKey et al., 1985) and other studies have shown that Head Start does have positive effects on children's health (Hale, Seitz, & Zigler, 1990; Haskins, 1989; Zigler, Piotrkowski, & Collins, 1994), their families (see Zigler & Styfco, 1993b), and the communities where they live (Kirschner Associates, 1970)—factors not studied for the experimental programs.

In sum, the sizable body of research on varying intervention programs tentatively shows enduring effects on school adjustment and other aspects of social competence (McCall, 1993). Findings concerning immediate program effects are much more definite: when children leave preschool they have better IQ test scores and school readiness skills. In other words, they are better prepared for school. In lamenting the loss of initial cognitive benefits, many critics have overlooked the contribution of early intervention toward realizing the first national education goal for the year 2000— that all children will enter school ready to learn.

There are several reasons that children leave preschool testing well and then may lose this advantage. One is that curricula and teaching practices in elementary schools may not continue the momentum toward success or build on the gains made in preschool. Another explanation is that the paper-and-pencil, standardized group achievement tests used in many studies are inappropriate for children in the early primary grades (for example, Meisels, 1992). This argument supports Barnett's (1992) position that the achievement gains made in preschool probably do not fade out at all. He suggests that their apparent loss is an artifact of measurement, statistical analysis, and sampling procedures. For example, poor achievers in both preschool graduate and comparison groups could be retained in grade and thus dropped from the evaluation, thereby minimizing the differences among the remaining students. A final reason for fade-out is that a year or two of preschool is simply not enough to counteract the deleterious effects of prior and continuing poverty. Whatever the cause, the fact is that children who attend quality preschools are ready to learn when they graduate, so intervention has accomplished its mission. If the advantage later fades, the fault lies beyond the preschool.

Prosocial Behavior

The primary goal of preschool education is to give children the background they need to succeed when they enter elementary school. Varying curricula, teaching philosophies, and learning practices are the defining features of most preschool programs. Some, however, offer more than basic education. Head Start, for example, has always taken a "whole child" approach to school readiness, with program components devoted to physical and mental health, parental involvement, and family support. Broader programs could logically be expected to have broader benefits than those confined to academics (Zigler & Styfco, 1994). Because intervention programs were created to affect school performance, however, few researchers have looked for outcomes beyond the realm of school. Those who have done so have discovered some surprising and welcome benefits, particularly in the area of delinquency—a behavior that is negatively correlated with success in school. (For reviews of the literature on early intervention and criminality, see Yoshikawa, 1994; Zigler, Taussig, & Black, 1992.)

The most frequently cited study of the effects of early intervention on delinquency is that of the Perry Preschool (Schweinhart, Barnes, & Weikart, 1993). This program was a high-quality preschool that most of the fifty-eight participants attended for two years. The well-trained teachers also conducted weekly home visits to teach the children's mothers to reinforce the curriculum at home. The program graduates as a group did better in school and beyond than did controls. They were retained in grade less often, received fewer special education services, were more likely to graduate from high school, and had higher employment rates and lower welfare usage. They were also less likely to be chronic troublemakers. Although over 60% of the program men had been arrested between one and four times, only 12% of them were arrested more times than that. Nearly 50% of the men in the control group had five or more arrests.

These positive program effects saved a great deal of taxpayer money. An economist on the research team, W. Steven Barnett (1993), estimated that every dollar spent on the preschool saved $7.16 in fewer special school services, less welfare use, higher employment, and of course, reduced crime. In fact, over 90% of the savings were in this area. Most of these benefits were projected savings to crime victims who did not become victims because the crime was not committed.

Although no other study has followed preschool graduates for such a long time and for so many possible outcomes, research on several other programs has produced results suggestive of reduced delinquency. One such effort was the Family De-

velopment Research Program at Syracuse University (Lally, Mangione, & Honig, 1988). The program began with young, poor single mothers who were in their last trimester of pregnancy. Most had not graduated from high school and many had histories of arrests or court appearances. Paraprofessionals worked with the families once a week to encourage good mother-child relationships and to help them access needed support services. The children received 4½ years of quality child care at the Syracuse Children's Center, beginning when they were 6 months old. Through the combination of attention to parent and child, the researchers hoped to change the permanent environment of the home and to enable parents to support their child's development.

That appears to have happened. Although the children did not do much better in school than controls, they were less likely to be seen at the county probation department. By the age of 13 to 16, only 6% of the children had been processed as probation cases, compared with 22% of the controls. Court and penal costs for each child in the program group averaged $186. These costs were ten times as much for each child in the control sample.

The Yale Child Welfare Research Program offered a program more for parents than for children (Provence & Naylor, 1983). Participants were young mothers raising children in high-risk environments. Services began prenatally and lasted until the children were 2½ years old. The services included parenting education and practical supports, such as help in accessing housing and food programs. Professionals also guided the mothers in making decisions about future education, career, and family goals. The children received pediatric services, and most attended child care which was an optional service made available to their parents. At the ten-year follow-up (Seitz, Rosenbaum, & Apfel, 1985), the intervention mothers had obtained more education than controls and had fewer children. Almost all of the program families were self-supporting by this time. Although the researchers did not assess delinquent behavior, teacher ratings showed that control boys were more likely to skip school and to show aggressive, acting-out, predelinquent behavior. The program boys required fewer remedial and supportive services, including court hearings, at an average savings of over $1,100 each academic year.

In the Houston Parent-Child Development Program (Johnson, 1989), paraprofessionals conducted home visits and weekend workshops with Mexican American families to teach them child management techniques and how to create a healthy home environment. The parents were involved for two years, while the children attended one year of nursery school. When they were in grade school, program children showed less aggression and fighting and were more considerate than controls. The differences in aggression disappeared seven to fifteen years after the program, but the home environment remained more supportive for the program children. A supportive home can be an important mediator in the prevention of delinquency.

Several other family support programs appear to have affected one or more of the risk factors associated with delinquency among children of young, poor mothers. The most striking result of the Nurse Home-Visitation Program at the University of Rochester (Olds, 1988) was a reduction in child abuse and neglect. Some researchers have linked severe abuse in childhood to delinquency and later criminality. The Gutelius Child Health Supervision study (Gutelius, Kirsch, MacDonald, Brooks, & McErlean, 1977) also provided support services to poor, single teenage mothers. By the time their children were 5 or 6 years old, they showed fewer behavior problems than controls. Early misconduct is a strong precursor of chronic delinquency (Loeber, 1991). Again, intensive parent education coupled with other family supports

seem to have lowered the risks in these children's environments.

How can programs designed to help children succeed in school or strengthen their families have such an effect on delinquent or predelinquent behaviors? The field is indebted to Hirokazu Yoshikawa (1994), who wrote a brilliant review of the risk factors in chronic delinquency. He grouped the risks into those associated with the child and those occurring within the child's family. Child correlates of delinquency include gender, low intelligence, poor school achievement, aggressiveness, and poor intersocial skills. Family correlates involve large family size, low socioeconomic status, low educational attainment among parents, poor parenting skills, and criminality in other household members. A third source of risks that can be added to Yoshikawa's analysis involves community factors, including poor schools, poor housing, lack of employment opportunities, and a lack of positive role models. These three types of causative agents obviously occur in combination to some extent. A poor child with a low IQ who attends a substandard school is likely to do poorly academically; uneducated parents with many children may not be able to find decent housing in an area with good schools; and so forth. The more risk factors that affect a child, the more likely she or he is to engage in delinquent behavior.

Yoshikawa presented a model that encompasses the multiple risk factors and described two pathways through which intervention might mediate their effects on delinquency. Programs aimed at reducing a child's risk factors might work to enhance cognitive and social development and school achievement. Programs that focus on family risks might attempt to improve parenting skills and socioeconomic status. Yoshikawa argued convincingly that interventions that take both pathways will be the most effective in preventing chronic delinquency and later adult criminality. Comprehensive, early childhood programs that provide preschool education as well as family support fill this bill. However, more research is needed to substantiate the link between early intervention and prosocial behavior. Until it is forthcoming, it seems reasonable to assume that children who begin school healthier, have the academic and social skills they need, have parents who are involved in their education, and have some of their families' needs met have gained some protection against the risks associated with later delinquency.

Perspectives on the Methods and Mission of Effective Intervention

The field of early childhood intervention has blossomed since the 1960s and has generated a wealth of knowledge and professional expertise. As will be discussed in turn, first it is now clear that programs must be comprehensive and of high quality to achieve desired ends. Second, because there are no magical periods in human development, programs must begin earlier and last longer than the year or two before a child who lives in poverty enters school. Third, programs that address the broad ecology in which the child develops will be the most effective. The final and perhaps the hardest lesson is not to expect miracles. Early intervention can help prepare children for school and enhance some aspects of their families' functioning, but it alone cannot end poverty and crime or guarantee successful schooling.

Comprehensive Programming

The literature on early intervention has generated some guiding principles that underlie the most salutary efforts (see National Head Start Association, 1990; Price, Cowen, Lorion, & Ramos–McKay, 1988; Schorr, 1988; Zigler & Berman, 1983; Zigler & Styfco, 1993a). One is that programs must be comprehensive in scope, attending to the many factors that underlie the complex phenomenon of school performance. All children need certain learning experiences to be ready for school, but poor children often have unmet health, nutrition, and social service needs as well. There is no question that children who are hungry, frequently ill, or have uncorrected vision or hearing problems will not be as good at learning as those who enjoy good health. And children who are homeless, witnesses or victims of abuse, or live in neighborhoods governed by gangs and guns will not be able to give their full attention to the teacher's lessons. The services poor children often need go beyond the traditional mission of the school, but their absence makes that mission unattainable.

Preschool programs have proliferated in recent years, but few of them provide comprehensive services. Of particular concern are the public prekindergartens implemented in many states after the adoption of the national education goals. In a 1989 survey by Mitchell, Seligson, and Marx, twenty-seven states funded preschool programs and twelve contributed to Head Start. Both types of effort typically serve 4-year-olds and, like Head Start, two-thirds of the state programs are for children deemed at-risk of having problems in elementary school. On the surface, the combined federal and state preschool developments suggest that universal enrollment will soon be a reality, and that the goal of having all children ready for school will indeed be achieved. However, not all of these programs provide the quality and quantity of services that are absolutely necessary to produce benefits.

Only half of the public prekindergartens are required to provide services that go beyond education (Mitchell et al., 1989). Few do so, and none approaches the level of services in Head Start (General Accounting Office, 1994). Further, the quality of the programs may not be sufficiently high to meet the needs of very young, at-risk children. For example, school districts in Texas with at least fifteen children who are 4 years old and poor, or with limited proficiency in English, must provide them with prekindergarten (Mitchell et al., 1989). Teacher/child ratios, however, are 1:22, over twice that recommended for preschool-age children and an untenable number for a group who may have some serious problems.

Group size is only one illustration of how public preschools are often designed in the mold of elementary schools. Many do not offer the developmentally appropriate, individualized instruction needed by very young children. There is fear among early childhood professionals that in public schools there will be a downward extension of the academic program from kindergarten and first grade to the preschool classrooms (see Bauch, 1988; Kagan & Zigler, 1987). Analysts worry that, "Without attention to the developmental nature of the programs offered, we do not believe they will work" (Farran, Silveri, & Culp, 1991, p. 71). Finally, parental involvement—particularly important in intervention with young children—is a practice that not all public schools have implemented or even fully accepted (Kagan, 1991).

Both the state and federal preschool efforts can be enhanced by ensuring that services for children are of sufficient quality to deliver the intended benefits. This point deserves emphasis because, in the recent Head Start expansion, efforts to serve more children proceeded more rapidly than efforts to serve them well. Years of inadequate funding, oversight, and training and technical assistance had left many Head Start centers struggling to provide adequate services, and some were unable to do so (Chafel, 1992; National Head Start Association, 1990). The direness of this situation cannot be overemphasized. The literature makes very clear that "only high quality programs consistently show success" (Weikart & Schweinhart, 1991, p. 58). Zigler testified before the U.S. Senate that "Head Start is effective only when quality is high. . . . Below a certain threshold of quality, the program is useless, a waste of money regardless of how many children

are enrolled" (U.S. Senate, 1990, p. 49). Quality improvement plans have now been drawn (Advisory Committee on Head Start Quality and Expansion, 1993). Their implementation may enable Head Start to become "a model of quality, a catalyst for change and a source of innovation" for the entire system of early childhood services (National Head Start Association, 1990, p. v).

State governments, too, would do well to take a closer look at their public prekindergartens to determine whether they have simply acted on the matter of school readiness or have acted wisely. Guidance is available from the Head Start Performance Standards, which are being revised at this writing, and from the accreditation criteria of the National Association for the Education of Young Children (Bredekamp, 1990). An emphasis on quality in preschool services is important not only to the children and families being served but also to the reputation of early intervention as an effective use of public funds.

Dovetailed Programming

The first major disappointment over Head Start came from the findings of the Westinghouse report that the academic gains children made in preschool appeared to be short-lived. Although many were quick to dismiss Head Start as a failure, advocates of early intervention suggested that the blame belonged to the elementary schools the children later attended. They were prepared for school when they arrived, but the education establishment failed to build on this advantage. Others argued that Head Start came too late— that by the time children began preschool their potential had already been dimmed by the harmful effects of poverty. Today, it is widely recognized that both sides were right. There are no magical periods in development. All stages of growth are important and require appropriate environmental nutrients.

The need for preventive intervention beginning very early in the child's life has now been firmly established. Recognizing that preventive services can be more effective, and more cost-effective, than remedial ones, Congress has expanded the number of Parent-Child Centers—Head Start's pioneer program for very young children and their families. An exciting new zero to three effort called Early Head Start has also been initiated with the Human Services Reauthorization Act of 1994. The Clinton administration followed the advice of the Carnegie Task Force on Meeting the Needs of Young Children, the Children's Defense Fund, and other advocacy and professional groups and convened a multidisciplinary committee to plan and implement this younger version of Head Start. Services for at-risk families will begin prenatally and will include nutrition, health care, parenting education, and family support. The rationale for the project is clear: waiting until a child is 3 or 4 years old is waiting too long. Children who are healthy, who have sound relationships with their primary caregivers, and who have received adequate nurturing and stimulation will have the socioemotional foundations needed for learning in preschool and beyond (Zero to Three, 1992).

For children who may still need services after infancy and preschool, the Head Start-Public School Early Childhood Transition Project (described by Kennedy, 1993) has been reauthorized by the 1994 act. The project follows Head Start graduates from kindergarten through third grade. Local Head Start and public school personnel work to introduce each child and family to the new school experience and to familiarize kindergarten teachers with the child's progress, program, and needs. Comprehensive services, parental involvement, and family support are continued for the next four years.

A small but convincing body of evidence supports the premise of the Transition Project—that longer, coordinated intervention produces longer-lasting gains. Results (reviewed by Zigler & Styfco, 1993b) of the Abecedarian Project, Success for All, the Chicago Child-Parent Centers, Follow Through, and Deutsch and Deutsch's early enrichment program confirm that the advantages derived from preschool can be sustained with dovetailed, school-age programming.

This research offers promise that the Transition Project will be effective in helping Head Start graduates be more competent students throughout school. If evaluation of the demonstration phase confirms this expectation, it will be compelling to move the project into the educational mainstream. At the Yale Bush Center, we have developed a plan to do so using current federal education expenditures (Zigler & Styfco, 1993a). A large part of the Department of Education's budget (over $7 billion annually) is spent on Title I of the Elementary and Secondary Education Act (ESEA) of 1965. Title I is a compensatory education program for economically and "educationally" deprived children in preschool through twelfth grade. Originally intended to enhance the educational services of impoverished school districts, the program now operates in the majority of the nation's schools—mostly as a pull-out program offering remedial instruction to children who have fallen behind the academic expectations of their grade level.

There has been little evaluation of Title I considering the size of the program, but what there is shows that most students do not exhibit a meaningful gain in achievement (see Arroyo & Zigler, 1993). The reasons for the lackluster results may be in the program's design: services are remedial rather than preventive and narrow instead of comprehensive; parental involvement is minimal; and health and family problems that can interfere with school performance are not addressed. Debate during reauthorization of the ESEA in 1994 focused on suggestions to revamp the program by training teachers and narrowing the target population (Commission on Chapter 1, 1992). Although such efforts may do some good, they do not bring the elements of effective intervention to Title I. To make a difference in the education of low-income children, we must put aside the ineffectual educational model of Title I and adopt on a large scale the proven model of comprehensive, family-focused services.

Although the Improving America's School Act of 1994 mandates that Title I do more to provide children with access to health and social services and to include their parents in the program, such stipulations have been poorly implemented in the past (Arroyo & Zigler, 1993). Our proposal is instead for Title I to follow Transition program plans and become the school-age version of Head Start. As Head Start eventually expands to serve all eligible children, Title I can continue their intervention in grammar school. Coordinated curricula and continued parental involvement and comprehensive services will then be firmly placed in schools that serve populations below the poverty line.

A national system of extended intervention, beginning with the zero to three program and followed by preschool Head Start and a Title I Transition, will do more than make a meaningful impact on the lives of at-risk children and their families. Together, the three programs will form a coherent federal policy to meet the needs of poor children beginning prenatally. Instead of funding a hodgepodge of programs with similar goals, tax dollars will be more efficiently spent on a system that can produce benefits greater than the sum of its parts.

Ecological Approach

Today, it is generally agreed that successful intervention programs target not only the child but also the family that rears the child. The seeds of this type of thinking can be traced to Head Start's commitment to parental involvement and family support. The need for these program components

was argued by one of Head Start's planners, Urie Bronfenbrenner, who at the time was conceptualizing his ecological approach to human development. Bronfenbrenner (1974, 1979) theorized that there is a complex interrelationship among children, their families, and their communities, so intervention must touch all of these systems to be effective.

The family systems approach provides a viable hypothesis to explain the long-term effects that have been found for early intervention. Several theorists (for example, Lally et al., 1988; Seitz, 1990; Zigler & Seitz, 1982) have advanced the view that persistent benefits cannot be due to a half-day program experienced by the child during one year of preschool, but rather are due to the parents. As a result of their involvement with the intervention, parents become more optimal socializers of the child throughout the rest of the day and hopefully throughout the child's course of development.

With families viewed as having the most important and lasting influence on the child, it is naturally important for them to be as strong and secure as possible. In perhaps the first effort to provide total family support, Head Start's Child and Family Resource Program made available a number of services for families with children ages 0 to 8. Each family could select those services (for example, health or child care) that could benefit them. The program has been partially revived as the Comprehensive Child Development Program for families and children from the prenatal period through age 5.

Thanks to the ecological model, we are now aware that the child's development is not only influenced by the family system but also by other systems far removed from the family's control. These include work, neighborhoods, the school, the media, health services, and child care. Thus, effective intervention must strive to address the entire ecology of the child to make it more conducive to human development. This is a formidable task, one that can be attempted only through strong collaborations between early childhood and other human services providers (Melaville with Blank, 1991).

The ecological model has clear implications that we not oversell what we can realistically accomplish with current early intervention programs. These programs simply cannot change enough of the ecology or the larger environment to make a real difference in the lives of children. The problems of many families will not be solved by early intervention efforts but only by changes in the basic features of the infrastructure of our society. No amount of counseling, early childhood curricula, or home visits will take the place of jobs that provide decent incomes, affordable housing, health care, good schools, or safe neighborhoods where children encounter positive role models. Quality early intervention can prepare children for school and help them meet social expectancies during the school years and perhaps beyond. But no program can enable children to develop optimally when their larger rearing environment is not conducive to optimal development.

References

Advisory Committee on Head Start Quality and Expansion. (1993). *Creating a 21st century Head Start.* Washington, DC: U.S. Department of Health and Human Services.

Arroyo, C. G., & Zigler, E. (1993). America's Title I/Chapter 1 programs: Why the promise has not been met. In E. Zigler & S. J. Styfco (Eds.), *Head Start and beyond: A national plan for extended childhood intervention* (pp. 73–95). New Haven, CT: Yale University Press.

Barnett, W. S. (1992). Benefits of compensatory preschool education. *Journal of Human Resources, 27,* 279–312.

Barnett, W. S. (1993). Benefit-cost analysis of preschool education: Findings from a 25-year follow-up. *American Journal of Orthopsychiatry, 63,* 500–508.

Bauch, J. P. (Ed.). (1988). *Early childhood education in the schools.* Washington, DC: National Education Association.

Bredekamp, S. (Ed.). (1990). *Accreditation criteria and procedures of the National Academy of Early Childhood Programs.* Washington, DC: National Association for the Education of Young Children.

Bronfenbrenner, U. (1974). Is early intervention effective? *Day Care and Early Education, 44,* 14–18.

Bronfenbrenner, U. (1979). *The ecology of human development.* Cambridge, MA: Harvard University Press.

Campbell, D. T., & Erlebacher, A. (1970). How regression artifacts in quasi-experimental evaluations can mistakenly make compensatory education look harmful. In J. Hellmuth (Ed.), *Compensatory education: A national debate* (Vol. 3, pp. 185–210). New York: Brunner/Mazel.

Chafel, J. A. (1992). Funding Head Start: What are the issues? *American Journal of Orthopsychiatry, 62,* 9–21.

Cicirelli, V. G. (1969). *The impact of Head Start: An evaluation of the effects of Head Start on children's cognitive and affective development.* Report presented to the Office of Economic Opportunity (Report No. PB 184 328), Westinghouse Learning Corporation. Washington, DC.

Commission on Chapter 1. (1992). *Making schools work for children in poverty.* Washington, DC: U.S. Department of Education.

Consortium for Longitudinal Studies. (1983). *As the twig is bent: Lasting effects of preschool programs.* Hillsdale, NJ: Erlbaum.

Datta, L. (1979). Another spring and other hopes: Some findings from national evaluations of Project Head Start. In E. Zigler & J. Valentine (Eds.), *Project Head Start: A legacy of the War on Poverty* (pp. 405–432). New York: Free Press.

Deutsch, M., & Deutsch, C. P. (1963). *Report to the Office of the Commission on Education.* Unpublished manuscript.

Farran, D. C., Silveri, B., & Culp, A. (1991). Public school preschools and the disadvantaged. *New Directions for Child Development, 53,* 65–73.

Garber, H. L. (1988). *The Milwaukee Project: Preventing mental retardation in children at risk.* Washington, DC: American Association on Mental Retardation.

General Accounting Office. (1994). *Early childhood programs: Many poor children and strained resources challenge Head Start* (Report No. GAO/HEHS-94-169BR). Washington, DC: Author.

Gutelius, M. F., Kirsch, A. D., MacDonald, S., Brooks, M. R., & McErlean, T. (1977). Controlled study of child health supervision: Behavioral results. *Pediatrics, 60,* 294–304.

Hale, B. A., Seitz, V., & Zigler, E. (1990). Health services and Head Start: A forgotten formula. *Journal of Applied Developmental Psychology, 11,* 447–458.

Haskins, R. (1989). Beyond metaphor: The efficacy of early childhood education. *American Psychologist, 44,* 274–282.

Herrnstein, R. J., & Murray, C. (1994). *The bell curve: Intelligence and class structure in American life.* New York: Free Press.

Hunt, J. McV. (1961). *Intelligence and experience.* New York: Ronald Press.

Hunt, J. McV. (1971). Parent and child centers: Their basis in the behavioral and educational sciences. *American Journal of Orthopsychiatry, 41,* 13–38.

Johnson, D. L. (1989, April). *Follow-up of the Houston Parent-Child Development Center: Preliminary analyses.* Paper presented at the meeting of the Society for Research in Child Development, Kansas City, MO.

Kagan, S. L. (1991). Moving from here to there: Rethinking continuity and transitions in early care and education. In B. Spodek & O. Saracho (Eds.), *Yearbook in early childhood education* (Vol. 2, pp. 132–151). New York: Teacher's College Press.

Kagan, S. L., & Zigler, E. (Eds.). (1987). *Early schooling: The national debate.* New Haven, CT: Yale University Press.

Kennedy, E. M. (1993). The Head Start Transition Project: Head Start goes to elementary school. In E. Zigler & S. J. Styfco (Eds.), *Head Start and beyond: A national plan for extended childhood intervention* (pp. 97–109). New Haven, CT: Yale University Press.

Kirschner Associates. (1970). *A national survey of the impacts of Head Start centers on community institutions.* Albuquerque, NM: Author.

Lally, R. J., Mangione, P. L., & Honig, A. S. (1988). The Syracuse University Family Development Research Program: Long-range impact on an early intervention with low-income children and their families. In D. Powell (Ed.), *Parent education as early childhood intervention: Emerging directions in theory, re-*

search and practice (pp. 79–104). Norwood, NJ: Ablex.

Loeber, R. (1991). Antisocial behavior: More enduring than changeable? *Journal of the American Academy of Child and Adolescent Psychiatry, 30,* 393–397.

McCall, R. (1993). *Head Start: Its potential, its achievements, its future* (A briefing paper for policymakers). Pittsburgh, PA: University of Pittsburgh Center for Social and Urban Research.

McKey, R. H., Condelli, L., Ganson, H., Barrett, B., McConkey, C., & Plantz, M. (1985). *The impact of Head Start on children, family, and communities: Final report of the Head Start Evaluation, Synthesis and Utilization Project.* Washington, DC: U.S. Government Printing Office. (DHHS Pub. No. OHDS 85-31193)

Meisels, S. J. (1992). Doing harm by good: Iatrogenic effects of early childhood enrollment and promotion policies. *Early Childhood Research Quarterly, 7,* 155–174.

Melaville, A. I., with Blank, M. J. (1991). *What it takes: Structuring interagency partnerships to connect children and families with comprehensive services.* Washington, DC: Education and Human Services Consortium.

Mitchell, A., Seligson, M., & Marx, F. (1989). *Early childhood programs and the public schools.* Dover, MA: Auburn House.

National Head Start Association. (1990). *Head Start: The nation's pride, a nation's challenge* (Report of the Silver Ribbon Panel). Alexandria, VA: Author.

Olds, D. L. (1988). The Prenatal/Early Infancy Project. In R. H. Price, E. L. Cowen, R. P. Lorion, & J. Ramos-McKay (Eds.), *Fourteen ounces of prevention: A casebook for practitioners* (pp. 9–22). Washington, DC: American Psychological Association.

Price, R. H., Cowen, E., Lorion, R. P., & Ramos-McKay, J. (Eds.). (1988). *Fourteen ounces of prevention: A casebook for practitioners.* Washington, DC: American Psychological Association.

Provence, S., & Naylor, A. (1983). *Working with disadvantaged parents and children: Scientific issues and practice.* New Haven, CT: Yale University Press.

Ramey, C. T., & Campbell, F. A. (1991). Poverty, early childhood education, and academic competence: The Abecedarian Project. In A. C. Huston (Ed.),

Children in poverty: Child development and public policy (pp. 190–221). New York: Cambridge University Press.

Schorr, L. B. (1988). *Within our reach: Breaking the cycle of disadvantage.* New York: Doubleday.

Schweinhart, L. J., Barnes, H. V., & Weikart, D. P. (1993). *Significant benefits: The High/Scope Perry Preschool Study through age 27. Monographs of the High/Scope Educational Research Foundation, 10.* Ypsilanti, MI: High/Scope Press.

Seitz, V. (1990). Intervention programs for impoverished children: A comparison of educational and family support models. *Annals of Child Development, 7,* 73–103.

Seitz, V., Abelson, W. D., Levine, E., & Zigler, E. (1975). Effects of place of testing on the Peabody Picture Vocabulary Test scores of disadvantaged Head Start and non–Head Start children. *Child Development, 46,* 481–486.

Seitz, V., Rosenbaum., L. K., & Apfel, N. H. (1985). Effects of family support intervention: A 10-year follow-up. *Child Development, 56,* 376–391.

Smith, M., & Bissell, J. S. (1970). Report analysis: The impact of Head Start. *Harvard Educational Review, 40,* 51–104.

Spitz, H. H. (1986). *The raising of intelligence: A selected history of attempts to raise retarded intelligence.* Hillsdale, NJ: Erlbaum.

U.S. Senate. (1990, August 3). *Human Services Reauthorization Act of 1990. Report to accompany H.R. 4151* (Report No. 101–421). Washington, DC: U.S. Government Printing Office.

Weikart, D. P., & Schweinhart, L. J. (1991). Disadvantaged children and curriculum effects. *New Directions for Child Development, 53,* 57–64.

Woodhead, M. (1988). When psychology informs public policy: The case of early childhood intervention. *American Psychologist, 43,* 443–454.

Yoshikawa, H. (1994). Prevention as cumulative protection: Effects of early family support and education on chronic delinquency and its risks. *Psychological Bulletin, 115,* 28–54.

Zero to Three: National Center for Clinical Infant Programs. (1992). *Heart start: The emotional foundations of school readiness.* Arlington, VA: Author.

Zigler, E. (1988). The IQ pendulum. Review of H. Spitz, *The raising of intelligence. Readings,* 3(2), 4–9.

Zigler, E., Abelson, W. D., Trickett, P. K., & Seitz, V. (1982). Is an intervention program really necessary to raise disadvantaged children's IQ scores? *Child Development, 53,* 340–348.

Zigler, E., & Berman, W. (1983). Discerning the future of early childhood intervention. *American Psychologist, 38,* 894–906.

Zigler, E., & Butterfield, E. C. (1968). Motivational aspects of changes in IQ test performance of culturally deprived nursery school children. *Child Development, 39,* 1–14.

Zigler, E., Piotrkowski, C. S., & Collins, R. (1994). Health services in Head Start. *Annual Review of Public Health, 15,* 511–534.

Zigler, E., & Seitz, V. (1982). Social policy and intelligence. In R. Sternberg (Ed.), *Handbook of human intelligence* (pp. 586–641). New York: Cambridge University Press.

Zigler, E., & Styfco, S. J. (1993a). Strength in unity: Consolidating federal education programs for young children. In E. Zigler & S. J. Styfco (Eds.), *Head Start and beyond: A national plan for extended childhood intervention* (pp. 111–145). New Haven, CT: Yale University Press.

Zigler, E., & Styfco, S. J. (1993b). Using research and theory to justify and inform Head Start expansion. *Social Policy Report,* 7(2).

Zigler, E., & Styfco, S. J. (1994). Is the Perry Preschool better than Head Start? Yes and no. *Early Childhood Research Quarterly, 9,* 269–287.

Zigler, E., Taussig, C., & Black, K. (1992). Early childhood intervention: A promising preventative for juvenile delinquency. *American Psychologist, 47,* 997–1006.

CHAPTER 7

Problems and Potentials of Youth Development: A Developmental Contextual Model for Research and Outreach Promoting Positive Youth Development

RICHARD M. LERNER
Boston College

Across the communities of our nation, children and adolescents are dying—from violence, from drug and alcohol use and abuse, from unsafe sex, from poor nutrition, and from the sequelae of persistent and pervasive poverty (Dryfoos, 1990; Hamburg, 1992; Huston, 1991; Lerner, 1993a, 1993b, 1995; McKinney, Abrams, Terry, & Lerner, 1994; Schorr, 1988; Wilson, 1987). And, if our youth are not dying, their life chances are being squandered—by school failure, underachievement, and dropout; by crime; by teenage pregnancy and parenting; by lack of job preparedness; by prolonged welfare dependency; by challenges to their health (such as, lack of immunizations, inadequate screening for disabilities, insufficient prenatal care, and lack of sufficient infant and childhood medical services); and by the feelings of despair and hopelessness that pervade the lives of children whose parents have lived in poverty and who see themselves as having little opportunity to do better—that is, to have a life marked by societal respect, achievement, and opportunity (Dryfoos, 1990; Huston, 1991; Huston, McLoyd, & Coll, 1994).

There are numerous manifestations of the severity and breadth of the problems besetting our nation's youth, families, and communities. To illustrate, consider the four major categories of risk

behaviors in late childhood and adolescence (Dryfoos, 1990):

1. Drug and alcohol use and abuse
2. Unsafe sex, teenage pregnancy, and teenage parenting
3. School underachievement, school failure, and dropout
4. Delinquency, crime, and violence

Clearly, participation in any one of these behaviors diminishes a youth's life chances. Indeed, engagement in some of these behaviors eliminates the young person's chances of even having a life. Such risks to the life chances of children and adolescents are occurring, unfortunately, at historically unprecedented levels.

Today, in the United States, there are approximately 28 million children and adolescents between the ages of 10 and 17. About 50% of these youth engage in *two or more* of the categories of risk behaviors just mentioned (Dryfoos, 1990)! Moreover, 10% of our nation's youth engage in all four categories of risk behaviors (Dryfoos, 1990).

These data indicate that risk behaviors are highly interrelated in children and adolescents. Half of our nation's youth are at least at moderate risk as a consequence of engaging in two or more risk behaviors. And one American youth in every ten is at very high risk as a consequence of "doing it all," of engaging in behaviors associated with every category of risk behaviors.[1]

Illustrations of the Risk Behaviors Engaged in by American's Youth[2]

Within each of the categories of risk behaviors, there are a burgeoning number of indications of the extensiveness of the problems besetting our nation's youth. Information derived from several recent publications provides dramatic illustrations of the breadth and depth of these problems. See, for example, Carnegie Corporation of New York, (1992, 1994), Carnegie Council on Adolescent Development (1989), Center for the Study of Social Policy (1992, 1993), Children's Defense Fund (1992), Dryfoos (1990), Hamburg (1992), Hernandez (1993), Mincy (1994), the National Research Council (1993), and Simons, Finlay, and Yang (1991).

Considering the category of drug and alcohol use and abuse, it has been reported that, in 1990, about 25% of 12- to 17-year-olds and more than 50% of 18- to 25-year-olds had used illicit drugs; about 10% of sixth-graders have initiated alcohol use. In addition, about 25% of 12- to 14-year-olds and more than 50% of seventh-graders in the United States are current users. About 40% of this population drink alcohol weekly. Approximately 92% of high school seniors report some experience with alcohol, and 33% use alcohol daily. In addition, 33% of high school seniors are "binge

drinkers," which is defined as having five or more drinks in a row. Also approximately 66% of high school seniors have some experience with cigarettes, and 19% smoke cigarettes daily.

Moreover, in the risk category of unsafe sex, teenage pregnancy, and teenage parenting, current information indicates the following: across the adolescent years, 80% of males and 70% of females have sexual intercourse; 20% of these youth have four or more sexual partners; youth between the ages of 15 and 19 account for 25% of the sexually transmitted diseases (STD) reported each year. Moreover, 6.4% of adolescent runaways (of which there are between 750,000 and 1 million each year in the United States) test positive for the AIDS virus. These runaway youth often engage in unsafe sex, prostitution, and intravenous drug use. Thus, each year in the United States up to 64,000 "time bombs" are going out onto the streets of our towns and cities and spreading a disease that will kill them and the people with whom they engage in unsafe sexual and intravenous drug use behaviors. One million adolescents become pregnant each year; about half have their babies. Indeed, about every minute an American adolescent has a baby; of adolescents who give birth, 46% go on welfare within four years; of *unmarried* adolescents who give birth, 73% go on welfare within four years; by age 18, 25% of American females have been pregnant at least once. Approximately 10,000 babies are born each year to unwed mothers who are under 15 years of age. In 1991, 531,591 babies were born to adolescents; of these adolescent mothers, 69% were unmarried. African American unwed females aged 15 to 19 years have a birth rate of about 118 per 1,000; the corresponding rates for white, non-Hispanic, and Hispanic unwed females in this age range are approximately 43 per 1,000 and 107 per 1,000, respectively. By age 19, 15% of African American males have fathered a child; the corresponding rates for Latinos and for white, non-Hispanics are about 11% and 7%, respectively. More-

---

[1]Throughout this chapter the terms *America* and *American* refer to the United States.

[2]The theory, data, and interpretations presented in this chapter are derived from a monograph by the author (Lerner, 1995) and are related to the presentation made by Lerner, Ostrom, & Freel (in press). These publications, as well as the author's work on the present chapter, were supported in part by the W. K. Kellogg Foundation and the National 4-H Council.

over, most of these men are absentee fathers. This typically results in their babies being born into and living in single-parent, female head-of-household families. There is a high probability that such households will be poor ones, and thus the children in such settings are likely to experience the negative effects of living in poverty.

In regard to the category of school failure, underachievement, and dropout, current information indicates the following: about 25% of the approximately 40 million children and adolescents enrolled in America's 82,000 public elementary and secondary schools are at-risk for school failure; each year about 700,000 youth drop out of school. About 25% of all 18- and 19-year-olds have not graduated from high school. At any point in time, about 18% of all 18- to 24-year-old dropouts and 30% of 25- to 34-year-old dropouts are under supervision of the criminal justice system. Among African Americans, the corresponding percentages are about 50% and 75%, respectively. During the 1980s, school dropout rates for African Americans living in inner cities increased to between 40% and 50%. High school dropout rates are 300% higher among poor young adults (of all races and ethnic backgrounds) than they are among nonpoor young adults. African Americans and Native Americans are about 200% more likely than European Americans to be high school dropouts, and Latinos are about 300% more likely. African American youth graduate from high school at about the same rate as do European American youth. Across the nation, the percentage of 18- to 24-year old European American and African American males who have not completed high school is about 24% and 32%, respectively. However, the number of years needed to graduate from high school is greater among African Americans: about 4.5 million 10- to 14-year-olds are one or more years behind in their modal grade level; African American and Latino teenagers are more likely than European Americans to be two or more

grades behind in school. In 1986, 57% of 10- to 15-year-old African Americans were two or more years behind their grade level; and in 1989, 75% of 25- to 34-year-old African Americans who completed high school worked, whereas 90% of European American high school graduates in this age range worked. African Americans who worked full time and full year earned only 81% as much as their European American counterparts. A male high school dropout earns $260,000 less than a high school graduate and contributes $78,000 less in taxes over his lifetime. For a female dropout, the comparable figures are $200,000 and $60,000, respectively. Unemployment rates for dropouts are more than double those of high school graduates; and each added year of secondary education reduces the probability of public welfare dependency in adulthood by 35%.

Finally, in regard to the risk category of delinquency, crime, and violence, current information indicates that 13- to 21-year-olds accounted for 35.5% of all nontraffic-related arrests in the United States during the 1980s, although this age group was only 14.3% of the population. As noted earlier, between 750,000 and 1 million youth run away from home each year. In the mid-1980s, 1.7 million arrests occurred among 10- to 17-year-olds. More than 500,000 of those arrested were 14 years of age or younger, and 46,000 were under the age of 10. In 1991, 130,000 youth aged 10 to 17 years were arrested for rape, robbery, homicide, or aggravated assault. This figure represents an increase of 48% since 1986; at any point in time, about 20% of all African American youth are involved with the criminal justice system. Between 1980 and 1990, arrest rates of African American adolescents charged with weapons violations, murder, and aggravated assault increased by 102%, 145%, and 89%, respectively. African Americans experience rape, aggravated assault, and armed robbery at rates that are approximately 25% higher than those for European Americans; rates of motor vehicle theft are about 70% higher; and rates of robbery victimization are about 150% higher. Finally, African American homicide rates are typically between 600% to 700% higher that those for European Americans, and African American males are at high risk for being victims of violent crime. For example, in 1988, for African American males aged 15 to 19 and 20 to 24, death rates from the use of firearms were about 80 per 100,000 and about 125 per 100,000, respectively; the corresponding rates for European Americans were about 30 per 100,000 for both age groups. Also in 1988, homicide death rates among African American males in these same age groups were about 80 per 100,000 and about 120 per 100,000, respectively; the corresponding rates for European American males in the two age groups were about 5 per 100,000 and about 18 per 100,000, respectively.

Temporal Trends in the Risk Behaviors Engaged in by Youth

The data given in the previous section indicate that the current status of American youth is exceedingly problematic. Indeed, these data suggest that nothing short of a "generational time bomb" (Lerner, 1993a) is confronting American society. With so many of our nation's youth beset with so many instances of behavioral risks, the United States is on the verge of losing much of its next generation—that is, the human capital upon which the future of our nation relies (Hamburg, 1992; Lerner, 1993a, 1993b). Moreover, the "fuse" on the time bomb appears to be growing appreciably shorter. Several sources of data indicate that many of the key problems of American youth are increasing at relatively rapid rates.

For instance, information from *Kids Count Data Book* (Center for the Study of Social Policy, 1993) indicates that, between 1985 and 1992, many of the problems of children and youth grew substantially worse. For instance, the rate of violent deaths of 15- to 19-year-olds increased by 13%; whereas for European American youth, the increased rate was 10%, and for African American youth in this age range, it was 78%. In addition, the percentage of youth graduating from high school decreased by 4%; the percentage of all births that were to single teenage mothers increased by 16% (with a 26% increase among European American youth and no increase among African American teenagers); the arrest rate among 10- to 17-year-olds increased by 48% (with European Americans increasing by 58% and African Americans by 29%); and the number of children in single-parent families increased by 9% (with the corresponding rates for European American and for African American children increasing by 9% and by 6%, respectively).

As noted earlier, these latter changes in family structure are associated with both poverty and with the interrelation of risk behaviors among children and adolescents. As noted by Schorr (1988), child poverty is the single most damaging structural feature of American society affecting the quality of youth development. Accordingly, it is important to discuss the prevalence and temporal trends associated with poverty among youth in the United States.

Youth Poverty

Youth poverty exacerbates the risk behaviors of adolescents, and poverty is a growing problem for America's youth (Huston, 1991; Lerner, 1993a). By the end of the 1980s, approximately 20% of America's children and adolescents were poor (Huston, 1991; Huston, McLoyd, & Coll, 1994; Simons et al., 1991). Moreover, data from *Kids Count Data Book* (Center for the Study of Social Policy, 1992) indicate that across the 1980s the percentage of youth living in poverty in the United States increased by 22%. Indeed, this national trend was present in 40 states and continues to increase across the nation (Huston, 1991). Furthermore, of the 12 million children under the age of 3, 25% live in poor families (Carnegie Corporation of New York, 1994). In addition, whereas the number of children under the age of 6 decreased by 10% between 1971 and 1991, the number of poor children in this age group *increased by 60%* (Carnegie Corporation of New York, 1994).

Youth poverty occurs in all geographic regions of the United States. In fact, the rates of poverty in rural areas of the Unites States are as high as those in the inner cities (Huston, 1991; Jensen, 1988). Moreover, poor families in rural areas receive fewer welfare benefits and are less likely to live in states that provide Aid to Families with Dependent Children (AFDC) (Huston, 1991; Jensen, 1988).

However, it must be stressed that the probability of being a poor child is not equal across racial or ethnic groups. According to the 1993 edition of *Kids Count Data Book,* across the 1987–1991 period, the average percentage of European American, African American, and Latino children who were poor was 11.4%, 44.1%, and 37.9%, respectively. Moreover, among Latino groups, Puerto Rican children experienced the highest rate of poverty (40.4%) and Cuban children experienced the lowest rate (19.7%) (U.S. Bureau of the Census, 1991). In addition, as reported in 1991 by the U.S. Bureau of the Census, Asian children and Native American youth experienced rates of poverty of 16.7% and 24.9%, respectively.

The percentages of youth in poverty across the 1987–1991 period represent increases in the rates of poverty over the last ten years for all racial/ethnic groups. For example, from 1979 to 1989, youth poverty grew worse by 9% for European Americans, by 5% for African Americans, and by 25% for Latinos (Center for the Study of Social Policy, 1993). In terms of absolute numbers, data from the 1990 census indicate the following for youth living in poverty: 5.9 million European Americans, 3.7 million African Americans, 346,000 Asian Americans, 260,000 Native Americans, and 2.4 million Latinos (Children's Defense Fund, 1992).

As noted by Huston (1991), race is the most striking and disturbing distinction between youth whose poverty is chronic and youth for whom poverty is transitory. For instance, Duncan (1991) reports data from the Panel Study on Income Dynamics indicating that the average African American child in the study spent 5.5 years in poverty; the average non–African American child in the study spent only 0.9 year in poverty. Furthermore, as with race and ethnicity, poverty is not equally distributed across age groups. In 1989, about 20% of children younger than age 6 were poor, and the corresponding rate of poverty for 6- to 17-year-olds was about 17%. In turn, the rates for Americans aged 18 to 64 and aged 65 years or older were about 11% and 13%, respectively (Children's Defense Fund, 1992).

The sequelae of poverty for youth are devastating. Indeed, as Hamburg (1992) notes:

> Almost every form of childhood damage is far more prevalent among the poor—from increased infant mortality, gross malnutrition, recurrent and untreated health problems, and child abuse in the early years, to education disability, low achievement, delinquency, early pregnancy, alcohol and drug abuse, and failure to become economically self-sufficient. (p. 48)

Similarly, as Schorr (1988) stresses, poverty creates several "rotten outcomes" of youth development. For example, poverty is associated with early school failure, unemployability, long-term welfare dependency, violent crime, and feelings of hopelessness and despair (McLoyd & Wilson, 1991; Schorr, 1988, 1992). Furthermore, McLoyd and Wilson (1991) and Klerman (1991) find that poor youth live at high risk for low self-confidence, conduct problems, depression, and peer conflict. In addition, poor youth are at-risk for encountering severe health problems (such as infant mortality and lack of immunization against common childhood diseases) and physical abuse, neglect, and unintended injury (Carnegie Corporation of New York, 1994; McLoyd & Wilson, 1991).

Moreover, as compared to their nonpoor agemates, poor youth are 50% more likely to have physical or mental disabilities, almost twice as likely to have not visited a doctor or dentist in the most recent two years of their lives, 300% more likely to be high school dropouts, and significantly more likely to be victims of violence (Simons et al., 1991). In addition, several familial risk factors are associated both with youth poverty and with a key covariate of poverty—poor school achievement.

To illustrate, there are three maternal risk factors associated with a youth's living in poverty and with him or her being in the lower half of the school class. These risk factors include the following:

1. The mother has fewer than twelve years of schooling.
2. The mother is not married to the child's father.
3. The mother was less than 20 years old when she had her first child.

According to the Center for the Study of Social Policy (1993), among all 7- to 12-year-old children living in the United States, there was a probability of .79 that the child would be poor if all three maternal risk factors were present. Similarly, the probability of being in the lower half of one's school class was .58 if all three factors were present. When any two of these risk factors were present, the probabilities of being poor or of being in the lower half of one's school class were .48 and .53, respectively. The corresponding probabilities involving the presence of only one risk factor were .26 and .47, respectively. Finally, when none of these risk factors were present, the probabilities of children in this age group being poor or being in the lower half of their class were .08 and .30, respectively.

Across the 1980s, the probability that there would be a link between youth poverty and the presence of maternal risk factors increased. That is, as the poverty rates of America's children worsen, now exceeding all other major industrialized nations (Huston, 1991), the structure of the family is also changing in ways that have placed poor youth and parents at greater risk of problems of family life and individual development. For instance, during the 1980s there was a 13% increase in the number of youth living in single-parent families, a trend present in 44 states. From 1987 to 1991, 18.1% of European American children, 30% of Latino children, and 56.7% of African American children were living in single-parent households (Center for the Study of Social Policy, 1992). Overall, approximately 25% of America's youth live in single-parent (and typically, female-headed) families, and poverty rates among female-headed, single-parent or male-headed, single-parent families are much higher (46.8% and 23.2%, respectively) than among two-parent families (9.0%) (Center for the Study of Social Policy, 1993; Hernandez, 1993). Indeed, the poverty rates in single-parent households were, by the beginning of the 1990s, 29.8% for European American families, 50.6% for African American families, and 53% for Latino families (U.S. Department of Commerce, 1991). Since the income of female-headed, single-parent households is often three or more times lower than two-parent households—and is also lower than single-parent, male-headed households—the fact that increasing numbers of youth live in these family structures means that the financial resources to support parenting are less likely to be available (Center for the Study of Social Policy, 1993).

Moreover, in 1990, 90.3% of youth were living with their parents, 7.3% were living with other relatives, and 2.3% were living outside of the family (Center for the Study of Social Policy, 1992).

However, only 41.9% of African American children, 67.7% of Latino children, and 78.5% of European American children between the ages of 10 and 14 lived with both their parents (Simons et al., 1991). In turn, only 41% of African American youth, 63% of Latino youth, and 76% of European American youth lived in two-parent households (Simons et al., 1991).

To summarize the costs—not only to youth but to society—of pervasive youth poverty, we note Hamburg's (1992) view:

> Not only are many more children growing up in poverty than was the case a decade or two ago, but many more are mired in persistent, intractable poverty with no realistic hope of escape. They are profoundly lacking in constructively oriented social-support networks to promote their education and health. They have very few models of competence. They are bereft of visible economic opportunity. The fate of these young people is not merely a tragedy for them, but for the entire nation: A growing fraction of our potential work force consists of seriously disadvantaged people who will have little if any prospect of acquiring the necessary competence to revitalize the economy. If we cannot bring ourselves to feel compassion for these young people on a personal level, we must at least recognize that our economy and our society will suffer along with them. Their loss is our loss. (p. 10)

Addressing the Crisis of America's Children Through an Integrative Theory of Human Development

Given the number of youth who are at such profound levels of risk, we are faced with a crisis so broad that the entire fabric of American society is in serious jeopardy (Simons et al., 1991). With so many communities facing the likelihood of losing much of their next generation to one or more

high-risk behaviors present among our nation's youth, *all* of our children are living in risk—of experiencing the adverse economic and employment conditions associated with living in a nation that is increasingly globally uncompetitive, has a diminished pool of future leaders, offers lowered standards of living, requires lower expectations about life chances, and provides fewer and fewer opportunities for healthy and wholesome development (Lerner, 1993a).

Simply put, America is wasting its most precious resource: the human capital represented by its youth (Hamburg, 1992; Lerner, 1993a, 1993b, 1995; Lerner & Miller, 1993). This destruction of human capital is a problem that cuts across race, ethnicity, gender, and rural and urban environments (Center for the Study of Social Policy, 1992, 1993; Simons et al., 1991). Accordingly, all of us, and certainly all of our children and adolescents, are now confronted by this crisis of youth development. Of course, the pervasiveness of this crisis does not diminish the need to prioritize our efforts. In fact, results of evaluation studies of preventive interventions indicate that great success can occur with programs directed to youth and families most in need (Dryfoos, 1990, 1994, 1995; Hamburg, 1992; Schorr, 1988). Nevertheless, the breadth of the problems affecting our nation's youth requires that we see the issues as pertaining to all of us, and not to only a segment or a subgroup of our society.

Yet, despite the magnitude of the crisis confronting all the youth of our nation, it is still the case that the majority of child and adolescent development research is not focused on the behavioral risks confronting the diverse youth of America; as a consequence, there are relatively few developmental studies of youth poverty and its sequelae. In fact, most studies published in the leading scientific journals in child development focus on investigations of European American, middle-class children (Fisher & Brennan, 1992; Graham, 1992; Hagen, Paul, Gibb, & Wolters, 1990). Moreover, most of these studies appraise children in laboratory settings, and most do not address topics that are relevant to developing, delivering, or sustaining programs that prevent risk behaviors or the sequelae of persistent and pervasive poverty (Fisher & Brennan, 1992; Graham, 1992; McKinney et al., 1994; McLoyd, 1994).

There is a considerable gap between the work of many of America's child and adolescent developmentalists and the problems facing the youth of America (Graham, 1992; McLoyd, 1994). A similar gap exists between those who seek to develop policies and programs that will help youth lead better lives within their families and communities and the scientists who can provide the intellectual base upon which to build these endeavors.

These gaps—between the major foci of contemporary child and adolescent development research and the needs of poor American youth, families, and communities (Graham, 1992; McLoyd, 1994)—exist despite the presence of alternative models for science and for outreach. In a report by the Michigan State University Provost's Committee on University Outreach (1993), *outreach* was conceived of as a form of scholarship that involves

> the generation, transmission, application, and preservation of knowledge for the direct benefit of audiences to whom and for whom the university seeks to extend itself in ways that are consistent with university and unit missions. (p. 2)

In other words, outreach involves the generation, transmission, application, or preservation of scholarship for purposes developed collaboratively with communities served by the university (Lerner & Miller, 1993; Lerner et al., 1994a). When outreach scholarship is conducted in regard to youth, their families, and their communities—or, more generally, in regard to human development—it may be

defined as the "systematic synthesis of research and application to describe, explain, and promote optimal developmental outcomes in individuals and families as they develop along the life cycle" (Fisher & Lerner, 1994, p. 4). This instance of outreach scholarship has been termed by Fisher and Lerner (1994) *applied developmental science.*

It is important to note that this view of outreach scholarship in the field of human development emerged within land-grant institutions' colleges of home economics, human ecology, family and consumer sciences, and human development (Lerner & Miller, 1993; Miller & Lerner, 1994). The perspectives about human development produced in these institutions have provided a vision of scholarship that integrates research and outreach (Boyer, 1990, 1994; Enarson, 1989; Lynton & Elman, 1987), a vision consistent with a statement of the National Council of Administrators of Home Economics Programs (1991):

> The mission of the profession in higher education is to conduct research and provide education programs that are integrative and are focused on reciprocal relationships among individuals, families, and their near environments toward improvement of the human condition within a dynamic world community. (p. 5)

A theory of child and family development—*developmental contextualism* (Lerner, 1986, 1991, 1995, 1996; Lerner & Kauffman, 1985; Lerner & Miller, 1993; Miller & Lerner, 1994)—has emerged within land-grant institutions promoting this home economics vision of integrative, reciprocal, and dynamic relations among developing individuals, families, and contexts (see, for example, Featherman, 1983). This theory embeds the study of children in the actual families, neighborhoods, and communities within which they live their lives. Moreover, the model—when fully implemented—synthesizes research with policy and program design, delivery, and evaluation and involves both multiprofessional collaboration and full partnership with the communities within which science and service are being conducted (Lerner & Miller, 1993). In other words, the people that science is intended to serve are full collaborators in the process of research and outreach.

This model may be of use in narrowing the gaps mentioned earlier between research and the practical needs of our nation's diverse youth and families. As such, we first provide some background to this perspective, and then describe the model's synthetic approach to research and application.

An Overview of Developmental Contextualism

Over the last two decades, the study of human development has evolved in at least three significant directions. These trends involve: (1) changes in the conceptualization of the nature of the person; (2) the emergence of a life-span perspective about human development; and (3) stress on the contexts of development. These trends were both products and producers of developmental contextualism. This perspective has promoted a rationale for a synthesis of research and outreach, a synthesis focused on the diversity of youth and on the contexts within which they develop.

Developmental contextualism stresses that bidirectional relations exist among the multiple levels of organization involved in human life (for example, biology, psychology, social groups, and culture) (Bronfenbrenner, 1977, 1979; Lerner, 1986, 1991, 1995). These dynamic relations provide a framework for the structure of human behavior (Ford & Lerner, 1992). In addition, this system is itself dynamically interactive with historical changes; this temporality provides a change component to human life (Dixon, Lerner, & Hultsch, 1991). In other words, within developmental contextualism a changing configuration of relation-

ships constitutes the basis of human life—of behavior and development (Ford & Lerner, 1992).

Developmental contextualism is a perspective about human development that takes an integrative approach to the multiple levels of organization presumed to comprise the nature of human life; that is, "*fused*" *and changing relations* among biological, psychological, and social contextual levels comprise the process of developmental change (Tobach & Greenberg, 1984). Rather than approach variables from these levels of analysis either in a reductionistic or in a parallel-processing way, the developmental contextual view rests on the idea that variables from these levels of analysis are dynamically interactive—they are reciprocally influential over the course of human ontogeny.

Accordingly, from a developmental contextual perspective, human behavior is both biological and social (Featherman & Lerner, 1985; Tobach & Schneirla, 1968). In fact, no form of life as we know it comes into existence independent of other life. No animal lives in total isolation from others of its species across its entire life span (Tobach, 1981; Tobach & Schneirla, 1968). Biological survival requires meeting the demands of the environment, or attaining a goodness of fit (Chess & Thomas, 1984; Lerner & Lerner, 1983, 1989; Thomas & Chess, 1977) with the context. Because the environment is populated by other members of one's species, adjustment to these other organisms is a requirement of survival (Tobach & Schneirla, 1968).

Human evolution has promoted this link between biological and social functioning (Featherman & Lerner, 1985; Gould, 1977). Early humans were relatively defenseless, having neither sharp teeth nor claws. Coupled with the dangers of living in the open African savanna, where much of early human evolution occurred, group living was essential for survival (Masters, 1978; Washburn, 1961). Therefore, human beings were more likely to survive if they acted in concert with the group than if they acted in isolation. Human characteristics that support social relations (such as attachment and empathy) may have helped human survival over the course of evolution (Hoffman, 1978; Hogan, Johnson, & Emler, 1978; Sahlins, 1978). Thus, for several reasons, humans at all portions of their life spans may be seen as embedded in a social context with which they have important relationships.

Much of the history of the study of human development prior to the mid-1970s was predicated on either organismic or mechanistic (reductionistic) models (Overton & Reese, 1973, 1981; Reese & Overton, 1970). In turn, it is accurate to say that since the 1970s developmental contextual conceptions have been increasingly prominent bases of scholarly advances in human development theory and methodology (Dixon & Lerner, 1992; Dixon et al., 1991; Lerner, Hultsch, & Dixon, 1983; Riegel, 1975, 1976a, 1976b; Sameroff, 1975, 1983). Indeed, the three themes in the study of human development define the place of developmental contextualism in theory and research over the last two decades. Accordingly, we will discuss each of these themes in some detail.

Children's Influences on Their Own Development

Children have come to be understood as active producers of their own development (Bell, 1968; Lerner & Spanier, 1978; Lewis & Rosenblum, 1974; Thomas, Chess, Birch, Hertzig, & Korn, 1963). These contributions occur primarily through the reciprocal relations individuals have with other significant people in their context; for children, these relationships would be with family members, caregivers, teachers, and peers, for example.

The content and functional significance of the influences people have on others and on themselves occur in relation to people's characteristics of individuality (Schneirla, 1957). Individual dif-

ferences in people evoke differential reactions in others, reactions that provide feedback to people and influence the individual character of their further development (Schneirla, 1957). Accordingly, individuality—diversity among people—is central in understanding the way in which any given person is an active agent in his or her own development (Lerner, 1982, 1991; Lerner & Busch-Rossnagel, 1981). In other words, diversity has core, substantive meaning and, as such, implications for all studies of human development.

A key feature of the importance of individual differences arises when one recognizes that, as a consequence of their individuality, children will present different stimulation to parents. However, the effect of the child's stimulation on the parent depends in part on the parent's own characteristics of individuality. To explain this point, it is useful to consider the second theme in the literature that helped crystallize the developmental contextual view of human development.

Development as a Life-Span Phenomenon

During the 1970s and 1980s, the emergence of interest in a life-span perspective about human development led to the understanding that development occurs in more than the childhood or adolescent years (Baltes, 1968, 1987; Block, 1971; Brim & Kagan, 1980; Elder, 1974, 1980; Featherman, 1983; Riley, 1979; Schaie, 1965). Parents as well as children develop as distinct individuals across their life span (Lerner & Spanier, 1978). Parents develop both as adults in general and, more specifically, in their familial and career roles (Vondracek, Lerner, & Schulenberg, 1986). Indeed, the influence of a child on his or her parents will depend in part on the prior experience each parent has had with the parental role and on the other roles in which the parents are engaged (such as worker, adult child, and caregiver for an aged parent) (Hetherington & Baltes, 1988). Thus, a person's unique history of experiences and roles, as well as his or her unique biological (genetic) characteristics, combine to make him or her unique—and with time, given the accumulation of the influences of distinct roles and experiences, increasingly more unique across the course of life (Lerner, 1988).

In essence, then, the literature on "child effects" and on the life-span perspective promotes a concern with individual differences; with variation in developmental pathways across life; and with the developmental contextual idea that changing relations between the person and his or her context provide the basis, across life, of the individual's unique repertoire of physical, psychological, and behavioral characteristics (Lerner, 1991). The recognition of this link between person and context was a product and a producer of the third theme emerging in the study of human development since the 1970s.

Development in Its Ecological Context

Since the 1970s, the study of children has become increasingly "contextualized," or placed within the broader "ecology of human development" (Bronfenbrenner, 1977, 1979; Elder, 1974; Garbarino, 1992; Pepper, 1942). This focus has involved a concern with the real-life situations within which children and families exist. It has also led to the study of the bidirectional relations between the family and the other social settings within which children and parents function; for instance, the workplace, the welfare office, the day care, the Medicaid screening office, and the formal and informal educational and recreational settings present in a neighborhood or a community (Lewis & Fiering, 1978; Lewis & Rosenblum, 1974).

The contributions of Urie Bronfenbrenner and his colleagues (Bronfenbrenner, 1979; Bronfenbrenner & Crouter, 1983; Garbarino, 1992) have been a major catalyst in promoting this contextu-

alization of human development, and in helping scholars understand why the study of development must move beyond its status during the 1970s, as "the science of the strange behavior of children in strange situations with strange adults for the briefest possible periods of time" (Bronfenbrenner, 1977, p. 513). Bronfenbrenner (1977, 1979, 1983) has argued that human development needs to be understood as it occurs in its real-world setting or *ecology.* He believes that this ecology of human development is composed of four distinct although interrelated systems.

The first, the *microsystem,* is composed of "the complex of relations between the developing person and environment in an immediate setting containing the person" (Bronfenbrenner, 1977, p. 515). For example, the family is the major microsystem for infant development in our society (Belsky, Lerner, & Spanier, 1984); it involves interactions between the child, his or her parents, and any siblings that are present in the home. Other microsystems of infant life include the day care, nursery, or school setting, which involve both child-teacher and child-peer interactions; and the playground, most often involving child-peer interactions.

An individual's microsystems may be interrelated. What occurs in a child's school may affect what happens in the family, and vice versa. Bronfenbrenner notes that such microsystem interrelations constitute a second ecological stratum termed the *mesosystem.* He defines the mesosystem as "the interrelations among major settings containing the developing person at a particular point in his or her life" (Bronfenbrenner, 1977, p. 515).

Often, what happens in a microsystem (for example, in an interaction between a child and a parent within the family context) may be influenced by events that occur in systems in which the child takes no part. Bronfenbrenner sees such influences as constituting a third system within the ecology of human development. He labels it the *exosystem* and defines it as "an extension of the mesosystem embracing . . . specific social structures, both formal and informal, that do not themselves contain the developing person but impinge upon or encompass the immediate setting in which the person is found, and thereby delimit, influence, or even determine what goes on there" (Bronfenbrenner, 1977, p. 515).

Finally, Bronfenbrenner notes that there exists a *macrosystem* within the ecology of human development. This system is composed of cultural values and beliefs, as well as historical events (wars, floods, famines), both of which may affect the other ecological systems. For instance, natural disasters may destroy the homes, schools, or other microsystems of a person or a group of developing people, or they may make certain necessities of life (food, fresh water) less available. In turn, cultural values influence the developing child in many ways. For example, cultural beliefs about the appropriateness of breast feeding and about when weaning from the breast should occur can affect not only the nutritional status of an infant but, because mother's milk may make some children less likely to develop allergies later in life, it can also affect their health status.

In short, Bronfenbrenner's model of the ecology of human development provides a means to represent the idea that the bidirectional socialization that occurs between children and other people (parents, peers, teachers) is embedded in a more complex system of social networks and of societal, cultural, and historical influences.

Levels of Embeddedness in the Ecology of Human Development

The core idea in developmental contextualism is that the organism (organismic attributes or, most generally, biology) and its context cannot be separated (Gottlieb, 1991, 1992; Lerner, 1984; Tobach, 1981). Both are fused across all of life, and thus across history.

We may speak of dynamic interactions between individuals and contexts that pertain to either *social* or *physical* (for instance, biological or physiological) relations. For example, in regard to social relationships, the parent "demands" attention from the child, but the child does not show it; this lights the parent's "short fuse" of tolerance; the parent scolds the child, who then cries; this creates remorse in the parent and elicits soothing behaviors; the child is calmed, snuggles up to the parent, and now both parties in the relationship show positive emotions and are happy (see Tubman & Lerner, 1994, for data pertinent to such parent-child relationships).

We may also illustrate dynamic interactions that involve not only the exchange of "external" social behaviors but also involve biological or physiological processes. For example, parental religious practices, rearing practices, or financial status may influence the child's diet and nutritional status, health, and medical care. In turn, the contraction of an infectious disease either by parent or child can lead to the other member of the relationship contracting the disease. Moreover, the health and physical status of the child influences the parent's own feelings of well-being and his or her hopes and aspirations regarding the child (Finkelstein, 1993).

Thus, the child's physiological functioning and developmental course are influenced by his or her behavioral and social context (in this example, parental) (see Finkelstein, 1993; Ford & Lerner, 1992; Howard, 1978). The inner and outer worlds of the child are fused and dynamically interactive. In addition, of course, the same may be said of the parent and, in fact, of the parent-child relationship. Each of these foci—child, parent, or relationship—is part of a larger, enmeshed *system* of fused relations among the multiple levels that constitute the ecology of human life (Bronfenbrenner, 1979).

Finally, all changes are embedded in history (Baltes, 1987; Elder, 1974; Elder, Modell, & Parke,

1993); that is, time cuts through all levels of organization. As such, the nature of parent-child relations, of family life and development, and of societal and cultural influences on the child-parent-family system is influenced by both "normative" and "nonnormative" historical changes (Baltes, 1987)—in other words, by "evolutionary" (gradual) and "revolutionary" (abrupt) historical changes (Werner, 1957). This system of multiple, interconnected, or "fused" (Tobach & Greenberg, 1984) levels comprises a complete depiction of the integrated organization involved in the developmental contextual view of human development (Lerner, 1986, 1991).

Conclusions

In developmental contextualism the development of youth is seen as occurring in relation to the specific features of their actual, "ecologically valid" context, that is, their specific family, neighborhood, society, culture, physical environments, and even the particular point in history within which they live (Lerner, 1986, 1991, 1992, 1994, 1996; McKinney et al., 1994). Moreover, because developmental contextualism sees human development as occurring within a systematically changing and complex (multilevel) system (Ford & Lerner, 1992), youth influence their contexts—for example, adolescents affect their parents—as much as their contexts (their parents) influence them (Lerner, 1982; Lerner & Busch-Rossnagel, 1981).

Developmental contextualism leads, then, to descriptions of both the problems and the potentials for healthy development that are associated with these bidirectional relationships between youth and their contexts (Lerner, 1994). Moreover, to explain development one must also turn to the system of relations between youth and their contexts. And, in order to test these explanations, one must change something about the actual context

within which youth live. These changes constitute both "experimental" manipulations designed to test theoretical ideas about the variables that influence the course of human development *and* interventions aimed at changing for the better the life paths of children and youth (Lerner, 1995; Lerner & Miller, 1993; Lerner et al., 1994a, 1994b). Depending on the level of organization involved in these contextual manipulations/interventions, we may label these planned changes into the course of human life as either policies or programs (Lerner et al., 1994a).

Thus, when we evaluate the efficacy of these interventions in regard to the changes in the human life course associated with them, we are learning something about the adequacy of particular policies and programs to effect desired changes among children and youth *and* we are learning something very basic about how human development occurs through changing relations between the developing person and his or her actual context (Lerner, 1991, 1994, 1996). In other words, within developmental contextualism there is a synthesis of "basic," theory testing research and "applied" scholarship (or "outreach") associated with program and policy design, delivery, and evaluation (Lerner, 1995; Lerner & Miller, 1993; Lerner et al., 1994a, 1994b).

Building on the seminal work of Dryfoos (1990, 1994), Schorr (1988), and Hamburg (1992), I use developmental contextualism to discuss both the features of successful prevention and development-enhancing programs for youth and the principles that seem to be key in the design and implementation of such programs. In addition, I discuss how the developmental contextual approach to integrating research and outreach can be used to assist universities in becoming productive partners in community coalitions aimed at addressing the problems and potentials of children and youth. I suggest that the means to do this is through pursuing what Weiss and

Greene (1992) term *participatory-normative evaluation* and what may be termed *development-in-context evaluation* (Lerner, Ostrom, & Freel, in press; Ostrom, Lerner, & Freel, 1995).

Using Developmental Contextualism as a Framework for Preventive and Enhancement Interventions

The problems of contemporary American children and youth were not produced by a single event or from a single cause. Poor parenting, poverty, inappropriate media influences, inadequate health care, problems of local, state, and federal economies, a failed educational system, racism, territoriality among social service and other youth and family-serving agencies, inadequate state and federal policies—none of these alone produced the problems faced by America's children. However, all these phenomena are a part of the developmental system within which America's children are embedded (Ford & Lerner, 1992), and it is this system that is implicated in the production of the problems of our nation's youth.

Key Principles for the Design of Successful Prevention Programs

Given, then, that development in the context of this system provides the bases of these problems, this same system has to be engaged in any comprehensive solution to these problems (Ford & Lerner, 1992; Lerner, 1994). As such, and as Dryfoos (1990) points out, *there is no one solution to a problem of childhood or adolescence.* The developmental system may be—and, for comprehensive and integrated solutions, must be—engaged at any of the levels of organization represented in the developmental contextual view of human development; including biological/physiological, psychological, interpersonal/familial, social network/community, institutional/societal, cultural,

physical ecological, and historical (Lerner, 1986, 1991, 1994). Thus, for any particular problem of youth behavior and development—for example, for youth violence—solutions may be sought by entering the system at the level of the individual, of his or her family, of the community, or of the societal/cultural context (for example, through working to affect social policies) (Mincy, 1994; Pittman & Zeldin, 1994).

Another reason that recognition of the potential for multiple solutions to a problem is important is that *high-risk behaviors are interrelated.* As noted by Dryfoos (1990), 10% of all 10- to 17-year-olds in the United States engage in behaviors associated with all four major categories of high-risk behaviors (unsafe sex, school failures, substance abuse, and delinquency and crime). Similarly, Schorr (1988) notes that poverty is associated with several "unwanted" behavioral outcomes; for example, school failure and dropout, unemployability, prolonged welfare dependency, and delinquency and crime.

The interrelation, and systemic bases, of high-risk behaviors means, then, that no one type of program is likely to be of sufficient scope to adequately address all the interconnected facets of a problem. Instead, as Dryfoos (1990) notes, *a package of services is needed within each community.* However, because of the systemic interconnections of the problems this package is to address, program comprehensiveness, in and of itself, will not be adequate. Rather, *an integration of services is required.*

Moreover, because of the systemic nature of the problems of children and youth, the integrated services that are provided to address these problems should be directed to this system, and not solely at the individuals within it. In other words, the relations—among individuals, institutions, and levels of the context—provide both the bases of and potential sources of change in the problems of children and youth. As such, *interventions should be aimed at changing the developmental system, within which people are embedded, rather than aimed at changing individuals* (Dryfoos, 1990).

Moreover, because of the systemic nature of youth problems and of their potential solutions, *the timing of interventions is critical* (Dryfoos, 1990; Lerner, 1984). That is, across life the developmental system not only becomes more organized, but this organization also involves, in a sense, overorganization; in other words, redundant as well as alternative portions of the system function to support developmental functioning (Hebb, 1949; Schneirla, 1957). For example, problem behaviors in adolescence may involve emotional shortcomings (such as low self-esteem) on the part of a youth *and* poor child-rearing skills on the part of his or her parents *and* negative appraisals about, and loss of hope for, the youth by school personnel *and* a peer group that promotes norm-breaking or even illegal behavior. Each part of this system may reinforce, support, or maintain the adolescent's problem behaviors. Accordingly, problems of behavior and development, once embedded in this redundantly organized system, are more difficult to alter than if the same problems were embedded in the system at an earlier portion of its development (Clarke & Clarke, 1976; Ford & Lerner, 1992; Lerner, 1984).

The developmental system remains open to intervention across the life span of individuals; that is, there is relative "plasticity" in human behavior and development across life (Lerner, 1984). Nevertheless, the developmental changes in the organization of a system over the course of life mean that to effect a given change in behavior or development, interventions occurring later in life require greater expenditures of effort, and require involvement of greater portions of the system, than is the case in earlier portions of the life span (Baltes & Baltes, 1980; Clarke & Clarke, 1976; Ford & Lerner, 1992; Lerner, 1984).

Accordingly, preventive interventions are more economical—in terms of time, scope, and other resources—than are ameliorative interventions.

An excellent illustration of this point is provided by Hamburg (1992). Young, pregnant adolescents have a higher probability of giving birth to a high-risk baby (a low-birth-weight or premature baby) than do postadolescent females. Hamburg (1992) notes that the total cost of good prenatal care for a pregnant adolescent would be much less than $1,000. However, the intensive care needed to keep a low-birth-weight or premature baby alive would be at least $1,000 a day for many weeks or months. Often, the initial hospital cost of such care is $400,000 (Hamburg, 1992). Thus, preventive prenatal care for pregnant adolescents would not only save a lot of money but would also eliminate the sequelae of emotional, behavioral, social, and physical problems—for both mother and infant—associated with the birth of a high-risk baby. Yet most pregnant adolescents, especially those under 15 years of age, receive either no prenatal care or inadequate care (Hamburg, 1992). Moreover, about 50% of pregnant adolescent African Americans do not receive prenatal care, or they receive care only in the last three months of pregnancy (Hamburg, 1992). Furthermore, poor, inner city, and isolated rural youth are among those most likely to have no or inadequate prenatal care (Hamburg, 1992).

Thus, as illustrated by the information Hamburg (1992) presents about the economic and human benefits of preventing high-risk births through prenatal care, preventive interventions—although insufficiently used—seem most efficacious in the promotion of healthy youth and family development. That is, although the relative plasticity of human behavior and development across the life span means that there is always some probability that the intervention can be successful, the nature of the developmental system indicates that prevention has the best likelihood of effecting desired changes.

Of course, a system that remains open to changes for the better also remains open to changes for the worse. Thus, the interventive means through which human behavior and development change is *not* akin to inoculation to disease. Accordingly, "one shot" interventions into human behavior and development are unlikely to effect enduring changes. Instead, interventions must be designed to be longitudinal in scope (Lerner & Ryff, 1978) or, as both Dryfoos (1990) and Hamburg (1992) note, *continuity of programming must be maintained across development.* Programs, conceived of as life-span "convoys of social support" (Kahn & Antonucci, 1980), should be implemented in order to protect and enhance the positive effects of preventive interventions.

Clearly, such continuity of effort is expensive. However, a commitment to life-span programming must be coupled with a commitment to *discontinue programs that have proved to be ineffective* (Dryfoos, 1990). Accountability—the requirement to deliver a high-quality program—is a necessary feature of professionally responsible, ethical, and humane programs (Hamburg, 1992). Moreover, if only those programs that have been shown to be effective are continued, then resources devoted to poor programs may be saved. Of course, making such decisions requires that appropriate evaluation information exists.

The Development-in-Context Evaluation (DICE) Model

Promoting positive individual and social development and change through the incorporation of participatory evaluation into program design and implementation is precisely what is considered within a developmental contextual view of evaluation (Lerner et al., in press; Ostrom et al., 1995). Indeed, from a developmental contextual perspective, which emphasizes a community-collaborative approach to the integration of research and outreach, *program- and community-specific evaluation is a requisite for all effective programming* (Dryfoos,

1990) and for an understanding the basic processes of human development (Lerner, 1991).

Accordingly, such evaluations will seek to understand how a successful program may be designed, implemented, assessed, and sustained in a specific community. To attain such knowledge, a *development-in-context evaluation* (DICE) model may be pursued (Lerner et al., in press; Ostrom et al., 1995). The DICE model is an instance of the kind of community-evaluator collaborative, participatory-normative approach to evaluation forwarded by Weiss and Greene (1992).

Moreover, the DICE model builds on the basic tenets of the philosophy of pragmatism in general (Dixon & Lerner, 1992), and on Charles Sanders Peirce's (1931) pragmatic maxim specifically. Peirce's conception of pragmatism focuses on the results or consequences that occur if one accepts and acts on any idea, theory, model, policy, or innovation. Several ideas flow from this seemingly straightforward maxim. The key ideas guiding the DICE model are discussed next.

A Template for Creating Collaborative Communities

The development-in-context evaluation model represents an instance of the community collaborative, participatory-normative approach to evaluation—and to program design, program development, and community empowerment—promoted by Weiss and associates (for example, Jacobs, 1988; Miller, 1993; Weiss, 1987a, 1987b; Weiss & Greene, 1992; Weiss & Jacobs, 1988). As such, evaluators following the DICE model will do the following:

1. Work with community members to identify the problems or issues to which the program will be directed
2. Engage the members of the community in the planning of the evaluation; in decisions about the nature of any preliminary, developmental, and outcome information sought about the

program; in the collection of relevant data; and in the documentation and interpretation of the information derived from the evaluation

3. Collaborate with the community in the utilization of the information derived from the evaluation; for example, in the execution of any "midcourse" corrections deemed necessary to enhance program effectiveness and/or in the identification of any changes that have resulted in the nature of the problem that led to the initiation of the program

Moreover, evaluations conducted within the framework of the DICE model build from a qualitative understanding of the community and of the goals for the program envisioned by community members. Such evaluations collaborate with the community throughout the entire process of gaining the knowledge that the evaluation seeks to obtain. This is why such evaluations involve at their core *co-learning* between the evaluators and the community. In addition, the community-collaborative approach of such evaluations builds the capacity of the community to sustain the program after the evaluation is completed; indeed, the community is empowered to incorporate continued evaluations into its future plans for the program (Lerner et al., in press; Ostrom et al., 1995).

Finally, such evaluations are predicated on attention to the diversity that exists within a specific community—to the specific goals, values, and meaning systems that are present in the community and that shape the program. Recognition of the importance of such diversity appears critical in the design of effective prevention programs. As noted by Dryfoos (1990), programs that pay attention to cultural and lifestyle diversity, as well as individual diversity, are more likely to succeed.

In sum, the concepts of developmental contextualism and the features and principles of successful prevention programs—especially when they involve a participatory, development-in-con-

text approach to evaluation—appear to be highly consonant. Accordingly, the application of developmental contextual ideas and the principles of successful programs should assist in the design, implementation, evaluation, and sustainability of programs effectively addressing the problems of children and adolescents. Although, by necessity, specific features of such programs will vary in relation to the particular target problem(s) being addressed and the particular community within which the program exists, it is clear from this discussion that these programs will share some general features. They will involve integrated, communitywide, multiagency (or institutional) collaborations that link youth, families, and the larger community together in a sustained effort.

I believe that, in general, partnerships between the research and extension communities are critical if the developmental contextual vision of integrated research and outreach—and, more specifically, of the participatory approach to evaluation involved in the DICE model—is to succeed in producing effective programs for America's children and adolescents. Moreover, research and extension partnerships will be the vital base upon which universities will be able to build effective means to respond to the problems facing America's children.

Such partnerships should begin with identifying issues through broadly constituted, community-university teams; these teams will be facilitated by land-grant universities' cooperative extension services in order to ensure that there is an arm of the university that has knowledge of, and legitimacy in, the community—indeed, extension is part of the community. University structures should then be developed to provide an integrated university capacity to work with communities around the issues raised in the identification process. Then, with community partners who invite collaboration, research and extension colleagues can join in the building of collaborative communities by starting integrated efforts at program development, program evaluation, and community empowerment for sustainability; these efforts are predicated on asset mapping for positive youth development. This process serves as a means to identify, organize, and *integratively* deploy the strengths of the community.

The sorts of thorough collaborations we envision both within universities and between universities and communities have not been attempted seriously. They may not work. However, the fragmented and uncoordinated state of current responses to the issues and needs of America's diverse children and families have not only not worked but have failed miserably. If we are to pull our youth, and our nation, back from the precipice of generation destruction on which it now hangs, we have to dare to envision and enact new models that have reason and evidence to support their viability. We believe that the thorough, participatory, and empowering collaboration involved in the DICE model is such an approach. Nothing short of the future of the United States may hang in the balance as we pursue tests of the usefulness of this model.

Conclusion

Ultimately, we must all continue to educate ourselves about the best means available to promote enhanced life chances among *all* of our youth, but especially among those whose potentials for positive contributions to our nation are most in danger of being wasted (Lerner, 1993a, 1995). The collaborative expertise of the research and extension communities can provide much of this information, especially if it is obtained in partnership with strong, empowered communities. Policies promoting such coalitions will be an integral component of a national youth development policy aimed at creating caring communities and having the capacity to nurture the healthy development of our children and youth.

There is no time to lose in the development of such policies. The United States as we know it—and, even more, as we believe it can be—will be lost unless we act now. The strengths and assets of all our universities, of all our institutions, and of all our people must be marshaled for this effort.

The agenda is clear and the means to achieve it appear available. We need only the will. This motivation will be readily evoked when Americans recognize the validity of the point made by Marian Wright Edelman (1992), president of the Children's Defense Fund:

> In the waning years of the twentieth century, doing what is right for children and doing what is necessary to save our national economic skin have converged. (p. 93)

Let us work together to save our youth, to save our families and communities, and, superordinately, to save our nation.

References

Baltes, P. B. (1968). Longitudinal and cross-sectional sequences in the study of age and generation effects. *Human Development, 11,* 145–171.

Baltes, P. B. (1987). Theoretical propositions of life-span developmental psychology: On the dynamics between growth and decline. *Developmental Psychology, 23,* 611–626.

Baltes, P. B., & Baltes, M. M. (1980). Plasticity and variability in psychological aging: Methodological and theoretical issues. In G. E. Gurski (Ed.), *Determining the effects of aging on the central nervous system* (pp. 41–66). Berlin: Schering.

Bell, R. Q. (1968). A reinterpretation of the direction of effects in studies of socialization. *Psychological Review, 75,* 81–95.

Belsky, J., Lerner, R. M., & Spanier, G. B. (1984). *The child in the family.* Reading, MA: Addison-Wesley.

Block, J. (1971). *Lives through time*. Berkeley, CA: Bancroft Books.

Boyer, E. L. (1990). *Scholarship reconsidered: Priorities of the professoriate*. Princeton, NJ: The Carnegie Foundation for the Advancement of Teaching.

Boyer, E. L. (1994, March 9). Creating the new American college [Point of View column]. *Chronicle of Higher Education*, p. A48.

Brim, O. G., Jr., & Kagan, J. (Eds.). (1980). *Constancy and change in human development*. Cambridge, MA: Harvard University Press.

Bronfenbrenner, U. (1977). Toward an experimental ecology of human development. *American Psychologist, 32*, 513–531.

Bronfenbrenner, U. (1979). *The ecology of human development*. Cambridge, MA: Harvard University Press.

Bronfenbrenner, U. (1983). The context of development and the development of context. In R. M. Lerner (Ed.), *Developmental psychology; Historical and philosophical perspectives* (pp. 39–83). Hillsdale, NJ: Erlbaum.

Bronfenbrenner, U., & Crouter, A. C. (1983). The evolution of environmental models in developmental research. In W. Kersen (Ed.), *Handbook of child psychology: Vol. 1. History, theories, and methods* (pp. 39–83) New York: Wiley.

Carnegie Corporation of New York. (1992, December). *A matter of time: Risk and opportunity in the nonschool hours*. Available from Carnegie Council on Adolescent Development, P.O. Box 753, Waldorf, MD 20604.

Carnegie Corporation of New York. (1994, April). *Starting points: Meeting the needs of our youngest children*. Available from Carnegie Corporation of New York, P.O. Box 753, Waldorf, MD 20604.

Carnegie Council on Adolescent Development. (1989). *Turning points: Preparing American youth for the 21st century*. Available from Carnegie Council on Adolescent Development, 11 Dupont Circle N.W., Washington, DC 20036.

Center for the Study of Social Policy. (1992). *Kids count data book*. Washington, DC: Author.

Center for the Study of Social Policy. (1993). *Kids count data book* (2nd ed.) Washington, DC: Author.

Chess, S., & Thomas, A. (1984). *The origins and evolution of behavior disorders: Infancy to early adult life*. New York: Brunner/Mazel.

Children's Defense Fund. (1992). *Child poverty up nationally and in 33 states*. Washington, DC: Author.

Clarke, A. M., & Clarke, A. D. B. (Eds.). (1976). *Early experience: Myth and evidence*. New York: Free Press.

Dixon, R. A., & Lerner, R. M. (1992). A history of systems in developmental psychology. In M. H. Bornstein & M. E. Lamb (Eds.), *Developmental psychology: An advanced textbook* (3rd ed., pp. 3–58). Hillsdale, NJ: Erlbaum.

Dixon, R. A., Lerner, R. M., & Hultsch, D. F. (1991). The concept of development in individual and social change. In P. Van Geert & L. P. Mos (Eds.), *Annals of theoretical psychology* (Vol. 7, pp. 279–323). New York: Plenum.

Dryfoos, J. G. (1990). *Adolescents at risk: Prevalence and prevention*. New York: Oxford University Press.

Dryfoos, J. G. (1994). *Full service schools: A revolution in health and social services for children, youth and families*. San Francisco: Jossey-Bass.

Dryfoos, J. G. (1995). Full service schools: Revolution or fad? *Journal of Research on Adolescence, 5*, 147–172.

Duncan, G. J. (1991). The economic environment of childhood. In A. C. Huston (Ed.), *Children in poverty: Child development and public policy* (pp. 23–50). Cambridge: Cambridge University Press.

Edelman, M. W. (1992). *The measure of our success: A letter to my children and yours*. Boston: Beacon Press.

Elder, G. H. (1974). *Children of the Great Depression: Social change in life experiences*. Chicago: University of Chicago Press.

Elder, G. H., Jr. (1980). Adolescence in historical perspective. In J. Adelson (Ed.), *Handbooks of adolescent psychology* (pp. 3–46). New York: Wiley.

Elder, G. H. Modell, J., & Parke, R. D. (1993). Studying children in a changing world. In G. H. Elder, J. Modell, & R. D. Parke (Eds.), *Children in time and place: Developmental and historical insights* (pp. 3–21). New York: Cambridge University Press.

Enarson, H. L. (1989). *Revitalizing the landgrant mission*. Blacksburg, VA: Virginia Polytechnic Institute and State University.

Featherman, D. L. (1983). Life-span perspectives in social science research. In P. B. Baltes & O. G. Brim, Jr. (Eds.), *Life-span development and behavior* (Vol. 5, pp. 1–57). New York: Academic Press.

Featherman, D. L., & Lerner, R. M. (1985). Ontogenesis and sociogenesis: Problematics for theory about development across the lifespan. *American Sociological Review, 50,* 659–676.

Finkelstein, J. W. (1993). Familial influences on adolescent health. In R. M. Lerner (Ed.), *Early adolescence: Perspectives on research, policy and intervention* (pp. 111–126). Hillsdale, NJ: Erlbaum.

Fisher, C. B., & Brennan, M. (1992). Application and ethics in developmental psychology. In D. L. Featherman, R. M. Lerner, & M. Perlmutter (Eds.), *Life-span development and behavior* (Vol. 11, pp. 189–219). Hillsdale, NJ: Erlbaum.

Fisher, C. B., & Lerner, R. M. (1994). Foundations of applied developmental psychology. In C. B. Fisher & R. M. Lerner (Eds.), *Applied developmental psychology* (pp. 3–20). New York: McGraw-Hill.

Ford, D. L., & Lerner, R. M. (1992). *Developmental systems theory: An integrative approach.* Newbury Park, CA: Sage.

Garbarino, J. (1992). *Children and families in the social environment* (2nd ed.). New York: Aldine de Gruyter.

Gottlieb, G. (1991). The experiential canalization of behavioral development: Theory. *Developmental Psychology, 27,* 4–13.

Gottlieb, G. (1992). *Individual development and evolution: The genesis of novel behavior.* New York: Oxford University Press.

Gould, S. J. (1977). *Ontogeny and phylogeny.* Cambridge: Belknap Press of Harvard University.

Graham, S. (1992). "Most of the subjects were white and middle class": Trends in published research on African Americans in selected APA journals, 1970–1989. *American Psychologist, 5,* 629–639.

Hagen, J. W., Paul, B., Gibb, S., & Wolters, C. (1990, March). Trends in research as reflected by publications in *Child Development:* 1930–1989. In *Biennial Meeting of the Society for Research on Adolescence,* Atlanta, GA.

Hamburg, D. A. (1992). *Today's children: Creating a future for a generation in crisis.* New York: Time Books.

Hebb, D. O. (1949). *The organization of behavior.* New York: Wiley.

Hernandez, D. J. (1993). *America's children: Resources from family, government, and the economy.* New York: Russell Sage Foundation.

Hetherington, E. M., & Baltes, P. B. (1988). Child psychology and life-span development. In E. M. Hetherington, R. M. Lerner, & M. Perlmutter (Eds.), *Child development in life-span perspective* (pp. 1–19). Hillsdale, NJ: Erlbaum.

Hoffman, R. F. (1978). Developmental changes in human infant visual-evoked potentials to patterned stimuli recorded at different scalp locations. *Child Development, 49,* 110–118.

Hogan, R., Johnson, J. A., & Emler, N. P. (1978). A socioanalytic theory of moral development. *New Directions for Child Development, 2,* 1–18.

Howard, J. (1978). The influence of children's developmental dysfunction on marital quality and family interaction. In R. M. Lerner & G. B. Spanier (Eds.), *Child influences on marital and family interaction: A life-span perspective* (pp. 275–298). New York: Academic Press.

Huston, A. C. (Ed.). (1991). *Children in poverty: Child development and public policy.* Cambridge: Cambridge University Press.

Huston, A. C., McLoyd, V. C., & Coll, C. G. (1994). Children and poverty: Issues in contemporary research. *Child Development, 65,* 275–282.

Jacobs, F. H. (1988). The five-tiered approach to evaluation: Context and implementation. In H. Weiss & F. Jacobs (Eds.), *Evaluating family programs* (pp. 37–68). Hawthorne, NY: Aldine de Gruyter.

Jensen, L. (1988). Rural-urban differences in the utilization of ameliorative effects of welfare programs. *Policy Studies Review, 7,* 782–794.

Kahn, R. L., & Antonucci, T. C. (1980). Convoys over the life course: Attachment, roles, and social support. In P. B. Baltes & O. G. Brim, Jr. (Eds.), *Life-span development and behavior* (Vol. 3). Hillsdale, NJ: Erlbaum.

Klerman, L. V. (1991). The health of poor children: Problems and programs. In A. C. Huston (Ed.), *Children in poverty: Child development and public policy,* (pp. 1–22). Cambridge: Cambridge University Press.

Lerner, R. M. (1982). Children and adolescents as producers of their own development. *Developmental Review, 2,* 342–370.

Lerner, R. M. (1984). *On the nature of human plasticity.* New York: Cambridge University Press.

Lerner, R. M. (1986). *Concepts and theories of human development* (2nd ed.). New York: Random House.

Lerner, R. M. (1988). Early adolescent transitions: The lore and the laws of adolescence. In M. D. Levine & E. R. McArarney (Eds.), *Early adolescent transitions* (pp. 1–40). Lexington, MA: D. C. Heath.

Lerner, R. M. (1991). Changing organism-context relations as the basic process of development: A developmental-contextual perspective. *Developmental Psychology, 27,* 27–32.

Lerner, R. M. (1992). *Final solutions: Biology, prejudice, and genocide.* University Park: Penn State Press.

Lerner, R. M. (1993a). Investment in youth: The role of home economics in enhancing the life chances of America's children. *AHEA Monograph Series, 1,* 5–34.

Lerner, R. M. (1993b). Early adolescence: Toward an agenda for the integration of research, policy, and intervention. In R. M. Lerner (Ed.), *Early adolescence: Perspectives on research, policy, and intervention* (pp. 1–13). Hillsdale, NJ: Erlbaum.

Lerner, R. M. (1994). Schools and adolescents. In P. C. McKenry & S. M. Gavazzi (Eds.), *Visions 2010: Families and adolescents* (pp. 14–15, 42–43). Minneapolis, MN: National Council on Family Relations.

Lerner, R. M. (1995). *America's youth in crisis: Challenges and options for programs and policies.* Thousand Oaks, CA: Sage.

Lerner, R. M. (1996). Relative plasticity, integration, temporality, and diversity in human development: A developmental contextual perspective about theory, process, and method. *Developmental Psychology, 32,* 781–786.

Lerner, R. M., & Busch-Rossnagel, N. A. (Eds.). (1981). *Individuals as producers of their development: A life-span perspective.* New York: Academic Press.

Lerner, R. M., Hultsch, D. F., & Dixon, R. A. (1983). Contextualism and the character of developmental psychology in the 1970s. *Annals of the New York Academy of Sciences, 412,* 101–128.

Lerner, R. M., & Kauffman, M. B. (1985). The concept of development in contextualism. *Developmental Review, 5,* 309–333.

Lerner, R. M., & Lerner, J. V. (1983). Temperament-intelligence reciprocities in early childhood: A contextual model. In M. Lewis (Ed.), *Origins of intelligence: Infancy and early childhood.* New York: Plenum.

Lerner, R. M., & Lerner, J. V. (1989). Organismic and social contextual bases of development: The sample case of early adolescence. In W. Damon (Ed.), *Child development today and tomorrow* (pp. 69–85). San Francisco: Jossey-Bass

Lerner, R. M., & Miller, J. R. (1993). Integrating human development research and intervention for America's children: The Michigan State University model. *Journal of Applied Developmental Psychology, 14,* 347–364.

Lerner, R. M., Miller, J. R., Knott, J. H., Corey, K. E., Bynum, T. S., Hoopfer, L. C., McKinney, M. H., Abrams, L. A., Hula, R. C., & Terry, P. A. (1994a). Integrating scholarship and outreach in human development research, policy, and service: A developmental perspective. In D. L. Featherman, R. M. Lerner, & M. Perlmutter (Eds.), *Life-span development and behavior* (Vol. 12, pp. 249–273). Hillsdale, NJ: Erlbaum.

Lerner, R. M., Ostrom, C. W., & Freel, M. A. (in press). Preventing health compromising behaviors among youth and promoting their positive development: A developmental-contextual perspective. In J. Schulenberg, J. L. Maggs, & K. Hurrelmann (Eds.), *Health risks and developmental transitions during adolescence.* New York: Cambridge University Press.

Lerner, R. M., & Ryff, C. D. (1978). Implementation of the life-span view of human development: The sample case of attachment. In P. B. Baltes (Ed.), *Life-span development and behavior* (Vol. 1, pp. 1–44). New York: Academic Press.

Lerner, R. M., & Spanier, G. B. (Eds.). (1978). *Child influences on marital and family interaction: A life-span perspective.* New York: Academic Press.

Lerner, R. M., Terry, P. A., McKinney, M. H., & Abrams, L. A. (1994b). Addressing child poverty within the context of a community-collaborative university: Comments on Fabes, Martin, and Smith (1994) and

McLoyd (1994). *Family and Consumer Sciences Research Journal, 23,* 67–75.

Lewis, M., & Fiering, C. (1978). A child's social world. In R. M. Lerner & G. B. Spanier (Eds.), *Child influences on marital and family interaction* (pp. 47–66). New York: Academic Press.

Lewis, M., & Rosenblum, L. A. (Eds.). (1974). *The effect of the infant on its caregivers.* New York: Wiley.

Lynton, E. A., & Elman, S. E. (1987). *New priorities for the university: Meeting society's needs for applied knowledge and competent individuals.* San Francisco: Jossey-Bass.

Masters, R. D. (1978). Jean-Dacques is alive and well: Rousseau and contemporary sociobiology. *Daedalus, 107,* 93–105.

McKinney, M., Abrams, L. A., Terry, P. A., & Lerner, R. M. (1994). Child development research and the poor children of America: A call for a developmental contextual approach to research and outreach. *Family and Consumer Sciences Research Journal, 23,* 26–42.

McLoyd, V. C. (1994). Research in the service of poor and ethnic/racial minority children: A moral imperative. *Family and Consumer Sciences Research Journal, 23,* 56–66.

McLoyd, V. C., & Wilson, L. (1991). The strain of living poor: Parenting, social support, and child mental health. In A. C. Huston (Ed.), *Children in poverty: Child development and public policy* (pp. 105–135). Cambridge: Cambridge University Press.

Michigan State University Provost's Committee on University Outreach. (1993). *University outreach at Michigan State University: Extending knowledge to serve society.* East Lansing: Michigan State University Press.

Miller, J. R., & Lerner, R. M. (1994). Integrating research and outreach: Developmental contextualism and the human ecological perspective. *Home Economics Forum, 7,* 21–28.

Miller, P. B. (1993). *Building villages to raise our children: Evaluation.* Cambridge, MA: Harvard Family Research Project.

Mincy, R. B. (Ed.). (1994). *Nurturing young black males: Challenges to agencies, programs, and social policy.* Washington, DC: The Urban Institute Press.

National Council of Administrators of Home Economics Programs. (1991, October). *Creating a vision: The profession for the next century* [Report of the working conference]. Pine Mountain, GA: Callaway Gardens.

National Research Council. (1993). *Losing generations: Adolescents in high-risk settings.* Washington, DC: National Academy Press.

Ostrom, C. W., Lerner, R. M., & Freel, M. A. (1995). Building the capacity of youth and families through university-community collaborations: The development-in-context evaluation (DICE) model. *Journal of Adolescent Research, 10,* 427–428.

Overton, W. F., & Reese, H. W. (1973). Models of development: Methodological implications. In J. R. Nesselroade & H. W. Reese (Eds.), *Life-span developmental psychology: Methodological issues* (pp. 65–86). New York: Academic Press.

Overton, W. F., & Reese, H. W. (1981). Conceptual prerequisites for an understanding of stability-change and continuity-discontinuity. *International Journal of Behavioral Development, 4,* 99–123.

Peirce, C. S. (1931). In C. Hartshorne, P. Weiss, & A. Burks (Eds.), *Collected papers of Charles Sanders Peirce* (Vol. 5, p. 86). Cambridge, MA: Harvard University Press.

Pepper, S. C. (1942). *World hypotheses.* Berkeley: University of California Press.

Pittman, K. J., & Zeldin, S. (1994). From deterrence to development: Shifting the focus of youth programs for African-American males. In R. B. Mincy (Ed.), *Nurturing young black males: Challenges to agencies, programs, and social policy* (pp. 165–186). Washington, DC: The Urban Institute Press.

Reese, H. W., & Overton, W. F. (1970). Models of development and theories of development. In L. R. Goulet & P. B. Baltes (Eds.), *Life-span developmental psychology: Research and theory* (pp. 115–145). New York: Academic Press.

Riegel, K. F. (1975). Toward a dialectical theory of development. *Human Development, 18,* 50–64.

Riegel, K. F. (1976a). The dialectics of human development. *American Psychologist, 31,* 689–700.

Riegel, K. F. (1976b). From traits and equilibrium toward developmental dialectics. In W. J. Arnold & J. K. Cole (Eds.), *Nebraska symposium on motivation* (pp. 348–408). Lincoln: University of Nebraska Press.

Riley, M. W. (Ed.). (1979). *Aging from birth to death.*

Washington, DC: American Association for the Advancement of Science.

Sahlins, M. D. (1978). The use and abuse of biology. In A. L. Caplan (Ed.), *The sociobiology debate.* New York: Harper & Row.

Sameroff, A. (1975). Transactional models in early social relations. *Human Development, 18,* 65–79.

Sameroff, A. J. (1983). Developmental systems: Contexts and evolution. In W Kessen (Ed.) & P. H. Mussen (Series Ed.), *Handbook of child psychology: Vol. 1. History, theory and methods* (pp. 237–294). New York: Wiley.

Schaie, K. W. (1965). A general model for the study of developmental problems. *Psychological Bulletin, 64,* 92–107.

Schneirla, T. C. (1957). The concept of development in comparative psychology. In D. B. Harris (Ed.), *The concept of development* (pp. 78–108). Minneapolis: University of Minnesota Press.

Schorr, L. B. (1988). *Within our reach: Breaking the cycle of disadvantage.* New York: Doubleday.

Schorr, L. B. (1992). Effective programs for children growing up in concentrated poverty. In A. C. Huston (Ed.), *Children in poverty: Child development and public policy* (pp. 260–281). Cambridge: Cambridge University Press.

Simons, J. M., Finlay, B., & Yang, A. (1991). *The adolescent and young adult fact book.* Washington, DC: Children's Defense Fund.

Thomas, A., & Chess, S. (1977). *Temperament and development.* New York: Brunner/Mazel.

Thomas, A., Chess. S., Birch, H. G., Hertzig, M. E., & Korn, S. (1963). *Behavioral individuality in early childhood.* New York: New York University Press.

Tobach, E. (1981). Evolutionary aspects of the activity of the organism and its development. In R. M. Lerner & N. A. Busch-Rossnagel (Eds.), *Individuals as producers of their development: A life-span perspective* (pp. 37–68). New York: Academic Press.

Tobach, E., & Greenberg, G. (1984). The significance of T. C. Schneirla's contribution to the concept of levels of integration. In G. Greenberg & E. Tobach (Eds.), *Behavioral evolution and integrative levels* (pp. 1–7). Hillsdale, NJ: Erlbaum.

Tobach, E., & Schneirla, T. C. (1968). The biopsychology of social behavior of animals. In R. E. Cooke & S. Levin (Eds.), *Biologic basis of pediatric practice* (pp. 68–82). New York: McGraw-Hill.

Tubman, J. G., & Lerner, R. M. (1994). Stability of affective experiences of parents and their children from adolescence to young adulthood. *Journal of Adolescent, 17,* 81–98.

U.S. Bureau of the Census. (1991, August). *The Hispanic population in the United States: March, 1991* (Current Population Reports, Series P-20, No. 455). Washington, DC: U.S. Government Printing Office.

U.S. Department of Commerce. (1991, August). *Poverty in the United States: 1990.* Washington, DC: Author.

Vondracek, F. W., Lerner, R. M., & Schulenberg, J. E. (1986). *Career development: A life-span developmental approach.* Hillsdale, NJ: Erlbaum.

Washburn, S. L. (Ed.). (1961). *Social life of early men.* New York: Wenner-Gren Foundation for Anthropological Research.

Weiss, H. B. (1987a). Family support and education in early childhood programs. In S. Kagan, D. Powell, B. Weissbourd, & E. Zigler (Eds.), *America's family support programs* (pp. 133–160). New Haven, CT: Yale University Press.

Weiss, H. B. (1987b). Evaluating social programs: What have we learned? *Society, 25*(1), 40–45.

Weiss, H. B., & Greene, J. C. (1992). An empowerment partnership for family support and education programs and evaluations. *Family Science Review, 5,* 131–148.

Weiss, H. B., & Jacobs, F. (Eds.) (1988). *Evaluating family programs.* Hawthorne, NY: Aldine.

Werner, H. (1957). The concept of development from a comparative and organismic point of view. In D. B. Harris (Ed.), *The concept of development* (pp. 125–148). Minneapolis: University of Minnesota Press..

Wilson, W. J. (1987). *The truly disadvantaged: The inner city, the underclass, and public policy.* Chicago: University of Chicago Press.

PART III

Care and Special Education: A Cultural Project

JAMES L. PAUL
University of South Florida

Diversity is one of the core challenges to educational philosophers, curriculum theorists, and teachers involved in restructuring public education. The increasing sociocultural complexity of schools and the economic conditions of our society at the end of the 20th century are raising fundamental questions about both the process and goals of education. The issues are not new but the context of the 1980s and 1990s has brought new meaning and urgency to the questions.

During the last half of this century we have lost our innocence about the moral and political force of pedagogy. Propelled by the civil rights reforms of the 1960s, a new and critical imagination about justice, fairness, equality, individual and collective interests, and care has emerged, along with both technical and heuristic tools for deeper and richer understandings of human communities. Examples of this new thinking include an appreciation for the nature and power of texts and subtexts in the classroom, a more valid understanding of the complexity and sociology of knowledge, the development and acceptance of research methods from anthropology and literary theory, and the growth of interest in ethics and education. Positivist research philosophy, which has generated useful knowledge about groups and the general case, has provided limited knowledge about local contexts and individual cases. During the past decade, the research and professional literature in many different disciplines has challenged the traditional hegemony of positivism. Some of the challenges have argued for alternatives to positivism, whereas others have focused more on the politics of knowledge and the need for a continuing dialogue on paradigms of knowledge and knowing, including positivism.

The policy tools of the social sciences continue to be blunt instruments (Gallagher, 1997) in helping us understand the moral and social well-being of individuals and collective interests, including gender, ethnic traditions, religious preference, and so forth. What we have not been able to discern with our senses, however aided by sophisticated technologies, has been left to political debate, which is structured by the values and interests of those in power at the time. The only knowledge that counted in these debates was what was shown to be objective and verifiable. While this view of knowledge continues to be an important feature of the political process, there is a growing diversity of voices being heard that give more contextualized and storied accounts of human communities. These accounts preserve the moral complexities and nuances of social advantage and exploitation often lost in the more technical discourses of the social sciences.

Although values, rather than data, have generally shaped public policy, matters of the heart are now of explicit consequence in debates about both social policy and science. This is especially evident in the rhetoric of the reform of public education. Those representing feminist and gay and lesbian perspectives have created more powerful voices in articulating different ways of knowing and an ethic of care as an alternative to the traditionally dominant ethic of justice. Ethnic minorities have found their own voices and have established powerful platforms to protect the integrity of their histories and their own linguistic, social, religious, and moral perspectives.

The wider conversation about human community has been aided by the dynamic integration of the two cultures of the sciences and the humanities. Anthropologists, moral philosophers, ethicists, epistemologists, literary theorists, and artists, for example, are now more likely to be found at the table previously reserved for social, behavioral, and neuroscientists in discussions of knowledge about human behavior.

The emerging discourses are rich and varied, including those that center on public education. There is concurrent advocacy for the interests of diverse groups and for connected communities. There is a challenge to the dominant groups of the past to share power, control, and resources with groups that have been disenfranchised. The focus is on eliminating hierarchies that are unfair and that disadvantage groups because of their minority status. The development of a connected, egalitarian community has emerged as an implicit goal in social policy. There are numerous policies and social technologies that reflect this aim, such as site-based management in schools, shared decision making, a focus on families, and collaborative strategies in classrooms and between schools and communities.

In the absence of predictive knowledge to guide social policy and practices such as education, the rules and guidelines for decisions are much more complex and require more perceptive discernment about individual and group interests. How are interests to be understood and adjudicated? Although ethical decisions can be aided by data, consideration must be given to the duties, values, and motivations of those making the decisions, and to the rights and interests of those affected by the decisions.

One diverse group of students in schools has been singled out for "special" education. How are their interests to be understood? How can a disproportionate amount of public resources needed for their education be justified? How should the departures of their education from the education of other students be evaluated? Changing views about individual differences—and the role of the sciences and humanities in addressing differences in morally, socially, and technically defensible ways—have had an impact on special education. The flaws of a system designed to be helpful in the learning and social development of children with disabilities have come more clearly into focus as the reforms of the past forty years have provided different lenses for seeing and interpreting our work. For example, we have become more aware of the role of culture and the dynamics of power in schools that influence our decisions about "preferred" practices. Although we have developed better methods of research and evaluation to improve practice, we have also become increasingly aware of the ethical implications of special education policies and practices.

There has been a growing awareness that children with disabilities and their families share in the spoils of the public policy discourse on diversity. Like minorities and other disenfranchised groups, their welfare in public services is largely determined by decisions made by others—those in the majority. This common plight of those in the minority, and the moral complexity of this sociopolitical context, frames this section on care and special education as a cultural project.

Special education policies define children with respect to impairments, inadequacies, or deficits in one or more aspects of social, psychological, and/or physical functioning. With the exception of students with special gifts and talents, all special education students are identified as having "less than" or the absence of something. They are, therefore, treated differently, and that difference reflects our values about what we regard as worthy as well as our science about what we regard to be true.

One of the most fundamental issues in special education has to do with the implicit presumptions about personhood: What does it mean to be

human? Most of the professional discourses on disability have been technical, empirical, legal, and, to a lesser extent, ethical. The storied nature of lives
lived with learning disabilities, emotional disorders, sensory impairments,
developmental disabilities, or other atypical challenges is often lost. What is
lost when the story is gone is the person, his or her gender, ethnicity, religious
beliefs, and other realities that identify her or him as unique and worthy. The
child learns at home—often in a faith community—the story she or he is in
and the role she or he is playing now and is expected to play in the future.
The personal, cultural, and religious stories are often in stark contrast to the
professional story of disability that defines the child as "different."

The school is a social, learning, and political community with a complex
cultural web of traditions. As a social community, it has traditions acknowledged with pride, such as the Euro-American heritage, and traditions often
insulted by ignorance, such as those of Native Americans or African Americans. The school has diversities of ethnicity, gender, faith perspectives, abilities, and other self-defining characteristics in need of support and affirma-
tion yet vulnerable to harm. As a learning community, the school is a place
where learners gather, where both visible and hidden curricula are studied,
and where texts and subtexts assign status to all members. It is a place where
there are unlimited opportunities to learn how to be more fully human as
well as how to insult, steal, cheat, and deceive. As a political community, the
school has all of the error and mischief of any other social system where
there are those who have power and those who do not, those committed to
justice and those who are not, those who care and those who do not. Because most of those who populate schools are children, and power is clearly
established in the adults who teach and make school policies, there is an
enormous potential for disservice to the interests of individuals. Fortunately, the risk of error is balanced by the opportunity to effect a more
thoughtful, informed, competent, and caring human community.

This section raises powerful questions about the intersections of professional practice, public education policy, and human community. Chapter 8
was prepared by Sonia Nieto, professor of education in the Cultural Diversity and Curriculum Reform Program in the School of Education, University of Massachusetts at Amherst. Her research interests include curriculum
issues in multicultural education, the education of Latinos in the United
States, and Puerto Ricans in children's books, and her writings have focused
on educational equity and social justice.

Nieto begins her discussion of diversity with the view that the daunting challenges of facing the increasing diversity among the student bodies

in elementary and secondary schools require colleges of education to transform the process of preparing the next generation of teachers. She examines the complex forces of institutional discrimination, focusing primarily on culture, language, and ethnicity. She emphasizes the sociopolitical context of schooling and the need for teacher education programs to consider the subtleties and force of school policies, pedagogy, and curricula in marginalizing and otherwise working against the interests of diverse student populations.

Chapter 9 addresses gender issues and is authored by Nel Noddings, the Lee L. Jacks Professor of Child Education at Stanford University and acting dean of education. Her research interests include feminist ethics, moral education, and mathematical problem solving.

Noddings critiques the idea of valued work and workers. Challenging the arrogance of the presumption that math and science achievement represents the pentacle of success in school, she argues for valuing the social graces, caring, art, and professions, such as teaching and social work. She addresses the larger theater of human affairs, where community is a way of life rather than an abstraction, where family is a social construction of the human community rather than only a genetic bond, where cultural and religious imagination lead to celebrations of mystery rather than to negatively valued stereotypes about faith perspectives, where curiosity is a virtue leading to hopeful possibilities rather than to negative judgments, where forgiveness is an act of will reserved for acts of injustice rather than a social mechanism to publicly acknowledge incompetence or irresponsibility, and where injustices can be recognized and redressed wherever they occur and from whomever they come without the mystification of those in power.

Chapter 10, which focuses on ethics, was prepared by Kenneth Howe, associate professor in the School of Education at the University of Colorado. Howe's research interests include educational philosophy, ethics, testing, and philosophy of inquiry.

In the complex matrix of competing interests and values in the diverse environments of schools, how can decisions be made that are fair, respectful of differences, and that affirm the rights of individuals? Howe presents a liberal-democratic framework for educational ethics and describes three major philosophical theories that comprise this framework—utilitarian, libertarian, and liberal-egalitarian—arguing that the liberal-egalitarian theory is superior. He also describes four ethical theories—critical theory, communitarianism, the ethics of care, and postmodernism—that have challenged the liberal-egalitarian framework on grounds that it is overly abstract, ahistorical, unresponsive to diversity, androcentric, Eurocentric, oppressive, and an apology for the status quo. Howe argues that these criticisms can be accommodated by liberal-egalitarian theory. He goes on to discuss the professional activities of special education as a context for ethical deliberation, and therefore, the need for teaching the ethics of special education.

References

Gallagher, J. (1997). The role of policy in special education reform. In J. L. Paul, M. Churton, W. Morse, A. Duchnowski, B. Epanchin, P. Osnes, & L. Smith (Eds.), *Special education practice Applying the knowledge, affirming the values, and creating the future.* Pacific Grove, CA: Brooks/Cole.

CHAPTER 8

Diversity: What Do Teachers Need to Know?

SONIA NIETO
University of Massachusetts at Amherst

From the time free and compulsory education became a fact of life in the 19th century, first in Massachusetts and then throughout the states, our society has had a social contract to educate all youngsters, not simply those who happen to be from economically privileged backgrounds or the cultural mainstream. In spite of this, too many students have traditionally been failed by our schools, and this is especially true of those from racially and culturally dominated and economically oppressed backgrounds. Research over the past half-century has documented a legacy of failure for students of all backgrounds, but particularly for those of Latino, African American, Native American, and poor white families and more recently for Asian and Pacific American immigrant students. Traditional explanations for this failure, especially beginning in the 1960s, have included theories of genetic inferiority, cultural deprivation, or family apathy to the benefits of education (Bereiter & Englemann, 1966; Jensen, 1969; Reisman, 1962).

Teacher education programs, reflecting the conventional wisdom that grew out of such theories, have been mired in assumptions about the necessity for assimilation and the role of schools as the standard bearers of a traditional and unchanging canon. In many teacher preparation programs, students of dominated cultures have been viewed as walking sets of deficits rather than as having cultures, languages, and experiences that could be helpful in their own learning and that could enrich the curriculum for all youngsters. Thus, although the blame for student failure has usually been placed squarely on the shoulders of students and their families, schools have been reluctant to face their own policies and practices as complicitous in creating a climate of failure. Colleges of education have been even slower to admit that their teacher education curriculum may be in need of reform.

How culture, ethnicity, language, and social class, among other differences, may influence student learning, and what teachers should learn about such differences in terms of school policies and practices, is the subject of this chapter. First, I will discuss what I mean by the terms *diversity* and *multicultural education*. I will then explore a number of school policies and practices and suggest questions that teacher educators can consider in order to change their own curriculum. In the process, I hope to challenge them to explore needed curricular, pedagogical, and structural changes that can transform professional preparation so it can better prepare future teachers to be effective, caring, and motivating for an increasingly diverse student body.

Defining Diversity

The term *diversity* is one of those catchwords of the late 20th century that is often used but seldom defined. From preschool through graduate school, diversity is either extolled as a virtue from which all can benefit or blasted as a code word for quotas and declining standards. In educational circles, and more specifically in teacher education, diversity has recently been sanctioned through numerous calls for curriculum inclusion and certification. Whether one is for or against diversity, however, it is important to begin with a common understanding of this term and to explore what implications it might have for teacher education programs.

As used in this chapter, *diversity* will refer to the range of differences that encompass race, ethnicity, gender, social class, ability, and language, among others. It is frequently used interchangeably with *multicultural education*, which, although assumed to speak to only racial and ethnic differences, is actually used more broadly by most of its proponents (Banks & Banks, 1995; Bennett, 1990; Gollnick & Chinn, 1994; Nieto, 1996; Perry & Fraser, 1993; Sleeter & Grant, 1994). Although multicultural educators differ in their focus and in the weight they may give to each of these differences, there is little argument that diversity and multicultural education usually focus on the same thing. This chapter is based on an inclusive definition of diversity, but I will focus primarily on culture, language, and ethnicity and how these issues can be included in teacher education programs, with the hope that the discussion will have implications for the many other differences with which our students come to school.

Sometimes, however, *diversity* is used as a euphemism in an attempt to soften the blow of racism. Because it is a difficult and conflicted issue to discuss, especially among Americans of European descent, racism is too often quickly dismissed in teacher education courses in an effort to move on to more pleasant and less painful issues of difference. In such cases, diversity may assume a celebratory aspect, and multicultural fairs, festivals, and holidays are often the result. But racism needs to be confronted directly, and no softening of terms can help.

In this chapter, racism and other forms of *institutional discrimination* based on the privilege of race, gender, language, and social class, among others, will be of paramount importance in treating differences and their role in teacher education. It is typical for discussions of racism to focus on biases and negative perceptions of *individuals* toward those of other groups. Such prejudiced or racist individuals as Archie Bunker, the television character in *All in the Family,* come to mind. However, although the beliefs and behaviors of such individuals may be hurtful, there is far greater harm done by institutions such as schools, housing, health, and the criminal justice system through their policies and practices. In the discussion that follows, we will be concerned primarily with *institutional racism and other forms of institutional discrimination;* that is, harmful policies and practices within institutions aimed at certain groups of people by other groups of people. Whereas *racism* is specifically directed against racial groups, *discrimination* is a more general term and will be used here to mean the same kind of belief systems and behaviors, both personal and institutional, directed against individuals and groups based on their gender (sexism), ethnic group (ethnocentrism), social class (classism), language (linguicism),[1] or other perceived differences.

The major difference between individual and institutional discrimination is the wielding of *power,* because it is primarily through the power of

---

[1]The term *linguicism,* coined by Tove Skutnabb-Kangas, refers to "ideologies and structures which are used to legitimate, effectuate and reproduce an unequal division of power and resources (both material and non-material) between groups which are defined on the basis of language" (Skutnabb-Kangas & Cummins, 1988, p. 13).

the people who control institutions such as schools that oppressive policies and practices are reinforced and legitimized. Consequently, when we understand racism as a *systemic* problem and not simply as an individual dislike for a particular group of people, we can better understand the negative and destructive effects it can have. This is not meant to minimize the powerful effects of individual prejudice and discrimination, which can be personally painful, or to suggest that they occur only in one direction; for example, from whites toward African Americans. There is no monopoly on prejudice and discrimination; they happen in all directions, and even within groups. However, interethnic hostility, personal prejudices, and individual biases, while negative and hurtful, simply do not have the long-range and life-limiting effects of *institutional racism* and *other forms of institutional discrimination*. Thus, because of the power of some groups over others, those groups with the most power in society are the ones that benefit from institutional discrimination, whether or not that is their intent. That is, males, Americans of European descent, the able-bodied, and English speakers are the beneficiaries of institutionally sexist, racist, or linguicist policies and practices.

In schools, testing practices may be racist and ethnocentric because students from dominated groups are stigmatized or labeled as a result of their performance on tests that favor the knowledge and experiences of the dominant group. What places some students at a disadvantage is not so much that particular teachers or even school systems may have prejudiced attitudes about them, but rather the negative impact of *particular institutions* on students from culturally dominated groups—in this case, the testing industry.

In addition to a focus on institutional discrimination in diversity, the *context* of education is also central. We cannot separate diversity from its sociopolitical context, just as we cannot understand the role diversity may play in our classrooms without considering how students are treated be-

cause *of the way their differences are perceived* rather than because of these differences per se. For instance, a student who speaks Haitian Creole and is economically poor may be viewed quite differently from one who speaks French and is economically and educationally privileged. Whether or not these two students are equally intelligent, capable of communicating in their native languages, or able to learn English competently are not the central issues. Rather, that one speaks a highly valued language whereas the other does not, and the economic disparities in their backgrounds, can create multiple cultural differences that are viewed not simply as differences but as deficits or strengths.

Given the differences in perceptions about student diversity—perceptions that are often based on elitist notions that have little to do with actual competence or intellectual capability—it is important to develop teacher education programs that look critically at the effect of school policies and practices on students. This exploration will help teacher educators and their students avoid what has been called the "holidays and heroes" approach to multicultural education (Banks, 1991) and instead will concentrate on how schools can create conditions that make it possible for all students to learn. What follows, then, is a definition of multicultural education that avoids the superficial trappings of simply adding foods, festivals, or ethnic tidbits to the curriculum.

Defining Multicultural Education: A Personal, Collective, and Institutional Odyssey

Defining multicultural education is a matter of a personal, collective, and institutional exploration. A static or imposed definition is contrary to the development of a multicultural perspective because it assumes a "program in place" or a package that is unchanged by the particular conditions and histories of teacher education programs and the participants in those programs. It is nevertheless necessary to begin with a common basis for understanding multicultural education if we are to develop teacher education programs that are responsive to student diversity. In this section, I will review my own definition of multicultural education and suggest implications for teacher education in the hope that other teacher education faculty will consider how their campuses might define and incorporate a multicultural perspective into their curriculum and pedagogy.

There are two central questions for faculty in teacher education programs to think about in this regard. The first concerns whether diversity or multicultural education should be added to the program through infusion or through specific courses. Each campus will differ in location, size, student body, and history of experience with diversity, but it is probably safe to say that a combination of infusion of diversity concerns along with specific courses about diversity is the most appropriate course of action in bringing these issues to the attention of future teachers. Nevertheless, the balance between infusion and specific courses will vary depending on the context of the specific institution. For example, a specific course on multicultural education may be required at the same time that all other courses are changed to reflect awareness of multicultural concerns.

A second question concerns the kinds of experiences in diversity that are most appropriate for future teachers. Although there can be no list of experiences that will be relevant for all students, it makes sense to provide experiences in education courses, prepracticum and practicum experiences, and in courses and other experiences outside the school or college of education. Each college will vary according to the resources it has in faculty expertise and in the diversity of populations accessible to students. Extracurricular experiences and a wide range of courses in the liberal arts that focus on diversity are also helpful in preparing future educators for teaching a diverse population.

The definition of multicultural education that drives each program may also vary because of context, experiences, and diversity of student body. The point, however, is to give time and attention to what multicultural education and diversity mean for a particular context. In arriving at my own definition of multicultural education, I began with the assumption that any worthwhile educational philosophy needs to be based on two central premises:

❑ To provide an equitable and high-quality education for all students
❑ To provide an apprenticeship for active participation in democracy to prepare students for their roles as active and critical citizens

Thus, my definition is as follows. *Multicultural education is a process of comprehensive and basic education for all students that challenges and rejects racism and other forms of discrimination in schools and society and accepts and affirms the pluralism (ethnic, racial, linguistic, religious, economic, gender, among others) that students, their communities, and teachers represent. Multicultural education permeates the curriculum and instructional strategies used in schools, as well as the interactions among teachers, students and parents, and the very way that schools conceptualize the nature of teaching and learning. Because it uses critical pedagogy as its underlying philosophy and focuses on knowledge, reflection, and action (praxis) as the basis for social change, multicultural education promotes the democratic principles of social justice.*

This definition is based on seven major characteristics that underscore the sociopolitical context of education: multicultural education is *antiracist education, basic education, important for all students, pervasive, education for all students, a process,* and *critical pedagogy.* These characteristics will not be described fully here, but readers are encouraged to investigate them further (see Nieto, 1996).

This definition, however, is not as important as the process I used to arrive at it. I began by exploring interrelated school policies and practices that either promote or hinder learning and the preparation of students for active participation in a democracy. I will review these policies and practices, suggesting pertinent questions for faculty to consider when going through their own process of defining multicultural education in order to build a solid knowledge base in diversity for teacher preparation.

School Policies and Practices and Implications for Teacher Education

There are a number of interrelated policies and practices that may influence student achievement and that should be examined by teacher educators in order to help determine how their own curriculum and pedagogy can be transformed. These include institutional racism and other forms of discrimination; expectations of student achievement; curriculum; pedagogy; tracking and ability grouping; testing; and student, teacher, and parent involvement in education. In considering each of these, I will include some questions and concerns that teacher educators may want to explore further.

Institutional Racism and Other Forms of Discrimination

Teachers and schools are not exempt from the effects of institutional racism and other forms of discrimination present in our society. Try as we might to shield children from the harmful effects of racism, we live in a society that is stratified by race, gender, and social class divisions, among others, and these must be taken into consideration in revamping teacher education programs. In addition, prospective teachers from the dominant group often fail to acknowledge their own privilege and thus develop what King (1991) has called *dysconscious racism;* that is, a limited and distorted view of racism based on a tacit acceptance of dominant white norms and privileges that fails to

take into account basic structural inequities of society. As a result, white preservice students cannot see how some people benefit from racism while others inevitably lose simply because of their race. Most teacher preparation programs do little to confront this issue.

Some related questions that need to be considered by teacher educators include the following.

❏ *How many of us as teacher educators have grappled with our own biases? How do we prepare future teachers to confront racism in their classrooms?*

This is not a question of developing a "touchy-feely" curriculum or "sensitivity training," but instead concerns designing curriculum and experiences for future teachers that ask them to think about privileges that are earned simply by belonging to particular social groups in society and how this impacts on student learning.

For example, students might be encouraged to look for biases in teacher education texts and curriculum materials. They might be required to document critical incidents in their prepracticum experiences that signal biases in instruction or in their interactions with students. Teacher educators can encourage future teachers to express and confront their biases by developing small-group study circles to tackle difficult issues such as these.

❏ *Do we include examples of racism and other types of institutional discrimination in U.S. educational history, including the legacy of segregation, tracking, and exclusion?*

Our educational history has a long and complex legacy of two competing ideologies: one concerns the push to equalize education and afford all children from all families the benefits of free, compulsory, and high-quality education; the other is a history of exclusion, domination, and inequality evident in such practices as "separate but equal" schooling, unequal economic resources for education, and ability grouping. It is as important to teach future teachers this checkered history as it is to teach child development and methods courses because it helps them confront mythologized and partial views of our educational history and therefore moves the conventional explanation for student failure from an individual problem to that of a structural one.

Expectations of Student Achievement

An issue related to racism and other forms of discrimination concerns expectations of student achievement based on students' race, gender, social class, and other differences. Expectations are often deeply held convictions, but rarely are they directly articulated. This makes them more difficult to confront and discuss.

It is important not to blame just teachers for having low expectations of particular students, because teachers are members of an unequal society and they learn to internalize and hold negative views of students that are reinforced daily by media and other institutions. Blaming teachers alone fails to take into account the fact that they are often the ones who care most about their students and struggle valiantly to teach them. Teachers are not blameless in having low expectations, but they are certainly not alone or completely responsible. Thus, rather than *teacher expectations,* the focus in professional development programs needs to be on *negative expectations of student achievement* and how these may jeopardize the academic success of young people of particular backgrounds.

Some questions that can guide teacher educators in developing their programs include the following.

❑ *How do we work with future teachers to help them think about what they expect of students and how students' cultural and socioeconomic backgrounds might influence this?*

Exposing students to the history of teacher expectancy effects is an important part of the teacher education curriculum. Although research on teacher expectations is not without its controversies and opinion is divided on how much of an impact teachers may have on the achievement of their students (Brophy, 1983; Eccles & Jussim, 1992; Goldenberg, 1992; Rosenthal, 1987; Rosenthal & Jacobson, 1968; Snow, 1969; Wineburg, 1987), prospective teachers need to be let in on such debates in order to be informed and aware of their own attitudes and prepared to make changes in their teaching practices and interactions with students.

When developing courses and other experiences in teacher education programs, faculty must consider how to help their students make unarticulated expectations more explicit so they can be more directly confronted. A focus on the pedagogy we use in courses (for example, using more small-group activities with less emphasis on lecture) can help make such discussions less uncomfortable for students. In addition, such strategies as journal writing can allow students the freedom to express attitudes and beliefs that they might be reluctant to express verbally. In turn, faculty can use such attitudes and beliefs as a basis for their curriculum—not pointing an accusatory finger at individual students but rather using such attitudes and beliefs to create learning experiences through which all students can learn to look critically at how their own attitudes and behaviors may impact negatively on the learning of some students.

❑ *What types of experiences do we give future teachers to have them look at interactions in classrooms, including their own, critically?*

Teacher educators may want to focus some of their attention on the types of activities and assignments they give their students outside of class as well, so that students become more aware of how their unstated expectations may have unanticipated and negative consequences. These activities and assignments might include keeping field notes on their work with particular students, videotaping their teaching, and observing and working with their peers to help discuss how expectations, both positive and negative, may influence their teaching.

Curriculum

It is unfortunate that teachers sometimes view curriculum development as little more than a technical activity rather than as a dynamic and potentially empowering decision-making process. Part of the blame lies in teacher education programs that stress stale methods courses rather than challenge their students to think more creatively about what knowledge is of most worth. The fact that teachers have tremendous power in determining the curriculum is likewise not often addressed, and most beginning teachers enter schools ready to be handed a "curriculum-in-place" that they must "deliver." New teachers often appreciate the curriculum-as-product rather than curriculum-as-process approach because of their inexperience and need for guidance, but it soon becomes tiresome and unchallenging.

In contrast to this static view of curriculum, prospective teachers need to learn that curriculum can be powerful and that they have an important role in developing it. They need to be given experiences in which they design curriculum that is rigorous, informative, and engaging to students. Given the multicultural nature of our society, they also need to learn how to best use and reflect students' experiences, lives, and talents in the curriculum.

There is a distinct mismatch between the curriculum of the school and the lives of many children. For example, although students may learn about their cities and towns, they may never come across the types of real people who make their communities come to life. Add to this the fact that the joys, dilemmas, and conflicts of communities

are seldom brought into the classroom in significant ways, and the result is that students report being bored because they see little in school that is of relevance to their lives (Grant & Sleeter, 1986; Poplin & Weeres, 1992). Alternatively, when students' strengths (such as native language proficiency or family skills) are unknown to teachers or not addressed in the curriculum (by using their native languages and other skills as valuable resources), schools lose the opportunity to make learning possible for these students (Commins, 1989; Moll, 1992).

Textbooks are an important part of the curriculum in most schools, and they, too, are implicated in teachers' understanding of the curriculum. In fact, if one were to ask teachers to describe their curriculum, many would point to their textbooks as the primary source of the knowledge and information presented to students. Yet textbooks, although more inclusive and representative of diversity than in the past, are still sadly lacking in appropriate content about differences and a critical perspective about the knowledge they do present (García, 1993; Sleeter & Grant, 1991). Not only do they still reinforce the dominance of European American perspectives and accomplishments but they usually present knowledge with such tremendous authority that the truths within their pages are rarely challenged.

How curriculum has traditionally been taught is therefore simply unacceptable for today's schools and classrooms. Some questions that teacher educators need to address in reforming their programs might include the following.

❏ *How can teacher preparation programs help future teachers develop a critical perspective about the curriculum?*

Built into teacher education courses and other experiences for prospective teachers should be specific activities through which they learn to view curriculum as a decision-making process in which their own creativity and talents can be used. This means providing numerous situations in which teacher education students actually develop curriculum, try it out, and adapt and modify it to best reach their particular students.

In addition, teacher education courses should provide experiences in which future teachers can confront their own biases and limitations so that they understand that the curriculum is never neutral but always represents a point of view and a vested interest. This is best learned when prospective teachers are given opportunities to review textbooks and other instructional materials critically, both at the university and in their field placements.

❏ *What knowledge do future teachers need to possess in order to develop affirming, inclusive, and rigorous curricula?*

One of the major dilemmas in multicultural education is that teachers cannot teach what they do not know, and most teachers have had little or no experience in knowledge that is outside the traditional canon. Undergraduate education and postbaccalaureate education in the field of education are ideal places in which to provide this type of knowledge and these perspectives to future teachers.

Teacher education programs cannot do it all. Close and collaborative arrangements with other departments and programs need to be developed to ensure that future teachers have a broad-based and comprehensive education in the arts, physical and biological sciences, and social sciences. For example, this means encouraging students to major in areas outside of education and urging them to take courses with content to which they have not been exposed previously, as well as courses that represent the traditional canon. Courses in anthropology and in African American, Latino, Asian, and women's studies, for example, provide alternative experiences because they concern perspectives frequently unknown to most students. An important function of teacher education is to encourage students to find ways to mesh the content they learn in different disciplines.

❏ *How can future teachers learn to accept the talents and skills students possess and incorporate them into the curriculum (rather than seeing students as a set of walking deficiencies)?*

A traditional response of teachers to accommodate for student differences is to water down the curriculum. Although this response may be due to their desire to equitably address differences, instead it can result in low expectations for some students and inequitable student outcomes. In addition, watered-down curriculum tends to be lifeless and dull, disengaging even more the students who need to be drawn into learning.

Prospective teachers can be guided to think critically about the conventional wisdom that students who are economically poor or who are from culturally and linguistically diverse families somehow lack the intellectual stamina to be productive learners. All good teachers know that learning begins where students are at, but because so many prospective teachers have not learned to recognize the particular skills of some students, they learn to view differences from a deficit perspective. That is, rather than seeing students who speak another language as, say, *Vietnamese-speaking* or *Spanish-speaking*, they think of them as *non–English-speaking*, and this in turn shapes how teachers think about what these students are capable of learning.

In both their teacher education courses and in their field placements, future teachers can be challenged to think about ways to develop curriculum that takes into account the skills and talents that students have as a basis for teaching them. In a study concerning the feelings and experiences of Latino students, a Dominican student called this building on their "already culture" (Zanger, 1993).

Pedagogy

It is unfortunate but true that teachers tend to teach as they themselves were taught. Given few alternative models, future teachers simply end up replicating stale and worn methods, and too many schools remain uninteresting and unchallenging places (Goodlad, 1984). This is particularly true of secondary schools, where subject matter controls pedagogy and teachers learn to believe that content is always more important than the form in which it is taught. Schools in economically disadvantaged communities are even more likely to rely on pedagogical strategies that focus on what Haberman (1991) has termed "the pedagogy of poverty"— that is, asking questions, giving directions, making assignments, and monitoring seatwork. Ironically, students who could benefit tremendously from creative, energetic, and challenging environments become even more bored by a pedagogy based on the assumption that children living in poverty cannot perform in such settings. Furthermore, classroom instruction at all levels is too often driven by standardized tests as gatekeepers to promotion and accreditation. Little wonder, then, that so many classrooms are characterized by the "chalk and talk" method of a century ago.

Although it is crucial that knowledge be made more accessible and engaging for students, this by itself is not what pedagogy is about. Pedagogy also concerns how teachers perceive the nature of learning and what they do to create conditions that motivate students to learn and become critical thinkers. For example, most classrooms still reflect the view that learning takes place best in a competitive and highly charged atmosphere, and techniques that stress individual achievement and extrinsic motivation are commonplace. Such policies as ability grouping, testing, and rote learning are the result.

Simply changing large-group instruction to small-group and cooperative groups is not the answer, however. Although cooperative learning is based on the premise that using the talents and skills of all students is important, it is too often accepted unproblematically by future teachers as the answer to all the problems in schools. Yet an examination of current school reform efforts found that, when done uncritically, small-group work can result in students becoming even more passive and dependent learners (McCaslin & Good, 1992). Viewing methods in a critical way is a potent reminder that methods should not become sacred cows, but instead must be understood as means to the end of learning (Bartolomé, 1994; Reyes, 1992).

Although future teachers should be encouraged to develop student-centered, empowering pedagogical strategies, they must also learn to view all pedagogical strategies as means, not as ends in themselves. Some questions to guide teacher educators include the following.

❑ *How can we get future teachers to increase their repertoire of pedagogical strategies and to avoid the limitations of "chalk talk"?*

The best way for teacher educators to challenge their students to develop other ways of teaching is to model the behavior in their own courses. The irony of using only a lecture format in courses that advocate student-centered learning cannot be lost on future teachers. If they are given few resources, they will go back to what is tried and familiar.

In addition, the placement of students in the field is crucial to the development of their pedagogical strategies and to how they think about student learning. It is not so important that future teachers learn the "jigsaw" approach to cooperative groups, for instance, but rather that they learn about the benefits and limitations of group work, among other strategies. For this to happen, they need to be placed with teachers who encourage them to be creative and take risks, and who themselves experiment with a wide variety of strategies.

❑ *What types of experiences do future teachers need to help them understand culturally responsive education?*

Modifying instruction to be more culturally appropriate is an important skill for teachers who work with students of diverse backgrounds, yet few prospective teachers learn about cultural differences or the types of strategies that can help more students be successful learners. First, future teachers need to be informed about how culture may influence student learning. Although it is limiting and ultimately counterproductive to perceive culture as *predictive* of learning styles or preferences, it is nevertheless important for future teachers to understand that culture may influence (although it does not determine) how their students learn. This approach takes the burden of complete responsibility for learning from the student so that it is shared by teachers as well. That is, teachers need to develop strategies that will speak to the preferred working and learning styles of *all* students, not just of some students, as is usually the case.

Part of the teacher education curriculum can focus on the growing body of research concerning culture-specific educational accommodations (Hollins, King, & Hayman, 1994; Irvine, 1992; Jacob & Jordan, 1993). In addition, future teachers need to practice in a variety of settings so they understand that what has been traditionally viewed as deviant behavior may in fact be culturally influenced. This implies that future teachers will be placed with teachers of different backgrounds who use a variety of strategies and approaches with their students.

Tracking and Ability Grouping

Tracking, the placement of students in groups of similar ability, has been found to be one of the most inequitable practices in schools (Braddock, 1990; Ekstrom, 1992; Goodlad, 1984; Oakes, 1985). Until recently, it has also been quite undisputed

and thought to be the most effective way to teach students of widely differing abilities. Yet it is clear from research on tracking that grouping decisions are often made on questionable grounds, and that those who most suffer the consequences of tracking are students who have had the least educational success in our schools, especially students from economically disadvantaged and culturally marginalized families. In fact, tracking decisions have generally reflected other inequities in society based on gender, race, and ethnicity. Thus, Latino, Native American, and African American children, and all children of low-income families, have been found to be at the lowest track levels, where they move slowly (if at all) out of those tracks, where they receive fewer resources and less innovative pedagogy and curriculum, and, as a result, where they develop poor self-esteem.

Some critical questions for teacher educators to consider about tracking would include the following.

❑ *What do future teachers need to understand about tracking and how can they learn from it?*

Prospective teachers should be given the opportunity to consider the debate on tracking in order to be aware of the research and to develop viable alternatives to it in their own classrooms. This means that tracking, rather than being taken for granted as the only way to group students, needs to be viewed critically as simply one option among several.

Simply rejecting tracking and accepting "detracking," however, is not the solution because it does nothing to prepare future teachers to plan their curriculum, organize their classrooms, or consider how to go about developing a learning environment in which all students can learn. In fact, if detracking is accepted without considering such issues as changes in pedagogy, materials, and curriculum, it may do more harm than good by exacerbating student failure and parent disapproval.

Therefore, teacher educators also need to present future teachers with concrete suggestions for making detracking work, including skills in cooperative learning, alternative assessment, and empowering pedagogy (Estrin, 1993; Sapon-Shevin, 1992; Wheelock, 1992).

❑ *How can we work with students to help them understand that tracking is part and parcel of multicultural education and the diversity initiative?*

Multicultural education is often understood in a superficial way and results in such activities as celebrations of holidays and "ethnic months" in the curriculum. But prospective teachers should know that multicultural education is not just about bulletin boards with beautiful pictures of children from around the world, curricula that include references to many differences, or nice assembly programs. Multicultural education means looking critically at such practices as tracking because traditionally, marginalized students are the ones who suffer the greatest consequences of these decisions. Thus, it is necessary to make the issue of tracking an explicit part of the teacher education curriculum through relevant readings, specific assignments, and work in classrooms.

❑ *What skills must we give students so that they can develop viable alternatives to tracking?*

A review of the effects of tracking needs to be part of the teacher education curriculum in order to counter a simplistic view of multicultural education. Another strategy is to require students to consider diverse approaches to teaching, including peer tutoring, cross-age and cross-grade teaching, and team teaching.

Testing

The relationship of testing to tracking has often been symbiotic. Tests, especially intelligence tests, have been used as the basis for segregating and sorting students, and this is especially true for those whose cultures and languages differ from the mainstream. It has been estimated that about 100 million standardized tests are given yearly, an average of 2.5 tests per student per year (Medina & Neill, 1990). In addition, "high-stakes" testing—connecting the success of students, teachers, and schools to test scores—is a particularly negative form of the testing explosion.

Testing may affect other factors that get in the way of equal educational opportunity. For example, testing can have a negative effect on curriculum and pedagogy because teachers feel forced to "teach to the test" rather than create more innovative and challenging curricula for their students. In fact, a decline in the use of teaching and learning methods (such as student-centered discussions, essay writing, research projects, and laboratory work) has been found to result when standardized tests are required (Darling-Hammond, 1991).

Questions that may be helpful in reforming the way teacher education programs focus on testing include the following.

❑ *How do we work with students so that they develop a critical eye toward assessment? What do students need to know about tests and the testing industry?*

Prospective teachers need to know that much of the testing frenzy is a direct result of the educational reform movement of the 1980s and 1990s, and they need to develop an awareness of the results of assessment policies and how they impact on other school policies and practices. Prospective teachers need to learn what tests are for, how they are used, and the limits and benefits of testing.

❑ *What skills do future teachers need to develop so that they learn to assess all students in an equitable manner?*

The stated purposes of testing are frequently at odds with the ways in which they are used. This has led some researchers to suggest that all norm-based assessments should be abandoned, especially for linguistically and culturally diverse students (Figueroa & García, 1994). It is therefore important for future teachers to know what alternatives to norm-based assessments exist, and to be familiar and comfortable with developing and using these alternatives, including portfolios, performance tasks, and student exhibitions (Ascher, 1990; Estrin, 1993).

Student, Teacher, and Parent Involvement

Schools are not generally organized to encourage active student, parent, or teacher involvement. Although nominally represented in the governance, none of these groups has the kind of direct representation that would make their voices important in the very way that schools are organized and run. Teacher education programs perpetuate this loss of leadership and involvement by providing student teachers with few opportunities to develop the important skills they will need to work with parents or with their own students to develop appropriate and exciting learning environments.

Most new teachers also know very little about their rights and responsibilities as professionals. Teachers often feel as if they have no autonomy, and this curbs their enthusiasm and creativity (Lee, Bryk, & Smith, 1993). This should not be surprising when we consider that student teachers are given little sense of their own efficacy in the teaching-learning process. Teacher education courses and other experiences can make a difference in how teachers view their own involvement and that of others in their classrooms and in schools in general. Relevant questions about parent, student, and teacher involvement, and how to include these in the teacher education curriculum, might include the following.

❑ *How do we prepare future teachers to make decisions and see themselves as creative professionals rather than as technical workers?*

Instead of thinking of themselves as passive recipients of knowledge, future teachers can learn to see themselves as creative and powerful agents for change. In readings, class activities, and fieldwork, prospective teachers should be given opportunities to make decisions about curriculum, pedagogy, and student learning.

In the teacher education curriculum itself, provisions can be made for students to take a key role in their own learning by having them make decisions about the goals they have for their professional development, the kind of research in which they are interested, and the courses they need to take in order to meet their goals. This approach challenges a static and unchanging teacher education curriculum and instead demands flexibility in developing each student's curriculum based on his or her particular situation. Courses can also include information on the profession of teaching per se so that future educators become more aware of the complexity of their roles.

❑ *What experiences do we provide future teachers so that they understand the important role of parents in educational decision making and help them confront their fear, anxiety, or superiority concerning parents?*

Teacher education curriculum can include information about parent involvement and the effect it can have on student achievement and on what teachers and schools can learn from students and how this can affect the curriculum and pedagogy (Epstein & Dauber, 1989; Henderson, 1987). Their fieldwork can include observation of parent-teacher meetings and attendance at PTO and school board meetings. In their classrooms, they should be encouraged to contact and work with parents, not only when there are problems with particular students but as a general way of operating to improve student learning.

❑ *How do we help future teachers to involve their students in curriculum planning and to let go of their own power in the classroom?*

Rather than thinking of learning as a one-way process in which students learn and teachers teach, prospective educators should think of learning as a reciprocal process (Freire, 1970). Using students' ideas, experiences, and interests can also help future teachers think creatively about how the curriculum can be more engaging for their students (Nieto, 1994). Again, placement of students in pre-practicum and practicum sites can go a long way in pairing them with teachers who believe that students can be effective in helping to plan the learning environment. In the final analysis, however, it will be through a transformation of the teacher education curriculum that future teachers can be assisted in developing the desire to work collaboratively with a wide range of students.

Conclusion

The foregoing discussion about diversity and the specific policies and practices that shape teacher education brings up a number of questions concerning the infusion of these issues in the teacher education curriculum and pedagogy. Given the tremendous variety of teacher education programs that currently exist, no set of changes will work for all. This discussion has not been aimed at providing a specific set of experiences, courses, or objectives for all programs. Curricular and institutional changes must be based on and consistent with the specific context of each program, including considerations of student profiles, the nature of the schools with which it collaborates, the experiences and expertise of the faculty, state guidelines and certification requirements, and, of course, the particular university or college in which the program is located.

The responsibilities of higher education in preparing teachers for the 21st century are awesome. Our society is faced with the daunting challenges of creatively facing the increasing diversity among the student body in elementary and secondary schools, and this diversity is a compelling reason for colleges of education to transform the process of preparing the next generation of teachers. Approaches that build on the experiences of teacher education students and that help them become better teachers of our diverse student populations in elementary and secondary schools are called for. The curriculum needs to be overhauled, of course, but even more important, our ideas about how teachers are prepared for the classroom need to undergo massive changes. Multicultural education and concerns about diversity are thus part of total school reform, not only for public elementary and secondary schools but for teacher education programs as well. Until faculty in teacher preparation programs develop the understanding that diversity means *all* of us, little change will occur in the learning environments and opportunities that are provided for the children in our schools.

References

Ascher, C. (1990). *Testing students in urban schools: Current problems and new directions.* New York: ERIC Clearinghouse on Urban Education, Teachers College, Columbia University.

Banks, J. A. (1991). *Teaching strategies for multiethnic education* (5th ed.). Boston: Allyn & Bacon.

Banks, J. A., & Banks, C. M. (1993). *Multicultural education: Issues and perspectives.* Boston: Allyn & Bacon.

Banks, J. A., & Banks, C. A. M. (Eds.). (1995). *Handbook of research on multicultural education.* New York: Macmillan.

Bartolomé, L. (1994). Beyond the methods fetish: Toward a humanizing pedagogy. *Harvard Educational Review, 64*(2), 173–194.

Bennett, C. I. (1990). *Comprehensive multicultural education: Theory and practice* (2nd ed.). Boston: Allyn & Bacon.

Bereiter, C., & Englemann, S. (1966). *Teaching disadvantaged children in the preschool.* Englewood Cliffs, NJ: Prentice-Hall.

Braddock, J. J., II (1990, February). *Tracking: Implications for student race-ethnic subgroups.* Baltimore, MD: Johns Hopkins University, Center for Research on Effective Schooling for Disadvantaged Students, Report No. 1.

Brophy, J. E. (1983). Research on the self-fulfilling prophecy and teacher expectations. *Journal of Educational Psychology, 75,* 631–661.

Commins, N. L. (1989). Language and affect: Bilingual students at home and at school. *Language Arts, 66*(1), 29–43.

Darling-Hammond, L. (1991). The implications of testing policy for quality and equality. *Phi Delta Kappan, 73*(3), 220–225.

Eccles, J., & Jussim, L. (1992). Teacher expectations: 2. Construction and reflection of student achievement. *Journal of Personality and Social Psychology, 63*(6), 947–961.

Ekstrom, R. B. (1992). Six urban school districts: Their middle-grade grouping policies and practices. In *On the right track: The consequences of mathematics course placement policies and practices in the middle grades* [Report to the Edna McConnell Clark Foundation]. New York: ETS and the National Urban League.

Epstein, J. L., & Dauber, S. L. (1989). Teacher attitudes and practices of parent involvement in inner-city elementary and middle schools [Report no. 33]. Baltimore Center for Research on Elementary and Middle Schools, John Hopkins University.

Estrin, E. T. (1993). *Alternative assessment: Issues in language, culture, & equity* [Knowledge Brief No. 11]. San Francisco: Far West Laboratory.

Figueroa, R. A., & García, E. (1994). Issues in testing students from culturally and linguistically diverse backgrounds. *Multicultural education, 2*(1), 10–19.

Freire, P. (1970). *Pedagogy of the oppressed.* New York: Seabury Press.

García, J. (1993). The changing image of ethnic groups in textbooks. *Phi Delta Kappan, 75*(1), 29–35.

Goldenberg, C. (1992). The limits of expectations: A case for case knowledge about teacher expectancy effects. *American Educational Research Journal, 29*(3), 514-544.

Gollnick, D. M., & Chinn, P. C. (1994). *Multicultural education in a pluralistic society* (4th ed.). New York: Macmillan.

Goodlad, J. (1984). *A place called school.* New York: McGraw-Hill.

Grant, C. A., & Sleeter, C. E. (1986). *After the school bell rings.* Philadelphia: Falmer Press.

Haberman, M. (1991). The pedagogy of poverty versus good teaching. *Phi Delta Kappan, 73*(4), 290–294.

Henderson, A. T. (1987). *The evidence continues to grow: Parent involvement improves student achievement.* Columbia, MD: National Coalition of Citizens in Education.

Hollins, E. T., King, J. E., & Hayman, W. C. (Eds.). (1994). *Teaching diverse populations: Formulating a knowledge base.* Albany, NY: SUNY Press.

Irvine, J. J. (1992). Making teacher education culturally responsive. In M. E. Dilworth (Ed.), Diversity in teacher education: *Teacher education yearbook 1* (pp. 79–92). San Francisco: Jossey-Bass.

Jacob, E., & Jordan, C. (Eds.). (1993). *Minority education: Anthropological perspectives.* Norwood, NJ: Ablex.

Jensen, A. R. (1969). How much can we boost IQ and scholastic achievement? *Harvard Educational Review, 39,* 1–123.

King, J. E. (1991). Dysconscious racism: Ideology, identity, and the miseducation of teachers. *Journal of Negro Education, 60*(2), 133–146.

Lee, V. E., Bryk, A. A., & Smith, J. B. (1993). The organization of effective secondary schools. In L. Darling-Hammond (Ed.), *Review of research in education* (pp. 171–267). Washington, DC: American Educational Research Association.

McCaslin, M., & Good, T. L. (1992). Compliant cognition: The misalliance of management and instructional goals in current school reform. *Educational Researcher, 21*(3), 4–17.

Medina, N., & Neill, D. M. (1990). *Fallout from the testing explosion* (3rd ed.). Cambridge, MA: FairTest.

Moll, L. C. (1992). Bilingual classroom studies and community analysis: Some recent trends. *Educational Researcher, 21*(2), 20–24.

Nieto, S. (1994). Lessons from students on creating a chance to dream. *Harvard Educational Review, 64*(4), 392–426.

Nieto, S. (1996). *Affirming diversity: The sociopolitical context of multicultural education* (2d rev. ed.). White Plains, NY: Longman.

Oakes, J. (1985). *Keeping track: How schools structure inequality.* New Haven, CT: Yale University Press.

Oakes, J. (1992). Can tracking research inform practice? *Educational Researcher, 21*(4), 12–21.

Perry, T., & Fraser, J. W. (1993). *Freedom's plow: Teaching in the multicultural classroom.* New York: Routledge & Kegan Paul.

Poplin, M., & Weeres, J. (1992). *Voices from the inside: A report on schooling from inside the classroom.* Claremont, CA: The Institute for Education in Transformation, Claremont Graduate School.

Reisman, F. (1962). *The culturally deprived child.* New York: Harper & Row.

Reyes, M. (1992). Challenging venerable assumptions: Literacy instruction for linguistically different students. *Harvard Educational Review, 62*(4), 427–446.

Rosenthal, R. (1987). Pygmalion effects: Existence, magnitude, and social importance. *Educational Researcher, 16*(9), 37–44.

Rosenthal, R., & Jacobson, L. (1968). *Pygmalion in the classroom.* New York: Holt, Rinehart & Winston.

Sapon-Shevin, M. (1992). Ability differences in the classroom: Teaching and learning in inclusive classrooms. In D. A. Byrnes & G. Kiger, *Common bonds: Anti-bias teaching in a diverse society* (pp. 39–52) Wheaton, MD: Association for Childhood Education International.

Skutnabb-Kangas, T., & Cummins, J. (1988). Multilingualism and the education of minority children. In T. Skutnabb-Kangas & J. Cummins (Eds.), *Minority education: From shame to struggle* (pp. 9–44). Clevedon, England: Multilingual Matters.

Sleeter, C. E., & Grant, C. A. (1991). Race, class, gender and disability in current textbooks. In M. W. Apple & L. K. Christian-Smith (Eds.), *The politics of the textbook.* New York: Routledge & Chapman Hall.

Sleeter, C. E., & Grant, C. A. (1994). Making choices for multicultural education: Five approaches to race, class, and gender (2nd ed.). New York: Macmillan.

Snow, R. E. (1969). Unfinished Pygmalion. *Contemporary Psychology, 14,* 197–200.

Wheelock, A. (1992). *Crossing the tracks: How "untracking" can save America's schools.* New York: Free Press.

Wineburg, S. S. (1987). The self-fulfillment of the self-fulfilling prophecy: A critical appraisal. *Educational Researcher, 16*(9), 28–37.

Zanger, V. V. (1993). Academic costs of social marginalization: An analysis of the perceptions of Latino students at a Boston high school. In R. Rivera & S. Nieto, *The education of Latino students in Massachusetts: Issues, research, and policy implications* (pp. 170–190). Boston: The Mauricio Gastón Institute for Latino Community Development and Public Policy, University of Massachusetts.

CHAPTER 9

Gender in the Classroom

NEL NODDINGS
Stanford University

Today, it is often taken for granted that girls as well as boys should be prepared for public life—for professions, politics, trades, and whatever else males have traditionally done. Of course, it hasn't always been this way, and teachers should know something about the history of female education, not only because it is a fascinating story but because that history has left a legacy of questions and issues with which we must grapple. I'll start this chapter with a brief historical overview and then consider topics that arise out of that discussion: women's intellectual and moral patterns, research on gender and education, problems in today's classrooms, and possibilities for curriculum change.[1]

Historical Background

The education of women has been a lively topic of discussion in Western history since the days of the Greeks. Of course, most of the recorded discussion

was conducted by men and, with a few notable exceptions, women had little formal influence on their own education until the 19th century.

Two contrasting positions on the education of women are found in the Greek philosophers Plato and Aristotle. In several works (for example, *Symposium, Meno,* and *Republic*), Plato used Socrates as a spokesperson for the view that there are no relevant differences between males and females in the qualities required for leadership in government. Women, Socrates declared, should be seen as eligible for the kind of education offered to male guardians of the state. Just like boys, girls should be evaluated for qualities of character and mind and selected for higher education on the basis of those qualities.

There has been plenty of debate in ensuing centuries over whether Plato really believed what he had Socrates say or whether he used his position on women as a mere strategy to solve other problems in his political philosophy, and, in any case, his view of women was not consistently positive. In many places, even Socrates is heard making derogatory remarks about women (see Okin, 1979).

For present purposes, two issues arise out of Plato's discussion. First, a question remains whether women are "just like men" with respect to intellectual and moral qualities (we'll explore that

[1]Some of the material in this chapter is taken directly from the following articles previously published by the author: "Gender and the Curriculum" (chapter 24), in P. Jackson (Ed.), *Handbook of Research on Curriculum* (New York: Macmillan and AERA, 1992), pp. 659–684; "The Gender Issue," *Educational Leadership,* December 1991/January 1992, pp. 65–70; and "Social Studies and Feminism," *Theory and Research in Social Education,* 20(3), 1992, pp. 230–241.

question in the next section). Second, a question that did not even occur to Plato has been posited by some of today's feminists: Aren't women's work and traditions sufficiently important in themselves to warrant inclusion in the curriculum? If women are to be "offered" the same education as men for public life, should not men be educated in the best of women's traditions? This second question is at the heart of one body of feminist thought today. (We'll discuss it in each of the following sections.)

In contrast to the enlightened view of Plato, Aristotle held a view more representative of his time. For him, women were inherently inferior to men—handicapped both morally and intellectually by their biology. Whereas for Plato and Socrates the deficiencies of women could properly be traced to their faulty education and not their bodies, Aristotle insisted that women are designed by nature to be oriented to things of the body and not of the mind. It is astonishing that vestiges of this view remain in 20th-century Western life. Even today there are those who believe that women are biologically unsuited for high political office and that the moral reasoning of typical women is less rigorous than that of men.

From the earliest days of Christianity, the Aristotelian view persisted, aggravated by the Augustinian doctrine of Original Sin and Eve's role in the Fall of Man. But alongside this deeply misogynist attitude ran the doctrine of "equality of souls" (McLaughlin, 1974). In soul, if not in body, women were thought to be equal to men. Indeed, women who were willing to forsake their usual bodily roles (marriage and childbearing) and enter the virginal life of a convent were accepted as "more like men." Some of these women were highly educated and exercised considerable authority in religious houses. It was not unusual for a woman to serve as head of a joint monastery-convent. McLaughlin (1974) says, "These women were learned in scripture; they taught; they administered great religious houses; they missionized alongside the men, and

without any hint in the sources that these public roles were improper for women" (p. 237). This was in the 7th and 8th centuries.

Later in the Middle Ages, the Aristotelian view again dominated. Now women in monastic life were considered a threat to male chastity and holiness, and the sexes were separated in their religious houses.

In the same period of time, women came to be described more and more narrowly as either saintly mothers, virgins, or whores. Notice that in all three categories, women were described in terms of their biology. Although most people today do not think of women this way, the language that developed in these categories persists. For example, in everyday language, there are only a few terms for promiscuous males (and not all of these are pejorative); however, there are many terms (all derogatory) for promiscuous women. Students today should be helped to understand the origins of such language and the great harm it has done to women (Spender, 1980). Consider also what it has meant to young women to have as their chief role model that biological impossibility, the Virgin Mother.

With the revival of art and literature after the Middle Ages, there was an increased interest in education, but the Renaissance did little to improve women's education. Indeed, one of the most terrible epochs of women's history is the period from the 14th through the 17th centuries. This was the time of the witch craze, and many thousands (perhaps millions) of women were tortured, burned, and hanged as witches. Although historians have identified a whole complex of causes for the witch craze (Klaits, 1985), some feminist writers think that a major cause was the desire of powerful men to wipe out every last trace of women's special knowledge as healers and the old female religions (Daly, 1973; Ehrenreich & English, 1973). Certainly the knowledge that had once produced the village wise woman disappeared and so, for the most part, did any female urge for autonomy. Lone women, particularly those who had any claim to power or property, were prime candidates for the witch-hunters. Thus, not only were most women deprived of formal education, but even the informal education associated with women's traditions was devalued.

One might think that the Enlightenment, the great Age of Reason, should have turned things in women's favor, and in fact the twin evils of superstition and Church authority were both weakened considerably. If women were still regarded as inferior, at least they were not branded as witches. But the Enlightenment brought out new versions of the old arguments on women's moral and intellectual deficiencies. Rousseau, the philosopher often praised for his innovative educational ideas, recommended an education for girls entirely different from the one he prescribed for boys. Whereas Emile was to be educated for independence, responsible citizenship, authority, and freedom, Sophie was to be trained for dependence, convention, chastity, coquetry, and a life of service (Martin, 1985).

In *A Vindication of the Rights of Woman*, Mary Wollstonecraft (1792/1975) presented a remarkable and cogent argument against Rousseau's prescription for Sophie's education. Wollstonecraft argued that women should have the same education as men—that their present condition of ignorance and apparent frivolity was a result of their faulty education, not an inferior nature. Give women a chance, she pleaded. If they failed, and Wollstonecraft was quite sure they would not, then at least men would be justified in assigning them a different and inferior education. This question—whether women should receive the same education as men or a different one—remained important well into the 20th century.

Immanuel Kant, one of the Western world's greatest philosophers, also had something to say about women's education. He remarked that a woman highly educated in the usual male disciplines "might as well even have a beard; for perhaps that would express more obviously the mien of profundity for which she strives" (1764/1983). It was also Kant who said that women often do what men would regard as the morally right thing out of a natural instinct for the beautiful. Such acts, according to Kant, deserve no *moral* credit. In the Kantian framework, an act is moral only if it is logically deduced to be one's duty and done for that reason. A debate over differences in men's and women's moral reasoning has recently taken on new life in the wake of Carol Gilligan's (1982) challenge to the developmental theory of Lawrence Kohlberg (1981).

During the 19th century, many women argued vigorously for women's rights to education and political equality. Most did not argue, as we do today, for full equality in professional and occupational life. Catherine Beecher (1842/1977), for example, wrote eloquently on the importance of women's roles as mothers, educators, and homemakers. In these roles, women were domestic economists, scientists, educators, and religious leaders, and they needed the best possible education in order to perform these functions well. Beecher advocated a separate and different education for women, not because they are in any way intellectually or morally inferior to men but because their work is so complex and of such vital importance.

As science displaced religion in the Western world's hierarchy of authority, Darwinian arguments on women's inferiority replaced the older patristic arguments. Now it was argued that evolution had prepared men for mental life and a wide range of cultural activities; it had specialized women for sex, childbearing, and homemaking. Many prominent psychologists and educators in the period around 1900 argued vehemently that women would be both physically and emotionally harmed by the rigors of the standard male curriculum, they would become uninterested in marriage, unfit to bear children, suffer mental collapse, and the like. Strong women educators such as M. Carey Thomas, president of Bryn Mawr, responded vigorously to such statements (see Cross, 1965).

Nevertheless, more and more women were being educated, and many entered academic life, primarily in women's institutions. Indeed, the period just before 1920 was something of a high point for women in academic life, especially in the literary field. By the 1950s, something of the feminine mystique, coupled with the "professionalization" of university fields, had once again overcome women's opportunities for higher education aimed at professional and academic life.

Both teachers and students should know something about women's long struggle for equality in education. But as the story of that struggle within Western culture is told, comparable stories about other cultures should also be discussed. While Western women lost their influence as village healers, for example, Native American women often held positions of authority and respect. Informal learning in their cultures was maintained and honored. Similarly, while white women in the United States struggled to be heard (even to be allowed to speak) in their own communities, African American women were often highly regarded leaders in their communities. The full range of stories should be told.

Predictably, many of the issues so important today have historical roots: Do women and men approach intellectual and moral problems differently? If so, are the differences innate or culturally induced? Should some of the values, tasks, and attitudes traditionally associated with women be included in the curriculum for both girls and boys? Should girls be educated in all-girl settings—especially in mathematics and science? We'll turn to these questions next.

Women's Intellectual and Moral Patterns

Some of the questions still hotly debated about differences between male and female thinking patterns, brain lateralization, and the like, are best left as open scientific questions. At this time, we simply do not know how many differences are traceable to biology, but it seems safe to say that the few intellectual differences we still recognize are very small. Differences in speech patterns, social preferences, leadership styles, ways of knowing, and approaches to moral problems are far more interesting.

In a fascinating study of women's intellectual development, Bellenky, Clinchy, Goldberger, and Tarule (1986) described several categories of women's ways of knowing:

> *Silence*, . . . women experience themselves as mindless and voiceless and subject to the whims of external authority; *received knowledge*, . . . women conceive of themselves as capable of receiving, even reproducing knowledge from the all-knowing external authorities. . . ; *subjective knowledge*, . . . truth and knowledge are conceived of as personal, private, and subjectively known or intuited; *procedural knowledge*, . . . women are invested in learning and applying objective procedures for obtaining and communicating knowledge; and *constructed knowledge*, . . . women view all knowledge as contextual, experience themselves as creators of knowledge, and value both subjective and objective strategies for knowing. (p. 15)

Bellenky and her colleagues also identified two modes of knowing which they have called "separate" and "connected" knowing. Separate knowing is characterized by the detachment and disinterest so highly valued in traditional masculine approaches to science. Connected knowing, in contrast, retains a connection, even a feeling, for the objects of study. Some readers of the Bellenky and colleagues (1986) study have interpreted connected knowing as a preference to work with others rather than alone, and this does seem to be one aspect of connected knowing. But an important aspect of connected knowing is the difference in attitude toward the objects of study. Barbara McClintock, the Nobel Prize winning geneticist, has been identified as a connected knower, not because she prefers to work with others but because she feels a deep connection or relation to the plants that she studies (see Keller, 1983).

The work of Bellenky and colleagues is important for several reasons. First, it has drawn the attention of educators to the plight of young women whose personal lives have forced them into silence, and it has reminded us that our way of educating encourages not only girls but also boys to simply receive and reproduce knowledge. Second, as we have begun to use the descriptive terms "separate" and "connected," we have become aware that many creative men are also connected knowers in the sense that refers to a relation with the objects of knowledge or creation. Further, some highly creative women are *not* connected knowers in the social sense. Third, because so many women *are* connected knowers in the social sense, educators have good reason to explore and further develop strategies and patterns of cooperative learning. Finally, even if the patterns described by Bellenky and colleagues turn out not to be distinctive of *women's* ways of knowing, their categories represent important patterns that educators should be aware of. Both girls and boys can profit from our sensitivity to various ways of knowing.

A similar claim can be made for studies in the moral domain. In 1982, Carol Gilligan published her now-famous *In a Different Voice,* which describes an alternative approach to moral problems. This approach was identified in interviews with women, but Gilligan does not claim that the approach is exclusively female, nor does she claim that all women use it. Still, the avalanche of re-

sponse from women who recognized themselves in Gilligan's description is impressive in itself. "This is me," many women responded. "Finally someone has articulated my way of handling moral problems."

Gilligan described a morality based on the recognition of needs, relation, and response. Women who use the different voice in moral matters refuse to leave themselves, their loved ones, and connections out of their moral reasonings. Their reasoning is contextual. When faced with standard, textbook-type dilemmas, such women often ask for more information. This seemingly odd response has led some investigators to suspect that earlier judgments on women's moral reasoning might be right after all. Perhaps women do not reason as well as men do in the moral domain. They certainly do not treat moral problems as though they were problems in geometry. Other respondents evaluate the different voice as an important contribution to moral dialogue. It brings moral reasoning into the real world where it belongs. Real moral problems are, after all, *not* like mathematical problems.

Much research and criticism has resulted from Gilligan's challenge to Kohlberg's (1981) description of stages of moral reasoning. In some early studies, it seemed (as recounted earlier) that women lag behind men in moral reasoning. Results suggested that the average woman attains only stage 3 on Kohlberg's scale, whereas the average man scores at stage 4. Gilligan's work suggests that there may be a separate and equally important pattern of development that grows out of the relatedness characteristic of Kohlberg's stage 3. Highly developed in the direction of care and response, this pattern of development is as healthy and ethically powerful as the pattern described by Kohlberg— one that culminates in the recognition and use of an abstract, universal principle of justice.

The debate over differences in men's and women's moral reasoning and over the relative merits of care and justice is still heated (Larrabee, 1993). However, for educators the main effects of the debate should be to make us more sensitive to wider possibilities in discussing moral life and moral education. Stories chosen for use in moral education (or "prosocial development") should illustrate both care and justice, and boys as well as girls should learn to exercise the thinking characteristic of both patterns.

It is also important to note that several writers have described the care orientation in African American culture. It appears in the novels and poetry of Alice Walker, Toni Morrison, Ntozake Shange, and Audre Lorde, and has also been noted in anthropological and sociological studies (see Harding, 1987). In discussing the care tradition, we have an opportunity to acknowledge both gender and cultural diversity.

Research on Gender and Education

It seems incredible to young women today that it was not until the second half of this century that women were admitted to the elite universities and professional schools in this country. Throughout the long struggle for political and educational equality, treatises were written on women's capacities and duties, and, with the advent of educational research, projects were undertaken to learn more about gender differences.

The concentration on gender differences led researchers to explore questions such as the following: Are males or females better at subject *X*? How much better? Why? Who has the greater aptitude for *Y*? Indeed, the topic of gender differences, remarked Susan Chipman (1988), has been "far too sexy a topic." Researchers and policymakers have concentrated on gender differences for over a century, and most of the differences uncovered have been small or unimportant. Years ago, sociologist Arlie Hochschild (1973) raised questions about the usefulness of research on gender differences in

the cognitive domain; more recently, Hyde (1981) has shown that the variance accounted for by gender runs between 1% and 5%. Yet such differences continue to intrigue professional educators, and some accounts even make front-page newspaper stories (Benbow & Stanley, 1980).

The difference between the research we will discuss here and the Bellenky and colleagues (1986) and Gilligan (1982) research is of great importance. In the latter form of research, we learn something about the patterns and quality of women's thinking and moral reasoning. A contrast to masculine ways is implied and sometimes even made explicit, but the central idea is to study and describe women's thinking in all its richness—to study it from its own perspective. This is truly transformational work. It does *not* ask, How similar are women to men? Rather, it attempts to watch and to listen to women as they think, feel, and act in real-life settings. Further, as we have seen, such research is beginning to stretch our imaginations with respect to what it means to be human. As a result, there should be greater possibilities for both women and men.

However, the research that begins with an implicit male model and then investigates differences has been influential in establishing policy and directing further research. Research on mathematical aptitude and achievement has been prominent. Because more boys than girls excel on tests such as the Scholastic Aptitude Test (SAT), some researchers have suggested that there may be a gene favoring males for mathematics (Benbow & Stanley, 1980), but these studies have concentrated on highly talented students who have chosen to pursue mathematics and to demonstrate their proficiency in it. As many researchers have pointed out, factors other than genetic predisposition are almost certainly operating by the time children enter junior high school, and many of these factors press young women to reject mathematics (Brush, 1985; Casserly & Rock, 1985). Research needs to be directed at why and how young women make these choices. If they reject mathematics because it seems unfeminine or because they are afraid that boys will not like them, then educators need to work on the self-image of girls and, perhaps, on the attitudes of boys toward bright females.

However, if girls are making positive, well-informed choices in favor of subjects other than mathematics, then we should learn more about these choices and what they can mean for girls' professional success. There are two points to be made here. First, we have to ask why mathematics represents the acme of achievement. Why not exquisitely polished interpersonal skills? Why not the sort of loving altruism that leads to competence in teaching and social work? It may be that mathematics holds its high place, in part, because males have been attracted to it and have dominated the field. Second, in our eagerness to give girls opportunities to participate and excel in mathematics, we should be careful not to let such participation define the self-worth of girls. Many bright girls are apparently being told by teachers and counselors that they are "too good" for fields traditionally associated with women and that they should plan careers in mathematically related fields. This message is potentially harmful for both the young women who receive it and for the professions ultimately deprived of their talent.

These points remind us that, as educators, we should respect and cultivate the full range of human capacities and talents, not the standard few long promoted by schools. It is not only cultural and gender diversity that should interest us but also the wonderful array of human capacities displayed in children who are not academically talented.

Another line of gender research has looked at the effects of single-sex schooling. Present research findings suggest that single-sex schooling may have advantages for females: such schools engender greater student satisfaction and higher educational aspirations (Lee & Marks, 1988), a stronger sense of community, and more desirable attitudes toward intellectual and social life (Gilroy, 1989; Lee & Bryk, 1986). However, most studies show that the positive effects of single-sex schooling are confined to females; coeducation seems better for many males (Jiminez & Lockheed, 1988). Apparently, boys are spurred on by the presence of girls, whereas girls are impeded, intimidated, and silenced by the presence of boys. Again, results of this sort suggest that teachers need to help girls find a voice and help boys monitor their own behavior to control the acts and attitudes that have such ill effects on girls.

Arguments for all-girl schools seem somewhat paradoxical. Feminists throughout the 19th and 20th centuries have worked hard for equality, and the most obvious road to equality has always seemed to be coeducation (Tyack & Hansot, 1990). Indeed, coeducation was probably the only way to ensure that girls would have the same facilities and resources as boys. (Even with coeducation, resources for boys far exceed those for girls in physical education, and the long-standing dominance of males in mathematics and the sciences has had a similar, if unintended, effect in those fields.) But now it seems that, given a similar curriculum and similar facilities, girls do better if males are not present.

A similar phenomenon has appeared in the education of African Americans. Although it was held (and perhaps rightly so) that separate education is inherently unequal, that proposition is now being questioned. Almost certainly the empirical part of the claim was accurate. In fact, facilities and resources for minority children were not, and still are not, equal to those enjoyed by white, middle-class students. But today we question whether separation is *inherently* unequal. Cannot black children learn well with all-black classmates? The liberal justice and generosity of the earlier judgment now seems tainted with more than a bit of arrogance.

As I understand it, a similar problem may exist in special education. On the one hand, it seems right to place children in the "least restrictive" environment consonant with their needs and to mainstream as many as possible. On the other hand, special environments that have been designed by people who know the needs of special children may be more liberating for these children than "regular" classrooms. Again, we may have allowed an implicit standard of normality to push us toward arrangements that are not necessarily in the best interests of all children.

Problems in Today's Classrooms

Recent research has shown that boys receive more attention than girls in our classrooms (Sadker & Sadker, 1986). Granted, some of this attention is negative; that is, boys are more often reproved for behavioral infractions. But, when analysis is restricted to intellectual interactions, boys still get significantly more attention than girls. Further, it has been shown that, when boys have academic difficulties, they are exhorted to work harder. When girls have similar problems, they are often advised to find studies more compatible with their "abilities," or they are praised for working hard even though the results are poor. Minorities get similar treatment, and minority females receive the least attention and encouragement. However, teachers can learn to do better, and many improve when these problems are drawn to their attention and fairer strategies are suggested (McCormick, 1994).

Girls suffer another kind of discrimination in schools because of the great emphasis on subjects long dominated by males. In the previous section, we discussed some of the research on gender differences in mathematics achievement. But why should such emphasis be placed on mathematics and science? They are important, of course. But in a time when more and more young people are drawn to crime and antisocial activities, why should math-

ematics be more important than social studies and humanistic studies? It is hard to deny the possibility that math and science are so emphasized *because* they have long been male strengths.

For many years, girls did somewhat better than boys on the verbal portion of the SAT. Now boys are doing better on both the math and verbal sections. Although I know of no research that yields a convincing explanation of this relative decline in women's achievement, it might well be that the great emphasis on math and science "for all" has distracted some girls from the studies in which they might have excelled. This has long been a problem for artistically oriented males as well. Men who are successful in literary and artistic fields often report having hated school. In our well-intentioned efforts to "give everyone a chance" at the high-paying jobs associated with technology, we may be depriving many children of opportunities to develop their own distinctive capacities.

Another feature of schooling that may have an adverse effect on girls' aspirations is the administrative hierarchy. As young children, both girls and boys are taught mainly by women. In high school, more males are available as teachers. But at all levels, the administrators are more likely to be male than female, and at the high school level and in superintendent positions, the proportion of males is overwhelming. Nothing in the structure of schooling suggests to young women that they should aim for positions of leadership. In all-female schools, the presence of more women in higher positions may contribute to the positive effects identified earlier.

In addition to doubts about their place in a male-dominated world, young women are still hard-pressed by the "feminine mystique" (Friedan, 1963). Even though the emphasis on domesticity has been greatly reduced (and, as we will see in the next section, this is not an unmixed good), the pressure to be thin, beautiful, and attractive to males is still very great. Susan Brownmiller (1984) has described the dilemma faced by most women. On the one hand, femininity has its pleasures and social advantages; on the other, it demands a great sacrifice:

> The world smiles favorably on the feminine woman: it extends little courtesies and minor privilege. Yet the nature of this competitive edge is ironic, at best, for one works at femininity by accepting restrictions, by limiting one's sights, by choosing an indirect route, by scattering concentration, and by not giving one's all as a man would to his own, certifiably masculine, interests. (pp. 15–16)

Girls need counseling not only on college and career opportunities but also on how to be both a woman and a person. They need to understand the history and the current power of the cultural construct we call femininity. And boys need to understand how our culture's view of masculinity limits their own possibilities and causes great harm to women. Surely boys need gender counseling if the following paragraph by Michael Kimmel (1993) represents a widespread understanding of masculinity:

> Sexual behavior confirms manhood. It makes men manly. Robert Brannon has identified the four traditional rules of American manhood: (1) No Sissy Stuff: Men can never do anything even remotely suggesting femininity. Manhood is a relentless repudiation and devaluation of the feminine. (2) Be a Big Wheel: Manhood is measured by power, wealth, and success. Whoever has the most toys when he dies, wins. (3) Be a Sturdy Oak: Manhood depends on emotional reserve. Dependability in a crisis requires that men not reveal their feelings. (4) Give 'em Hell: Exude an aura of manly daring and aggression. Go for it. Take risks. (p. 123)

Part of today's curriculum should surely be devoted to helping young people understand and cope with the cultural constructions surrounding masculinity and femininity.

Including Women's Traditions in the Curriculum

Women's struggle for equality has involved a deep paradox. Even when women are considered equal (for example, Plato's female guardians), they are judged *equal to men*. A model created and shaped by masculine culture is the one to which women must aspire. Western culture, at its most generous, invites women to be like men; it does not invite men to be like women.

The stage was set for discussion of this problem in our earlier analysis of women and mathematics. Instead of asking why women lag behind men in mathematics, we might ask why men lag behind women in early childhood education, nursing, social work, and similar activities. The attitudes and tasks traditionally associated with women have long been undervalued. Surely, bearing and raising children, caring for the ill and the elderly, supporting neighborhood institutions, and homemaking are essential and beautiful activities. It is hard to imagine a healthy society in which no one attends to such tasks or cares for the society's vulnerable members. Yet these central concerns of human life are almost entirely absent from the school curriculum. Male culture has produced the curriculum. What might the curriculum look like if women's culture provided the standard?

In speaking of "women's culture," we must be careful. Women, like men, are all different. It is misleading to talk of a unitary "women's experience" or "women's culture." Nevertheless, certain societal expectations have affected the lives of all women in the Western world. Whether or not particular women became mothers or were involved in caregiving occupations, they all faced the expectation that women would do such caregiving. Women's culture has emerged out of this expectation, the work itself, and resistance to it. Thus, when I speak of women's culture, I refer to this common experience.

Suppose this culture were fully articulated. Suppose the voice of care were heard. What might be included in the curriculum?

There might be much more emphasis on what we once called "private" life as contrasted with "public" life. As we know, the sharp separation between the two breaks down under analysis, but the tradition that sustains the separation is still dominant. Surely, if we had started with private life, the school curriculum would be very different from the one actually developed (Noddings, 1992; Thompson, 1992).

Instead of the emphasis on preparation for occupations and citizenship, there might be one on family membership and homemaking. When I refer to *homemaking*, I am not suggesting a return to Catherine Beecher's plan of domestic economy as the center of women's education. Rather, I am suggesting an education that prepares both girls and boys for the hard work of establishing and maintaining a home.

There is nothing inherently anti-intellectual in the topic of homemaking. The topic can include economics, art, nutrition, geography, history, technology, and literature. It can and should be multicultural. Perhaps, most wonderful of all, it can be philosophical. What does it mean to "make a home"? Must a home's occupants be members of a nuclear family? Why is a "home for the aged" not considered a home by many of its occupants? Why is a nation often referred to as a homeland, and how does love for a homeland sometimes contribute to disagreements and even war? Why is exile such a terrible punishment? By emphasizing the intellectual here, I do not mean to denigrate the practical but simply to pique the interest of those who might otherwise brush aside the notion of including homemaking in the curriculum.

Of course, we should teach the practical elements of homemaking as well. I'm not sure these skills were ever taught well in ordinary homes, and today it seems certain that many children are not learning them. We should teach homemaking in such a way that students become competent homemakers and also learn to see both the personal and global tragedies of homelessness, whether that homelessness is caused by poverty, psychological neglect, mental illness, or war—whether it is the literal absence of shelter or the dreadful alienation of psychological separation.

Citizenship, from this perspective, is not all we have in common as adults. We should want our children to be prepared as competent parents, homemakers, spouses, neighbors, and friends. They should be responsible pet owners (if they own pets), considerate and appreciative users of the natural and human-made environments, intelligent believers or nonbelievers in the religious domain. These are common human activities. Are they not as important as voting and knowing the name of one's congressional representative?

Another topic that women's culture surely emphasizes is intergenerational life. In schools, this would involve a study of life stages as well as of intergenerational responsibility. How do infants grow? When should children be taught to read? What are the special problems of adolescence? Of young adulthood? When does old age begin? A fascinating set of topics for multicultural education might include demographic and statistical studies, systems of medical care, the history of childhood, attitudes toward death and helplessness, responsibilities of the old for the young, and vice versa. Such study might also include field experience in the form of community service.

Especially important to the development of young women are stories about women who have composed lives of their own (Bateson, 1990) while supporting husbands, raising children, and contributing to local communities. Other impressive accounts describe the life stages of women in both literary and practical language (Lindbergh, 1955). At least some of this literature should become part of the standard curriculum.

The recommendation to include descriptions and analyses of women's lives from the perspective of women and women's culture is very different from the usual approach of simply adding women to the traditional masculine story. In that approach, textbook writers do not change the standard material; they merely search for women whose participation in public life has been overlooked. Thus, women are mentioned more often and appear in illustrations, but they are not honored for the accomplishments connected to women's culture (Tetreault, 1986).

Even in discussions of war and peace, women are infrequently given their due. One reason for this, of course, is that social studies curricula have put much more emphasis on war than on peace. The story of women's efforts in behalf of peace is impressive (Brock-Utne, 1985; Elshtain, 1987; Reardon, 1985; Ruddick, 1989); often it is heroic, and both girls and boys should be familiar with it.

In connection with the study of peace, it is important to note that most feminists do not regard peace as the mere absence of war. As long as substantial numbers of people live in daily fear of violence, the world is not "at peace." Eliminating the violence that women suffer at the hands of men is part of the peace movement and an essential part of gender education. Both men and women have much to learn in this area, and the study of peace must be extended beyond an analysis of nations at war to a careful and continuing study of what it means to live without the fear of violence.

Schools must give more attention to issues and practices that have long been central in women's experience, especially to child-rearing, intergenerational responsibility, changes induced by life stages, and concern about violence. Given current worries about poverty, crime, child abuse, and declining levels of education, our society may be ready to raise its evaluation of "women's work."

Conclusion

We have analyzed and discussed several important topics and issues concerning the education of women: the history of female education and some competing views on what should be included in that education; women's patterns of intellectual and moral reasoning; parallels between the problems of women and those of other minority groups; educational research on gender; special issues arising in today's classrooms; and the possibilities of including substantial parts of women's culture in the school curriculum. It has been suggested that all educators should be familiar with this material and that both girls and boys should receive a powerful and rich gender education.

References

Bateson, M. C. (1990). *Composing a life.* New York: Plume.

Beecher, C. (1977). *A treatise on domestic economy.* New York: Schocken Books. (Original work published 1842)

Bellenky, M. F., Clinchy, B. C., Goldberger, N. R., & Tarule, J. M. (1986). *Women's ways of knowing.* New York: Basic Books.

Benbow, C. P., & Stanley, J. C. (1980). Sex differences in mathematical ability: Fact or artifact? *Science, 210,* 1262–1264.

Brock-Utne, B. (1985). *Educating for peace: A feminist perspective.* New York & Oxford: Pergamon Press.

Brownmiller, S. (1984). *Femininity.* New York: Linden Press/Simon & Schuster.

Brush, L. R. (1985). Cognitive and affective determinants of course preferences and plans. In S. F. Chipman, L. R. Brush, & D. M. Wilson (Eds.), *Women and mathematics: Balancing the equation* (pp. 123–150). Hillsdale, NJ: Erlbaum.

Buchwald, E., Fletcher, P. R., & Roth, M. (Eds.). (1993). *Transforming a rape culture.* Minneapolis, MN: Milkweed Editions.

Casserly, P., & Rock, D. (1985). Factors related to young women's persistence and achievement in advanced placement mathematics. In S. F. Chipman, L. R. Brush, & D. M. Wilson (Eds.), *Women and mathematics: Balancing the equation.* Hillsdale, NJ: Erlbaum.

Chipman, S. F. (1988). Far too sexy a topic [Review of J. S. Hyde & M. C. Linn (Eds.), *The psychology of gender*]. *Educational Researcher, 17*(3), 46–49.

Cross, B. M. (Ed.). (1965). *The educated woman in America.* New York: Teachers College Press.

Daly, M. (1973). *Beyond God the father.* Boston: Beacon Press.

Ehrenreich, B., & English, D. (1973). *Witches, midwives, and nurses.* Old Westbury, NY: Feminist Press.

Elshtain, J. B. (1987). *Women and war.* New York: Basic Books.

Friedan, B. (1963). *The feminine mystique.* New York: Norton.

Gilligan, C. J. (1982). *In a different voice.* Cambridge: Harvard University Press.

Gilroy, M. K. (1989). *The effects of single-sex secondary schooling: Student achievement, behavior, and attitudes.* Ann Arbor: University of Michigan Press.

Harding, S. (1987). The curious coincidence of feminine and African moralities. In E. F. Kittay & D. T. Meyers (Eds.), *Women and moral theory* (pp. 296–315). Totowa, NJ: Rowman & Littlefield.

Hochschild, A. A. (1973). A review of sex role research. In J. Huber (Ed.), *Changing women in a changing society* (pp. 249–267). Chicago: University of Chicago Press.

Hyde, J. S. (1981). How large are cognitive gender differences? *American Psychologist, 36,* 892–901.

Jiminez, E., & Lockheed, M. E. (1988). *The relative effectiveness of single-sex and coeducational schools in Thailand* [Working paper for Policy, Planning and Research]. Washington, DC: The World Bank.

Kant, I. (1983). Of the distinction between the beautiful and the sublime in the interrelations of the two sexes. In M. B. Mahowald (Ed.), *Philosophy of women.* Indianapolis, IN: Hackett. (Original work published 1764)

Keller, E. F. (1983). *A feeling for the organism: The life and work of Barbara McClintock.* New York: W. H. Freeman & Co.

Kimmel, M. S. (1993). Clarence, William, Iron Mike, Tailhook, Senator Packwood, Spur Posse, Magic . . . and us. In E. Buchwald, P. R. Fletcher, & M. Roth (Eds.), *Transforming a rape culture* (pp. 121–138). Minneapolis, MN: Milkweed Editions.

Kittay, E. F., & Meyers, D. T. (Eds.). (1987). *Women and moral theory.* Totowa, NJ: Rowman & Littlefield.

Klaits, J. (1985). *Servants of Satan.* Bloomington: Indiana University Press.

Kohlberg, L. (1981). *The philosophy of moral development.* San Francisco: Harper & Row.

Larrabee, M. J. (Ed.). (1993). *An ethic of care.* New York & London: Routledge.

Lee, V. E., & Bryk, A. S. (1986). Effects of single-sex secondary schools on student achievement and attitudes. *Journal of Educational Psychology, 78*(5), 381–395.

Lee, V. E., & Marks, H. M. (1988). Sustained effects of the single-sex secondary school experience on attitudes, behavior, and values in college. Ann Arbor, MI: Center for the Study of Higher and Postsecondary Education, University of Michigan.

Lindbergh, A. M. (1955). *Gift from the sea.* New York: Random House.

Martin, J. R. (1985). *Reclaiming a conversation.* New Haven, CT: Yale University Press.

McCormick, T. (1994). *Creating the nonsexist classroom: A multicultural approach.* New York: Teachers College Press.

McLaughlin, E. C. (1974). Equality of souls, inequality of sexes: Women in medieval theology. In R. R. Ruether (Ed.), *Religion and sexism* (pp. 213–266). New York: Simon & Schuster.

Noddings, N. (1992). *The challenge to care in schools.* New York: Teachers College Press.

Okin, S. M. (1979). *Women in Western political thought.* Princeton, NJ: Princeton University Press.

Reardon, B. A. (1985). *Sexism and the war system.* New York: Teachers College Press.

Ruddick, S. (1989). *Maternal thinking: Towards a politics of peace.* Boston: Beacon Press.

Sadker, M., & Sadker, D. (1986). Sexism in the classroom from grade school to graduate school. *Phi Delta Kappan, 67*(7), 512–515.

Spender, D. (1980). *Man-made language.* London: Routledge & Kegan Paul.

Tetreault, M. K. (1986). The journey from male-defined to gender-balanced education. *Theory into Practice, 25,* 227–234.

Thompson, P. J. (1992). *Bringing feminism home.* Charlottetown, Canada: Home Economics Publishing Collective.

Tyack, D., & Hansot, E. (1990). *Learning together: A history of coeducation in American public schools.* New Haven, CT: Yale University Press & Russell Sage Foundation.

Wollstonecraft, M. (1975). *A vindication of the rights of woman* (C. H. Poston, Ed.). New York: Norton. (Original work published 1792)

CHAPTER 10
Liberalism, Ethics, and Special Education

KENNETH R. HOWE
University of Colorado at Boulder

This chapter characterizes the present scene with respect to educational ethics. Although aspiring to comprehensiveness, its scope is limited in two ways. First, it emphasizes philosophical perspectives, largely ignoring other perspectives—for instance, religious, psychological, and legal—that are also important and illuminating. Second, it emphasizes elaborating a liberal-democratic framework, the kind of framework dominant in Western democracies.

The discussion is divided into four sections.[1] The first characterizes the liberal-democratic tradition in terms of the three philosophical theories that have dominated it: utilitarian, libertarian, and liberal-egalitarian. I focus on the internal disagreements among these theories, particularly with respect to how they balance the liberal values of liberty and equality, and argue that the liberal-egalitarian framework is superior to the other two.

The second section briefly considers four theories that currently challenge the liberal-democratic tradition; namely, critical theory, communitarianism, the ethics of care, and postmodernism. Each of these theories advances one or more of the following objections to the liberal-democratic tradition: it is overly abstract, ahistorical, unresponsive to diversity, androcentric, eurocentric, oppressive, and an apology for the status quo.

The third section concedes many of these criticisms, particularly with respect to libertarian and utilitarian frameworks. I advance the view, however, that the liberal-democratic tradition (at least in a liberal-egalitarian form) can be revised to accommodate these criticisms. Such an accommodation involves acknowledging the important insight of challenges to classic liberalism (to abstract ethical theory in general) that ethical deliberation is situated in particular contexts that involve particular people with particular histories, genders, cultures, and so forth.

Among the contexts for ethical deliberation are professional activities, which add yet another set of particularistic factors. The final section briefly considers the implications of the preceding sections as they apply specifically to special education as an area of applied and professional ethics. Four questions are addressed: Why teach the ethics of special education? What should be taught? How should it be taught? To whom should we teach it? I detach the answers I give, as far as I am able, from broader theoretical commitments to liberalism or its competitors.

---

[1]The first three sections of this chapter are adapted from Howe (1993).

Three Predominant Philosophic Theories in the Liberal-Democratic Tradition

Today, the term *liberal* is typically used to describe the end of the political spectrum—the opposite of *conservative*. Given this usage, liberals endorse (whereas conservatives oppose) governmental intervention to solve social problems, schemes to redistribute income from the rich to the poor, scrupulous protection of civil liberties, and a host of other "liberal" positions. But the term *liberal* also has a long history in political theory in which it is used to describe a broad political tradition that encompasses both liberals *and* conservatives in the above uses of the terms. What makes views "liberal" in this sense is a shared commitment to the fundamental liberal principles of liberty and equality; they diverge, often dramatically, regarding how to interpret and balance these principles.

Utilitarianism

Utilitarianism is an ethical theory that determines the rightness of given actions and policies on the basis of their consequences. In particular, an action or policy is right if, from among the available alternatives, it is the one that maximizes total benefit, or, more technically, satisfies the "Principle of Utility." For example, consider the policy debate that is now raging over "schools of choice" schemes. For a utilitarian, whether implementing schools of choice is the morally best policy will depend on whether such an educational policy shift would result in the best overall consequences. If, all things being equal, schools of choice maximized student achievement, economic competitiveness, and the other things for which they are touted, then they would be endorsed by utilitarians.

In making their calculations, utilitarians incorporate the principle of equality by insisting that everyone's (and some utilitarians would include animals') benefit be included and equally weighted. John Stuart Mill (1863/1961b), probably the most well-known utilitarian of all, takes it as a given that "the interests of all are to be regarded equally" (p. 435). Thus, like any theory in the liberal-democratic tradition, utilitarianism precludes providing special privileges to individuals on the basis of considerations such as birthright, social rank, and the like.

As all liberal theorists must, utilitarians also incorporate the liberal value of liberty. In a much cited passage from *On Liberty*, Mill (1849/1961a) voices his unusually strong (for a utilitarian) commitment:

> [T]he sole end for which mankind are warranted, individually or collectively, in interfering with the liberty of action of any of their number is self protection . . . the only purpose for which power can be rightfully exercised over any member of a civilized community, against his will, is to prevent harm to others. . . . He cannot rightfully be compelled to do or forbear because it will be better for him to do so, because it will make him happier, because, in the opinion of others, to do so would be wise, or even right.

Mill was one of the earliest and most influential utilitarians. Since his time, utilitarianism has dominated the liberal-democratic tradition (Rawls, 1971) and continues to exert considerable influence. It has come under increasing criticism, however, for the manner in which it construes both liberty and equality—not surprisingly, libertarians focus their criticisms on a perceived compromising of liberty; egalitarians focus theirs on a perceived compromising of equality. These criticisms will be developed later in a way that will help explicate libertarianism and egalitarianism and help further explicate utilitarianism as well. There is a further criticism, however, that may be most fruitfully introduced here: it is by no means clear, much less uncontroversial, what the benefit (or good) to be maximized should be.

Historically, the most common criterion of the good has been happiness. But this criterion needs to be operationalized in some fashion if it is to permit utilitarian calculations. Individual preferences, as determined by polls, for example, is one modern suggestion. But relying on mere preferences obliterates the distinction between what is legitimate or worthwhile for people to value and what is not. The upshot is that a vulgar hedonistic society—for instance, one that valued only money and the pleasure it could buy—would be judged morally best if this is what served to maximize the satisfaction of preferences among its members. To take a more extreme case, one could imagine a society in which the satisfaction of preferences was maximized by sanctioning the practices of slavery and fights to the death between gladiators.

This is an unwelcome conclusion, but trying to avoid it (as Mill did in *Utilitarianism*, 1863/1961b) by somehow ranking certain preferences as worthwhile or "progressive" and others as vulgar leads to the difficult problem of determining just who is to decide and how they might justify foisting their judgment on others, particularly in a liberal democracy where people are presumably afforded the freedom to decide for themselves what vision of happiness to pursue.

This problem is perhaps the most fundamental one for utilitarianism, because it calls into question the feasibility of utilitarianism's brand of "consequentialism"—relying solely on the Principle of Utility to determine whether an action or policy is morally right. Utilitarianism appears to be unable to capture, in its own terms, the difference between *mere preferences* and *legitimate claims*. What seems to be required to capture this distinction is a "nonconsequentialist" theory that appeals to principles and rights that may override the Principle of Utility. For example, the right not to be enslaved must be observed regardless of whether the institution of slavery might be widely endorsed and might maximize economic benefits. Though they differ quite substantially in other ways, libertarians and liberal-egalitarians alike reject utilitarianism in favor of nonconsequentialism.

Libertarianism

For libertarians (see, for example, Nozick, 1974), liberty is the overriding value, and maximizing it is the best way to avoid showing disrespect for people's dignity by treating them paternalistically—as if they were children or incompetent to judge for themselves what is in their own best interests. According to Nozick, only a "minimalist" or "nightwatchman" state can be justified, in which the state's power to infringe on individual liberty is limited to protecting the rights of citizens to be free from crime, foreign aggression, and interference in freely executing agreements and transferring goods. Thus, unlike utilitarians, libertarians face no difficulty regarding how to define what the criterion of benefit should be, for they object in principle to interference by governments in the freely chosen activities of its citizens in order to distribute society's benefits for the purpose of achieving some "end state," such as maximum benefit.

Because libertarianism is thus a nonconsequentialist view, it is not patterns of results that determine the rightness of policies and actions, but the procedures that govern exchanges and agreements among free citizens. Libertarians would endorse Mill's stance on liberty but would reject his stance on the Principle of Utility as the overriding principle for deciding right from wrong. In terms of the example of schools of choice, Mill might very well endorse them on the grounds that the liberty to choose would result in maximizing total benefit. However, if schools of choice did not maximize overall benefit, and if Mill nonetheless remained true to the Principle of Utility as the overriding ethical principle, then he would be required to endorse some other policy on public education. A thoroughgoing libertarian, on the other hand, would object to rendering liberty an *extrinsic value* that is held hostage to producing the right kind of results. Such a libertarian would defend a policy of schools of choice solely on the basis of the *intrinsic value* of granting liberty to students (more likely, their parents) to choose the kind of education they judged best. Whether such a policy led to bad results (such as a large difference in achievement among identifiable groups, for instance) would be moot.

Just as libertarians take a different view from utilitarians regarding the liberal value of liberty, they take a different view regarding the liberal value of equality. Libertarians also rule out such things as birthright and social rank as justifying inequality, but it is only legitimate interests—interests tied to maximizing liberty versus interests in being given an equal claim to the overall benefits produced by others—that must be given equal protection. In this way, a libertarian conception of equality is formal rather than substantive, and this conception of equality renders it illegitimate for governments to do anything more in the name of equality than to play the "nightwatchman" role described earlier.

Liberal-Egalitarianism

I have chosen the term *liberal-egalitarianism* (a term also used independently by Kymlicka, 1990) to refer to the third view I wish to describe in the liberal-democratic tradition. The view is liberal insofar as it is committed to the two liberal values of liberty and equality. It may be distinguished from stricter versions of egalitarianism, however, because, like all liberal theories, it does not hold

that inequality must always be eliminated. Instead, it holds that inequality is only prima facie objectionable and therefore may be justified. I will explicate this view in terms of the criticisms it advances against utilitarianism and libertarianism, respectively.

It is important to observe that the type of equality endorsed by utilitarianism does not entail that a policy cannot be right if its result is that different individuals and groups enjoy different levels of benefits. Imagine that schools of choice were to result in a nation composed of 10% rich entrepreneurs, scientists, and engineers and 90% poor service workers and homeless people and that this result maximizes benefits. Setting aside how benefit might be measured (the GNP is one measure that is implicitly endorsed these days in popular arguments lauding competitiveness, and so on), it is consistent with utilitarianism (indeed, it is required by the Principle of Utility, as described earlier) to endorse a policy of schools of choice given these results. For it is the total benefits, not how evenly they might be distributed, that forms the basis of utilitarian calculations.

Liberal-egalitarians find this consequence of utilitarianism unacceptable. Although they do not preclude employing the Principle of Utility, they contend that it can be superseded or "trumped" by rights (for example, Dworkin, 1979) as well as by principles of justice (for example, Rawls, 1971). Such liberal-egalitarians would object to the scenario just described regarding a policy of schools of choice on the grounds that it is inconsistent with a correct interpretation of equality.

Dworkin (1979), for instance, distinguishes "equal treatment" from "treatment as an equal." Equal treatment is the interpretation of equality implicit in utilitarianism, in which everyone's interests are given equal weighting. The problem with this interpretation is that it cannot protect essential interests, or rights, which should outweigh or "trump" those that are less essential, or, indeed, illegitimate. For example, if a policy of schools of choice were to maximize overall benefit but also result in racial discrimination, the essential interest in, and right to, nondiscrimination would "trump" the Principle of Utility for a thinker such as Dworkin. He would be willing to accept (indeed, would insist on) foregoing the Principle of Utility in order to respect rights.

In contrast to the equal treatment interpretation of equality, the treatment as an equal interpretation is sensitive to the relative legitimacy of different interests and is closely tied to the concept of "equal respect." Under this interpretation, it is difficult to imagine how a society composed of 10% haves and 90% have-nots could show equal respect for its members and thus be ethically defensible, particularly if it failed to do all it could to ensure that those most in need were given the opportunity to share in its fruits.

This point leads rather naturally to the principle of equal opportunity and to the views of John Rawls (1971). For utilitarians, equal opportunity, like any other principle, is subordinate to the Principle of Utility. Thus, although utilitarians can (and most no doubt do) endorse it, because it ultimately must be sanctioned by the Principle of Utility, its existence is precarious. For example, consider the flurry of government support for social programs in general and educational programs in particular following the riots of the late 1960s. Such programs can be (and, in fact, often were) justified on the utilitarian grounds that equalizing opportunity would lead to a reduction of violence, an increased quality of life for all, identifying and developing talent that would otherwise be wasted, and so forth. Of course, support for such programs has since eroded, and utilitarian reasoning has been an accomplice in this erosion. Today, the perception by many citizens as well as policymakers is that such programs do not work

or, worse, may even be counterproductive (Murray, 1984), and thus should be abandoned.

Rawls is able to avoid such waffling on a commitment to the principle of equal opportunity because his theory exempts the requirements of social justice, of which equal opportunity forms a part, from utilitarian calculations. For him, equal opportunity is required for individuals to have a fair chance to enjoy a reasonable amount of society's goods; for example, employment, income, health care, education, and self-respect. And he requires more than equal opportunity in the formal sense described in connection with libertarianism's conception of equality; he requires a substantive sense that he calls "fair equality of opportunity." This conception is based on Rawls' belief that people are not responsible for disadvantages that arise from natural and social contingencies over which they have no control—who their parents are, how talented they are, whether they have a disability—and that justice requires social institutions and practices that mitigate these disadvantaging contingencies, sometimes in opposition to the Principle of Utility.

Like libertarianism, then, liberal-egalitarianism is nonconsequentialist in the sense that it subordinates the Principle of Utility to rights and justice. Unlike libertarianism, however, it rejects a merely formal interpretation of equality that tends to render liberty hollow. Dworkin (1979) and Kymlicka (1990), in particular, contend that equality is the fundamental value in liberalism, and that instead of existing in tension with liberty such that trade-offs have to made, liberty cannot be viewed apart from equality. Liberal-egalitarians in general hold that liberty must be "worth wanting" (Dennett, 1984). For this reason, liberal-egalitarians, (as opposed to libertarians) are disposed to advocate intervening in social activities in order not only to ensure equality but (and what for them often amounts to the same thing) to ensure that citizens are empowered with a kind of liberty in which, as Dewey (1930) says, "human desire and choice count for something" (p. 10).

Consider once again the example of schools of choice, and recall that a utilitarian would endorse them if they maximized benefit and a libertarian would endorse them if they maximized liberty. Liberal-egalitarians tend to be much more suspicious and dismissive of such a policy than either utilitarians or libertarians. Amy Gutmann (1987), for instance, contends that the first obligation of public schooling is to ensure that as many children as possible reach the "democratic threshold"—a level of educational success that prepares them to engage as equals in the political processes that shape their lives—and uses this criterion as the standard against which to judge educational policy. A policy of schools of choice is thus required to pass a stiffer test than those associated with either utilitarian or libertarian reasoning, because the requirement of as many children as possible attaining the democratic threshold—attaining the requisites of equality—must be figured in, and it supersedes the values of maximizing benefit and of maximizing liberty.

I have devoted a fair amount of space to the difficulties that beset utilitarianism and libertarianism, and it is thus fitting that I say something about the difficulties that beset liberal-egalitarianism. Gutmann's "democratic threshold" provides a clue to the general types of difficulties it involves. Whereas utilitarians may appeal to the Principle of Utility to set policy and libertarians may appeal to minimally constrained choice, liberal-egalitarianism is more complex and more difficult to apply, insofar as it must give some account of what counts as the criterion of a "fair share" (for example, Kymlicka, 1990) of society's goods and resources, a criterion that both must check these other forms of reasoning but that nonetheless must permit justified inequalities. For example, how far must public schools go to ensure that a

child with severe emotional disturbances attains the "democratic threshold," receives his or her "fair share" of educational resources, before it gives up? What *is* the "democratic threshold" anyway?

The kind of detailed analysis required to meet these difficulties would be beyond the scope of this chapter. Generally speaking, liberal-egalitarianism has become the dominant strain in the liberal-democratic tradition in the second half of the 20th century, propelled largely by Rawls. In my view, liberal-egalitarianism represents the liberal-democratic tradition at its best and most defensible. On balance, its difficulties are less serious than those associated with utilitarianism and libertarianism, particularly regarding what equality requires.

Current Challenges to the Liberal-Democratic Tradition

Perspectives on educational ethics have both external and internal aims, by which I mean they concern themselves both with what kind of citizens education should develop and with what educational methods should be employed. Of course, these two aims are intimately related, and how they are fleshed out will depend on the political tradition within which they are couched. In Plato's *Republic,* for instance, the external aim depends on what class of citizens education is being provided for—the rulers, the military, or the producers—and the internal aims are adjusted accordingly.

In the case of educational ethics rooted in the liberal-democratic tradition, the external aim is to develop citizens who are capable of exercising their liberty as equals in a democratic society, and, unlike Plato's aristocratic form of government, this aim is common to all students. The internal aim is to ensure that educational practices, as far as possible, not only serve this external aim but also exemplify it. Thus, although educational theorists in the liberal-democratic tradition certainly have their disagreements (recall the schools of choice example), they nonetheless agree on certain fundamentals; for example, that public education must produce citizens who can think for themselves and who are thus self-determining. Accordingly, thinkers in this tradition have a long history of criticizing doctrinaire educational practices that suppress, distort, or refuse to entertain questions about truth and about what kinds of lives are worth leading and that, accordingly, deny students the opportunity to develop their own, well-considered views.

In virtue of its commitments to liberty and equality, liberal educational theory is committed to some form of neutrality vis-à-vis the good and virtuous life, and it is just such a commitment that engenders the central problem for a liberal theory of educational ethics (Strike, 1982): how a system of public education can be both guided by liberal-democratic principles and remain neutral regarding what vision of the good it should promote.

Skepticism surrounding liberalism's capacity to adequately respond to this problem has increased markedly over the last several decades. Liberal political theory in general and liberal educational theory in particular have increasingly been charged with class, gender, and cultural biases, each of which is inconsistent with the tradition's avowed commitment to equality. These criticisms often take the form of documenting the various and overlapping disparities that exist in educational opportunities and achievement among girls versus boys, men versus women, minority cultures versus white culture, the working class versus the middle class, and so forth. Where criticisms of liberal educational theory take these kinds of disparities as the basis for calls to achieve much greater equality across groups by equalizing educational opportunities, they do not fundamentally challenge the liberal tradition. Instead, they demand that it live up to its promise. But there are deeper forms of criticism that not only go beyond, but are

often at odds with, the liberal presuppositions in the kind of criticism just described.

Marxist theorists in education (Bowles & Gintis, 1976, 1989) have historically criticized liberalism for ignoring the manner in which class membership advantages or disadvantages persons in liberal-democratic, typically capitalistic, societies. Inspired by Marxist analysis, but finding it too deterministic and simplistic, critical theorists in education have extended it to include such factors as gender, race, culture, and ethnicity (Apple, 1993; Burbules, 1993; Young, 1990). These thinkers assign a large role to economic class, but they also emphasize how the factors of gender, race, culture, and ethnicity interact with class to "distort" communication and disadvantage social groups vis-à-vis the dominant culture. For example, "castelike" minorities—minorities that have involuntarily become a part of the political-economic system, such as certain Hispanics and African Americans (Ogbu & Matute-Bianchi, 1986)—are faced with the dilemma of either playing by the rules of the dominant culture and compromising their cultural identity or refusing to play and paying a price for preserving it. African Americans, for instance, can either embrace the practice of "acting white" to succeed in school or embrace an "oppositional" stance that often dooms them to poor performance. A related set of problems faces indigenous peoples such as North American aboriginals (Kymlicka, 1991).

From another direction, feminist scholars (for example, Bellenky, Clinchy, Goldberger, & Tarule, 1986; Gilligan, 1982; Noddings, 1984) have claimed that there are certain ways of thinking and relating to others, as well as certain interests, that are peculiar to women's experience, and that an appreciation of these differences is rarely reflected in institutional norms and in the laws (for example, Noddings, 1990; Okin, 1989; Salamone, 1986). For its part, the educational system in particular tends to implicitly embrace the gendered attitudes and practices of society at large and to respond to and sort girls and women accordingly, both in their roles as educators and in their roles as students (Apple, 1988; Kelly & Nihlen, 1982; Oakes, 1990; Sadker & Sadker, 1986; Shakeshaft, 1986; Weiler, 1988; Weis, 1988). Moreover, women are faced with a sort of "double bind"—insofar as they must pay a price when they *do* play by the existing rules—because certain traits are "genderized" (Martin, 1982) such that women are judged differently from men for exhibiting what otherwise seems to be the same behavior.

From a third direction, communitarians (MacIntyre, 1981; Sandel, 1982) criticize liberalism for presupposing a conception of individuals as disconnected atoms, each pursuing his or her self-interests. Given such a view, shared conceptions of good persons and good lives are precluded. As a consequence, so the argument goes, ethical reasoning collapses into "emotivism"—a mere power struggle among individuals to satisfy their preferences. Furthermore, lacking agreement on what good persons and good lives are, the possibility of creating an "educated public"—a public that has some shared starting point and some shared standards for moral-political deliberation and negotiation—is also precluded (MacIntyre, 1987).

Finally, from a fourth direction, postmodernism criticizes liberalism for ignoring the tight connections between rationality and knowledge, on the one hand, and power, on the other. In the postmodern view, the curriculum and instruction of liberal educational theory are rooted in the conceptions of rationality and knowledge of the dominant group, conceptions that are employed to marginalize and delegitimize other forms of rationality and knowledge as irrational and relativistic (for example, Lather, 1991).

Critics of liberalism from these four general perspectives can substantially disagree, including among themselves. Nonetheless, they converge on one or both of two general criticisms.

The first is that, by remaining neutral, liberalism incorporates a conception of the individual that is atomistic, ahistoric, and egoistic. Given this conception, individuals are free to constantly reassess their vision of the good and their practices independent of the time, place, and human connections within which they find themselves. Whether such individuals are a psychological possibility is questionable. In any case, such individuals, as well as a society composed of them, are morally undesirable.

Consider the moral education technique of values-clarification, often identified with the principle of neutrality (Raths, Harmin, & Simon, 1978). Practitioners of values-clarification are given explicit instructions not to impose traditional values on students, even moral values such as rules against cheating on tests. Instead, they are instructed to confine themselves to merely pointing out the personal consequences for students of behaving in one way versus another. The nature of moral agents assumed by values-clarification thus seems to be just as the critics contend.

The second general criticism is that, contrary to its ostensive aim and purported neutrality, the liberal quest for equality merely serves to ensconce the status quo, rendering upper-class white males the standard of comparison and requiring disempowered groups (such as the working-class, cultural minorities, and women) to play by existing rules that they had no part in formulating and whose interests such rules do not serve.

Consider Hirsch's (1988) call for the universal distribution of "cultural literacy." Hirsch makes free use of the principles and rhetoric of the liberal-democratic tradition, contending that it is only by acquiring "cultural literacy" that the disadvantaged can participate in democratic processes and enjoy equality of opportunity. Hirsch's solution to the challenge posed by multiculturalism is thus to eliminate it by using public education to promote cultural uniformity based on the existing dominant beliefs and practices. According to Hirsch, extending cultural literacy to minorities not only benefits them in particular but is required in order to preserve democracy. Although Hirsch himself doesn't directly do so, Hirschian-like arguments may easily be extended to girls and women. Such an argument would hold that girls and women should become equal to men in various areas of literacy: for example, mathematics and science, where they have traditionally fared poorly.

Thus, Hirsch advocates precisely the kind of view that is vulnerable to the general criticism discussed earlier. In particular, because the game is rigged in a way that favors the historically dominant group, equal opportunity to measure up to what that group has unilaterally decided is worthwhile can be quite hollow. In this way, Hirsch's proposal incorporates a significant gender and cultural bias. What follows is that his version of liberal education fails to adequately resolve the fundamental tension between the requirement of neutrality regarding what public education promotes as the good and the liberal principles of liberty and equality.

Liberal Responses

The picture painted by the critics of liberalism's conception of neutrality, especially by communitarians, is at best a caricature. The kind of neutrality presupposed by the technique of values-clarification is indeed untenable, but it is easy to formulate a version of liberal neutrality that is much more substantive than this, and yet is considerably less culturally loaded than Hirsch's concept of cultural literacy. Liberal neutrality needn't imply that individuals are ahistoric, egoistic atoms, but only that they are capable of assessing the life situations in which they find themselves and of criticizing and changing those that are unacceptable (Kymlicka, 1991; Rawls, 1993). Consider young women thrust into a school community

characterized by a significant degree of gender bias. Aren't they capable of questioning the kind of identity that such a community foists upon them? And shouldn't they be empowered to initiate progressive change?

Whereas contemporary liberals dismiss the criticism that liberalism presupposes a view of moral agents as atomistic, ahistoric, and egoistic, they concede the second general criticism: that liberalism has been largely oblivious to the peculiar difficulties presented by cultural and gender differences. However, they deny that this is a fatal flaw. For instance, Will Kymlicka (1990, 1991) contends that an adequate response to these difficulties is implicit in the writings of prominent liberal-egalitarians such as Rawls and Dworkin. (See also Okin, 1989, who advances arguments similar to Kymlicka's, though she confines herself exclusively to gender.) Specifically, Kymlicka (1991) ties the issue of affording self-respect to women and minorities to the principle of granting them equality, and argues that granting them equality requires giving them a voice in political decision making that is sensitive to their peculiar histories and perspectives. In this connection he observes:

> [I]t only makes sense to invite people to participate in politics (or for people to accept that invitation) if they will be treated as equals. . . . And that is incompatible with defining people in terms of roles they did not shape or endorse. (p. 89)

Extending Kymlicka's argument to encompass public education, his observation may be slightly reformulated to read as follows: It only makes sense to invite people to participate in *schooling* (or for people to accept that invitation) if they will be treated as equals. . . . And that is incompatible with defining people in terms of roles they did not shape or endorse. In contrast to Hirsch's vision of the liberal educational ideal—one that merely explicates and further entrenches the status quo—the vision that grows out of a view like Kymlicka's is one that affords everyone equal respect, including minorities and women, and ensures that their interests will be protected in a process of negotiating educational ideals.

This tack embraces the heart of liberalism, particularly the commitment to equality, but attempts to eliminate gender and cultural biases that stand in the way of realizing true equality. As I intimated earlier, however, eliminating such biases does not entail embracing a *completely* neutral mission for public education. Liberal educational theorists of all stripes remain committed to the aim of educating individuals to become competent citizens in a liberal-democratic society. The trick is not to eliminate the commitment to the liberal educational ideal but to define it in such a way that it does not deny certain identifiable groups (such as women and cultural minorities) genuine equality. Rather than complete neutrality, the commitment to liberal educational theory requires circumscribing democratic negotiations in terms of liberal principles, and the correct interpretation and application of such principles require much greater attention to voices that historically have been muted or not heard at all.

Whether liberal-egalitarianism successfully accommodates the insights of its competitors I leave for readers to judge, and as grist for further reflection and dialogue. It should be noted, however, that far from being apologists for the status quo, the transformations of society's institutions in general, as well as its educational institutions in particular, called for by liberal-egalitarians are nothing short of radical by comparison to what typically passes as "liberal" in the current political arena.

The Ethics of Special Education

I focus the remainder of this chapter on the ethics of special education, and begin with the general observation that whatever general theoretical perspective is embraced—liberalism, critical theory, communitarianism, the ethics of care, or postmodernism—one cannot escape the tension that exists between questions concerning the basic structure of society and its schools and questions concerning what to do in concrete situations. This tension has important implications for how to conceive the ethics of special education.

On the one hand, there are questions that are broad in scope concerning public policy toward special education and what its national mission should be, exemplified, for example, in legislation such as The Education for All Handicapped Children Act (PL 94-142). These questions profoundly affect the interests of a large number of people and frame day-to-day practice. Because they are so broad in scope, individual educators are relatively powerless to influence how they are decided. Moreover, the loyalties they demand from individual educators are to abstract principles and to unidentified individuals—individuals on the other side of the district, the state, the country, or the globe.

On the other hand, there are questions that are narrow in scope concerning particular schools, classrooms, and students, exemplified, for example, in the question of whether teachers should be particularly aggressive in garnering extra resources for their particular school, classroom, or student. In contrast to broad questions of public policy, individual educators have significant influence in deciding these narrower questions. Moreover, they are decided on the basis of loyalties to identified individuals with whom concrete relationships and obligations have been established. The trade-off—the tension—is that answers to these narrower questions may exclude attention to the broader questions and may exclude the interests of all those unidentified individuals. The reverse can also happen, in which commitment to abstract principles and unidentified individuals is permitted to override one's more intimate, concrete relationships and obligations.

In my estimation, it is unlikely that any theoretical breakthrough in ethical theory will be forthcoming that can completely eliminate this tension. But this should not serve to halt deliberating about and teaching the ethics of special education. Instead, we can make peace with the existence of a plurality of ethical perspectives that cannot always be rendered consistent (Strike, 1993a), give up the quest for "moral harmony" (Hampshire, 1983), and proceed.

In this spirit, I now turn to the four questions posed at the outset: (1) Why teach the ethics of special education? (2) What should be taught? (3) How should it be taught? (4) To whom should we teach it?

1. Why teach the ethics of special education? It has become commonplace for educational philosophers to observe that education is inherently a moral activity. It follows that ethics should be studied by all educators—teachers and administrators alike, preservice and inservice. But why focus on special education in particular?

Ethics is increasingly being recognized as highly context-sensitive. This general observation explains why different fields of applied and professional ethics have grown up around business, law, journalism, nursing, and medicine. As in these other fields, the history, mission, and bureaucratic organization of special education (though not unrelated to public education in general) are distinctive. Recognition of this distinctiveness is reflected by the fact that, also similar to these other fields, special education has its own professional organizations and its own ethical codes.

2. What should be taught? The content of the ethics of special education should be drawn from its most frequent and pressing problems and should be divided into three categories: broad-scope issues, narrow-scope issues, and issues that lie between (Howe & Miramontes, 1992). The first two categories include issues at the ends of a continuum corresponding to the tension between ethical perspectives described earlier. The third includes issues that most clearly place individuals midway between these two extremes, a kind of predicament that is characteristic of the role-related obligations that attend professional activities in general. For example, HMO physicians must attend to the needs of patients in front of them while balancing them against the needs of other patients in the HMO—if too many resources are spent on this patient, there won't be enough for the next. Special education teachers must engage in similar reasoning regarding their students. Although not immune from being tugged in both directions in our personal lives (Should I buy my son a new pair of soccer shoes when other people are starving?), this predicament is more frequent and more difficult to ignore in carrying out our professional responsibilities.

As for sequencing these three categories, philosophers are likely to want to begin at the most abstract level and work their way to the more concrete levels, whereas special educators (and perhaps students) are likely to want to do the reverse. But the order in which the three categories are pursued is probably not essential. I can imagine beginning with abstract issues of policy, and then seeing how policies constrain what can be done in concrete situations, or, alternatively, beginning with concrete situations and seeing how these bump up against policy. Either sequence could be effective. The proviso is that whatever sequence is chosen, it must give sufficient attention to the full spectrum of issues. Otherwise, students of the ethics of special education will fail to gain a full appreciation of its scope, coherence, and relevance.

3. How should it be taught? The ethics of special education should be taught in a highly dialogical and participatory manner, a suggestion that applies to ethics teaching in general. It is only by employing such a method that participants are provided with the experience needed to gain the "dialogical competence" required of ethical deliberation and negotiation in a pluralistic society (Strike, 1993b).

Cases drawn from practice, policy, and law provide a particularly good vehicle for this method. They readily lend themselves to a dialogical approach, and are motivating because they depict real-life problems.

4. To whom should it be taught? Virtually everyone in public education is affected by special education, particularly since the advent of inclusion. Thus, the audience for the ethics of special education should be very general. (For example, at my university all preservice teachers are required to take a course titled "The Exceptional Child," which includes the history of and rationale for inclusion.) This is not to suggest that those most directly involved in special education should not study the ethics of special education in greater depth than those less directly involved. However, the task of special educators is made all the more difficult when only they understand the egalitarian underpinnings of special education and only they have the skills and dispositions required to work out compromises.

Conclusion

Not too long ago *Time* magazine carried a story on a 12-year-old girl, suffering from spastic cerebral palsy and progressive scoliosis, whose parents requested that her "Do Not Resuscitate" (DNR) order be honored while she was at school (Van Biema, 1993). Recently, I engaged in a conversation about this case (sometimes a bit heated) over dinner with Tonda Potts (my wife and director of special education in a local district), Ofelia Miramontes (my colleague and co-author of *The Ethics of Special Education),* and Bill Barkley (Ofelia's husband and a biologist in private business).

Whether the DNR order was otherwise justified was not an issue. The issue was whether carrying out DNR orders is the sort of thing that should be going on in schools. Tonda and Ofelia had no trouble coming to the conclusion that the school should refuse to honor the parents' wishes. It was obvious to them that permitting a child to die in school would destroy the trust of children and was contrary to the mission of education, particularly special education. Trotting out the celebrated Karen Ann Quinlan case, I responded that "this is contrary to our mission" is exactly the response that hospitals used to give (and some no doubt still do) to patients' requests to refuse medical treatment. I advocated listening carefully to the parents and finding some way to accommodate their wishes, and Bill largely agreed with me. Over the next hour or so, the conversation took a number of twists and turns, but wound up pretty much in the same place that it started.

There are two morals I would like to draw from this story. First, although we took a few cheap shots at one another (Ofelia and Tonda berated Bill and me with sarcasms and laughed out loud at our supposed naiveté, whereas "wimpy paternalists" was one of my more memorable expressions), none of us wound up thinking the others were evil demons or flat wrong. On the contrary, we gained an appreciation of one another's views and, at the same time, lost some confidence in the unassailability of our own. This is a kind of success, short of agreement, that can attend a dialogical approach to ethics.

Second, that the occasion would even arise to have such a conversation says a lot about the present situation in which special education finds itself vis-à-vis ethics. If it ever made sense to put the ethics of special education on "automatic pilot,"[2] that time has surely passed.

---

[2]I owe this expression to Benjamin and Curtis (1986), who use it in connection with nursing ethics.

References

Apple, M. (1988). *Teachers and texts: Political economy of class and gender relations.* New York: Routledge & Kegan Paul.

Apple, M. (1993). *Official knowledge: Democratic education in a conservative age.* New York: Routledge & Kegan Paul.

Bellenky, M., Clinchy, B., Goldberger, N., & Tarule, J. (1986). *Women's ways of knowing.* New York: Basic Books.

Benjamin, M., & Curtis, J. (1986). *Ethics in nursing* (2nd ed.). New York: Oxford University Press.

Bowles, S., & Gintis, H. (1976). *Schooling in capitalist America.* New York: Basic Books.

Bowles, S., & Gintis, H. (1989). Can there be a liberal philosophy of education in a democratic society? In H. Giroux & P. McLaren (Eds.), *Critical pedagogy, the state, and cultural struggle.* Albany, NY: State University of New York Press.

Burbules, N. (1993). *Dialogue in teaching.* New York: Teachers College Press.

Dennett, D. (1984). *Elbow room: The varieties of free will worth wanting.* Cambridge, MA: MIT Press.

Dewey, J. (1930). *Human nature and conduct.* New York: Random House.

Dworkin, R. (1979). *Taking rights seriously.* Cambridge, MA: Harvard University Press.

Gilligan, C. (1982). *In a different voice: Psychological theory and women's development.* Cambridge, MA: Harvard University Press.

Gutmann, A. (1987). *Democratic education.* Princeton, NJ: Princeton University Press.

Hampshire, S. (1983). *Morality and conflict.* Cambridge, MA: Harvard University Press.

Hirsch, E. D. (1988). *Cultural literacy.* New York: Vintage Books.

Howe, K. (1993). The liberal-democratic tradition and educational ethics. In K. Strike & L. Ternasky (Eds.), *Ethics for professionals in education* (pp. 27–42). New York: Teachers College Press.

Howe, K., & Miramontes, O. (1992). *The ethics of special education.* New York: Teachers College Press.

Kelly, G., & Nihlen, A. (1982). Schooling and the reproduction of patriarchy: Unequal workloads, unequal rewards. In M. Apple (Ed.), *Cultural and economic reproduction in education.* Boston: Routledge & Kegan Paul.

Kymlicka, W. (1990). *Contemporary political theory: An introduction.* New York: Clarendon Press.

Kymlicka, W. (1991). *Liberalism, community and culture.* New York: Clarendon Press.

Lather, P. (1991). *Getting smart.* New York: Routledge & Kegan Paul.

MacIntyre, A. (1981). *After virtue.* Notre Dame, IN: University of Notre Dame Press.

MacIntyre, A. (1987). The idea of an educated public. In G. Haydon (Ed.), *Education and values.* London: Institute of Education, University of London.

Martin, J. R. (1982). The ideal of the educated person. In D. DeNicola (Ed.), *Proceedings of the thirty-seventh annual meeting of the Philosophy of Education Society* (pp. 3–20). Normal, IL: Philosophy of Education Society.

Mill, J. S. (1961a). On liberty. In J. S. Mill & J. Bentham, *The utilitarians* (pp. 475–600). Garden City, NY: Doubleday. (Original work published 1849)

Mill, J. S. (1961b). Utilitarianism. In J. S. Mill & J. Bentham, *The utilitarians* (pp. 402–472). Garden City, NY: Doubleday. (Original work published 1863)

Murray, C. (1984). *Losing ground: American social policy 1950–1980.* New York: Basic Books.

Noddings, N. (1984). *Caring: A feminist approach to ethics and moral education.* Berkeley: University California Press.

Noddings, N. (1990). Feminist critiques in the professions. In C. Cadzen (Ed.), *Review of research in education* (Vol. 16, pp. 393–424). Washington, DC: American Educational Research Association.

Nozick, R. (1974). *Anarchy, state, and utopia.* New York: Basic Books.

Oakes, J. (1990). Opportunities, achievement, and choice: Women and minorities in science and mathematics. In C. Cadzen (Ed.), *Review of research in education* (Vol. 16, pp. 153–222). Washington, DC: American Educational Research Association.

Ogbu, J., & Matute-Bianchi, M. (1986). Understanding sociocultural factors: Knowledge, identity, and school adjustment. In *Beyond language: Social and cultural factors in schooling language minority students* (pp. 73–142). Los Angeles: Evaluation, Dissemination and Assessment Center, California State University.

Okin, S. M. (1989). *Justice, gender, and the family.* New York: Basic Books.

Raths, L., Harmin, M., & Simon, S. (1978). *Values and teaching* (2nd ed.). Columbus, OH: Charles E. Merrill.

Rawls, J. (1971). *A theory of justice.* Cambridge, MA: Harvard University Press.

Rawls, J. (1993). *Political liberalism.* New York: Columbia University Press.

Sadker, M., & Sadker, D. (1986). Sexism in the classroom: From grade school to graduate school. *Phi Delta Kappan, 67,* 512–516.

Salamone, R. (1986). *Equal education under the law.* New York: St. Martin's Press.

Sandel, M. (1982). *Liberalism and the limits of justice.* New York: Cambridge University Press.

Shakeshaft, C. (1986). A gender at risk. *Phi Delta Kappan, 67,* 499–503.

Strike, K. (1982). *Educational policy and the just society.* Chicago: University of Illinois Press.

Strike, K. (1993a). Ethical discourse and pluralism. In K. Strike & L. Ternasky (Eds.), *Ethics for professionals in education* (pp. 176–188). New York: Teachers College Press.

Strike, K. (1993b). Teaching ethical reasoning using cases. In K. Strike & L. Ternasky (Eds.), *Ethics for professionals in education* (pp. 102–116). New York: Teachers College Press.

Strike, K., & Soltis, J. (1985). *The ethics of teaching.* New York: Teachers College Press.

Van Biema, D. (1993, October 11). An education in death. *Time,* p. 60.

Weiler, K. (1988). *Women teaching for change.* South Hadley, MA: Bergin and Garvey.

Weis, L. (Ed.). (1988). *Class, race, and gender in American education.* Albany, NY: State University of New York Press.

Young, R. (1990). *A critical theory of education.* New York: Teachers College Press.

PART IV

The Future of Special Education

JAMES L. PAUL AND HILDA ROSSELLI-KOSTORYZ
University of South Florida

Up to this point, the primary focus of this book has been knowledge bases in the social and neurosciences and the humanities that, arguably, form the foundations of the philosophy, research, and practice of special education. An assumption underlying the development of this book is that the knowledge and perspectives grounding special education research and practice have "drifted" or become disconnected from those foundations. Over time, as the body of research in special education has grown, researchers have increasingly depended on the accumulated knowledge about special education to guide future research. Similarly, the philosophy of inquiry guiding the research has been sustained across time and across areas of interest. Special education practice, on the other hand, has been unevenly guided by intervention research and by prevailing philosophies of practice that have varied with changes in the political and social ecology.

Just as educators attempted early in this century to integrate several disciplines—sociology, anthropology, philosophy, and history—into the social foundations of education, special educators have attempted to integrate different disciplines, and fields of study within disciplines, in understanding and addressing the needs of children with disabilities. Some of the most influential disciplines have been psychology (especially clinical, experimental, ecological, and developmental psychology), neurology, child psychiatry, sociology, and social work. Basic topics of interest that have focused research, policy, and practice in special education have included, for example, intelligence, behavior, learning, deviance, development, and systems.

Although there are many ways of structuring discussions of the knowledge bases of special education, authors in this section have organized the discussion into three categories: systems knowledge, developmental knowledge, and behavioral knowledge. The fourth chapter in this section, Chapter 14, adopts a stance outside the traditional knowledge foundations of special education. In this chapter the postmodern perspective is examined, along with implications for related special education knowledge with philosophical moorings outside of the modern *Weltanschauung* that generated that knowledge.

In Chapter 11, Duchnowski and Kutash draw from their policy studies and their research on caregiving systems to propose a systems-based design for research in special education. They begin by acknowledging the grim news on outcomes for special education students, attributing some of the responsibility to the research base that informs the practice. In their opinion, research has focused the field too much on a simple action model that examines what a teacher does to a student, while giving less attention to the more complex social systems in which the child lives. Echoing Fuchs and Fuchs's call to the special education research community, Duchnowski and Kutash propose moving toward systems-oriented research.

Duchnowski and Kutash's call to action is responsive to the need for reform in special and general education, as well as the need to forge more effective links between research and practice. Unfortunately the research community has not been viewed as a significant source for solutions to the challenges of public education, including special education. The authors decry the lack of confidence in, and public policy commitment to, data-based, solution-generating systems research. Like Fuchs and Fuchs, they point to several successful interventions that have affected academic performance and improved the behavior of students with disabilities. They concede that the bleak picture of overall outcomes may be a function of the field's lack of large-scale comprehensive systems research.

The authors then draw on the work of Malouf and Schiller in their explication of the poor linkage between research and practice. Notable contrasts between research and practical knowledge have caused an alienation between those whose business it is to provide empirical validation and those to whom fall the responsibilities of implementing research findings. Duchnowski and Kutach are sympathetic but caution against a lessening of methodological rigor that would ultimately diminish the value of "craft knowledge."

The authors propose a move away from microresearch to multidisciplinary and collaborative research. They also call for a more concerted effort to examine service delivery systems within larger operating social systems. This contextualized approach to service reform requires a different type of rigor, characterized by cross-sector collaborative ventures, long-term design, revised views of families, and a need for flexible policies governing research funds.

The authors point out the difficulties encountered by such research; noting, for example, that consensus-building is necessary across various disciplines, stakeholders, and perspectives. Unlike the fixed treatment model, there is no single independent variable, much less a single dependent variable. Even the role of the researcher is fraught with dilemmas experienced by participant observers. Yet, a vision is offered by Duchnowski and Kutash of a systems-oriented research agenda that encompasses the use of participatory research teams, mixed methodologies within a longitudinal context, as well as agreement between stakeholders on valuable outcomes—all within contexts that consider individual, family, and system levels.

The authors conclude their discussion by using the Child and Adolescent Service System Program (CASSP), and several projects funded by private foundations, to illustrate their vision. These examples are promising and emphasize the need for further conceptualization and description of systems in order to regird the future of special education research.

Chapter 12 offers another call to change, this time within research on human development, learning, and special education. Marfo and Boothby focus on relating knowledge bases in behavioral science to the knowledge bases in special education and developmental disabilities. They emphasize the value of advancements in developmental psychology and the cognitive sciences to special education, highlighting a number of examples found in Chapters 4 through 7, as well as three additional areas: ecological and contextualist theories of development, resiliency, and changing conceptions of cognitive competence.

Marfo and Boothby begin by carefully analyzing research efforts to attribute achievement to either genetic or environmental influences. Although the discussion is clearly not over, as evidenced by the recent responses to *The Bell Curve,* the authors point to the contributions of interactionist theorists, such as Sameroff, Bronfenbrenner, and Lerner, who have influenced the fields of special education and developmental disabilities. Though special education researchers have not totally embraced these frameworks, the authors blame this lag on the complexity of ecological-contextualist perspectives, which can pose dilemmas for researchers. What follows is an intriguing reanalysis of Head Start research, applying the ecological-contextualist framework. A second example draws from Marfo's work on an efficacy research model for assessing intervention outcomes that suggests at least five classes of independent variables and at least two classes of outcome variables. Marfo identifies significant influences (such as family commitment to an intervention and parents' beliefs about child development) that his model would consider. He proposes that this type of an approach would also strengthen the relevance of classroom- and school-based research.

According to Marfo and Boothby, the emerging lines of inquiry on resiliency also hold promise for special education and developmental disabilities. They recount how the use of correlates of success support a competence model of children's functioning, a theme that parallels the recommendation by Duchnowski and Kutash to build on the strengths of families. This view is considered novel when compared to the historically negative view of disability embraced by the fields of special education and psychology.

The third convincing example offered relates advancements in cognition and learning to assessment and instruction. Paralleling the discussion of Viens, Chen, and Gardner (see Chapter 5) and many others, Marfo and Boothby reiterate the need for special education to move toward newer directions for assessing intellectual functioning. They also call for a more deliberate and careful linking between cognitive theories and instructional strategies, cautioning against shallow educational applications that precede necessary conceptual bridges between a given body of knowledge and the specific applications derived from it. They offer a framework initially proposed by Lauren Resnick for determining whether a given theory has all the necessary ingredients to allow direct application to instructional settings. What still may be needed is further explication of the theories of competence, acquisition, or intervention before useful interpretation for daily classroom application can be achieved.

Another powerful research theme emerges from this chapter with the discussion of the rather "cavalier" overall treatment of culture, which disregards much of what has been learned from cross-cultural studies. This "culture gap," as Marfo and Boothby have labeled it, has been widely ignored in North American psychology because we have succumbed to assumptions of universality, endogenous development, and optimality. These assumptions are outlined in-depth by the authors as evidence that cross-cultural researchers have not paid enough attention to specific dimensions of culture that account for observed differences in individuals from differing cultures. Of equal destructive value has been the field of special education's inclination to infer deficits from differences, which has not boded well for children from differing cultural or economic backgrounds.

Finally, Marfo and Boothby examine the "local" research influences that have limited the field of special education and development disabilities. "Politicization of inquiry" is explored through two examples from the literature illustrating how political influences can and do exert undue pressures on the conduct of research. The remaining influence, that of the "interventionist culture," is embedded deep within the fundamental role of special education; yet, as the authors note, it has the potential for masking the need for larger, more radical social reform.

Chapter 13 follows the call for new research directions in behavior analysis, one of the more grounded forces influencing special education. Dunlap and Kern argue that the current and future relevance of behavioral perspectives to the field represents an important area of exploration as the field of special education reinvents itself in response to social, cultural, and political influences. The authors provide a useful review of the principles of applied behavior analysis, noting the strengths derived from its grounding in scientific method and conceptual basis in operant psychology. Methodological characteristics related to observation and measurement to assess the impact of environmental manipulations are also noted. Dunlap and Kern both believe that the single-subject characteristic and the dynamic nature of behavioral analysis lend themselves well to addressing the needs of students with disabilities, particularly in the context of inclusive education. They also view the empirical nature of behavioral analysis as compatible with the recent shift toward accountability, enabling researchers to systematically evaluate the effectiveness of an intervention. The authors also remind us that functional analysis, another outgrowth of the field, has resulted in more logical and more successful approaches to improving student behavior.

New challenges exist as applied behavior analysis is considered in settings that differ dramatically from traditional special education settings. Dunlap and Kern also note that dramatic shifts in demographics and increases in violent behaviors have precluded the traditional responses of schools that resulted in special education placements. They view the field as poised on a threshold at which behavior analysis must demonstrate its usefulness in broader applications that involve a variety of settings and individuals responsible for implementation.

In response, the authors call for more studies of utilization and relevance, offering several methodological approaches that facilitate this type of research. They also encourage assessment of the social validity of applied behavior analysis, as well as studies focusing on its effectiveness as understood by "goodness-of-fit" variables. Though strongly in support of the role of measurement in applied behavior analysis, both Dunlap and Kern caution against excessive methodological inhibitions that may overpower more useful insights regarding human development and interaction, particularly those that are more illusive in nature.

In Chapter 14, Danforth concludes this section with a stimulating discussion of postmodernism, narrative, and hope in special education. Danforth writes from a postmodern perspective and uses narrative inquiry to explore the storied lives of individuals with emotional disturbances.

In this chapter, Danforth uses an address given by Carl Becker to explore the thesis that every person in education may be an educator; thus inviting the participation of those traditionally thought of as outsiders, such as families, paraprofessionals, and students themselves. This poses an invitation to all of us to make the construction of what is true, real, and worthy a communal and intentional activity. Danforth also examines "disability stories" that have attempted to connect what happens in schools or classrooms to plausible categorical explanations. This he attributes to our historical roots in psychology, with generally unacknowledged interests in administrative and social control.

A story by Salman Rushdie is also explored in this chapter for its potential in sense making of what Danforth calls the untrue stories that may still provide hope and value for the future. In Rushdie's *Haroun and the Sea of Stories,* Danforth deftly interprets Rushdie's message regarding democratic dialogue. Danforth also explores the role of "laminations" as a social, linguistic process of symbolic layering absent the modernist's additional search for objectivity and reason.

In closing, he does not stipulate what stories should be told but rather encourages a move away from hegemonic modern narratives toward smaller, more personal stories that share communal meaning and that embrace solidarity. In this manner, persons with disabilities will be included in the range of "us" and will be considered equal, yet not the same.

As promised, this collection of chapters seeks to intrigue, awaken, provoke, and stimulate consideration of the future of special education as informed by research and practice shaping the field. There has been no attempt at a grand synthesis and no search for deep currents of thought connecting these different bodies of research. The perspectival differences are relatively clear.

Yet, several common messages bear mention across the seemingly diverse chapters in this section. The type of socially constructed story that Danforth proposes is echoed in Duchnowski and Kutash's call for systems-based research as well as the ecologically constructed view and politicization of inquiry discussed by Marfo and Boothby. The student's journal exploring his disability (in Danforth's Chapter 14) is hauntingly linked to Marfo's discussion of resiliency, Duchnowski and Kutash's experiences with CASSP, and Dunlap and Kern's support for functional analysis taken to a more personal level. Dunlap and Kern's view of functional analysis bridges several of the chapters as it calls us to more thoughtful consideration of context in interpreting even the most empirically based research. Duchnowski and Kutash's call for more thoughtful involvement of families as partners in research is again echoed in the careful consideration of family beliefs, culture and tradition espoused by Marfo and Boothby. Likewise, Marfo and Boothby's comments regarding the culture gap overlap with Duchnowski and Kutash's call for culturally competent services and Danforth's view of solidarity. Though not in agreement on many fronts, there are common threads across the authors that speak to the need for reconsidering the full array of voices and influences impacting the education of children with disabilities. Perhaps by spanning across differing ideologies and philosophies we have captured a hopeful glimpse of the future of special education.

CHAPTER 11

Future Research in Special Education: A Systems Perspective

ALBERT J. DUCHNOWSKI
University of South Florida

KRISTA KUTASH
University of South Florida

The purpose of this chapter is to cast special education research within a larger systems perspective and to describe the role of special education research as a critical partner in improving outcomes for children with disabilities as well as in effectively contributing to systemic reform in the nation's public schools. The need to accomplish this is more urgent than ever in the history of modern special education. In the mid 1990s, special educators find themselves under critical attack from the media (Shapiro et al., 1993), advocates (Fuchs & Fuchs, 1994), and the families of the children they serve (Duchnowski, Berg, & Kutash, 1995). Although some of the criticism may not be fully supported by the facts (Fuchs & Fuchs, 1995), it is clear that each annual report to Congress by the Office of Special Education and Rehabilitative Services (OSERS) reveals that children who have disabilities and who are placed in special education programs do not fare well while they are in school or when they leave school (Edgar, 1987; Hasazi, Gordon, & Roe, 1985). We propose that the unsatisfactory levels of program effectiveness are due in part to some limitations in the research base that informs special education practice. Specifically, researchers have focused almost exclusively on the microlevel—that is, the child-teacher dyad in the special education

classroom. The disability under examination has usually been conceptualized as a unitary entity, such as a "learning disability," "behavior disorder," or "mental retardation." The interventions evaluated have focused almost exclusively on what a teacher does during a specified time in the classroom. This is in contrast to more recent perspectives of children with disabilities as having complex combinations of strengths as well as deficits that cross several modalities, as being members of a social system composed of family and peers, and in some cases, in terms of having a chronic disability that may not be able to be totally cured but rather ameliorated to the point where a satisfactory level of quality of life may be achieved with a minimum of external supports.

To test our thesis, we propose an increased emphasis on systems research in special education. Such a research initiative would be characterized by a more global focus on the total ecology of children who have disabilities and their families, examining the interaction of the multiple service components that make up their programs, and would employ multisource, multimethod designs that ideally have a longitudinal data collection component. Such an initiative would include projects that aim to contribute new information to the knowledge base as well as those that systematically evaluate existing programs.

It has become almost a tradition that articles published in social science research journals conclude with some variation of the theme that "more research is needed." This is true regardless of the topic under investigation and it certainly holds true in the area of educational research, including special education. Recently, Fuchs and Fuchs (1994) published an excellent review of the facts and emotion surrounding the inclusion movement in special education and concluded with a thought-provoking and articulate version of the call for more research and action. After a comprehensive and exhaustive review of least-restrictive environment, the regular education initiative, and the inclusion movement, they concluded the following:

> Special education has big problems, not the least of which is that it must redefine its relationship with general education. Now is the time to hear from inventive pragmatists, not extremists on the right or the left. Now is the time for leadership that recognizes the need for change; appreciates the importance of consensus building; looks at general education with a sense of what is possible; respects special education's traditions and values and the law that undergirds them; and seeks to strengthen the mainstream, as well as other educational options that can provide more intensive services, to enhance the learning and lives of all children. (p. 305)

We believe that the message offered by Fuchs and Fuchs is not limited to those researchers who examine issues of place but rather can serve as a call to action for the entire special education research community. They articulate the framework for a strategy to systematically improve special education with innovative pragmatism that we propose can be significantly advanced by an increase in systems-focused research.

Special Education Research and Practice: Current Status

Although it is not our purpose to present a review of special education research in this chapter, some observations and summary conclusions are necessary to establish a context for our thesis promoting systems-oriented research. First, the conclusion by Fuchs and Fuchs (1994) that special education has many problems and is in need of some type of reform is shared by virtually all major researchers in the field (see, for example, Kauffman, 1993). Although both the nature and the degree of the reform are the subject of much debate, the need is not. Second, the link between research and practice in this field has been and continues to be weak (Malouf & Schiller, 1995). Research knowledge has had only a minor affect on education practice even when there has been a significant body of research about important problems of interest to practitioners and policymakers (Huberman, 1990; Shavelson, 1988).

Thus, we have a situation in which the state of practice is problematic and the field does not readily turn to the research community for help. This is in spite of the fact that the special education research community has accumulated an impressive knowledge base that has been empirically derived. For example, Fuchs and Fuchs (1995) make the point very well by summarizing the extent of such support in content areas ranging from reading comprehension and written language to spelling and handwriting. They go on to cite a dozen articles, each of which is a quantitative synthesis of numerous studies (sometimes more than 100 studies) that examine interventions that positively affect academic progress and behavior improvement in children who have disabilities.

With such an extensive empirical base supporting special education practices, why is the field in trouble and why do researchers have such a minor role in improving the situation? There are several factors to consider in answering these questions. The current era of reform in education is global in both the goal of reform and in the strategy used to reach it. The reform spurred on by "A Nation at Risk" (National Commission on Excellence in Education, 1983) and other related studies and reports focuses on the place of the United States in a global economy and the fact that America's children are not perceived as being competitive in the world market. The proposed strategy to improve the United States's competitive edge is to restructure America's schools. This is a strategy that proposes changes in school governance, standards, curriculum, and the involvement of parents and the community. It became apparent that special education and the challenges of educating children with disabilities were not addressed by this global strategy of reform (National Council on Disabilities, 1989).

With the onset of the 1990s, however, the public's desire for accountability in education spread to special education. As stated earlier, the annual reports submitted by OSERS continued to document the poor outcomes of children with disabilities compared to their non-disabled peers. The results from the National Longitudinal Transition Study (Wagner, 1993) also documented the poor outcomes of children in special education programs after they transitioned from school. Also, in December 1993 the cover story of *U.S. News & World Report* focused on the apparent ineffectiveness of special education (Shapiro et al., 1993). Special education has problems.

There is an inconsistency here, however, in that there is an impressive research base supporting special education interventions, yet aggregate student outcomes are disappointing. Furthermore, the field does not embrace or use extensively the findings of researchers anyway. There is now extensive literature examining this poor link between research and practice in special education

and many attempts to explain it (see, for example, Huberman, 1990). In a recent review of the relationship between research and practice, Malouf and Schiller (1995) emphasized the contrast between research knowledge and practice knowledge, a contrast that has increasing support (see, for example, Goldenberg & Gallimore, 1991). Briefly, research knowledge is viewed as being linear, it is the result of empirical validation, and it is disseminated to the practitioner who should replicate it in the classroom. In contrast, practice knowledge arises from the act of teaching "and can acquire functionality and validity independent of formal research or theory. Expressions such as 'wisdom of practice,' 'practical knowledge,' 'craft knowledge,' and 'practice knowledge' have proliferated" (Malouf & Schiller, 1995, p. 415). Malouf and Schiller point out the limits of science when empirically derived knowledge is applied to the complexities of the real world, where treatments interact with individual characteristics of people. When research knowledge is applied to a local context it is often found to be unrealistic by practitioners and not immediately helpful.

Systems-Oriented Research: A Linear Alternative

We are impressed by the knowledge base that has accumulated in special education and puzzled by its failure to generate acceptable outcomes for children with disabilities. In addition, we are concerned not about the proliferation of constructs such as practice knowledge, but by the observation that these constructs acquire validity without formal research. By formal research, we do not mean only experimental designs that employ randomly assigned participants, but rather systematic investigations that use rigorous methods, both quantitative and qualitative, that value data that are believable and generalizable (Miles & Huberman,

1994). In addition, we do not deny the importance of the local context and the necessity to take it into account when testing for generalizability.

How might the apparent paradoxes and conflicting perspectives of knowledge in special education be resolved? We offer several suggestions. First, the microaspect of much of special education research may contribute to its limited utility for driving practice. Children with disabilities tend to have complex, coexisting problems requiring a multifaceted intervention plan. Although academic deficit is one aspect of disability, social and adaptive functioning are equally important factors, and the need for related services is real. In spite of the reluctance of resource-poor schools to recognize this complexity of disabilities on Individual Educational Plans (IEPs), children need these services. In addition, families (parents, relatives, unrelated caregivers, and siblings) cannot be ignored or blamed but need to be part of the research that develops or evaluates interventions. No agency has the resources or expertise to implement effective interventions alone. Collaboration is necessary and adds a multidisciplinary aspect to research endeavors.

We propose that special education be conceptualized as an intervention embedded in a service delivery system. Consequently, future research in special education must attend to systems issues in order to more adequately affect implementation and to evaluate effectiveness. This can be done in a context of reform of both regular and special education as well as in those social and health care agencies that serve children with disabilities and their families; or, *the system* that serves children with disabilities and their families.

Service Reform: Creating a System

Research and evaluation efforts have a unique and powerful role as the concepts of accountability, service integration, community-based services,

and the like, sweep service delivery activities. As with previous research and evaluation activities, there is increasing pressure from various stakeholders to determine the worth and merit of these efforts and to help shape these evolving concepts within service delivery systems. Unlike research and evaluation activities of the past, however, the pressure is to understand these human service activities within a "systems" perspective. That is, pressure is being placed to understand service delivery within the operating systems in which they exist, rather than the fragmented and reductionistic perspectives that historically have operated for children and their families.

This focus on service reform is not a new concept to services researchers or evaluators, many of whom have identified service delivery reform as a necessary step to reach the goals outlined by program developers to serve children and families effectively. Research demonstrates that the majority of children and families currently receiving services have multiple needs that can be met only by receiving services across an array of child and family service agencies. In Virginia, for example, it was found that 14,000 families received services from at least one of the leading child-serving agencies; that is, child welfare, education, mental health, or juvenile justice. However, when the data were reviewed to identify families served by one or more agencies, the unduplicated count dropped to 4,993 families served (Boyd, 1994). Additionally, studies of the characteristics of children receiving services reveal that children involved in one service agency are often involved in other service agencies either historically or concurrently.

While there is no uniform definition of service reform, there are characteristics that help distinguish these efforts from the discrete, categorical programs of the recent past. The Harvard Family Research Project has outlined seven characteristics of service reform (Shaw, 1995). The first characteristic is that these reform efforts are ultimately outcomes focused and aimed at improving the lives of children and families by restructuring existing services into a system. This characteristic embraces the need for increased accountability within services for children and families. Attention is being shifted from how many families are served by a program to the outcomes achieved by the families served by a service delivery system. This focus on outcomes has caused agencies to concentrate on developing programs that work collaboratively across different child-serving agencies. The second characteristic stresses that service reform efforts go beyond coordinating existing services to generating a new set of integrated and user-friendly services. Efforts at merely coordinating services have revealed that many needs of children and families were not being met. Therefore, collaborative, multiagency services have had to evolve in order to meet these often complex needs of families. The third characteristic is that service reform efforts require participation from a diverse and usually large group of stakeholders with an increased emphasis on public accountability. Within service reform efforts, families of children with disabilities, for example, are seen as partners with government policymakers and agency representatives and are critical in the design and implementation, as well as in determining the desired outcomes (Duchnowski, Dunlap, Berg, & Adeigbola, 1995). Historically, families have been seen as either the "cause" of their child's disability or as exacerbating it, and have been the target of blame by professionals in the field. Despite overwhelming evidence to the contrary, new professionals are still taught that parents cause or contribute to their child's disability, and they perceive all parents as a single stereotype (Freisen & Koroloff, 1990). Currently, families are seen as advocates, at the least, and at best, as equal partners with professionals in designing services as well as in designing research

and evaluation activities. In this new role, the focus is on the strengths of families and on building strategies to include family members in the service delivery process.

The need to work collaboratively across child-serving agencies has created the need to design cross-agency, cross-sector governance entities, the fourth characteristic of service reform initiatives. Historically, agencies have had limited opportunity to work collaboratively; therefore, the organizational support of working together has not existed. Thus, new organizational units that bring agency directors together have begun to be created. These new governance entities have developed at state and local levels in many states. Eligibility requirements—the fifth characteristic—have often limited families' access to child-serving agencies. Current service reform efforts are usually large in their scope, either in serving wide geographic areas or in the goals or outcomes to be achieved.

The sixth characteristic of service reform efforts is that they are not seen as a time-limited, experiential effort, but rather as a long-term change in the way agencies deliver services. This leads to the seventh characteristic of service reform efforts—they require major shifts in financing at the local, state, and sometimes federal levels. It is widely recognized that financing has the potential for driving treatment decisions. That is, how funds are allocated influences the availability, type, and duration of services (Saxe & Cross, 1992). One of the major strategies in this area is the creation of policies that encourage flexible funding that meets the needs of youth rather than the program guidelines of a child-serving agency. In a 1993 national survey of state child mental health directors on fiscal strategies used to promote community-based services for children, thirty state directors (60%) reported the use and availability of flexible funds for the care of children. Further, twenty-three directors (46%) reported that the "pooling" of funds across child-serving agencies had been implemented in order to meet the needs of children in their states (Kutash, Rivera, Hall, & Friedman, 1994).

Challenges in Researching System Reform Efforts

This new view of collaboratively educating and providing services to children with disabilities and their families has also created some challenges in carrying out research and evaluation activities in studying their effectiveness. Although there are always challenges in researching complex interventions, Knapp (1995) outlines several issues specifically confronting researchers attempting to study comprehensive service delivery systems for children and families. The first issue is how various disciplines and perspectives should be integrated into the design and interpretation of the research efforts. This issue is basic in service reform efforts, for these efforts are, by definition, the combination of diverse disciplines, perspectives, and stakeholders. Each discipline, agency staff member, and client and his or her family has its own perspective that should be integrated and reflected in evaluation and research activities.

Another issue confronting the study of systems reform is the fact that these efforts are characterized by multiple efforts, often delivered simultaneously, in order to meet the complex needs of children with disabilities. This replacement of a "fixed treatment" (traditional in experimental designs) with a "menu of possibilities" accompanied by "a series of supports that facilitate consumers' interaction with these possibilities" (Knapp, 1995, p. 7) makes characterizing and measuring the independent variable (or what is under study) within system reform research a common challenge in studying this type of reform.

Similarly, researchers and evaluators are challenged by the process of isolating the dependent variable (or variables) when efforts are aimed at meeting multiple needs. Clearly, determining the ultimate outcomes or effects of collaborative, comprehensive service systems is a complex task. There are often multiple goals and outcomes inherent in this type of service delivery system that are interdependent on each other.

Given the difficulty in characterizing the independent and dependent variables, it should be no surprise that attributing results to influences is also a challenge in this type of research effort. Within this type of effort, what can be credited for the benefits experienced by children and their families?

The final challenge is that of capturing the often sensitive and sometimes subtle processes between the service providers and the participants of the program under study. Often, the issues being examined between participant and provider are private matters and not readily open for inspection by outside evaluators. Although this area is not new for many investigators, it does, however, compound the other challenges of isolating the independent and dependent variables by highlighting the sensitive nature of service delivery.

Fitting the Pieces Together for Special Education

Given the considerations discussed in the previous sections, can systems-oriented research programs be developed to investigate how to best serve children who have disabilities and need special education services? We think they can, and the results of such research initiatives have the potential to significantly affect practice so that the outcomes for children with disabilities will be improved.

Research Teams

The type of research program we propose cannot be executed by a single individual. The "lone wolf" researcher needs to be replaced by a multidisciplinary team joined by consumer/stakeholders. Ideal teams have expertise in regular and special education, relevant related services such as mental health and general health care, and qualitative and quantitative methods. Teachers and families have an opportunity to give input at all stages of the research. This adds an element of authenticity and practicality that is usually missing in special education research yet maintains the rigor needed for believability and generalizability. Such research teams are already in place in a variety of settings, such as professional development schools (Paul, Duchnowski, & Danforth, 1993), and have begun to produce results (Paul, Epanchin, Rosselli, & Duchnowski, in press).

Consensus building is an important component of this type of research team. For example, how do we know when something works? The team, including family members and teachers, will need to grapple with the elusive question, What are desirable outcomes? Interestingly, the field has not prescribed a formula answer to the question of outcome determination (Kauffman, 1993).

True participatory projects can develop in such a team atmosphere. The perspectives of parents and teachers as well as the perspectives of quantitative and qualitative researchers will shape the final research protocol and enhance validity.

Comprehensive Focus

Earlier, we criticized special education research as being limited to teacher-child interactions. In a systems approach, the program under investigation is comprehensive. Issues of assessment must be addressed as well as those relating to the intervention. For example, assessments should be conducted in the multiple contexts in which the child functions (home, school, and community) and linked to the desired outcomes. Intervention outcomes should be linked to changes at the individual, family, and system levels.

Obviously, such research is not of the "quick and dirty" variety. For something as complex as a special education program, it will probably take from three to five years of sustained effort to realize meaningful change (Malouf & Schiller, 1995). All the logistic ramifications of such endeavors must be addressed.

Organizational Capacity

Most research in special education is conducted in a higher education setting. Do all colleges and universities that currently support special education research have the capacity to conduct systems research as outlined here? Probably not. Could such an initiative develop an elite research cadre that could become a closed network and receive the lion's share of research support? We feel that a system of peer review with the highest standards of integrity would prevent this from occurring. In addition, we are not proposing an abandonment of research that is clinical and focused on child-teacher interaction, but rather a shift in effort. The special education research effort is, in a sense, out of balance. The majority of research is micro, with limited attention to mechanisms of large-scale implementation. An increase toward more comprehensive systems research may result in better practice on a scale that is detectable in terms of improved outcomes for children with disabilities.

The training of researchers for this type of investigation is another related challenge. Research universities with doctoral-level training programs have the capacity to train a new generation of researchers who could conduct the types of studies we feel are needed. Training that crosses the current boundaries of departments and colleges should be a characteristic of such programs (Paul et al., in press).

A Neighborhood Focus

Research that examines special education as a system should consider the neighborhood or broader community that is being served by the program. Neighborhood schools, consolidated rural schools, and city schools to which children are selectively bussed to maintain racial balance all have their own set of factors that affect program implementation. Research projects that do not address these issues will be limited in influencing practice. The related issue of culturally competent services must also be considered in such systems-oriented projects to achieve maximum impact.

Although the linear model may seek general laws and principles, no one should expect to develop a "silver bullet" intervention to treat all children with disabilities. The context formed by such factors as community values, racial and ethnic representation, resource availability, and the presence or absence of a progressive shared vision is a variable that cannot be ignored by researchers. Obviously, the introduction of such a contextual factor presents challenges to design control. We do not think they are insurmountable, but this does call for some of the "inventive pragmatism" that Fuchs and Fuchs recommend (Fuchs & Fuchs, 1995, p. 305).

Family and Teacher Involvement

There have been several references made to involving teachers and family members in systems-oriented research. This is because such research should be participatory and consumer-oriented in order to achieve the level of comprehensiveness necessary to evaluate a service delivery system and to raise the degree to which innovative research affects practice. Malouf and Schiller (1995) note that one factor that limits the research-to-practice link is that many researchers expect teachers to adopt innovative practices by essentially replicating studies in their classrooms. This is to be done, usually, with no increase in support or necessary resources. The result is usually an abandonment of the intervention soon after the researchers return to the university. When teachers and administrators are part of the team, issues of generalizability, dissemination, and training for implementation can become part of the total research package. If teachers have ownership of a research project, they become effective advocates before the school board to seek resources to implement an intervention that has been empirically tested in their schools.

The role of families in research is equally important. As noted earlier, the role of families is changing (Duchnowski et al., 1994). Families can contribute to several facets of a research project, ranging from developing family friendly protocols to formulating authentic research questions. Researchers must cultivate their relationships with families and adopt a collaborative stance toward their participation. Family members who feel like partners with researchers will also be powerful advocates for adoption and implementation of research-based interventions.

Improving the System of Care for Children Who Have Serious Emotional Disabilities: Building the Research Base

During the past ten years there has been a significant increase in activity across the country to improve services for children who have serious emotional disabilities and their families. This movement has been supported by a coalition of policymakers, family members, practitioners, researchers, and other advocates. The Child and Adolescent Service System Program (CASSP), a federal initiative, has been the core of this activity (Day & Roberts, 1991), and there has always been a strong value to base system development on a firm empirical base (Stroul & Friedman, 1986). There is a developing literature in this field that contains some examples of the systems-oriented research that we are recommending for the entire field of special education, beyond individual categories of disability. Some of the initial findings from this research have been published in a special issue of the *Journal of Emotional and Behavioral Disorders* (Kutash, Duchnowski, & Sondheimer, 1994).

A characteristic of these studies is that they target children who have multiple problems and that involve several agencies, such as education, child welfare, and mental health. These studies demonstrate an understanding of the need to include family issues in the research (Evans et al., 1994; Koroloff et al., 1994; Scherer, Brondino, Henggeler, Melton, & Hanley 1994), the linking of services between schools and social service agencies (Catron & Weiss, 1994), and the need to employ rigorous designs to study complex, multisystem service delivery (see, for example, Clark et al., 1994).

In addition to these service systems studies, two major initiatives funded by private foundations have been implemented across the country and demonstrate the type of systems orientation that we propose in their evaluation components. The first to be initiated is the Robert Wood Johnson Foundation Children's Demonstration. This is a multisite study of comprehensive service delivery models that are composed of all the child-serving agencies (Beachler, 1990). The evaluation includes quantitative measures of child outcomes as well as assessment of indicators associated with system improvement. Pre- and posttest procedures are used, as well as case study material. More recently, the Annie E. Casey Foundation has funded a Children's Mental Health Initiative focused on developing a neighborhood-based service delivery system (Kutash, Duchnowski, Meyers, & King, in

press). Although the evaluation of this project is still in process, the characteristics of multimethod and multidisciplinary perspectives are very much apparent (Friedman & Hernandez, 1993).

Conclusion

Although the projects just mentioned are, at best, "suggestive" that the systems approach has promise, they are indicative that it can work. We are at a point in the field of special education where we need to take a good look at how we do our business. We propose that it is time to diversify our activities and deploy more resources in the direction of a systems-oriented research and evaluation initiative. We are at the early stages of such research and at the level where much conceptualization and rigorous description is needed (Knapp, 1995). The network of collaborators and research partners must be expanded and attention must be given to developing new researchers in this endeavor. In a time when the future of special education can be described as "headed toward the rocks," some guidance and stability can be supplied by an influx of solid research and evaluation data. We join Fuchs and Fuchs in the call for inventive pragmatists to lead the way.

References

Beachler, M. (1990). The mental health services program for youth. *Journal of Mental Health Administration, 17,* 115–121.

Boyd, L. A. (1994). *Integrating system of care for children and families: An overview of values, methods, and characteristics of developing models, with examples and recommendations.* Tampa, FL: Department of Child and Family Studies, University of South Florida.

Catron, T., & Weiss, B. (1994). The Vanderbilt school-based counseling program: An interagency, primary care model of mental health services. *Journal of Emotional and Behavioral Disorders, 2*(4), 247–253.

Clark, H. B., Prange, M. E., Lee, B., Boyd, L. A., McDonald, B. A., & Steward, E. S. (1994). Improving adjustment outcomes for foster children with emotional and behavioral disorders: Early findings from a controlled study on individualized services. *Journal of Emotional and Behavioral Disorders, 2*(4), 207–218.

Day, C., & Roberts, M. (1991). Activities of the child and adolescent service system program for improving mental health services for children and families. *Journal of Clinical Child Psychology, 20,* 340–350.

Duchnowski, A. J., Berg, K., & Kutash, K. (1995). Parent participation in and perception of placement decisions. In J. M. Kauffman, J. W. Lloyd, D. P. Hallahan, & T. A. Astuto, *Issues in educational placement: Students with emotional and behavioral disorders* (pp. 183–196). Hillsdale, NJ: Erlbaum.

Duchnowski, A. J., Dunlap, G., Berg, K., & Adeigbola, M. (1995). Rethinking the role of families in the education of their children: Policy and clinical issues. In J. Paul, D. Evans, & H. Rosselli (Eds.) *Restructuring special education* (pp. 105–118). New York: Harcourt Brace Jovanovich.

Edgar, E. (1987). Secondary programs in special education: Are many of them justifiable? *Exceptional Children, 53*(6), 555–561.

Evans, M. E., Armstrong, M. I., Dollard, N., Kuppinger, A. D., Huz, S., & Wood, V. M. (1994). Developing and evaluation of treatment foster care and family-centered intensive case management in New York. *Journal of Emotional and Behavioral Disorders, 2*(4), 228–239.

Freisen, B., & Koroloff, M. (1990). Family-centered services: Implications for mental health administration and research. *Journal of Mental Health Administration, 17,* 13–25.

Friedman, R. M., & Hernandez, M. (1993, October). *Special challenges in evaluating multi-site system reform efforts: A focus on mental health services.* Paper presented at the fifteenth annual research conference of the Association for Public Policy Analysis and Management, Washington, DC.

Fuchs, D., & Fuchs, L. S. (1994). Inclusive school movement and the radicalization of special education reform. *Exceptional Children, 60*(4), 293–309.

Fuchs, D., & Fuchs, L. S. (1995). Special Education can work. In J. M. Kauffman, J. W. Lloyd, D. P. Hallahan, & T. A. Astuto, *Issues in educational placement: Students with emotional and behavioral disorders* (pp. 363–378). Hillsdale, NJ: Erlbaum.

Goldenberg, C., & Gallimore, R. (1991). Local knowledge, research knowledge, and educational change: A case study of early Spanish reading improvement. *Educational Researcher, 20*(8), 2–14.

Hasazi, S. B., Gordon, L. R., & Roe, C. A. (1985). Factors associated with the employment status of handicapped youth exiting from high school from 1979 to 1983. *Exceptional Children, 51,* 455–469.

Huberman, M. (1990). Linkage between researchers and practitioners: A qualitative study. *American Educational Research Journal, 27*(2), 363–391.

Kauffman, J. M. (1993). How we might achieve the radical reform of special education. *Exceptional Children, 60*(1), 6–16.

Knapp, M. S. (1995). How shall we study comprehensive, collaborative services for children and families? *Educational Researcher, 24*(4), 5–16.

Koroloff, N. M., Elliott, D. J., Koren, P. E., & Freisen, B. J. (1994). Connecting low income families to mental health services: The role of the family associate. *Journal of Emotional and Behavioral Disorders, 2*(4), 240–246.

Kutash, K., Duchnowski, A. J., Meyers, J., & King, J. (in press). Community and neighborhood based services for youth. In S. W. Henggeler & A. B. Santos (Eds.), *Innovative models for mental health treatment for "difficult to treat" clinical populations.* Washington, DC: American Psychiatric Press.

Kutash, K., Duchnowski, A. J., & Sondheimer, D. L. (1994). Building the research base for children's mental health services. *Journal of Emotional and Behavioral Disorders, 2*(4), 194–197.

Kutash, K., Rivera, R. V., Hall, K. S., & Friedman, R. M. (1994). Public sector financing of community-based services for children with serious emotional disabilities and their families: Results of a national survey.

Journal of Mental Health Administration, 21(3), 262–270.

Malouf, D. B., & Schiller, E. P. (1995). Practice and research in special education. *Exceptional Children, 61*(5), 414–424.

Miles, M. B., & Huberman, M. (1994). *Qualitative data analysis: An expanded sourcebook* (2nd ed.). Thousand Oaks, CA: Sage.

National Commission on Excellence in Education. (1983). *A nation at risk: The imperative for educational reform.* Washington, DC: U.S. Government Printing Office.

National Council on Disabilities. (1989). *The education of students with disabilities: Where do we stand?* Washington, DC: Author.

Paul, J., Duchnowski, A. J., & Danforth, S. (1993). Changing the way we do business: One department's story of collaboration with public schools. *Teacher Education and Special Education, 16,* 95–109.

Paul, J., Epanchin, B., Rosselli, H., & Duchnowski, A. J. (in press). The transformation of teacher education and special education: Work in progress. *Remedial and Special Education.*

Saxe, L., & Cross, T. (1992). Financing mental health care for children and adolescents: A gestaltist view of fragmented research and services. *Proceedings of the National Institute of Mental Health and the Maternal and Child Health Bureau Workshop: The Financing of Mental Health Services for Children and Adolescents.*

(pp. 149–153). Bethesda, MD: National Center for Education in Maternal and Child Health.

Scherer, D. G., Brondino, M. J., Henggeler, S. W., Melton, G. B., & Hanley, J. H. (1994). Multisystemic family preservation therapy: Preliminary findings from a study of rural and minority serious adolescent offenders. *Journal of Emotional and Behavioral Disorders, 2*(4), 198–206.

Shapiro, J. P., Loeb, P., Bowermaster, D., Wright, A., Headden, S., & Toch, T. (1993, December). Separate and unequal: How special education programs are cheating our children and costing taxpayers billions each year. *U.S. News & World Report, 115*(23), 46–60.

Shavelson, R. J. (1988). Contributions of educational research to policy and practice: Constructing, challenging, changing cognition. *Educational Researcher, 17*(7), 4–11, 22.

Shaw, K. M. (1995). Challenges in evaluating systems reform. *Harvard Family Research Project Evaluation Exchange: Emerging Strategies in Evaluating Child and Family Services, 1*(1), 2–3.

Stroul, B. A., & Friedman, R. M. (1986). *A system of care for severely emotionally disturbed children and youth.* Washington, DC: Georgetown University Child Development Center, CASSP Technical Assistance Center.

Wagner, M. (1993). *Trends in the post-school outcomes of youth with disabilities.* Menlo Park, CA: Stanford Research Institute.

The Behavioral Sciences and Special Education Research: Some Promising Directions and Challenging Legacies

Kofi Marfo
University of South Florida

Louise H. Boothby
University of South Florida

Introduction

The broader goal of the knowledge project from which this book and its companion (Paul, Churton, Morse, Duchnowski, Epanchin, Osnes, & Smith, 1997) emerged was to articulate a new vision for special education as the next millennium approaches. The project's authors have attempted to cast both the current status of the field and the new visions being sought for it within the context of various disciplines acknowledged to exert significant influences on research and practice involving children with special needs. This is the key rationale for assembling chapters on "basic knowledge" from multiple disciplinary perspectives. Behind this unique endeavor is the hope that as the special education leaders of tomorrow become increasingly cognizant of the philosophical, methodological, and practical implications of these knowledge bases, the insights, lessons, and cautions they draw from them will be applied responsibly to shape the future of the field of special education.

No meaningful discussion of a future vision for special education will be complete without serious attention to critical issues relating to knowledge production. The primary purpose of this chapter, then, is to address issues pertinent to the knowledge production enterprise within special education and its related subfields (such as devel-opmental disabilities, learning disabilities, behavioral and emotional disorders, early intervention, and early childhood special education). Special education research is used in this chapter to refer broadly to educational research activity involving developmental, learning, and instructional or intervention issues relating to individuals with special needs. It would not be unusual for a chapter devoted to research issues in a book of this nature to focus on the philosophical underpinnings of inquiry, on methodological contributions, or on a state-of-the-art appraisal of empirical literature. This chapter takes none of these approaches exclusively. Although philosophical and methodological issues are raised, the primary focus is on relating the *knowledge base* in the behavioral sciences (specifically, developmental psychology and cognitive science) to *knowledge production* in the field of special education.

This chapter is developed around three central premises. The first is that special education has benefited tremendously (and will continue to do so) from advances occurring in developmental psychology and cognitive science. Consistent with this premise, the first major task undertaken in this chapter is to highlight selected areas of significant promise where theoretical and empirical advances in the behavioral sciences can be incorporated productively into existing lines of special education inquiry to contribute new understandings about children with special needs. The second premise is that by adopting or relying extensively on certain aspects of the research traditions and knowledge bases of the behavioral sciences, special education has set itself up to fail in areas where the behavioral sciences have also failed. As an illustration of this premise, we identify legacies from the behavioral sciences that special education researchers may do well to either avoid or refine if they are to respond meaningfully and productively to some of the most critical philosophical and ethical challenges facing the field today. The third premise is that special education has accumulated some problematic legacies of its own. Although these legacies may have part of their roots in other disciplines, or in the inquiry process itself, they cannot be blamed easily on specific external disciplinary influences. In consonance with this third premise, we identify and discuss two illustrative examples of these *local* legacies. Before addressing the issues previewed here, we pause to provide a brief orientational caveat for the reader.

Paradigm Wars and Transport Models of Knowledge Production: An Orientational Caveat

Although the logic of this chapter may sound reasonable—in terms of the search for productive as well as potentially problematic influences that theories and lines of inquiry in other disciplines exert on the field of special education—we must acknowledge some of the problems entailed in such an exercise. In light of the larger paradigm debates that have engulfed the consciousness of special education scholars and leaders in recent years (see Geber, 1994; Heshushius, 1986, 1989; Poplin, 1988; Poplin & Stone, 1992; Skrtic, 1995), there can be an appearance of inherent contradiction in wanting to chart new waters—paradig-

matically speaking—while simultaneously looking to aspects of the *establishment knowledge bases* for insights and directions. The project giving rise to this publication, as we have already noted, was about creating a future vision for special education. In a number of academic settings, including our own (see Chapter 14; Paul & Morse, 1997; Rhodes, 1990), much of this future vision is being framed in the context of shifts and/or extensions in paradigms from postpositivistic inquiry traditions to relativist-constructivist forms of inquiry and scholarship.

Our contribution to this textbook is premised on the position that all forms of inquiry—along with the epistemological and ontological perspectives that undergird them—have important contributions to make to the ongoing quest for a better understanding of the development and education of children with special needs. However, we must approach each paradigm from a critical perspective, examining closely its underlying assumptions and presuppositions, in the hope of understanding the types of questions for which each can be appropriately employed to generate reasonable insights. Indeed, the worst thing that can happen to our field at this critical juncture in its history is to either continue the institutionalization of traditional hegemonies with adamance or replace old hegemonies with new ones. It is instructive, in this connection, to share some observations made by Sigmund Koch (1985) in a paper originally presented at the 1979 convention of the American Psychological Association in commemoration of the 100th anniversary of the formal founding of scientific psychology:

> Characteristically, psychological events . . . are multiply determined, ambiguous in their human meaning, polymorphous, contextually environed or embedded in complex and vaguely bounded ways, and evanescent and labile in the extreme. This entails some obvious constraints upon the task of the in-

quirer and limits upon the knowledge that can be unearthed. Different theorists will—relative to their different analytical purposes, predictive or practical aims, perceptual sensitivities, metaphor-forming capabilities, and preexisting discrimination repertoires—make asystematically different perceptual cuts upon the same domain. They will identify "variables" of markedly different grain and meaning contour, selected and linked on different principles of grouping. The cuts, variables, [and] concepts will in all likelihood establish different universes of discourse, even if loose ones. . . . Corollary to such considerations, paradigms, theories, models . . . can never prove preemptive or preclusive of alternate organizations. (p. 93)

With this caveat in mind, the yardstick for judging the potential contribution of any line of inquiry should be seen to hinge not on the mere paradigmatic rubric under which the research falls but on the meaningfulness, clarity, and rigor with which the substantive questions are addressed. Certainly, these are the criteria by which the contributions of the behavioral sciences to special education research and practice should be appraised.

Promising Directions from the Behavioral Sciences

During the last three decades, significant advances in theorizing and empirical analysis have been made in a number of behavioral science fields that have relevance for knowledge production in our field. For good reason, a comprehensive review of the relevant behavioral science literatures is not necessary here. Five earlier chapters (Chapters 3–7) present outlines and thorough discussions of some of the key advances occurring in developmental psychology and cognitive science during the course of this century. For example, in his extensive review and commentary on the ecology of the family as a context for human development, Bronfenbrenner

identifies key advances and trends in thinking, not only about families but also about the relative role of biology and environmental contexts in development (see Chapter 3). Steven Hooper's review of the fast-developing field of child neuropsychology outlines developments in the study of brain-behavior relations and demonstrates the growing clinical application of developments in neuropsychology to the solution of problems affecting children with special needs, particularly those with learning disabilities (see Chapter 4). Howard Gardner and his associates (Chapter 5) present an extensive review of major trends in the study of human intelligence. Edward Zigler's chapter on early intervention (Chapter 6) provides a vivid illustration of the linkage between developmental science and social policy and of the challenges involved in designing comprehensive evaluations of intervention programs emanating from the confluence of developmental science and social policy. Finally, Richard Lerner provides a practical demonstration of how the adoption of a contextualist paradigm can help to reorient developmental science toward the solution of real-world problems facing children, youth, and families in contemporary society (see Chapter 7). These chapters provide excellent background reading for some of the issues raised in this chapter. However, the discussion, as a whole, goes significantly beyond the literature covered by those five chapters.

The central thesis driving the discussion in this section is that researchers whose work focuses on developmental, learning, and instructional issues affecting children with special needs have yet to take full advantage of the developments identified here to shed new levels of understanding on the developmental and educational challenges facing these children. To illustrate this point, we draw examples from three areas: ecological, transactional, and contextualist theories of development; theorizing and research on resilience; and changing conceptions of cognitive competence.

Capitalizing on the Benefits of Ecological, Transactionalist, and Contextualist Frameworks

Developmental scientists have spent a good part of this century attempting to explicate the mechanisms by which complex biological processes transact symbiotically with a broad range of environmental-contextual variables to drive development along multiple pathways. Until about the early 1970s, however, much of this work was dominated largely by "partisan" efforts to assess the relative contributions of genetic and environmental influences on development. The questions driving much of this research were, Which one is more important? and By how much does one or the other influence development? (Thomas, 1992). It was not uncommon for researchers in either camp of the debate to concentrate on producing evidence to demonstrate the magnitude of influence represented by their own position. Thus, in the 1920s and 1930s, scholars such as Burks (1928), Leahy (1955), and Shuttleworth (1935) reported data suggesting the overwhelming influence of genetic forces on human mental ability, while others (for example, Skeels, 1940; Skeels & Dye, 1939; Skodak, 1939) reported data in support of greater environmental influence. Intriguingly, the relatively more contemporary debate between Hans Eysenck and Leon Kamin (see Eysenck & Kamin, 1981) and the debate sparked more recently by the publication of *The Bell Curve* (Herrnstein & Murray, 1994) both illustrate the phenomenal longevity of the passions engendered around the two historical positions.

Generally speaking, however, we now appear to have moved significantly beyond the era when the obviously dialectical relationship between the organism and its environment was discussed from the rather mechanistic "nature versus nurture" perspective, as if nature and nurture can be defined independently of each other (see Sameroff, 1990). The foundations for this shift were laid by interactionist theorists who, while recognizing the indispensability of hereditary and environmental forces, suggested that heredity sets the boundaries of potential development, with environmental forces determining how much of that potential will be realized (for example, Montagu, 1959). With the acknowledgment that boundaries differ for different characteristics or domains of development and that the potential defined by heredity is manifested differently at different times within the life span as a function of environmental context (see Thomas, 1992), the stage was set not only for a more dynamic view of the heredity/environment interaction process but for more in-depth analyses of the nature and mechanisms of environmental influences.

During the course of the last two decades, specific formulations of environmental influences on development have emerged within developmental psychology. Among the key formulations are Sameroff's *transactional model of development* (Sameroff & Chandler, 1975; Sameroff & Fiese, 1990), Bronfenbrenner's *ecological systems theory* (Bronfenbrenner, 1977, 1979, 1986, 1989), and Lerner's *developmental contextualism* (see Chapter 7; Lerner, 1991; Lerner & Kauffman, 1985; Lerner & Lerner, 1989). At the heart of each of these frameworks is a fundamental belief in the concept of development as the product of a dynamic, symbiotic relationship between inner biological workings and external social and environmental forces. However, the primary focus of each framework has been to explicate the processes and dynamics by which environmental-contextual factors impinge on development throughout the life span. While sharing these and other common attributes, each of the frameworks has areas of unique emphasis. For example, Sameroff has built a compelling theoretical case—based on analyses of prior research examining the relationship between early risk conditions of a biological nature and competence in later years—to highlight the limitations, if not the utter futility, of the *main effects* model of predicting future developmental outcomes solely on the basis of either early biological attributes of the child or intervention-induced competencies in the early years. Bronfenbrenner has paid particular attention to a delineation of varying levels of the ecology of human development, noting the manner in which dynamics within and between the various levels (microsystems, mesosystems, and exosystems) exert their influence on the child's development. In more recent formulations of the transactional framework, Sameroff (1990) has employed the concept of *environtype*—defined as "the social organization that regulates the way human beings fit into society" (p. 104)—to encapsule the ecological levels described by Bronfenbrenner. Finally, Lerner's emphasis is on defining human development in terms of the changing relations between "the developing person and his or her changing context" (Lerner & Fisher, 1994, p. 505), such that no meaningful understanding of human development is possible without considerable attention to issues of contextual variability and diversity in life circumstances.

That these theoretical frameworks have found appeal with scholars in the field of special education is not difficult to demonstrate. While Lerner's work has not received as much attention as the others, Sameroff's transactional model and Bronfenbrenner's ecological systems theory have been drawn upon quite extensively in the conceptualization of various forms of intervention. Perhaps the early intervention field is the clearest example of the phenomenal impact that transactional and ecological theories have had on these two fields. For example, in conceptualizations of early intervention practice (see Marfo & Cook, 1991; Sameroff & Fiese, 1990), the transactional model has, in recent years, superseded the "theory" of *plasticity of the central nervous system* and the related *critical periods* argument. Bronfenbrenner's ecological systems theory, on the other hand, has been used extensively to rationalize home-based, family

focused, social support, and behavioral-ecological interventions (see Dunst & Trivette, 1988, 1990; Vincent, Salisbury, Strain, McCormick, & Tessier, 1990). Outside the early intervention field, manifestations of the impact of ecological and systems theories are seen in the growing interest in integrating social, mental health, and educational services to simultaneously serve children, families, and communities. The growing prominence of wraparound intervention models and the emergence of integrated systems of care and the concept of full-service schools (see Duchnowski, Kutash, & Knitzer, 1997; Malysiak, in press) are illustrative examples.

A missing link. The enthusiasm with which ecological and contextualist frameworks are being embraced in the conceptualization of interventions and services has, intriguingly, not been matched with corresponding eagerness among special education researchers to modify and/or extend their research questions and designs to forge a more sophisticated understanding of the role of changing contextual influences in children's development and learning. To some extent, this is not surprising; even within developmental psychology itself, models of empirical analysis capable of addressing the complexity of ecological-contextualist[1] perspectives continue to lag significantly behind theoretical formulations. Nevertheless, the incorporation of the ecological-contextualist orientation into research paradigms in special education and its related subfields is a necessary direction. Such a direction will accentuate the importance of change-related and relational questions (see Lerner, 1991) and place desirable emphasis on understanding the

---

[1]We have used the term *ecological-contextualist* to designate a perspective combining viewpoints currently expressed in three overlapping frameworks: Sameroff's transactional model, Bronfenbrenner's ecological systems theory, and Lerner's developmental contextualism.

manner in which variables pertaining to the developing child, the changing context of development, and intervention processes and contexts work synergistically to impact both the child and her or his developmental environment. We will now attempt to describe one version of what intervention research would look like if the ecological-contextualist framework were applied faithfully, even at an elementary level.

Example 1: Head Start. Our first example is drawn from Head Start, a familiar national program that has been the subject of intense debate over the past thirty years. One of the most frequently criticized aspects of the earliest efficacy studies of Head Start programs is the myopic preoccupation with gains in IQ. Although Zigler and other scholars (see Chapter 6; Zigler & Seitz, 1980; Zigler & Trickett, 1978) have perhaps dealt exhaustively with this widely acknowledged limitation—and have actually suggested new directions for research that have already yielded supportive evidence on the impact early intervention programs make on non-IQ variables—we find it useful to revisit this matter as we attempt to subject efficacy research to an ecological-contextualist analysis.

First, framed in ecological-contextualist terms, Head Start will not be conceptualized as a stand-alone, one-shot program that is offered in the preschool years and is expected to make a lasting impact on a whole range of school-related competencies. Instead, Head Start will be the first phase of a series of planned interventions that begin even prior to age 3 and continue through at least the primary grades. Each component of the series will be designed to be responsive not only to the changing needs of the developing child but also to the changing challenges of the formal schooling process for children growing up in an increasingly diverse society. Essentially, this is one of the key recommendations that Zigler makes in Chapter 6.

Of course, his own analysis is driven by an ecological-contextualist perspective.

Second, an ecological-contextualist program of Head Start efficacy research will pay significant attention to at least three key contexts: (1) the family and community contexts in which Head Start children live their lives; (2) the programmatic and service delivery context, including curricular models, instructional practices, quality of personnel, and the quality of the social and physical climate of the classroom; and (3) the broader sociopolitical milieu within which fiscal policy and pedagogical canons are embedded. The first will require that attention be paid to gathering data on supports, stresses, and routines within families and neighborhoods (or communities) that have the potential to impact program benefits to individual children. The second will entail documentations involving such dimensions as the intensity of programming, the quality of instructional staff, the appropriateness of curriculum content and instructional strategies, and the degree to which the key program feature of family involvement is actually accomplished. The third context, particularly suited to cost-effectiveness and policy analyses, requires efficacy researchers to pay attention to exosystemic realities upon which the very viability of Head Start as a national social policy experiment rests.

Finally, an ecological-contextualist program of research will pay as much attention to Head Start's impact on the child's developmental ecology as it does to the program's direct impact on child outcomes. At the heart of the ecological-contextualist orientation is the maxim that "interventions should be aimed at changing the developmental system within which people are embedded" (see Chapter 7). Program goals relating to family involvement, health, and nutrition offer partial mechanisms by which Head Start could change the developmental environments of the children it serves. Changes occurring in child care practices (including increased vigilance on health and nutrition), beliefs about child development, and values about education can constitute critical mediator variables with significant potential to foreshadow long-term improvements in children's development, learning, and quality of life. Documentations involving these variables must become integral elements of any comprehensive efficacy study or program evaluation.

Armed with the foregoing data—and with data pertaining to individual children's cognitive, academic, social, health, and nutritional characteristics—researchers will be in a better position than we have ever been in the past thirty years to appraise more meaningfully the contributions of Head Start and similar programs to the development of children, families, and communities.

In the next section, we provide a specific, albeit rather modest, example of how efficacy research is being reconceptualized in relation to early intervention services for children with special needs and their families.

Example 2: Early intervention and children with disabilities. Disturbed by efficacy researchers' excessive preoccupation with causal inferences in the past, Marfo and his associates (Marfo & Dinero, 1991; Marfo et al., 1992) have suggested an efficacy research model that is consistent with the ecological-contextualist orientation. The model builds on the design contributions of Dunst (1986), who has also lamented the way researchers have relied solely on *main effects* conceptual models in their examination of child and family outcomes. In *main effects* models, changes occurring in the recipients of intervention are presumed to be the direct effects of the intervention. Marfo and his associates have argued, to the contrary, that an intervention program is only one of many variables that can impinge on child development and family functioning. Additionally, the variety of

factors that influence child and family functioning often work synergistically rather than in isolation. Consequently, a useful efficacy model is one that enables researchers to understand the manner in which combinations of program and nonprogram variables are related systematically with various outcome measures.

One such model has been proposed by Marfo and his associates. The model suggests that, at the very minimum, a framework for assessing intervention outcomes might include five classes of independent variables (entry-point child characteristics, family demographic variables, family ecological variables, intervention program variables, and nonprogram auxiliary service variables) and at least two classes of outcome variables (child outcomes and parent/family outcomes). The framework posits that these five classes of independent variables might interact in ways that not only influence child development but also shape the manner in which an intervention program may operate for a particular family.

To illustrate, the child's developmental status at the time of program entry may place limits on how much developmental progress can be expected, shape parental expectations regarding intervention outcomes for the child, and thereby possibly influence how much commitment parents make to the intervention process. Parents' commitment to the intervention program may itself be influenced as much by factors external to the program as it is by those related to the program. For example, parents' knowledge and beliefs about child development as well as their expectations about the child's future may be as instrumental in determining parental commitment to intervention activities as their perceptions about the quality of programming and staff expertise.

Similarly, the amount and quality of developmentally enhancing environments and experiences to which parents expose their children outside the intervention context are crucial ingredients of developmental progress. However, these attributes may themselves be influenced by participation in the intervention program, by belief systems and/or expectations, and by such demographic variables as level of education and family income. Finally, the potential influence of various routine medical, developmental, and social services accessible to families outside the intervention program must be recognized and assessed.

In one empirical validation of an earlier version of this model (Marfo et al., 1992), two intervention outcomes—child developmental outcome and parental satisfaction—were assessed in relation to three classes of variables: child, program, and family ecology. Child characteristics included entry-level chronological and developmental ages. Program variables included duration of the intervention, parental knowledge gain, and perceived intervention worker competence. Family ecology was measured in terms of parental expectations regarding future outcomes for the child, quality of the home environment, and family resources. Regression techniques were used to assess the unique as well as the combined contributions of the three classes of independent variables to the prediction of children's rate of development and parental satisfaction with the intervention. The following captures the key elements of Marfo and associates' (1992) findings that are pertinent to the discussion here:

> In all cases, explanation of the variance in an outcome variable was maximized by considering the combined influence of different classes of variables. More importantly, however, nonprogram variables consistently contributed substantial amounts of variance in each of the . . . outcome variables. Indeed, in the case of the two indices of child developmental outcome, the contributions of the child and family ecologic classes of variables were even more substantial than that of the program class. (p. 41)

The ecological-contextualist orientation has relevance for classroom- and school-based research as well. In a sense, it is perhaps in this arena that the orientation has had the least impact. A child's behavior, performance, and experiences within the context of the classroom and school environment as a whole are shaped as much by the child's own personal attributes as they are by a complex combination of contextual variables—among them, the social climate of the classroom or school; the child's own social networks; the teacher's behaviors and attitudes toward the child; the degree of individual attention and respect accorded the child; and the strength of the child's identification with the school as a safe and culturally responsive place to learn and build relationships. Perhaps it is time to acknowledge that too much of our past research efforts have been spent on identifying child-level factors associated with learning and behavior problems in the school context and not enough attention has been paid to exploring the possibility that many of these problems may represent manifestations of relatively transient or endemic contextual constraints to which children are subjected.

Learning from Research on Resilience and Protective Factors

The special education enterprise has focused too much on what is *wrong* with children. The phenomenal preoccupation with deficits and their remediation has indeed blinded our field to many useful insights that might come only through direct examination of the person-level adaptive strengths and context-level buffering systems accounting for why some children with special needs or risk conditions do enjoy better-than-expected developmental and educational outcomes. From this perspective, the field has a lot to learn from the growing body of research on resilience and protective factors.

Over the past twenty-five years, the fields of developmental psychopathology and mental health have witnessed a significant expansion of orientation that is only now beginning to impact research in related fields. What Lois Murphy (1962) characterized as "the language of adequacy to meet life's challenges" has finally become a legitimate subject matter of psychological science. Largely through the pioneering work of scholars such as Garmezy (1974, 1981), Anthony (1974, 1978), Rutter (1979, 1981), and Werner (Werner & Smith, 1982), the study of resilience has attained significant prominence as a mainstream area of inquiry within developmental psychology, family studies, and education. Countering the predominant endemic emphasis that has been placed on negative outcomes in the past, research on resilience seeks to understand those positive personal and contextual factors that tend to inoculate certain individuals against the potentially deleterious effects of different forms of disadvantage—biological, social, economic, and so on.

Underlying this line of inquiry is the orientation so succinctly summarized by Richters and Weintraub (1990): "Among children who are exposed to even the most harrowing experiences one can always find a subset who seem resilient—that is, who do not manifest subsequent maladjustment [and who have often been] found to have different preexisting personality characteristics, relationships, available resources, and background experiences than those who do succumb" (p. 79). Research questions in this area have taken the form: "Why, under conditions of heightened stress and hazard, do many children successfully navigate these treacherous waters and often emerge stronger?" (Felner, 1991, p. xi). Thus, although the target group for resilience research is children who manifest significant vulnerability for potential negative outcomes, the focus of the research has been on what is right, rather than what is wrong, about them (Werner, 1990).

Thus far, the research on resilience shows a wide range of population foci and methodological variability. However from the prospective and retrospective studies of resilient offspring of psychotic parents (Garmezy, 1987), alcoholic parents (Werner, 1986), and abusive parents (Farber & Egeland, 1987) to the short-term longitudinal studies of children of divorced parents (Hetherington, Cox, & Cox, 1982) and teenage parents (Furstenberg, 1980), the primary goal has been to identify the correlates of successful outcomes, in the belief that understanding the associated protective factors will enable us to help other children to become less vulnerable or more resilient (Werner, 1990). We believe that the basic logic undergirding resilience studies in the populations mentioned here should have intuitive appeal to researchers in special education and its related subfields. Embedded in this line of inquiry is a competence model of children's functioning with explanation of the nature and correlates of successful developmental outcomes as its major preoccupation (see Sameroff & Seifer, 1990).

Research concerned with resilience in special and compensatory education could follow quite an array of directions. To illustrate, we will consider one example from each of two populations: children with disabilities and children who are at environmental risk for educational failure. Much of intervention programming in special education is built around normative developmental and learning patterns that are deemed to be absent or deficient in individuals with disabilities. This is not surprising, because much of what we investigate about individuals with disabilities is driven by a deficit orientation. Are there dimensions of behavior and competence in the performance repertoires of individuals with disabilities that, while deviating from known norms, are nevertheless functionally adaptive and should therefore be nurtured rather than suppressed? Do our traditional concepts and values regarding typical and atypical behavior and development blind us from noticing and building on alternative forms of behavior that are more likely to enhance adaptation in individuals with special needs? Questions such as these should lead to lines of inquiry in which the study of naturally occurring adaptive behaviors in individuals with special needs has intrinsic appeal in its own right. Among the potentially fruitful directions is inquiry that focuses attention on specialized areas of strength for specific populations of children with special needs. David Gibson's research at the University of Calgary is a good example. In addition to identifying developmental domains and attributes in which children and youth with Down syndrome are particularly vulnerable, Gibson (1991) has delineated areas pertaining to sensorimotor function, memory function, and visual cognition where these children have unusual strengths. Gibson's work underscores the potential role of etiology-specific analyses in inquiry focusing on resilience. Research of this nature has the potential to create a context in which knowledge of children's unusual strengths and natural adaptive behavior tendencies contributes as much to the design of interventions as does our current knowledge of what is wrong with them. As Gibson (1991) points out, incorporating areas of relative strength into intervention programs should generate leverage for learning.

Inquiry that is driven by an interest in resilience could also be fruitful for our field in the area of interventions for at-risk children and youth. School-based programs for at-risk children and youth typically deal, remedially and preemptively, with the effects of high-risk environments on children's learning capabilities. As we will argue in a later section of this chapter, such interventions are inadequate to the extent that they fail to change the conditions placing the children at-risk in the first place. Research focusing on resilience could help rectify this problem, even if only partially, by shed-

ding better light on the broader personal and contextual variables that impinge on the school behavior and performance of children at-risk. The purpose of this line of inquiry will be to obtain insights from the lives and experiences of children who overcome the odds associated with environmental disadvantage to succeed in and out of school. Not all children who grow up in poor families or neighborhoods experience difficulties in school. For those who have successful in-school and out-of-school experiences, what characteristics of the children themselves, their families, their peer relations, their neighborhoods, and their school relations serve to buffer them against the effects of environmental disadvantage? The answers that come from research of this nature could help us rethink the focus and content of current interventions for at-risk children.

Relating Advances in Cognition and Learning to Assessment and Instruction

The profound advances in theorizing and research on human cognition and learning within the behavioral sciences have already made a significant impact on special education practice and research. In this section, we will restrict our comments and observations to two specific areas where we think greater advantage needs to be taken of the emerging knowledge bases in the behavioral sciences to overcome identified challenges. The two areas include the assessment of cognition and research on the application of emergent theory to the design of instruction.

Assessment of cognition: Breaking the ubiquity of the intelligence quotient. As illustrated in Chapter 5, the psychometric perspective on human intelligence has long ceased to be the sole framework for thinking about children's cognitive abilities (see also Neisser et al., 1996; Wagner & Sternberg,

1984). Contemporary alternative frameworks view intelligence not as a unitary entity but as a complex set of competencies across diverse domains (for example, Gardner, 1983, 1993); not as an immutable quality but as a malleable process that is under both biological and experiential-contextual influences (Feuerstein, Rand, Hoffman, & Miller, 1980; Haywood & Switzky, 1986; Sternberg, 1986; Sternberg, Ketron, & Powell, 1982); and not merely as a product but as a dynamic process, the on-line features of which are as important and interesting as its outcome (Kail & Bisanz, 1982; Sternberg, 1980, 1985). Much of what we know and believe about human intelligence today undermines the utility of the intelligence quotient as a comprehensive measure of children's cognitive competence; yet IQ remains ever-ubiquitous in special education practice and research.

This is a significant challenge for the field of special education, especially in light of the broader social and moral questions raised by the history of the intelligence testing movement in this country. Intelligence testing in special education is not merely another legacy from psychological research; underlying this legacy are some fundamental political realities at the macro-societal level that are responsible in large part for the dominance of the psychometric tradition. Over the course of the past two decades, much has been written about the intelligence quotient and the politics of race and social class in this country (Gould, 1981; Kamin, 1974, 1975; Reed, 1987). Historical analyses of the sociopolitical perspectives and scholarly works of some of America's pioneers of the intelligence testing movement—notably, Carl Brigham, Henry Goddard, Lewis Terman, and Robert Yerkes—underscore the remarkable creativity with which the "science" of intelligence testing was used at the turn of the century to propagate a view of intellectual ability and civic worth as "biological capacities distributed unevenly among classes and ethnic groups" and, thereby, to advocate "the 'naturalness' of social class and racial caste" (Reed, 1987, p. 77).

The recent publication of *The Bell Curve* (Herrnstein & Murray, 1994) is a reminder that the politics of prejudice, in the context of which the intelligence testing movement was embraced in this country at the turn of the century, is alive and well. While the methods, arguments, and conclusions presented by Herrnstein and Murray have been critiqued and countered quite effectively by a number of scholars (such as LeVine & Lun, 1994; Neisser et al., 1996), no amount of counteranalysis can undo the historical image of intelligence testing as both a sorting and a subjugative tool. Unfortunately, special education has come to be seen increasingly as one of the new arenas for waging the politics of intelligence, race, and social class. Both this historical reality and the inherent limitations of the psychometric perspective, as noted at the beginning paragraph of this section, provide good reason for special education researchers to pursue alternative approaches to the assessment of cognition.

Fortunately, the behavioral sciences have now spawned enough new thinking on human cognition to move the assessment of intellectual functions in new directions. For example, contemporary information-processing and metacognitive theories offer useful insights on the assessment of cognitive functions in ways that permit the delineation of the influences of contextual, task, and person-level factors on cognitive performance. Indeed, these frameworks further permit the differentiation of person-level factors in terms of the relative contributions of component variables, such as awareness about self in relation to task demands, selection and deployment of strategies, and the use of executive control processes to monitor and evaluate performance. Thus, it is now possible to obtain richer and more differentiated indicators of cognitive activity in meaningful contexts and in ways that make it possible to link assessment information on individual children to intervention or instruction.

The principle of individualization has been the bedrock of special education practice since the field's inception. However, individualized instruction continues to be hampered by the perennial reality that much of our extant assessment practices—especially those pertaining to cognitive competence—have little relevance for instructional planning and delivery. Even newer assessment tools ostensibly built on cognitive process theories, such as the Kaufman Assessment Battery for Children (Kaufman & Kaufman, 1983), have not really moved us any closer toward attaining a better marriage of assessment and instruction. Thus, the need remains for special education researchers to take better advantage of current and emerging conceptualizations of cognitive competence to develop and validate idiographic, process-oriented tools and strategies for the assessment of cognition around contextually meaningful tasks.

Contributions to classroom instruction and instructional research. The cognitive education movement, which has become so widespread in North America since the 1960s, bears clear testimony to the powerful impact that research in the behavioral sciences has had on the field of education. In this section, our goal is to draw attention to potential problems in the derivation of educational and instructional applications from theory and research in the behavioral sciences. Here, the issues we raise have relevance beyond special education; consequently, our discussion is directed at instructional designers and instructional researchers in general. We raise two principal issues, both of which are stated as criticisms of efforts to apply theoretical frameworks in the cognitive tradition to classroom instruction. The first is that applied researchers are often too eager to apply the *raw* contents of cognitive theories and related experimental findings without first pausing to consider

what necessary conceptual bridges need to be built to enhance the viability of the application within the real world of classrooms (Marfo, Mulcahy, Peat, Andrews, & Cho, 1991). The second is that free-standing, intervention-oriented instructional programs—that is, those driven largely by concepts and principles from single theoretical frameworks—have proliferated at the expense of comprehensive models of instruction, which seek to incorporate sound principles and propositions from a broad range of theoretical perspectives into general instructional practice. We examine each of these criticisms next.

Bridges to instructional application. We do not have to look very far for examples of how educators' infatuation with newer theoretical frameworks has had the tendency to culminate, in the immediate short term, in rather literal and often shallow educational applications. Readers may recall the "cognitive rush" of the 1960s when Piaget's cognitive developmental theory was first introduced in North America. Piaget's preoccupation was to explain the mechanisms by which children's thought processes developed. Although it was generally acknowledged that some general principles of educational relevance could be derived from the theory (Ginsburg, 1981), Piaget's genetic epistemology was essentially a developmental theory, not a learning or instructional theory. While more reasonable and better conceptualized applications of Piaget's theory emerged with time, many of the initial efforts to apply Piaget's theory to education emphasized the attainment of specific Piagetian operations as key educational outcomes.

The current obsession with cognitive and metacognitive strategy instruction shows how history is repeating itself. The late 1970s saw a convergence of evidence from various lines of inquiry suggesting that besides native ability, learnable cognitive functions (such as specific strategies for executing a task) and executive routines (such as schemes for monitoring and evaluating the efficiency and effectiveness of deployed strategies) played a central role in cognitive performance (Belmont & Butterfield, 1971; Belmont, Butterfield, & Borkowski, 1978; Butterfield, Siladi, & Belmont, 1980; Campione & Brown, 1978; Flavell, 1979). The *training paradigm* (that is, designs in which subjects trained to use cognitive and metacognitive strategies are compared with naive or untrained subjects) was a prominent feature of the experimental research for investigating the role of cognitive and metacognitive strategies in cognitive performance. It was not surprising, therefore, that the direct instruction in cognitive strategies came to be viewed as a promising form of intervention for children who did not utilize such strategies spontaneously. Reminiscent of the literal application of Piaget's theory in the 1960s, educational researchers have built cognitive strategy intervention programs around those cognitive and metacognitive strategies that have frequently been shown through experimental, laboratory-based research to be associated with efficient information processing and performance.

Such programs are not likely to gain respect as theoretically sound and viable instructional systems as long as they are built around isolated strategies compiled from experimental research. What, then, is the key to harnessing the rich theoretical and empirical knowledge base on cognitive and metacognitive strategies into meaningful and potentially effective instructional programs? Part of the answer to this question is that applied researchers must seek to build strong conceptual bridges between a given body of knowledge and the specific applications derived from it. In the context of the present discussion, the first step is to consider a framework for linking emergent cognitive theories to instructional practice. Lauren Resnick (1984) offers one sketch of such a framework in a discussion of applied developmental theory—a framework that is useful for thinking

about the application of cognitive learning theories as well. Whether the purpose of the application is facilitative (such as the enhancement of functioning in children who are developing or learning normally) or remedial (such as helping children whose development or learning manifests difficulties), it should be guided by three elements: a theory of competence, a theory of acquisition, and a theory of intervention. A theory of competence is needed to explain both the overt behaviors and the underlying competencies to be gained through instruction. Next, it is important to articulate clearly the processes and mechanisms by which those behaviors and competencies come to be acquired. Without such a theory of acquisition, it is difficult to frame the intervention in ways that meaningfully address the needs, strengths, and limitations of individual children. The final element—the theory of intervention—spells out the kinds of actions that can be taken to aid the acquisition or improvement of the competencies.

In earlier work, Marfo and associates (Marfo et al., 1991) presented Resnick's three elements as a useful set of criteria for ascertaining whether a given theory has all the necessary ingredients to allow direct application to instructional settings, or whether additional conceptual work is needed to articulate more explicitly whatever theories of competence, acquisition, and intervention may be embedded in the original formulation. Case's (1978, 1980a, 1980b) reconceptualization of Piaget's theory is a good example of the kind of conceptual work that bridges the gap between a purely developmental theory and instructional practice. By recasting Piagetian schemas and operations in information-processing terms, Case made it possible to frame intellectual development not only in terms of the species-specific, normative and universal processes underlying the emergence of intellect, but also in terms of explicit competencies and strategies that children acquire and deploy in their day-to-day encounters with their experiential world. Case's work has thus shed better light on those dimensions of the cognitive developmental process that can be facilitated through planned as well as unplanned interventions.

Toward comprehensive instructional models. There are two identifiable traditions within the cognitive education movement: the *thinking-skills approach* and the *cognitive/learning strategies approach* (Marfo et al., 1991). Rooted in both cognitive science and philosophy, the thinking-skills tradition emphasizes the teaching of traditional critical, analytical, and productive thinking skills. Representative programs include Philosophy for Children (Lipman, 1985; Lipman, Sharp, & Oscanyan, 1980), Productive Thinking (Covington, Crutchfield, Davies, & Olton, 1974), CoRt (de Bono, 1985), and Problem Solving and Comprehension (Whimbey & Lockhead, 1982). The cognitive/learning strategies tradition, in turn, has its roots in cognitive psychology, particularly in conventional information-processing and metacognitive theories, and, to a limited extent, in neuropsychologically based models of cognition (for example, Das, Kirby, & Jarman, 1975, 1979). A distinguishing feature of the cognitive/learning strategies tradition is that it concerns itself not only with the improvement of basic cognitive functioning per se, but also with the application of cognitive functions and strategies to the improvement of academic learning and performance. Among the more prominent programs within this tradition are Reciprocal Teaching (Palinscar, 1986; Palinscar & Brown, 1984), Informed Strategies for Learners (Paris, Cross, & Lipson, 1984), Dansereau's Learning Strategies Course (Dansereau, 1978, 1985), and the Learning Strategies Curriculum (Deshler, Warner, Schumaker, & Alley, 1983).

Within special education, programs in the thinking-skills tradition tend to be used predominantly (although not exclusively) with gifted and talented students, whereas the cognitive/learning strategies programs are used more frequently with children who have learning problems. The University of Kansas Learning Strategies Curriculum (Deshler et al., 1983)—used largely with children with learning disabilities—and Palinscar's Reciprocal Teaching—originally validated on academically at-risk children in Title I programs—are among the most visible strategy-based instructional approaches for special populations. However, there are numerous unpublished programs in the field, including teacher-selected compendiums of mnemonic, comprehension, problem-solving, and writing strategies.

The key issue here is that, despite the proliferation and steady use of these programs over the past twenty years, they have remained very much in the realm of specialized interventions offered in special time slots—sometimes in special settings—for specialized populations. Educational and instructional psychology texts are increasingly devoting more space to contemporary cognitive theories and their instructional applications; however, the concepts, principles, and underlying assumptions of cognitive education remain to be integrated systematically into regular instructional practice. While not disputing the short-term remedial value of detached or free-standing, strategy-based intervention programs, we believe their long-term efficacy is bound to be compromised because they are not likely to be implemented consistently and systematically over a sufficiently long period of time to effect fundamental changes in children's processing and performance styles. Worse still, as is increasingly being acknowledged (for example, Joyce, 1985; Mulcahy, Marfo, Peat, Andrews, & Clifford, 1986), the practice of teaching thinking-skills and cognitive/learning strategies outside the regular curriculum creates a false dichotomy between academic content and cognitive activity, leaving students with the erroneous mind-set that the learning of academic subject matter and the active engagement of cognitive processes to think, plan, and solve problems are two separate activities.

The challenge for instructional researchers within and outside special education is thus clear. Programmatic instructional research is needed not only to build sound theoretical bridges between the growing cognitive science knowledge base and instructional practice, but also to design comprehensive models of instruction that enable all teachers to apply cognitive principles and strategies—along with sound practices from other realms of inquiry—in their day-to-day teaching. If this goal is accomplished, the need for extensive dependence on free-standing, packaged intervention programs will be diminished, and the transition toward inclusion of large numbers of children with special needs into regular classrooms will perhaps be smoother for all categories of teachers.

Problematic Legacies from the Behavioral Sciences

Along with the adoption of the mainstream research methodologies of the behavioral sciences, special education and its related subfields have also inherited or reinforced traditions that continue to place severe limitations on the ability of these fields to address some of the most fundamental challenges to the equitable delivery of quality services for all children and their families. In this section we focus on two specific legacies with profound significance for any discussion of future visions regarding research in special education and its related subfields. The first relates to the dearth of attention to cultural variables within these two fields. The second deals with the manner in which *difference* is handled by researchers and practitioners alike.

The Culture Gap in the Developmental Science Knowledge Base

The importance of culture has been acknowledged throughout the history of psychology (see Betancourt & Lopez, 1993), and in more recent decades the growing prominence of ecological-contextualist perspectives within developmental psychology has further accentuated awareness about culture and its influences on human development and learning (for example, Bronfenbrenner, 1979, 1986). It is a matter of profound paradox, therefore, that the systematic study of culture continues to receive scant attention within North American psychology. In this section, we argue that the cavalier treatment of culture in studies of development and learning is one of the unfortunate legacies that special education and its related subfields have inherited from the behavioral sciences. We take the position that solutions to some of special education's most challenging issues—such as problems in cognitive assessment, overrepresentation of children from minority backgrounds in specific program areas, the higher drop-out rate among children from ethnic minority and low socioeconomic backgrounds, the problem of attaining cultural sensitivity and appropriateness in classrooms and other intervention settings—call for deeper understandings of the cultural contexts within which children and schools function. These understandings will not come from the mainstream behavioral science knowledge base because, as we have stated, within the North American context the behavioral sciences have a poor record on the systematic study of cultural variation in relation to the development and use of competence in school and nonschool environments.

The obvious implication of the foregoing assertion is that researchers in special education and its related subfields have to incorporate cultural studies into their future research agenda. To do this successfully, scholars need to turn to cross-cultural research and to other disciplines (such as anthropology and sociology) for lessons and directions. It is mostly in the context of cross-cultural research—the kind that compares human development across cultures located in different nations or continents—that our knowledge of the developmental influences of culture has been amassed. For example, from the extensive cross-cultural research knowledge base that now exists across a variety of disciplines, we have learned the following: (1) cultures all over the world provide alternative pathways to optimal human development, and (2) the different values, norms, practices, and experiences associated with different cultures produce distinct differences in the ways in which individuals from different cultural groups acquire and/or express skills and competencies across all developmental domains.

It is also through cross-cultural research that we learn about some of the fundamental reasons that developmental researchers have failed so abysmally to address cultural variation within the context of pluralistic America. The demographic landscape of the United States, especially following the phenomenal trends in immigration throughout the second half of this century, is now a microcosm of the global cultural landscape. Notwithstanding this reality, closer examination of the American developmental science scene shows that neither the conduct of developmental research nor the application of this research to the solution of developmental problems (that is, intervention) reveals sufficient regard for the two principles stated above. Thus, although the cross-cultural developmental knowledge base includes the contributions of numerous American researchers, the insights offered by this knowledge base have not been applied effectively to advance research on cultural influences on human development within the American context.

This poor regard for cultural variation and its potential differential impact on development has been explained in a number of ways. Betancourt and Lopez (1993) see the "lack of a clear definition and understanding of culture from a psychological perspective" as a major impediment to the integration of cultural concepts in the formulation of developmental frameworks. They note that in much of the empirical research involving groups whose identities are defined in terms of race, ethnicity, or socioeconomic status, researchers often make inferences about cultural influences without even defining culture (Betancourt & Lopez, 1993). According to this perspective, definitional problems have made it difficult to make sense of even the relatively small body of research purporting to examine the role of culture in human development within the United States.

While the definitional problem is an important one, there is an even more formidable challenge—namely, the presence of several previously ubiquitous assumptions that, for the better part of this century, permeated developmental thinking and drew attention away from cultural and contextual factors in development. Robert LeVine (1989) has identified three such assumptions: (1) the assumption of endogenous development, (2) the universality assumption, and (3) the optimality assumption. Each of these assumptions is next briefly described and appraised.

The endogenous development assumption. The assumption of endogenous development holds that the key changes and patterns observed in the behavioral development of humans are largely driven by a prewired biological schedule, with environmental stimulation contributing only minimally to their emergence. It is this kind of assumption that led Arnold Gesell and others who have followed in his footsteps to identify developmental milestones and behavioral norms for various age groups of children without giving serious consideration to cultural and other environmental sources of variation. Thus, although Burton L.

White (cited in Thomas, 1992) once described Gesell's work as "the most widely utilized source of information on the *human infant*," the inference that this pioneering work has universal generalizability and application, even within American society, is certainly untenable because of the culturally restricted samples from which Gesell's developmental milestones emerged.

The universality assumption. The universality assumption derives its force from the assumption of endogenous development. By virtue of viewing specific developmental processes as being engendered by underlying biological mechanisms, many developmental theorists made universal claims about the timing and sequencing of cognitive, personality, and socioemotional milestones based exclusively on Western samples (LeVine, 1989). For quite some time, the stages and processes of intellectual development described by Piaget were deemed to be universally true of cognitive development across cultures. As has become evident through the work of cross-cultural research specialists on Piagetian theory (for example, Dasen, 1972, 1974), Piaget's model has not been successfully replicated across all cultures, leading Dasen to observe that "social and cultural factors are more important for cognitive development than Piaget had hypothesized" (Dasen, 1974, p. 407). Similar challenges to the universality assumption have been posed in the area of infant-mother attachment through some recent comparisons of results from Ainsworth's *strange situation* test between American and German dyads (see LeVine, 1989; LeVine & Norman, 1994). It is important to note that the universality assumption has been challenged in arenas other than culture. For example, Gilligan's feminist critique of Kohlberg's theory of moral development (see Gilligan, 1982) challenges the universal applicability of Kohlberg's stages of moral development across gender, even within the same cultural context.

The optimality assumption. This assumption has to do with claims and expectations regarding what environmental conditions are deemed necessary for the attainment of optimal development. North American developmental psychology has tended to manifest the guiding philosophy that optimal development consists of the skills possessed by white, middle-class children (Tulkin & Konner, 1976). LeVine (1989) captures this assumption even more vividly:

> Many child development specialists implicitly assume that the conditions of infants and children among educated middle-class Anglo-Americans represent, or at least approximate, the optimal environment for individual development in humans—in terms of parental commitment, health care, nutrition, living space, domestic facilities, physical protection, emotional warmth, cognitive stimulation, communicative responsiveness, and social stability. *Deviations from this pattern are interpreted not as alternative pathways for normal child development but as conditions of deficit or deprivation, representing less adequate environments in which to raise children . . .* [italics added for emphasis]. (p. 54)

From a theoretical perspective, the impact of the first two assumptions on developmental research has been weakened dramatically in recent decades. The last of these three assumptions—that pertaining to the conditions for optimal development—is perhaps the one that remains most intractable and pervasive, although in rather subtle ways. Because developmental research remains mostly normative and because most normative models of development and learning are built around white, middle-class samples, the yardstick for judging optimality has revolved around middle-class Euro-American culture. In special education, the optimality assumption permeates practice not only in the area of assessment but also in the realms of developmental and instructional interventions. The standards by which we judge all children—and, subsequently, their families—seem to be those derived from middle-class Euro-American cultural norms.

To turn this tradition around, it is not sufficient to merely espouse belief in the power of all cultures to promote optimal development. Developmental and instructional researchers alike must pay serious attention to the accumulation of cultural knowledge bases through which we can come to better understand not only the culture-specific norms for constituent ethnocultural groups but also the universal norms that cut across the larger mosaic of cultures. The lines of inquiry that develop in pursuit of this goal must heed one fundamental lesson from the history of cross-cultural research. Cross-cultural researchers have been faulted, and rightly so, for not paying sufficient attention to delineating the specific dimensions of culture that account for observed behavioral and developmental differences between participants from different cultural backgrounds (see Betancourt & Lopez, 1993). It is absolutely necessary that new research agendas focusing on cultural variation be able to perform more fine-grained analyses of the manner in which specific aspects of culture relate to children's developmental and learning characteristics or needs. Equally important is inquiry directed at in-depth examinations of the degree of compatibility between the educational system and the culture of schools on the one hand, and the culturally determined modes of learning and interpersonal relationships within distinct subcultures on the other. Insights arising from this line of inquiry are critically needed to enhance the relevance, meaningfulness, and effectiveness of the schooling process for children from all ethnocultural backgrounds (see Tharp, 1989).

The Tradition of Inferring Deficit from Difference

An equally important and related legacy is the tradition of inferring *deficits* from *differences*, a deeply entrenched problem in behavioral science research.

The extensive application of nomothetic contrastive research designs—along with related statistical tools—in the behavioral sciences has remarkably increased the ease with which differences among populations can be tested *scientifically*. Although the central assumption of homogeneity of variance underlying such nomothetic comparisons is often not satisfied, behavioral scientists frequently make value judgments from observed differences—often with little awareness that the basis for their judgments has more to do with their own culturally-biased notions of normative behavior than with the science of statistical comparison.

The exact origin of this tradition within the behavioral sciences is not altogether clear, but the cross-cultural psychology literature offers some useful insights on its nature and magnitude. There is substantial evidence that the problem of inferring deficits from differences is more insidious in intranational cultural comparisons than it is in international cross-cultural comparative research. As Tulkin and Konner (1976) have observed, American social scientists appear "reasonably tolerant of . . . practices observed in other cultures which would be devalued if reported in a minority group in the United States" (p. 137). Marfo (1993) has labeled this the problem of *differential cultural relativism*, drawing examples from Tulkin and Konner's (1976) work to support this characterization. In their review of cross-cultural research on parent-child interaction, Tulkin and Konner have demonstrated that researchers finding differences in interactional behaviors between American parents and parents from other nations (for example, The Netherlands, Japan, Germany) have consistently explained the differences in terms of cultural variations in the parents' conceptions of childhood and child behavior. Inferences about better or worse patterns of interaction are typically not made in these types of comparisons.

In contrast, when differences are observed in the interactional behaviors of middle-class parents and lower-income or ethnic minority parents within the United States, the interactional styles of the middle-class parents tend to be used as the yardstick for inferring deficiencies in and designing interventions for the lower-income or ethnic minority parents. Readers will recall the plethora of studies revealing significant SES-related differences in the quality of mother-child interactions in the 1960s. As a result of these studies, a variety of intervention programs emerged, such as Phyllis Levenstein's Verbal Interaction Project (Levenstein, 1970), that targeted lower-income families. Children from these family backgrounds were invariably considered to be at-risk for later developmental and learning problems, in part because their mothers' interaction styles were different from—and therefore deemed to be deficient in relation to—those observed in predominantly white middle-class families.

Within special education, the problem of inferring deficiencies from differences is endemic and is considered to be at the heart of the overrepresentation of minorities in special classes or programs. It is important to point out, however, that this problem is not unique to comparisons involving race, ethnicity, or social class. For example, in research on interactions involving parents and their children with developmental disabilities, we find that the basis for differential relativism is not race, ethnicity, or social class but rather the status of being the parent of a child with special needs. Thus, relative to the interactional styles of parents of typically developing children, deviations in the behaviors of parents of children with disabilities are seen as deficiencies rather than as positive adaptations to the unique interactional characteristics of the infant or child with special needs (see Marfo's [1990, 1992, 1992] research on parental directiveness).

Moving away from the tradition of equating difference with deficit is a formidable challenge, not only for special education and other human service professions but also for developmental psychology and the behavioral sciences in general. Our specific concern in this chapter, however, is for special education researchers to recognize the massive disservice that is done to thousands of children and their families whose futures are jeopardized daily because of the manner in which children's behavior and performance in the classroom situation are judged by standards that are often alien to their own cultural, familial, and personal realities.

Special Education's Own Challenging Legacies: Social Policy, Advocacy, and Intervention Research

Not all the challenges faced by special education are the result of external influences. As the field has developed, it has spawned its own problematic legacies. In this final section of the chapter, we discuss two subjects considered to be among the major philosophical and ethical quandaries facing the field. The first legacy we discuss—the politicization of inquiry—is not unique to special education; however, we believe that the essential nature of special education as a "helping profession with a unique history" renders the field especially vulnerable to the nurturance of this kind of predicament. The second legacy we discuss is a problem that is intricately embedded within special education's interventionist culture; namely, the ethical challenges that arise out of having too much faith in our field's ability to solve problems that have their roots within the larger ecological contexts over which educators have little control.

The Politicization of Inquiry

There is perhaps no research, especially in education and the social sciences, that is not prone to subjective biases. The questions we ask, how we ask them, and the methods we choose to answer them all involve decision-making processes that entail personal subjective judgments. However, certain forms of research appear particularly susceptible to biases that transcend the personal subjectivity of the researcher. In special education, intervention research represents one area where the confluence of science, social policy, and advocacy presents real ethical dilemmas with profound potential to jeopardize the confidence that can be placed in accumulated knowledge bases. Intriguingly, much of the critical reflection on intervention research that frequently occurs within and outside our field takes place around conceptual, methodological, and analytical issues (Dunst, 1986; Dunst, Snyder, & Mankinen, 1987; Kiesler, 1966; Marfo & Kysela, 1985; Simeonsson, Cooper, & Scheiner, 1982). As we explore avenues for enriching special education research with insights and lessons drawn from the behavioral sciences, we cannot afford to lose sight of the threats to validity that can and do result from the politicization of scientific inquiry. One reason intervention research is particularly vulnerable to politicization is that investigators frequently find themselves occupying the multiple roles of scientist, social policy advocate, and stakeholder in the intervention program under investigation. We draw examples from the early-intervention area to illustrate how these multiple roles can exert biasing influences on both the production and consumption of efficacy research.

It has been suggested (Marfo & Cook, 1991) that the political context within which the earliest efficacy studies on early-intervention programs for children with disabilities were spawned accounted, in part, for the remarkable tolerance of poorly designed investigations. Two objectives undergirding these early studies are clearly discernible. There was certainly the twin scientific objective of seeking (1) to demonstrate that the processes and outcomes of early-intervention programs could be investigated with objectivity and scientific rigor and (2) to generate data that could lead to the development of more effective intervention models and strategies. However, there was

also a political objective, borne largely out of anxiety, to demonstrate to legislators and policymakers at a critical point in the fiscal history of the early-intervention movement that continued funding and possible expansion of services were justified (Marfo & Cook, 1991). It appears that the scientific objective may have often been overpowered by the political objective. As both researchers and policymakers tied fiscal support for programs with the outcomes of efficacy research, even if only symbolically, the risk of biasing research toward producing supportive evidence was bound to increase. It is not surprising, therefore, that the vast majority of the research proclaiming the effectiveness of early intervention prior to the mid-1980s is now generally deemed to be too methodologically flawed to be interpretable (see Dunst, 1986; Dunst, Snyder, & Mankinen, 1987).

Politicization of inquiry at the consumption level has been equally problematic. Sixteen years ago, a study conducted in Canada compared a group of 9-month-old infants with Down syndrome in a center-based developmental intervention program with a control group after six months of intervention for the experimental group (Piper & Pless, 1980). Finding no statistically significant differences between the two groups on subtests of the Griffiths Scale, the authors concluded that the efficacy of the form of intervention evaluated in their study was "doubtful." For some fifteen years, the Piper and Pless (1980) study was perhaps the most frequently criticized efficacy study on record (see Marfo & Cook, 1991). It attracted swift and formal reactions in professional journals (Bricker, Carlson, & Schwartz, 1981; Sheehan & Keogh, 1981). To be fair to the critics, Piper and Pless were excessive in claiming, on the basis of a single study producing counterintuitive findings that "the efficacy of *this form of intervention* is doubtful" (p. 467). As Sheehan and Keogh (1981) observed, by drawing this sweeping conclusion, the researchers had gone beyond their data.

However, a close examination of the core criticisms of this study tells another story. The key elements of the various critiques are as follows: (1) the intervention was relatively short (Bricker, Carlson, & Schwartz, 1981; Sheehan & Keogh, 1981); (2) the sample size was small (Sheehan & Keogh, 1981); (3) neither the intervention effort itself nor the treatment variables under evaluation were described in sufficient detail to warrant precise interpretation of the findings (Bricker, Carlson, & Schwartz, 1981); (4) the Griffiths Scale may not have been sensitive enough to register changes triggered by the treatment (Bricker, Carlson, & Schwartz, 1981); (5) the statistical techniques used in the study were not particularly powerful (Sheehan & Keogh, 1981); and (6) given that the researchers did not collect any process data, they erred in interpreting the absence of experimental effects as evidence of inefficacy; their outcome could very well have been the result of factors related to the quality of treatment implementation (Marfo & Kysela, 1985).

It is a matter of profound irony that every one of the foregoing criticisms could be raised about most of the extant studies reporting positive intervention results. Indeed, in some ways the Piper and Pless (1980) study was perhaps one of the better scientifically designed studies of its time. As Janet Carr (1985) has aptly pointed out, the study was almost unique in its use of blind assessment to ensure that findings were not contaminated by the assessor's knowledge of which children were in the experimental or control group. The notoriety of the study appears, then, to be clearly related more to the unpleasantness of its findings than to its relative methodological deficiencies (Marfo & Cook, 1991).

A more recent example from the early-intervention literature also underscores the potential influences that considerations of a political nature can exert on the consumption of research. Between 1984 and 1986, a series of meta-analytic reviews of early-intervention efficacy studies, carried out at the Utah State University Early Intervention Research Institute (EIRI) appeared in several sources (Casto & Lewis, 1984; Casto & Mastropieri, 1986; White, Mastropieri, & Casto, 1984). The findings from these studies challenged and contradicted deeply entrenched beliefs and practices within the field. Among them were the following:

1. Although parents can be effective intervenors, "they are probably not essential to intervention success" because "those intervention programs which utilize parents are not more effective than those which do not" (Casto & Mastropieri, 1986, p. 421).
2. Contrary to the conventional belief that earlier exposure to intervention is better, it appears that for children with special needs, later exposure is associated with better outcomes.
3. More structured programs are only marginally superior to less structured programs.

As expected, these findings triggered much debate, controversy, and sharp criticism within the field. The reactions have been formal as well as informal, with the latter—often unleashed in the hallways and backrooms of professional meetings—revealing more overtly the fears and anxieties of the *advocacy self* of researchers and practitioners in the field. The published reactions (for example, Dunst & Snyder, 1986; Strain & Smith, 1986) have followed the normal scientific tradition of subjecting major investigations to critical analysis in the interest of assessing their contributions to the advancement of the field. For example, the Dunst and Snyder (1986) critique is consistent, in its thoroughness and harshness, with earlier integrative critiques in which they and other associates indicted most extant efficacy studies on grounds of methodological inadequacy. Thus, Dunst and his associates have been as critical of the meta-analytic studies used by the EIRI researchers to cast doubts on entrenched beliefs and practices as they have been of the corpus of earlier research purporting to validate these beliefs and practices.

Within the scientific community, subjecting counterintuitive findings to scrutiny is a normal—indeed, a responsible and desirable—act of scholarship. Without it, the advancement of knowledge in any field could be severely imperiled. Hopefully, this is the role that the formal critics of the EIRI studies have played, especially in their critical assessment of the validity and usefulness of applying meta-analysis as a tool for synthesizing a corpus of research studies deemed to be so diverse, in terms of the nature of the interventions involved, the categories of children served in the programs, and the methodological adequacy of the individual studies included in the analysis. As implied earlier in this discussion, however, the extensive informal and anxiety-laden response to the EIRI findings, from researchers and practitioners alike, tells a different story—one of tacit and insidious hostility that has been sufficient to make the individual researchers behind these counterintuitive findings feel ostracized in their immediate scientific community.

During the course of this decade, advocates, researchers, and practitioners in the early-intervention field have had good cause to be anxious about the future of federal support for services. Two factors combine to accentuate the anxiety engendered by the EIRI findings. The first is the timing—the fact that they were emerging at a politically vulnerable era in the history of U.S. social policy. The second has to do with the perceived clout of the Early Intervention Research Institute itself. As a well-funded national center of excellence with the unique mission to conduct large-scale, multisite investigations of early-intervention efficacy, its perceived potential to influence federal policy and budgetary appropriations may have contributed to the level of anxiety generated by the findings.

Is it likely, then, that these anxieties are at least part of the driving force behind the reactions to the scientific credibility of the EIRI studies? We do not pose this question to indict or accuse the individual scholars who reacted critically and formally to the EIRI studies. To the contrary, we believe that their formal critiques have advanced our field significantly by sensitizing researchers to a wide range of conceptual, methodological, and analytical issues associated with the synthesis of original research. We pose the question to underscore how important it is for us to be constantly cognizant of the subjective dimensions of the scientific enterprise. What would the reactions to the EIRI meta-analytic studies be if their findings were consistent with conventional wisdom in the field? Would the same concerns about the validity and meaningfulness of a meta-analysis be raised in relation to the heterogeneous nature of the studies included in the analysis? Or would the findings be embraced despite the observation that most of the individual investigations included in the analysis were too methodolgocially flawed for their results to be taken seriously? The answers to these questions will determine the extent to which our concern about the politicization of scientific inquiry may be justified in this particular instance.

Ethical Challenges to the Interventionist Culture

Although this chapter has raised mostly research issues, there are deep philosophical quandaries facing the field of special education as a whole that have significant relevance for any discussion on research. One such quandary requiring the attention of researchers whose interests lie in experimentation with or evaluation of varying forms of intervention relates to special education's intrinsic culture of intervention. Like many other applied fields, special education makes its fundamental contributions to society through the medium of intervention. By clearly relating knowledge about the strengths and limitations of individuals or groups with knowledge regarding strategies for enhancing their adaptation and performance, special education has improved the quality of life for millions of children and youth and their families.

However, a counterpoint to the obviously laudable goals, values, and accomplishments of the field is the reality that special education's culture of intervention also has the potential—in some areas—to erect significant, even if subtle, barriers to more ecologically far-reaching systemic interventions. At the risk of stirring up panic and pandemonium among stakeholders of the intervention funding enterprise, we suggest that some forms of contemporary intervention programming for *at-risk* children and youth illustrate this potential for well-intentioned special education programs, including those with demonstrated efficacy, to do as much harm as good in the long run.

To clarify this point, let us examine the concept of *at-risk* in relation to the focus of programs typically used to intervene with children so classified. The concept of *at-risk* held great promise for bringing balance to, if not redeeming, special education's unfortunate image as a field founded on an idiographic deficit model. In contrast to traditional categorical labels such as mental retardation, learning disabilities, emotional disturbance, behavior disorders, and so on— which tended to locate the problem within the child—the *at-risk* concept externalizes the child's problem. The term connotes that an otherwise developmentally normal child is placed at-risk for developmental problems or educational failure by some adverse environmental condition, such as poverty, family stress, diminished or lack of opportunity as a function of minority group membership, and so on.

The definitional perspective presented in the foregoing paragraph suggests at least two levels of intervention. From an ecological-contextualist standpoint, the first level of intervention for at-risk children should be a radical one (that is, one that gets to the very roots or origins of the problem) that directly targets the environmental conditions that place children at-risk. Responsibility for such radical interventions lies not with schools or similar agencies but at the broader societal level. Such responsibility should manifest itself in the form of political courage and will (on the part of society and its institutions of governance) to adopt fundamental social policies aimed at obliterating or reducing the prevalence of poverty, reducing economic and psychological pressures on the family, and accentuating equality of opportunity across different segments of the population.

The second level of intervention takes the form of programs designed to ameliorate or prevent the undesirable impact of risk conditions on individual children or groups. Interventions delivered through school-based special education programs and community-based early-intervention services for infants and preschool children operate at this second level. Remarkably, however, the ultimate success, and indeed meaningfulness, of these child-focused interventions hinge not only on the integrity of these interventions themselves but also on the extent to which society as a whole is able to dismantle the social conditions that place the children at-risk in the first place. As long as environments of social risk remain ubiquitous, the potential impact of interventions on children is likely to be muted for many of them.

Having framed the issue in this manner, what are the ethical challenges to special education's interventionist culture? Intervention programs designed to either remediate the manifest deleterious effects of social risk conditions or prevent the potential impact of such conditions are an important service to children at-risk and should continue to be an important focus of school- and community-based programs. But as Zigler (Chapter 6) points out so aptly, "intervention can help prepare children for school and enhance some aspects of their families' functioning, but it alone cannot end poverty and crime and guarantee successful schooling." Serious ethical challenges arise when intervention programs are raised to a level of primacy that has the potential to mask or diminish the imperative for radical social reform.

We argue that social scientists and educational researchers can and do participate in the process of raising interventions for at-risk children to the level of primacy that is of concern to us here. Through their advocacy and their research claims, researchers have a significant impact on legislators and policymakers and, as a result, on overall budgetary appropriations. Indeed, researchers, through their professional organizations, make the findings of their research the basis for their lobbying for resources to support various forms of interventions. Should researchers not take some responsibility for society's inadequate attention to fundamental social reform if their advocacy and lobbying promote school- and community-based interventions over fundamental social reform? As Head Start and other programs for disadvantaged children have achieved the status of significant national strategies for addressing the challenges of poverty and social inequity in American society, what role should social scientists and educational researchers play to ensure that these strategies are pursued in tandem with fundamental policies and accompanying resource appropriations to reduce poverty and social disadvantage in the first place? How can we play a meaningful role in designing effective interventions for at-risk children without participating in the institutionalization of our interventions as society's only solutions to the problems of poverty, social disadvantage, and family stress? Special education researchers, like all other researchers in the behavioral and social sciences, can no longer claim innocence about these issues.

Conclusion

A significant portion of this chapter was devoted to exploring linkages between the knowledge bases of the behavioral sciences—particularly developmental psychology and cognitive science—and special education research. This exploration was done with two purposes in mind. The first was to underscore the beneficial influences of the behavioral sciences, through identification and discussion of illustrative domains of inquiry where special education research stands to benefit significantly from key theoretical and empirical advances. Three such domains were highlighted: the trend toward explication of ecological and contextual influences on human development, the emerging resilience orientation to the study of long-term outcomes of developmental risk, and the ascendancy of contemporary *process* approaches to the study of human cognition. Noting the limited attention to context in special education research, we suggested that incorporating insights gained from these areas of behavioral science research into special education inquiry should yield new understandings about children with special needs and their families.

With regard to advances in the study of cognition, we examined implications for assessment as well as instruction. In the assessment area, the need to break the ubiquity of the intelligence quotient was emphasized, while recommendations were made for a movement toward the development and validation of process-oriented, contextually meaningful strategies for obtaining individualized measures of cognition. In the instructional domain, the case was made that educational researchers need to become more concerned about building pedagogically sound conceptual bridges from cognitive theories and their related empirical validations to classroom applications. Such conceptual bridging is necessary to ensure that intervention goals and strategies are firmly grounded in a sound understanding of the nature and manner of acquisition of the competencies that are the targets of instructional interventions. Without such conceptual grounding, it is often impossible to assess the effectiveness of instruction with any degree of certainty. Equally emphasized was the need to move beyond the proliferation of free-standing strategy-based intervention programs for specialized populations toward comprehensive instructional models that take advantage of insights from multiple theoretical perspectives to enrich the teaching/learning process for the benefit of all children in all settings.

The second purpose was to warn special education researchers about legacies from the behavioral sciences that have not served our field well. We identified two legacies from which special education research must depart: (1) the paradoxical dearth—considering the growing prominence of ecological-contextualist perspectives—of attention to cultural knowledge within mainstream developmental science, and (2) the related tradition of inferring deficits from differences. With regard to the former, we examined several key factors contributing to the low priority status accorded cultural variables in mainstream developmental science, and offered some general guidelines and proposals for advancing cultural knowledge within special education. In addressing the legacy of inferring deficits from between-groups differences, we drew attention to the problem of *differential cultural relativism* to sensitize researchers to contradictions inherent in current interpretations of cross-national and intranational cultural research findings. The solution to the problem of differential cultural relativism comes from understanding that cultural variation, as a source of explanation for behavioral and performance differences, has relevance not only for cross-national comparisons but also for subcultural comparisons within the same society.

Of equal interest to us were some of special education's own problematic legacies. The final section of the chapter underscored political and ethical challenges that are intricately embedded in intervention research. First, we showed how the occupation of multiple roles by researchers (as sci-

entists, social policy advocates, and stakeholders in specific interventions) can lead to unintended politicization of the inquiry process, blinding researchers to otherwise blatant methodological and conceptual shortcomings in their own work, and thereby threatening the validity and meaningfulness of the resulting knowledge base. Second, we called on special education researchers to give serious consideration to the broader ethical challenges embedded in the field's interventionist culture. In particular, we cautioned against the danger of raising developmental and educational interventions to a level of primacy that ultimately masks the broader moral and political imperative for radical systemic reform and social policies necessary at all levels of government to improve the quality of life for all children and their families, and thus reduce the need for massive interventions. This viewpoint establishes an important social policy advocacy role for researchers, one that requires them to develop interventions meeting the highest standards of excellence, while using their collective professional wisdom and power to shape fundamental social policies on children and families.

The issues discussed in this chapter have profound implications for the way we think about the culture of knowledge production in special education. To make the field more sensitive to cultural and contextual issues, theoretically credible models are needed to integrate psychological and cultural knowledge in studies of children with special needs and their families. Equally necessary is openness to the adoption of methodologies that are best suited to cultural studies. Both the development of these theoretical models and the adoption of new methodological tools will require a deeper commitment to collaborative research that draws on expertise from a variety of disciplines. As the knowledge production culture within special education comes to be increasingly characterized by an interdisciplinary and collaborative research ethos, we can expect to see forms and outcomes of inquiry that are better suited to addressing the complex array of real-world problems facing the field.

There are significant implications for the preparation of future researchers as well. On the basis of the range of issues considered in this chapter, it is perhaps an understatement to suggest that the traditional insular model of advanced graduate preparation in special education must give way to one that emphasizes and fosters interdisciplinary studies. Doctoral programs must embrace more actively and deliberately the contributions of the behavioral and social sciences, the arts, and the humanities to special education inquiry. In recent years, educational researchers have become increasingly responsive to methodologies (such as qualitative, interpretive, and narrative) that are firmly established in the social sciences and the humanities. Programs that build strong bridges with these disciplines should be able to diversify and strengthen their research training significantly, and thereby assure the field strong future research leadership. Research training can no longer be defined solely in terms of the acquisition and deployment of procedural and analytical techniques. Critical historical and philosophical analyses of the nature of inquiry must become an integral part of the research education process. Similarly, as the discussions in the third part of this chapter underscored, programs must also pay sufficient attention to the moral and ethical dimensions of the research enterprise.

There is perhaps no one right way to build a culture of doctoral-level research education that incorporates the features outlined here. The full-time doctoral program at the University of South Florida has been designed with these new directions in mind. Among the key features of this program are the following: an explicit valuing of diverse forms of inquiry; the use of joint appointments of faculty from other disciplines to accentuate the program's ability to nurture and support the work of students interested in pursuing alternative forms of inquiry; a strong student cohort culture; a collaborative research environment with active student involvement in thematic areas of inquiry; individualized mentoring and apprenticeship in research and teaching; a seminar on the nature of inquiry taught by an interdisciplinary group of faculty; and opportunities for interdisciplinary work through the department's joint specialization agreements with doctoral programs in such fields as anthropology, measurement, and reading. The field needs more model programs with sufficient longevity to ascertain what kind of impact this approach to advanced graduate education is likely to have on the culture and outcomes of special education research.

References

Anthony, E. J. (1974). The syndrome of the psychologically invulnerable child. In E. J. Anthony & C. Koupernik (Eds.), *The child in his family: Vol. 3. Children at psychiatric risk* (pp. 529–544). New York: Wiley.

Anthony, E. J. (1978). From birth to breakdown: A prospective study of vulnerability. In E. J. Anthony, C. Koupernik, & C. Chiland (Eds.), *The child in his family: Vulnerable children* (pp. 273–285). New York: Wiley.

Belmont, J. M., & Butterfield, E. C. (1971). Learning strategies as determinants of memory deficiencies. *Cognitive Psychology, 2,* 411–420.

Belmont, J. M., Butterfield, E. C., & Borkowski, J. G. (1978). Training retarded people to generalize memorization methods across memory tasks. In M. M. Gruneberg, P. E. Morris, & R. M. Sykes (Eds.), *Practical aspects of memory* (pp. 418–425). London: Academic Press.

Betancourt, H., & Lopez S. R. (1993). The study of culture, ethnicity, and race in American psychology. *American Psychologist, 48,* 629–637.

Bricker, D., Carlson, L., & Schwartz, R. (1981). A discussion of early intervention for infants with Down syndrome. *Pediatrics, 67,* 45–46.

Bronfenbrenner, U. (1977). Toward an experimental ecology of human development. *American Psychologist, 32,* 513–531.

Bronfenbrenner, U. (1979). *The ecology of human development.* Cambridge, MA: Harvard University Press.

Bronfenbrenner, U. (1986). Ecology of the family as a context for human development: Research perspectives. *Developmental Psychology, 22,* 723–742.

Bronfenbrenner, U. (1989). Ecological systems theory. In R. Vasta (Ed.), *Six theories of child development: Revised formulations and current issues* (pp. 187–219). Greenwich, CT: JAI Press.

Burks, B. S. (1928). The nature and influence of nature and nurture upon mental development. In National Society for the Study of Education (Ed.), *Nature and nurture: Part 1. Their influence upon intelligence* [27th Yearbook of the National Society for the Study of Education]. Bloomington, IL: Public School Publishing.

Butterfield, E. C., Siladi, D., & Belmont, J. M. (1980). Validating theories of intelligence. In H. Reese & L. Lipsitt (Eds.), *Advances in child development and behavior* (Vol. 15, pp. 96–162). New York: Academic Press.

Campione, J. C., & Brown, A. L. (1978). Toward a theory of intelligence: Contributions from research with retarded children. *Intelligence, 2,* 279–304.

Carr, J. (1985). The development of intelligence. In D. Lane & B. Stratford (Eds.), *Current approaches to Down's syndrome* (pp. 167–186). New York: Praeger.

Case, R. (1978). A developmentally based theory and technology of instruction. *Review of Educational Research, 48,* 439–463.

Case, R. (1980a). The underlying mechanisms of intellectual development. In J. R. Kirby & J. B. Biggs (Eds.), *Cognition, development, and instruction* (pp. 3–21). New York: Academic Press.

Case, R. (1980b). Implications of a neo-Piagetian theory for improving the design of instruction. In J. R. Kirby & J. B. Biggs (Eds.), *Cognition, development, and instruction* (pp. 161–186). New York: Academic Press.

Casto, G., & Lewis, A. C. (1984). Parent involvement in infant and preschool programs. *Journal of the Division for Early Childhood, 9,* 49–56.

Casto, G., & Mastropieri, M. A. (1986). The efficacy of early intervention programs: A meta-analysis. *Exceptional Children, 52,* 417–424.

Covington, M. V., Crutchfield, R. S., Davies, L., & Olton, R. M. (1974). *The productive thinking program: A course in learning to think.* Columbus, OH: Charles E. Merrill.

Dansereau, D. F. (1978). The development of a learning strategy curriculum. In H. F. O'Neil (Ed.), *Learning strategies* (pp. 1–29). Hillsdale, NJ: Erlbaum.

Dansereau, D. F. (1985). Learning strategies research. In J. W. Segal, S. F. Chipman, & R. Glaser (Eds.), *Thinking and learning skills: Vol. 1. Relating instruction to research* (pp. 209–239). Hillsdale, NJ: Erlbaum.

Das, J. P., Kirby, J. R., & Jarman, R. R. (1975). Simultaneous and successive synthesis: An alternative model for cognitive abilities. *Psychological Bulletin, 82,* 87–103.

Das, J. P., Kirby, J. R., & Jarman, R. R. (1979). *Simultaneous and successive cognitive processes.* New York: Academic Press.

Dasen, P. R. (1972). Cross-cultural Piagetian research: A summary. *Journal of Cross-Cultural Psychology, 3*(1), 23–29.

Dasen, P. R. (1974). The influence of ecology, culture and European contact on cognitive development in Australian Aborigines. In J. W. Berry & P. R. Dasen (Eds.), *Culture and cognition: Readings in cross-cultural psychology* (pp. 381–408). London: Methuen.

de Bono, E. (1985). CoRt thinking program. In J. W. Segal, S. F. Chipman, & R. Glaser (Eds.), *Thinking and learning skills: Vol. 1. Relating instruction to research* (pp. 363–388). Hillsdale, NJ: Erlbaum.

Deshler, D. D., Warner, M. M., Schumaker, J. B., & Alley, G. (1983). Learning strategies intervention model: Key components and current status. In J. McKinney & L. Feagans (Eds.), *Current topics in learning disabilities* (Vol. 1, pp. 245–283). Norwood, NJ: Ablex.

Duchnowski, A., Kutash, K., & Knitzer, J. (1997). Integrated and collaborative community services in exceptional student education. In J. L. Paul, M. Churton, W. Morse, A. Duchnowski, B. Epanchin, P. Osnes, & L. Smith (Eds.), *Special education practice: Applying the knowledge, affirming the values, and creating the future* (Chapter 11). Pacific Grove, CA: Brooks/Cole.

Dunst, C. J. (1986). Overview of the efficacy of early intervention programs. In L. Bickman & D. L. Weatherford (Eds.), *Evaluating early intervention programs for severely handicapped children and their families* (pp. 79–147). Austin, TX: Pro-Ed.

Dunst, C. J., & Rheingrover, R. (1981). An analysis of the efficacy of infant intervention programs with organically handicapped children. *Evaluation and Program Planning, 4,* 287–323.

Dunst, C. J., & Snyder, S. W. (1986). A critique of the Utah State University early intervention meta-analysis research. *Exceptional Children, 53,* 269–276.

Dunst, C. J., Snyder, S. W., & Mankinen, M. (1987). Efficacy of early intervention. In M. C. Wang, M. C. Reynolds, & H. J. Walberg (Eds.), *Handbook of special education* (Vol. 3, pp. 259–294). New York: Pergamon Press.

Dunst, C. J., & Trivette, C. M. (1988). Determinants of parent and child interactive behavior. In K. Marfo (Ed.), *Parent-child interaction and developmental disabilities: Theory, research, and intervention* (pp. 3–31). New York: Praeger.

Dunst, C. J., & Trivette, C. M. (1990). Assessment of social support in early intervention programs. In S. J. Meisels & J. P. Shonkoff (Eds.), *Handbook of early childhood intervention* (pp. 326–349). New York: Cambridge University Press.

Eysenck, H., & Kamin, L. (1981). *The intelligence controversy.* New York: Wiley.

Farber, E. A., & Egeland, B. (1987). Invulnerability among abused and neglected children. In E. J. Anthony & B. Cohler (Eds.), *The invulnerable child* (pp. 253–288) New York: Guilford Press.

Felner, R. D. (1991). Foreword. In W. A. Rhodes & W. K. Brown (Eds.), *Why some children succeed despite the odds* (pp. ix–xi). New York: Praeger.

Feuerstein, R., Rand, Y., Hoffman, M. B., & Miller, R. (1980). *Instrumental enrichment: An intervention program for cognitive modifiability.* Baltimore: University Park Press.

Flavell, J. H. (1979). Metacognition and cognitive monitoring: A new area of cognitive-developmental research. *American Psychologist, 34,* 906–911.

Furstenberg, F. F. (1980). Burden and benefits: The impact of early childbearing on the family. *Journal of Social Issues, 36,* 64–87.

Gardner, H. (1983). *Frames of mind: The theory of multiple intelligences.* New York: Basic Books.

Gardner, H. (Ed.). (1993). *Multiple intelligences: The theory in practice.* New York: Basic Books.

Garmezy, N. (1974). The study of competence in children at risk for severe psychopathology. In E. J. Anthony & C. Koupernik (Eds.), *The child in his family: Vol. 3: Children at psychiatric risk* (pp. 77–97). New York: Wiley.

Garmezy, N. (1981). Children under stress: Perspective on antecedents and correlates of vulnerability and resistance to psychopathology. In A. I. Rabin, J. Aronoff, A. M. Barclay, & R. A. Zucker (Eds.), *Further explorations in personality* (pp. 196–269). New York: Wiley.

Garmezy, N. (1987). Stress, competence, and development: Continuities in the study of schizophrenic adults, children vulnerable to psychopathology, and the search for stress resistant children. *American Journal of Orthopsychiatry, 57,* 159–174.

Geber, M. M. (1994). Postmodernism in special education. *Journal of Special Education, 28,* 368–378.

Gibson, D. (1991). Down syndrome and cognitive enhancement: Not like the others. In K. Marfo (Ed.), *Early intervention in transition: Current perspectives on programs for handicapped children.* (pp. 61–90) Westport, CT: Praeger

Gilligan, C. (1982). *In a different voice: Psychological theory and women's development.* Cambridge, MA: Harvard University Press.

Ginsburg, H. P. (1981). Piaget and education: The contributions and limits of genetic epistemology. In I. E. Sigel, D. M. Brodzinsky, & R. M. Golinkoff (Eds.), *New directions in Piagetian theory and practice* (pp. 315–330). Hillsdale, NJ: Erlbaum.

Gould, S. J. (1981). *The mismeasure of man.* New York: Norton.

Haywood, H. C., & Switzky, H. N. (1986). The malleability of intelligence: Cognitive processes as a function of polygenic-experiential interaction. *School Psychology Review, 15,* 245–254.

Herrnstein, R., & Murray, C. (1994). *The bell curve.* New York: Free Press.

Heshusius, L. (1986). Pedagogy, special education, and the lives of young children: A critical and futuristic perspective. *Journal of Education, 168,* 25–38.

Heshusius, L. (1989). The Newtonian-mechanistic paradigm, special education, and contours of alternatives: An overview. *Journal of Learning Disabilities, 22,* 403–415.

Hetherington, E. M., Cox, M., & Cox, R. (1982). Effects of divorce on parents and children. In M. Lamb (Ed.), *Non-traditional families* (pp. 223–285). Hillsdale, NJ: Erlbaum.

Joyce, B. (1985). Models for teaching thinking. *Educational Leadership, 42,* 4–7.

Kail, R., & Bisanz, J. (1982). Information processing and cognitive development. In H. W. Reese (Ed.), *Advances in child development and behavior* (Vol. 7, pp. 45–81). New York: Academic Press.

Kamin, L. J. (1974). *The science and politics of psychology.* Potomac, MD: Erlbaum.

Kamin, L. J. (1975). Social and legal consequences of I.Q. tests as classification instruments: Some warnings from our past. *Journal of School Psychology, 13,* 317–323.

Kaufman, A. S., & Kaufman, N. L. (1983). *Kaufman Assessment Battery for Children.* Circle Pines, MN: American Guidance Service.

Kiesler, D. J. (1966). Some myths about psychotherapy research and the search for a paradigm. *Psychological Bulletin, 65*(2), 110–136.

Koch, S. (1985). The nature and limits of psychological knowledge. In S. Koch & D. E. Leary (Eds.), *A century of psychology as a science* (pp. 75–97). New York: McGraw-Hill.

Leahy, A. M. (1955). Nature-nurture and intelligence. *Genetic Psychology Monographs,* Vol. 17, pp. 236–308.

Lerner, R. M. (1991). Changing organism-context relations as the basic process of development: A developmental contextual perspective. *Developmental Psychology, 27,* 27–32.

Lerner, R. M., & Fisher, C. B. (1994). From applied developmental psychology to applied developmental science: Community coalitions and collaborative careers. In C. B. Fisher & R. M. Lerner (Eds.), *Applied developmental psychology* (pp. 505–522). New York: McGraw-Hill.

Lerner, R. M., & Kauffman, M. B. (1985). The concept of development in contextualism. *Developmental Review, 5,* 309–333.

Lerner, R. M., & Lerner, J. V. (1989). Organismic and so-cial contextual bases of development: The sample case of adolescence. In W. Damon (Ed.), *Child development today and tomorrow* (pp. 69–85). San Francisco: Josey-Bass.

Levenstein, P. (1970). Cognitive growth through verbal interaction with mothers. *American Journal of Orthopsychiatry, 40,* 426–432.

LeVine, R. A. (1989). Cultural environments in child development. In W. Damon (Ed.), *Child development today and tomorrow* (pp. 52–68). San Francisco: Josey-Bass.

LeVine, R. A., & Lun, W. (1994). *Human nurture: A view from psychosocial anthropology.* Unpublished manuscript, Harvard Graduate School of Education and Chinese University of Hong Kong.

LeVine, R. A., & Norman, K. (1994, June). *Culture and attachment: The case of German infant care.* Paper presented at the biennial meeting of the International Society for the Study of Behavioral Development, Amsterdam, The Netherlands.

Lipman, M. (1985). Thinking skills fostered by Philosophy for Children. In J. W. Segal, S. F. Chipman, & R. Glaser (Eds.), *Thinking and learning skills: Vol. 1. Relating instruction to research* (pp. 83–108). Hillsdale, NJ: Erlbaum.

Lipman, M., Sharp, A. M., & Oscanyan, F. S. (1980). *Philosophy in the classroom* (2nd ed.). Philadelphia: Temple University Press.

Malysiak, R. (in press). Same as it ever was? The hope and challenge for the wrap-around model. In B. Friesen (Ed.), *Building from family strengths: Research and programs in support of children and their families* (6th Annual Conference Monograph). Portland OR: Portland State University.

Marfo, K. (1990). Maternal directiveness in interactions with mentally handicapped children: An analytical commentary. *Journal of Child Psychology and Psychiatry, 31,* 531–549.

Marfo, K. (1991). The maternal directiveness theme in mother-child interaction research: Implications for early intervention. In K. Marfo (Ed.), *Early intervention in transition: Current perspectives on programs for handicapped children* (pp. 177–203). Westport, CT: Praeger.

Marfo, K. (1992). Correlates of maternal directiveness in interactions with developmentally delayed children. *American Journal of Orthopsychiatry, 62,* 219–233.

Marfo, K. (1993, May). Multiculturalism and early childhood education: Implications for personnel preparation. Paper presented at the Invitational Conference on the Impact of Culture on the Early Childhood Education Curriculum, University of British Columbia, Canada.

Marfo, K., & Cook, C. (1991). Overview of trends and issues in early intervention theory and research. In K. Marfo (Ed.), *Early intervention in transition: Current perspectives on programs for handicapped children* (pp. 3–40). Westport, CT: Praeger.

Marfo, K., & Dinero, T. E. (1991). Assessing early intervention outcomes: Beyond program variables. *International Journal of Disability, Development and Education, 38,* 289–303.

Marfo, K., Dinero, T. E., Browne, N., Gallant, D., Smyth, R., & Corbett, A. (1992). Child, program, and family ecological variables in early intervention. *Early Education and Development, 3,* 27–44.

Marfo, K., & Kysela, G. M. (1985). Early intervention with mentally handicapped children: A critical appraisal of applied research. *Journal of Pediatric Psychology, 10,* 305–324.

Marfo, K., Mulcahy, R., Peat, D., Andrews, J., & Cho, S. (1991). Teaching cognitive strategies in the classroom: A content-based instructional model. In R. F. Mulcahy, R. H. Short, & J. Andrews (Eds.), *Enhancing learning and thinking* (pp. 67–95). New York: Praeger.

Montagu, A. (1959). *Human heredity.* New York: Harcourt Brace Jovanovich.

Mulcahy, R. F., Marfo, K., Peat, D., Andrews, J., & Clifford, L. (1986). Applying cognitive psychology in the classroom. *Alberta Psychology, 13*(3), 9–11.

Murphy, L. (1962). *Paths toward mastery.* New York: Basic Books.

Neisser, U., Boodoo, G., et al. (1996). Intelligence: Knowns and unknowns [Report of an American Psychological Association Task Force]. *American Psychologist, 51,* 77–101.

Palinscar, A. M. (1986). Metacognitive strategy instruction. *Exceptional Children, 53,* 118–124.

Palinscar, A. M., & Brown, A. L. (1984). The reciprocal teaching of comprehension fostering and compre-

hension monitoring activities. *Cognition and Instruction, 1,* 117–175.

Paris, S. G., Cross, D. R., & Lipson, M. Y. (1984). Informed strategies for learning: A program to improve children's reading awareness and comprehension. *Journal of Educational Psychology, 76,* 1239–1252.

Paul, J. L., Churton, M., Morse, W., Duchnowski, A., Epanchin, B., Osnes, P., & Smith, L. (Eds.). (1997). *Special education practice: Applying the knowledge, affirming the values, and creating the future.* Pacific Grove, CA: Brooks/Cole.

Paul, J. L., & Morse, W. C. (1997). Creating and using knowledge for special education practice: The conundrum and the promise. In J. L. Paul, M. Churton, W. Morse, A. Duchnowski, B. Epanchin, P. Osnes, & L. Smith, (Eds.), *Special education practice: Applying the knowledge, affirming the values, and creating the future* (Chapter 1). Pacific Grove, CA: Brooks/Cole.

Piper, M. C., & Pless, I. B. (1980). Early intervention for infants with Down syndrome. *Pediatrics, 65,* 463–468.

Poplin, M. S. (1988). Holistic/constructivist principles of the teaching/learning process: Implications for the field of learning disabilities. *Journal of Learning Disabilities, 21,* 401–416.

Poplin, M. S., & Stone, S. (1992). Paradigm shifts in instructional strategies: From reductionism to holistic/constructivism. In S. Stainback & W. Stainback (Eds.), *Controversial issues confronting special education: Divergent perspectives* (pp. 153–179). Boston: Allyn & Bacon.

Reed, J. (1987). Robert M. Yerkes and the mental testing movement. In M. M. Sokal (Ed.), *Psychological testing and American society: 1890–1930* (pp. 75–94). New Brunswick, NJ: Rutgers University Press.

Resnick, L. B. (1984). Toward an applied developmental theory. In B. Gholson & T. L. Rosenthal (Eds.), *Applications of cognitive-developmental theory* (pp. 263–280). Orlando: Academic Press.

Rhodes, W. C. (1990). From classic to holistic paradigm. In P. Leone (Ed.), *Understanding troubled and troubling children* (pp. 154–172). Newbury Park, CA: Sage Publications.

Richters, J., & Weintraub, S. (1990). Beyond diathesis: Toward an understanding of high-risk environments. In J. Rolf, A. S. Masten, D. Cicchetti, K. H. Neuchterlein, & S. Weintraub (Eds.), *Risk and protective factors in the development of psychopathology* (pp. 67–96). New York: Cambridge University press.

Rutter, M. (1979). Protective factors in children's responses to stress and disadvantage. In W. M. Kent, & J. E. Rolf (Eds.), *Primary prevention in psychopathology. Vol 3: Social competence in children* (pp. 49–74). Hanover, NH: University Press of New England.

Rutter, M. (1981). Stress, coping and development: Some issues and some questions. *Journal of Child Psychology and Psychiatry, 22,* 323–356.

Sameroff, A. J. (1990). Neo-behavioral perspectives on developmental theory. In R. M. Hodapp, J. A. Burack, & E. Zigler (Eds.), *Issues in the developmental approach to mental retardation.* New York: Cambridge University Press.

Sameroff, A. J., & Chandler, M. J. (1975). Reproductive risk and the continuum of caretaking casualty. In F. D. Horowitz, M. Hetherington, S. Scarr-Salapatek, & G. Siegel (Eds.), *Review of child development research* (Vol. 4, pp. 187–244). Chicago: University of Chicago Press.

Sameroff, A. J., & Fiese, B. H. (1990). Transactional regulation and early intervention. In S. J. Meisels & J. P. Shonkoff (Eds.), *Handbook of early childhood intervention* (pp. 119–149). New York: Cambridge University Press.

Sameroff, A. J., & Seifer, R. (1990). Early contributions to developmental risk. In W. M. Kent & J. E. Rolf (Eds.), *Primary prevention in psychopathology. Vol 3: Social competence in children* (pp. 52–66). Hanover, NH: University Press of New England.

Sheehan, R., & Keogh, B. K. (1981). Strategies for documenting progress of handicapped children in early education programs. *Educational Evaluation and Policy Analysis, 3*(6), 59–67.

Shuttleworth, F. K. (1935). The nature versus nurture problem: II. The contributions of nature and nurture to individual differences in intelligence. *Journal of Educational Psychology, 26*(9), 655–681.

Simeonsson, R. J., Cooper, D. H., & Scheiner, A. P. (1982). A review and analysis of early intervention programs. *Pediatrics, 69,* 635–641.

Skeels, H. M. (1940). Some Iowa studies of the mental growth of children in relation to differentials of the environment: A summary. In G. M. Whipple (Ed.), *Intelligence: Its nature and nurture (Thirty-ninth Yearbook of the National Society for the Study of Education,* pp. 281–308). Bloomington, IL: Public School Publishing.

Skeels, H. M., & Dye, H. B. (1939). A study of the effects of differential stimulation on mentally retarded children. *American Journal of Mental Deficiency, 44,* 114–120.

Skodak, M. (1939). Children in foster homes: A study of mental development. *University of Iowa Studies in Child Welfare, Vol. 16* (entire issue).

Skrtic, T. (1995). The crisis in professional knowledge. In E. L. Meyen & T. M. Skrtic, *Special education and student disability: An introduction* (4th ed, pp. 568–607). Denver: Love Publishing.

Sternberg, R. J. (1980). Sketch of a componential theory of human intelligence. *Behavioral and Brain Sciences, 3,* 573–584.

Sternberg, R. J. (1985). *Beyond IQ: A triarchic theory of human intelligence.* New York: Cambridge University Press.

Sternberg, R. J. (1986). *Intelligence applied: Understanding and increasing your intellectual skills.* San Diego: Harcourt Brace Jovanovich.

Sternberg, R. J., Ketron, J. L., & Powell, J. S. (1982). Componential approaches to the training of intelligent performance. In D. K. Detterman & R. J. Sternberg (Eds.), *How and how much can intelligence be increased?* Norwood, NJ: Ablex.

Strain, P. S., & Smith, B. J. (1986). A counter-interpretation of early intervention effects: A response to Casto and Mastropieri. *Exceptional Children, 53,* 260–265.

Tharp, R. G. (1989). Psychocultural variables and constants: Effects on teaching and learning in schools. *American Psychologist, 44,* 349–359.

Thomas, R. M. (1992). *Comparing theories of child development* (3rd ed.). Belmont, CA: Wadsworth.

Tulkin, S. R., & Konner, M. J. (1976). Alternative conceptions of intellectual functioning. In A. Skolnick (Ed.), *Rethinking Childhood: Perspectives on development and society* (pp. 128–148). Boston: Little, Brown.

Vincent, L. J., Salisbury, C. L., Strain, P., McCormick, C., & Tessier, A. (1990). A behavioral-ecological approach to early intervention: Focus on cultural diversity. In S. J. Meisels & J. P. Shonkoff (Eds.), *Handbook of early childhood intervention* (pp. 173–195). New York: Cambridge University Press.

Wagner, R. K., & Sternberg, R. J. (1984). Alternative conceptions of intelligence and their educational implications. *Review of Educational Research, 54,* 179–223.

Werner, E. E. (1986). Resilient offspring of alcoholics: A longitudinal study from birth to age 18. *Journal of Studies on Alcohol, 47,* 34–40.

Werner, E. E. (1990). Protective factors and individual resilience. In S. J. Meisels & J. P. Shonkoff (Eds.), *Handbook of early childhood intervention* (pp. 97–116). New York: Cambridge University Press.

Werner, E. E., & Smith, R. S. (1982). *Vulnerable, but invincible: A longitudinal study of resilient children and youth.* New York: McGraw-Hill.

Whimbey, A., & Lockhead, J. (1982). *Problem solving and comprehension* (3rd ed.). Philadelphia: Franklin Institute Press.

White, K., Mastropieri, M., & Casto, G. (1984). An analysis of special education early childhood projects approved by the Joint Dissemination Review Panel. *Journal of the Division for Early Childhood, 9,* 11–26.

Zigler, E., & Seitz, V. (1980). Early childhood intervention programs: A reanalysis. *School Psychology Review, 9,* 354–365.

Zigler, E., & Trickett, P. K. (1978). IQ and social competence, an evaluation of early intervention programs. *American Psychologist, 33,* 789–798.

CHAPTER 13

Behavior Analysis and Its Relevance to Special Education

GLEN DUNLAP
University of South Florida

LEE KERN
Children's Seashore House, Philadelphia

Introduction

Intervention strategies derived from a behavioral perspective have been prominent in special education for several decades, and that status is likely to be maintained for the foreseeable future. There is every reason that it should. Behavioral orientations embody important principles, practices, and methodologies that are demonstrably and indisputably valuable in analyzing and developing student behavior. Indeed, behavioral perspectives and procedures have been increasingly pervasive in educational endeavors pertaining to behavior management, general pedagogy, measurement and accountability, as well as the development of precise, specialized instructional technique.

Although behavioral interventions have been salient ingredients in special education for some time, there are nevertheless legitimate questions regarding the future relevance of behavioral approaches as the discipline of special education reconsiders its objectives and adjusts to a multiplicity of societal and contextual transformations. The very nature of special education is being altered by numerous social, cultural, and political influences (Paul, Rosselli, & Evans, 1995). The outcomes realized by special education are under scrutiny, as are the strategies designed to produce those outcomes.

All of these concerns affect the extent to which behavioral perspectives will contribute to special education as the next generation of students, educators, and schools emerge.

In this chapter, we offer a discussion and exploration of the current and future relevance of behavioral perspectives to special education. We begin with a brief presentation of some essential principles and features of the behavioral paradigm and then review some general considerations that attest to the relevance of behaviorism in special education. In the final section, we present a discussion of three general directions that must be addressed by behavioral researchers and practitioners if the orientation's relevance is to be increasingly meaningful.

Before proceeding, we need to explain that the term we will use to refer to behavioral orientations and procedures in special education is *behavior analysis* and, more specifically, *applied behavior analysis*. Many terms have been used over the years, including *behavioral psychology, operant conditioning, behaviorism, behavior modification,* and numerous others. All of these terms are applicable, but they sometimes carry inappropriate connotations or imply an overly restricted purview. *Applied behavior analysis* is a preferred term because it emphasizes the empirical and analytical aspects of the approach and also stresses the applied nature of its orientation (Baer, Wolf, & Risley, 1968, 1987).

Principles and Features of Applied Behavior Analysis

There are several basic principles that set behavior analysis apart from other approaches to understanding behavior. These pertain primarily to how behavior is viewed in the context of the surrounding environment and the manner in which behavior is studied. In this section, we describe some principles and features of behavior analysis that help define its unique position in psychology, education, and related disciplines.

Scientific Foundation

Behavior analysis is philosophically consistent with a positivist orientation. That is, the behavioral approach adheres to the position that there is order and lawfulness to behavior, and that behavior can be understood in much the same manner as other natural phenomena. Furthermore, behavior analysis asserts that the laws that govern behavior are detectable through systematic methods of empirical inquiry, including experimentation.

The belief that behavior can be understood directly, through scientific methods, distinguishes behavior analysis from those views that regard behavior as a phenomenon of secondary interest, occurring as a result of unobservable psychological or biological processes. Although behavior analysts do not discount the existence of internal processes, they emphasize the point that behavior, in and of itself, is a legitimate focus of investigation and that, for the most part, internal phenomena are not necessary considerations for pursuing behavioral knowledge. The assumptions represented by this outlook have freed behavior analysts from unresolvable hypotheses and speculations, and have permitted the establishment of research standards and a basis for consensus within the discipline.

The science of behavior analysis has been essentially the study of relations between environmental variables and dimensions of behavior (Cooper, Heron, & Heward, 1987). Typically, an event or circumstance in the environment is defined as the independent variable, and an index of change in behavior is delineated as the dependent variable. Because both constituents of the relation must be measurable, the independent variable has been limited primarily to aspects of the external environment; however, improved measurement procedures could well extend this to include physiological variables. Experimental procedures, including the mechanisms of systematic replication, provide a means for developing a body of scientific knowledge that is cumulative and that, ideally, leads to an improved ability to predict and influence behavior. This grounding in the scientific method offers behavior analysis a powerful advantage for contributing valid and replicable information and useful technologies to the practice of special education.

A Conceptual Basis in Operant Psychology

The conceptual framework of behavior analysis is drawn from learning theory and, in particular, operant psychology (Ferster, Culbertson, & Boren, 1975). The premise underlying operant psychology is that organisms learn to "operate" on the environment to produce desired consequences and to avoid or escape undesired consequences. In essence, behavior can be understood by identifying these desired and undesired consequences and specifying the manner in which they exert influence over behavior. Armed with this information, consequences and other environmental stimuli can be manipulated to produce desired behavior change.

The most fundamental principle of behavior analysis is reinforcement. Thus, a great deal of the research and practice in applied behavior analysis has focused on the ways in which behaviors are developed and maintained through programmed or naturally occurring reinforcement contingencies. Indeed, strategies for identifying and delivering reinforcers to enhance performance and to shape improved repertoires of responding constitute a major emphasis throughout human service domains.

Operant psychology also provides a structural foundation for research and development pertinent to the antecedent and contextual features of the environment. Behavior is organized in accordance with the surrounding environment, and indeed, much learning accomplished by individuals can be seen as a process of developing discriminations and associations between environmental opportunities. A prominent subject of behavior analytic research and technology has been the mechanisms involved in arranging stimuli to facilitate instruction. Increasingly, a related focus has been on the influence and interactions of ecological and contextual stimuli (Wahler & Fox, 1981).

Although behavior analysis is not necessarily restricted to data that are conceptually predicted by a particular paradigm, the principles of operant psychology have represented the dominant conceptual system that has united research findings and suggested procedural advances. The technology of applied behavior analysis is fundamentally that of operant psychology.

Methodological Characteristics

An essential and salient feature of behavior analysis is its methodology. The methodological characteristics of a behavior analytic approach include operational definitions of relevant variables, strategies for measuring the occurrence of those variables, an insistence on reliability, and a vital collection of experimental designs that are used to validate identified phenomena and to build accumulations of conceptual and practical data. These methodological features are integral to the discipline of behavior analysis. They embody the empiricism, accountability, precision, and scientific advancement that define the orientation.

Consistent with the scientific method of generating information, behavior analysis adheres to several guidelines in observation. First, observations rely on operational definitions. Behaviors are defined in an objective manner and with reference to observable characteristics. Attributes that are not observable or measurable (such as intent) are excluded. Behavior analysts believe that operational definitions are critical for obtaining unambiguous and replicable findings. That is, behaviors should be defined so that multiple observers agree, through direct observation, on whether or not the behavior has occurred. This criterion allows individuals in different settings to study the same behavior and heightens the chances of establishing replicable principles of behavior.

Behavior analysts rely on quantifiable measures of behavioral change to assess the impact of environmental manipulations. Behaviors of interest can be evaluated along a variety of dimensions. For example, behaviors with short, discrete beginnings and endings lend themselves well to frequency counts. Others are better quantified by the duration of time during which they occur. Still others can be measured according to dimensions such as amplitude or intensity. Quantifying and recording behavior permits an objectivity in evaluating whether behavior changes over time or in response to a specific intervention.

Central to measurement in behavior analysis is reliability. Because direct observations are conducted by human observers, there exists the possibility of error. To help guard against error, interobserver agreement (or interobserver reliability) checks are conducted. These checks serve several purposes that are important for research and practical purposes. Agreement obtained across observers eliminates a potential source of variability and helps to eliminate biases that individual observers may introduce. Reliability also provides feedback as to whether a target behavior has been adequately defined.

One of the crucial components of behavior analytic methodology is the collection of *single-subject* (or *within-subject*) *experimental designs* (Hersen & Barlow, 1976). These designs allow experimental replication to occur by controlling the application of an independent variable on the behavior of an individual subject. Thus, there is no requirement for a large subject pool that is demanded by traditional group designs. Single-subject designs permit a focus on the individual case, and they can be used in virtually any circumstance in which one wishes to verify the effectiveness of an intervention. In this respect, it is important to note that a distinctive feature of behavior analysis, as well as its methodology, is that the uniqueness of the individual is consistently emphasized and respected. This characteristic has blended agreeably with special education and the idiosyncratic behaviors and circumstances that special education students frequently exhibit.

Dynamic Characteristics

The methodological features just described provide the groundwork for ongoing development and refinement of principles and procedures. In behavior analysis, the inherent association of analysis (methodology) and implementation delivers a potential for continuous improvement and refinement. As with other lines of applied science, the focus and products of behavior analysis are malleable. Data from a variety of sources can serve as an impetus for improvement. For example, consumer feedback can communicate dissatisfaction with the effectiveness or applicability of a procedure. Similarly, parametric analyses can provide data regarding the relative contributions

of procedural variations, and error analyses can illuminate sources of inadequacy in a procedure's application with an individual, a group of individuals, or in a defined set of circumstances. These types of circumstances serve as triggers to develop improvements.

As with any branch of science, the process of experimentation produces an ongoing process of change and, as a result, a continual evolution in the knowledge and technology that it generates. There are numerous illustrations within the brief history of applied behavior analysis. For example, the goal of producing generalization represented a conspicuous deficiency in many behavior-oriented programs for many years (Lovaas, Koegel, Stevens, & Long, 1973); however, focused research over two decades produced many pivotal findings and technical improvements (see Dunlap, 1993). Similarly, behavior analytic approaches to behavior management have been transformed extensively in a relatively brief period of time (Carr, Robinson, & Palumbo, 1990).

Some Issues of Relevance

Special education as an independent enterprise in the field of education is a rather recent development. Our changing societal values reflect a broader understanding and acceptance of human differences. The social commitment to individuals who learn in different ways and at different paces has been accompanied by the need to examine and modify traditional teaching strategies. There are several features of behavior analysis that are consistent with this philosophical emphasis in educating individuals with disabilities. These features will be discussed in the following section.

Emphasis on Individualization

Historically, systems of education have sought to educate the masses. Those who failed to learn with the masses were excluded. In recent history, schools have become increasingly inclusive. It is no longer acceptable practice to reject individuals from the public education system whose behavior or learning style differs from what is considered the norm. Recognition and acceptance of individual differences is reflected in special education legislation. Perhaps the most significant legislation affecting children in educational settings is Public Law 101-476 (formerly Public Law 94-142), the Individuals with Disabilities Education Act (currently due for reauthorization). This legislation requires that an Individualized Education Program (IEP) be developed for each child receiving special education services. Embedded within this legislation is the view that the needs of individuals with disabilities can be understood and met.

The relatively recent movement in favor of educational inclusion for children with special needs has required a reexamination of teaching practices. Inclusive systems of education hold that all individuals have the right to public education. As the axiom of inclusion has been embraced, it has also become clear that children with learning and behavioral challenges have special needs that are often idiosyncratic. To meet the educational needs of these children, they must be viewed as individuals. Behavior analysis, which focuses on the individual with respect to assessment, intervention, and evaluation, is strongly compatible with this ideology. Underlying the single-subject approach that characterizes behavior analysis is the recognition of individual differences, and embedded within this approach is a methodology to ensure that interventions result in behavior change for each and every individual. This approach is uniquely suited to meet diverse and specialized student needs.

The Importance of Empiricism

The empirical approach that typifies behavior analysis is consonant with the accountability demanded in the field of special education. In response to a history of poor care and inadequate

educational opportunities for children with disabilities, P.L. 101-476 also requires that children's educational and behavioral progress be documented. A student's current level of performance in academic areas (such as reading, math, communication, and so on) and nonacademic areas (e.g., daily living skills, mobility, prevocational-vocational skills, and so on) must be measured and documented. Specific goals and objectives that describe achievement that will be made in each of these areas must be written. Assessments must then be conducted after a prespecified period of time (generally one year) to ensure that goals have been met. At the root of behavior analysis is direct observation to document lawful relationships. Specifically, some type of measurement system is used to chronicle behavior change. This rigorous approach to documentation is consistent with the demands placed on special education to provide evidence that certain outcomes have been achieved.

Development of Replicable Instructional Practices

An additional, and equally important, purpose of empiricism and documentation is to verify that an instructional program or behavioral intervention actually results in improvements in an individual's behavior. To do so requires that procedures be specifically delineated and implemented in a consistent manner. When traditional strategies fail to help children learn or behave acceptably, teachers often implement a cornucopia of interventions. In the rush for effective interventions, it is frequently the case that strategies are not allotted a fair or thorough evaluation. At other times, an assembly of interventions may be implemented simultaneously, making it difficult to determine the effectiveness of any single approach. Behavior analysis lends a systematic and well-proven set of strategies for evaluating the effectiveness of an intervention.

A variety of educational practices and procedures derived from applied behavior analysis are prevalent in educational settings. For example, reinforcement procedures (such as point and token systems) were developed directly from principles of behavior analysis. Popular instructional practices (such as precision teaching and social skills packages), systematic prompting procedures, and task analyses are rooted in the concepts of applied behavior analysis. In fact, the prevalence of special techniques and broad strategies that are derived directly from behavior analysis is so pervasive that it would be virtually impossible to chronicle (Sulzer & Mayer, 1972).

Focus on Function over Form

Frequently, a focus of educational programming pertains to decreasing inappropriate behaviors of children and adolescents with disabilities. Often, inappropriate behaviors are the result of repeated failure at academic tasks or with social interactions. Sometimes the behaviors themselves are the reason for special needs identification. Regardless, changing these behaviors becomes an educational goal. In recent years, applied behavior analysis has shifted considerably in its approach to challenging behavior. Treatment failures and short-lived successes have taught us that meaningful and durable behavior change is dependent on an understanding of the conditions under which a behavior occurs and the variables maintaining that behavior. That is, behavior change should not be attempted in the absence of an assessment to identify functional relationships between an individual's behavior and events or conditions that are present in his or her environment (Foster-Johnson & Dunlap, 1993). This approach to challenging behavior has been termed *functional assessment* (Repp & Horner, in press).

Recent research conducted in classroom settings has shown promising outcomes with this approach. Legislation in several states now mandates that a functional analysis be conducted prior to implementing any behavior change program. The logic of this approach is to conduct assessments that indicate the function a particular behavior serves for an individual. Then, the results of the assessment can be used to develop interventions that are linked to the behavior's function. For example, if a boy displays aggression in a classroom, a functional assessment might indicate that the aggression occurs when the boy is asked to perform tasks. Further analyses might show that aggression occurs only during tasks that require ambulation, such as clearing materials from the floor of the classroom. The boy's teacher might recognize that the child's gait is unsteady and that the movements required to perform the activity are difficult for him. Thus, a logical and reasonable intervention linked to the assessment might be to request fewer tasks requiring ambulation and to teach the boy to ask for a break when the activity becomes excessively arduous.

This approach to improving student behavior has advanced behavior management in several ways. First, interventions based on individualized assessment data are more likely to promote the use of positive approaches. In the absence of an assessment-based understanding, inappropriately punitive procedures (such as time-out) are sometimes used as a default option. Such options have no relationship to the purpose of the behavior, and thus they have a limited likelihood of effectiveness and an increased chance of aggravation. Second, because such assessment-based approaches stress function over form, they are more likely to result in effective and durable interventions. Interventions can be developed that teach students functionally equivalent responses as alternatives to the problem behavior (Carr, 1988). In this way, enduring changes and developing competencies are more likely to be seen.

The development and advancement of functional assessment procedures in the field of behavior analysis blends well with reforms in the field of special education. Not only does this approach meet the requirements of new legislation, it also conforms to the intent of education. It is an endeavor with the goal of producing durable and meaningful changes in the lives of students (and all people) with disabilities.

Issues and Directions for Applied Behavioral Research

Although there is much evidence to attest to the current relevance of behavior analysis to special education, the future will bring a number of new challenges. In order to maintain relevance, behavior analysis must enhance its responsiveness to the developing requirements and changing contexts presented by the special education enterprise. Fortunately, the experimental nature of behavior analysis and its practical methodologies make it extraordinarily well suited to meet such challenges. In this section, we discuss some issues and directions that may be particularly important for applied behavior analysis if it is to demonstrate continued contributions in support of educational practice for students with special needs.

The Changing Contexts of Special Education: Social Demographics, Educational Reform, and Inclusion

A pervasive and general challenge facing applied behavior analysis has to do with the changing character of special education as it relates to widespread movements of educational reform and to the changing demographics of our society. Thus far, the contributions of behavior analysis to special education have been demonstrated predominantly in the specialized and structured settings that have distinguished special education classrooms. They have been demonstrated with favorable student-teacher ratios, and typically within a homogeneous set of expectations and cultural contexts. However, the context within which special education is defined and practiced is rapidly changing. These changes will present behavior analysts with a new set of challenges.

Although it is impossible to forecast all the social, cultural, and political influences that will affect special education in the coming decades, there are some trends that seem dominant and salient for this discussion. First, there is a strong reform movement in education that is creating decentralization, an emphasis on local autonomy and school-level authority, and an accompanying urgency to serve all students' educational needs at the level of neighborhood schools. Relatedly, a substantial effort has promoted educational (physical and social) inclusion as an integral framework for educating students, regardless of the student's disabilities. Proponents of full inclusion emphasize that social competence, friendships, and a tremendous variety of subtle proficiencies cannot be developed satisfactorily in segregated special education settings. Although there are controversies regarding the efficacy of these reformations (Kauffman & Hallahan, 1995), and the extent to which they should be implemented, it seems clear that the future will bring increasingly blurred distinctions between special and general education, and that integrated services will be a more dominant feature of educational practice nationwide.

There are also significant changes occurring with regard to the demographics and behavioral predilections of our schools' student bodies. In many areas of our country, there is a conspicuous infusion of minority cultures such that, in aggregate, students from minority backgrounds are representing the majority of the student population. The increasing diversity of student populations presents numerous challenges including multilingualism, different bases of information and approaches to the acquisition and processing of knowledge, and culturally disparate ethical and spiritual roots. At the same time, social and economic forces have led to an alarming increase in juvenile crime, substance abuse, violence, noncompliance, and general belligerence on school campuses. The problem of classroom management has exploded into a crisis of such magnitude that it is no longer feasible to refer all serious offenders to separate special education programs.

Although highly individualized and technical interventions will still be required for students with extreme support needs, there is a growing urgency to develop, demonstrate, and implement approaches that have broader applicability. Thus far, the predominant focus of applied behavior analysis has been the individual student; however, the blending of special and general education, as well as the growing proportions of students with special needs within general education, suggests that behavior analysis could contribute significantly if it developed its tools and technologies to address broader concerns.

Applied behavior analysis can emphasize the development and systematic evaluation of interventions that are designed to affect relevant performances of groups of students at the classroom level, or even the campus level. The flexible experimental methodologies of single-subject designs can be employed very well with the aggregate of larger units of behavior serving as dependent measures.

Another consideration that relates to decentralization and greater generality is that the interventions of applied behavior analysis will need to be implemented by a larger and less specialized group of agents. As greater numbers of students with special intellectual, emotional, and behavioral challenges occupy our general education classrooms in our local schools, their primary source support will come less frequently from distinctively trained providers. Thus, a challenge for behavior analysis will be to produce and promote strategies that are increasingly accessible and robust in their effectiveness.

It will also be essential that procedures be developed and analyzed within the contexts of inclusionary and neighborhood schools. To date, many behavioral interventions have been applied within separate classrooms and facilities, but there is no guarantee that such procedures would be applicable or desirable within situations that have very different demands and less favorable student-teacher ratios, and that are open to greater public scrutiny. The contextual relevance of behavioral procedures is an essential consideration for the continuing relevance of behavior analysis.

Research on Utilization

The extent to which products and perspectives of applied behavior analysis contribute to the practice of special education is an empirical question that should be a focus of applied behavioral inquiry. Indeed, some steps have been taken in this direction; however, those steps are arguably inadequate, especially given the rapidly changing contexts just described. As we suggested previously, the methods of behavior analysis are uniquely appropriate for investigating issues pertinent to utilization and for instituting technical adjustments designed to increase the magnitude and favor with which procedures are adopted. There may be little that behavior analytic researchers and educators can do to improve the relevance of their discipline more directly than to conduct direct analyses of procedural utilization and, at least, to include secondary analyses of utilization in ongoing programs of behavioral assessment, intervention, and dissemination.

The study of utilization, and of the variables that affect utilization, is a concern that is well suited to the methods of behavior analysis. For example, the extent to which a technique or strategy is used in a classroom or on a campus is a definable variable that can be measured without difficulty. Similarly, procedural components or contextual factors that might affect the procedure's use can usually be factored out in a time-series analysis of the procedure's application, and reversal or probe designs can be used to establish the internal validity of identified ingredients. In this manner, the utilization of a behavioral practice can be evaluated and enhanced, thus building relevance.

A significant addition to the field of applied behavior analysis, and to the pursuit of utilization, entered the field about twenty years ago when Wolf (1978) and others (for example, Kazdin, 1977) introduced the notion of assessing social validity. The assessment of social validity is intended to evaluate the acceptability or viability of an intervention (Schwartz & Baer, 1991), or to determine the extent to which consumers are satisfied with the goals, techniques, and outcomes of an intervention (Wolf, 1978). The assessment of social validity is typically accomplished through the administration of interviews or questionnaires. Schwartz and Baer (1991) point out that the process of social validation should consist ideally of two phases: (1) an accurate and representative sample of opinion and (2) procedural changes that are introduced in response to assessment data. This sequence appears to be a superb approach to the issue of relevance and utilization, and in fact there are some good examples of how this can improve the acceptability of interactions and the efficacy of interventions (Minkin et al., 1976). It can be argued that applied behavior analysis, and special education, would be well served if this two-phase model was employed even more frequently and assiduously when behavioral interventions are developed and disseminated. Indeed, interventions derived from any orientation would benefit from this type of systematic analysis and refinement.

There are many factors that behavior analysts need to ponder as they examine issues pertinent to utilization. Naturally, there is the issue of effectiveness. It is unlikely that teachers, administrators and other personnel will adopt a practice if it is not effective in achieving desired outcomes. Furthermore, even if the practice *is* effective, it is still unlikely to be employed if the level of benefit is unfavorably balanced with the degree of effort, inconvenience, and/or resources that are required for implementation. The extent to which behavioral procedures will be used is also determined by a broad set of "goodness-of-fit" variables (Albin, Lucyshyn, Horner, & Flannery, 1996; Bailey, 1987) that describe the congruence between available intervention options and characteristics of the intervention agents (for example, special educators), settings, and systems. Goodness-of-fit variables that are relevant to the use of behavioral procedures may include the skills and knowledge of the teachers, the extent to which the procedures can be accommodated within the established schedule and flow of the classroom routine, and the philosophical and cultural frameworks of all the key personnel. The procedures should also be compatible with the goals of the students, teachers, families, and administrators, and they should contribute to a positive feeling among those responsible. If procedures lead to stress and unpleasant conflicts, it is unlikely that they will be used, even if they produce anticipated changes in students' behavior. The point is that utilization is a function of multiple variables, and each of these variables is susceptible to systematic investigation. This topic should be an important and fruitful area for behavior analytic researchers who are interested in the application of their discipline to the education of students with special needs.

Measurement of Broader Dependent Variables and Meaningful Outcomes

A final issue that we wish to visit regarding the relevance of behavior analysis to special education pertains to measurement. It is axiomatic that behavioral approaches are defined by their measurement systems and that the range of behavioral applications is similarly delineated (Horner, 1991). As long as a behavior or an event in the environment can be observed and measured reliably, it is a proper subject for analysis and modification. However, if a phenomenon is illusive to consistent definition in empirical terms, then that phenomenon is considered to be outside the realm of systematic inquiry.

The devotion to reliable measurement is a crucial ingredient of behavior analysis and it embodies its essential, scientific authority. A corpus of replicable findings that accumulate toward deeper and more expansive knowledge cannot be produced without a foundation of interpretable and replicable systems of measurement. This is the indispensable core of behavior analysis. At the same time, however, the constraints that measurement impose on the domain of behavior analysis can be viewed as restricting its relevance to the concerns of human development and interaction. Consumers (such as special educators) can interpret the contributions of applied behavior analysis as relatively narrow or trivial if the discipline cannot illuminate broader and more holistic purposes.

The challenge of measurement is extremely complex, involving difficult issues having to do with the integrity of science and the relationship of science to application. This has been an implicit dilemma and tension within applied behavior analysis for many years (Hayes, Rincover, & Solnick, 1980). The science of applied behavior analysis cannot be compromised by imprecise measures, yet the quest for optimal practice cannot be blinded by excessive methodological inhibitions. The relevance of behavior analysis to special education involves science and application. From both perspectives, there are important directions that behavior analysis can embrace in an effort to extend its value to the world of special education.

One concern of practitioners and advocates is that evaluative criteria used to judge interventions be broadened to encompass more meaningful outcomes (Meyer & Evans, 1993a, 1993b). In many cases, and certainly when large-scale efforts are involved, it is no longer sufficient to rely on indices of single, precisely defined responses or on scores from standardized tests. Consumers are seeking more comprehensive indications of lifestyle effects (Horner, 1991), including desired changes in behavior patterns, scholastic achievement, classroom placement, attitudes, relationships, school- and community-based activities, and other goals. Special education is obliged to become accountable for broader outcomes and to broader audiences. Therefore, the goals it embraces, and the measurement procedures that accompany those goals, must reflect this elevated level of accountability.

Many of the important objectives of special education are illusive to the necessary precision of operational definitions and reliable measurement. Teachers want their students to develop an enhanced "self-concept"; they attempt to develop "rapport" with students who are difficult to "connect" with; they want to generate academic "interests"; they seek to reduce "anxiety" in troubled students; and they wish that their alienated students would acquire genuine "friendships." An increasing number of educators regard the development of "relationships" as a critically important context and outcome in a student's school experience (Dunlap, 1996). All of these targets, however, are difficult to operationalize and measure, and therefore they have eluded the systematic attention of behavior analysts. Instead, behavioral research (and practice) has redefined and/or approximated these objectives by referring to observable components and manifestations (for example, social interactions, task engagement) of these more general constructs. This is altogether appropriate from a functionalist perspective, and it is an approach that has generated considerable advances; however, the microanalytic aspects of this tactic can appear tangential or evasive to educators concerned with more exhaustive aims.

The relevance to special education will be heightened if behavior analysis can further develop its strong legacy of measurement to incorporate more disparate phenomena that are central to special education concerns. There are numerous ways to approach this issue. Social validation (Schwartz & Baer, 1991; Wolf, 1978) of intervention goals and results provides one avenue. Other approaches might be to incorporate broader measures of ecological context (Greenwood & Carta, 1987) and distal events (Wahler & Fox, 1981) and to include assessment strategies and instruments commonly associated with other traditions (Walker & Severson, 1990). Regardless of how it is handled, the point we wish to make is that measurement is central to the definition and perception of applied behavior analysis, and the further that measures can extend the realm of behavior analysis into concordance with the dominant objectives of special education, the more relevant will be the connection.

Conclusion

Applied behavior analysis has a prosperous history of important contributions to special education. It has presented a set of operational principles and philosophical assumptions, a dynamic methodology that is uniquely designed to advance knowledge and practice, and a technological collection of procedures for providing instruction and changing student behaviors. The greatest strength of applied behavior analysis is that its principles and methodologies allow and encourage continuous refinement and enhancement of the available technology. Because of this regenerative quality, applied behavior analysis would seem to have the capacity to maintain a position of relevant association with special education for the foreseeable future.

In this chapter, we have cited some directions we believe will be most productive for applied behavior analysis to pursue if it is to heighten its contributions to special education. In particular, we have discussed issues relating to the changing context of education and school reform, the changing demands of an increasingly diverse student body, the need to study utilization of behavioral procedures, and the importance of measurement schemes in the application of behavioral perspectives and techniques. There are many emphases that we have not included, such as conceptual investigations into basic learning processes, primarily because their relevance was judged to be less immediate. However, we wish to acknowledge that the discipline of applied behavior analysis is multifaceted and that many of its various endeavors have products to contribute. The present discussion has only skimmed the interrelationships of behavior analysis and special education.

References

Albin, R. W., Lucyshyn, J. M., Horner, R. H., & Flannery, K. B. (1996). Contextual fit for behavioral support plans: A model for "goodness of fit." In L. K. Koegel, R. L. Koegel, & G. Dunlap, (Eds.). *Positive behavioral support: Including people with difficult behavior in the community* (pp. 81–98). Baltimore: Paul H. Brookes.

Baer, D. M., Wolf, M. M., & Risley, T. R. (1968). Some current dimensions of applied behavior analysis. *Journal of Applied Behavior Analysis, 1*, 91–97.

Baer, D. M., Wolf, M. M., & Risley, T. R. (1987). Some still-current dimensions of applied behavior analysis. *Journal of Applied Behavior Analysis, 20*, 313–327.

Bailey, D. B. (1987). Collaborative goal setting with families: Resolving differences in values and priorities for services. *Topics in Early Childhood Special Education, 7*, 59–71.

Carr, E. G. (1988). Functional equivalence as a mechanism of response generalization. In R. H. Horner, G. Dunlap, & R. L. Koegel (Eds.), *Generalization and Maintenance: Lifestyle Changes in Applied Settings* (pp. 221–241). Baltimore: Paul H. Brookes.

Carr, E. G., Robinson, S., & Palumbo, L. W. (1990). The wrong issue: Aversive versus nonaversive treatment. The right issue: Functional versus nonfunctional treatment. In A. C. Repp & N. Singh (Eds.), *Perspectives on the use of nonaversive interventions for persons with developmental disabilities* (pp. 361–379). DeKalb, IL: Sycamore.

Cooper, J. C., Heron, T. E., & Heward, W. L. (1987). *Applied behavior analysis*. Columbus, OH: Charles E. Merrill.

Dunlap, G. (1993). Promoting generalization: Current status and functional considerations. In R. Van Houten & S. Axelrod (Eds.), *Effective behavioral treatment: Issues and implementation* (pp. 269–296). New York: Plenum.

Dunlap, G. (1996). Discussion of social inclusion. In L K. Koegel, R. L. Koegel, & G. Dunlap (Eds.), *Positive behavioral support: Including people with difficult behavior in the community* (pp. 372–377). Baltimore, MD: Paul H. Brookes.

Ferster, C. B., Culbertson, S., & Boren, M. C. P. (1975). *Behavior principles* (2d ed.). Englewood Cliffs, NJ: Prentice-Hall.

Foster-Johnson, L., & Dunlap, G. (1993). Using functional assessment to develop effective, individualized interventions. *Teaching Exceptional Children, 25*, 44–50.

Greenwood, C. R., & Carta, J. J. (1987). An ecobehavioral analysis of instruction within special education. *Focus on Exceptional Children, 19*, 1–12.

Hayes, S. C., Rincover, A., & Solnick, J. V. (1980). The technical drift of applied behavior analysis. *Journal of Applied Behavior Analysis, 13*, 275–286.

Hersen, M., & Barlow, D. H. (1976). *Single case experimental designs*. New York: Pergamon Press.

Horner, R. H. (1991). The future of applied behavior analysis for people with severe disabilities: Commentary 1. In L. H. Meyer, C. Peck, & L. Brown (Eds.), *Critical issues in the lives of people with severe disabilities* (pp. 607–611). Baltimore: Paul H. Brookes.

Kauffman, J. M., & Hallahan, D. P. (Eds.) (1995). *The illusion of full inclusion: A comprehensive critique of a current special education bandwagon*. Austin, TX: Pro-Ed.

Kazdin, A. E. (1977). Assessing the clinical or applied importance of behavior change through social validation. *Behavior Modification, 1*, 427–452.

Lovaas, O. I., Koegel., R. L., Stevens, J. Q., & Long, J. S. (1973). Some generalization and follow-up measures on autistic children in behavior therapy. *Journal of Applied Behavior Analysis, 6*, 131–166.

Meyer, L. H., & Evans, I. M. (1993a). Meaningful outcomes in behavioral intervention: Evaluating positive approaches to the remediation of challenging behaviors. In J. Reichle & D. P. Wacker (Eds.), *Communicative approaches to the management of challenging behavior* (pp. 407–428). Baltimore: Paul H. Brookes.

Meyer, L. H., & Evans, I. M. (1993b). Science and practice in behavioral intervention: Meaningful outcomes, research validity, and usable knowledge. *Journal of the Association for Persons with Severe Handicaps, 18*, 224–234.

Minkin, N., Braukman, C. J., Minkin, B. L., Timbers, G., Timbers, B. J., Fixsen, D. L., Phillips, E. L., & Wolf, M. M. (1976). The social validation and training of conversational skills. *Journal of Applied Behavior Analysis, 9*, 127–139.

Paul, J. L., Rosselli, H., & Evans, D. (Eds.). (1995). *Integrating school restructuring and special education reform*. New York: Harcourt Brace Jovanovich.

Repp, A. C. & Horner, R. H. (Eds.). (in press). *Functional analysis of problem behavior: From effective assessment to effective support*. Pacific Grove, CA: Brooks/Cole.

Schwartz, I. S., & Baer, D. M. (1991). Social validity assessments: Is current practice state of the art? *Journal of Applied Behavior Analysis, 24*, 189–204.

Sulzer, B., & Mayer, G. R. (1972). *Behavior modification procedures for school personnel*. Hinsdale, IL: Dryden Press.

Turnbull, A., & Turnbull, H. R. (1990). A tale about lifestyle change: Comments on "Toward a technology of 'nonaversive' behavioral support." *Journal of the Association for Persons with Severe Handicaps, 15*, 142–144.

Wahler, R. G., & Fox, J. J. (1981). Setting events in applied behavior analysis: Toward a conceptual and methodological expansion. *Journal of Applied Behavior Analysis, 14*, 327–338.

Walker, H. M., & Severson, H. H. (1990). *Systematic screening for behavior disorders user's guide and administration manual*. Longmont, CO: Sopris West.

Wolf, M. M. (1978). Social validity: The case for subjective measurement, or how behavior analysis is finding its heart. *Journal of Applied Behavior Analysis, 11*, 203–214.

CHAPTER 14

Postmodernism, Narrative, and Hope in Special Education

SCOT DANFORTH
University of Missouri–St. Louis

Stories and Hope in Special Education

The idea that liberal societies are bound together by philosophical beliefs seems to me ludicrous. What binds societies together are common vocabularies and common hopes. The vocabularies are, typically, parasitic on the hopes—in the sense that the principal function of the vocabularies is to tell stories about the future outcomes which compensate for present sacrifices. . . . To retain social hope, members of such a society need to be able to tell themselves a story about how things get better, and see no insuperable obstacles to this story's coming true. (Rorty, 1989, p. 86)

If nothing else, a postmodern philosophy of special education would assert that our current governing story, the guiding and dominating scheme of modern social science, no longer provides a valuable basis for hope and unity in the struggle to educate children described as "disabled." Postmodernists typically eschew any such guiding story as deceptive and totalizing, as not providing universal or useful facts but a harmful hegemony arbitrarily foisting some knowledges and vocabularies over others of lesser sociocultural power. As a result, one postmodern goal is to encourage a professional shift from the primary explanatory story of modern social science to a pluralistic, conversational arena in which a multitude of smaller, situated stories may be told by the diversity of participants in special education (Gergen, 1991, 1994; Rosenau, 1992). We might say that the modernist's failed goal of finding objective truth is replaced by the postmodernist's attention to moral and political tasks of supporting human freedom and community.

Quite simply, the modern social science story— "grand narrative" (Gergen, 1991) or "metanarrative" (Lyotard, 1984)—has held that the utilization of specific, refined modes of human rationality (objectivity, neutrality, method, and so on) allows for independent reality to be mentally understood and symbolically and linguistically represented in text. Truth is accessible to those professionals trained in modern social science techniques. This social science progressively outlines "what is the case" and "the actuality of the matter"—the "objective facts" that may be passed along to well-trained practitioners in the form of concepts, practices, instruments, and techniques. A special education armed with such a host of "objective facts" or "truths" has been assumed to be a hopeful force; a knowledgeable group that may tackle difficult problems of learning, development, and social interaction.

Postmodern special educators (see Chapter 2; Danforth, Rhodes, & Smith, 1995; Duplass & Smith, 1995; Sailor & Skrtic, 1995; Skrtic, 1991) contend that the hope of educating and supporting children considered disabled can no longer be fueled and conceptualized through the modern social science story, that "insuperable obstacles to this story's coming true" have indeed arisen. As the "facts" produced by special education research have been conceived as useful tools to be carried by working practitioners, so those tools have turned out to be instrumental oddities and institutional cruelties in specific, daily realization. Teachers implement (or imitate) "best practices" only to find themselves attempting to technically adjust complex human and social webs with crude sledgehammers and dull butter knives. These initially hopeful teachers may have little recourse but to either blame themselves for misusing appropriate tools or blame their students for being too "disabled" to benefit from the correct prescription.

Two specific forms of stories deserve our attention at this point in the analysis. First, I have alluded to the "metanarrative" or overriding story of modernism as a dominating force in special education. I will briefly address the crumbling of the modernist foundational story, what Skrtic (1991) describes as the "crisis in modern knowledge" (p. 3), hoping not to bore the reader with well-worn arguments about paradigms and epistemology. This will lead to my explication of one postmodern epistemological and practical alternative based on the work of historian Carl Becker.

Following the Becker discussion, I will explore the second form of dominant special education narrative, what is perhaps best described as a series of similar stories that have grown out of the modern social science and continue as assumed universal tales of human capacity and character. These narratives are the disability stories, the standard models, labels, conditions, or categories that allow special educators to easily "understand" a child's identity, learning, and needs through the contours and boundaries of a deficit vocabulary.

If I am able to convince you of the questionable truthfulness and politics of both the grand narrative and the disability stories, you will then join me in wondering what we are to do without universal truth. Are there no true stories? If not, of what value are fictional narratives? I will borrow Salman Rushdie's (1991) adventurous novel *Haroun and the Sea of Stories* as a useful text for our exploration of the postmodern question, "What's the use of stories that aren't even true?" (Rushdie, 1991, p. 20).

The Trouble with Truth

A conceptual shift, "tectonic" in its implications has taken place. We ground things, now, on a moving earth. There is no longer a place of overview (mountaintop) from which to map human ways of life, no Archimidean point from which to represent the world. (Clifford, 1986, p. 22)

To university special educators, it may seem that truth, or at least the academic production of researched truth, has recently weathered a difficult storm. The relativists, constructivists, and qualitativists have been held off and subdued into accepting more conforming (or at least more quiet) positions within the fold. While I would contend that such a comfortable stance ignores developments in academic circles for much of this century, there exists ample evidence to support this view within the narrow boundaries of special education writing. The so-called "paradigm dialogue" (Guba, 1990) of the 1970s and 1980s seems to have subsided, allowing experimental and behavioral psychology to continue as the cornerstones of special education research.

Even efforts to expand special education beyond the borders of rigid positivism tend to stumble and regress to the modernist status quo. In a recent issue of *Remedial and Special Education* (May 1995), a promising and intriguing set of papers (see especially Anderson & Barrera, 1995; McPhail, 1995; Wanswart, 1995) attempted this very expansionist goal. The lead article (Reid, Robinson, & Bunsen, 1995) stands as a pyrrhic exemplar of the constrained conservativism that seems dominant in the field, a tentative sort of philosophical travel that somehow only brings one back to the modernism one had hoped to leave behind (see Howe, 1985). After providing brief and clear descriptions of critical theory, postmodern philosophy, and interpretive research, Reid and associates (1995) spend the remainder of their paper explaining how qualitative research can be restricted to "the Science Tradition" through adherence to traditional standards of objectivity, validity, and reliability. They give a glimpse of the postmodern, only to shoo us back into the secure educational psychology textbook special educators know all too well.

Yet, if my university special education colleagues and I wander dangerously across our doorstep to sample life at the academy, we may find epistemological crisis beyond mere squabblings over quantitative and qualitative methods, extending to powerful doubts concerning the project of finding and explaining truth itself. A number of movements, described as postmodern or poststructuralist, have struck at the very core of modern academic disciplines, contesting and undermining the underlying assumption that an objective world is knowable and may be established through the workings of a neutral, rational science. Gergen (1991), in his analysis of the academic upheaval, states:

> Most of the cherished beliefs that undergird the traditional goals of research and teaching are in eclipse. Some consider the demise of traditional assumptions to be an event little short of catastrophe, to part with the longstanding ideals of truth and understanding is to invite chaos, first in the academic

world and then in society generally. Others feel an innervating sense that history is at a turning point, that a new and exciting era is in the making. (p. 82)

Skrtic (1991) notes that special education is among a group of professions based in modern social science that have suffered a crisis of legitimacy since the 1960s. This crisis goes hand in hand with the dramatic critique of academic social sciences following Kuhn's (1962) hermeneutic analysis of the paradigmatic nature of science. A paradigm is a worldview, an assumed way of seeing, perceiving, and speaking that allows one to order experience into rational and livable explanations. Typically, an individual has little or no awareness of the paradigm she or he is utilizing to construct experience, because that paradigm melds finely with the experience itself. Only through intense sociological, political, and philosophical critique have various dominant paradigms of modernism been outlined (Anderson & Barrera, 1995; Skrtic, 1991).

Postmodernists are often refuted to be persons who claim to hold a "better" paradigm, a new process holier than the modern, mechanistic way of constructing meaning, a more "truthful" outline for delineating "what the case is." More accurately, we should understand postmodernism as nonfoundational, maintaining that no means of describing reality holds universal privilege over alternatives. All descriptions are viewed as provisional, arising from specific subject positions and reflecting not merely "the truth of the matter" but also the subjectivity of the individual, the physical and sociocultural contexts, the language community of the speaker, and the historical situation in which the representation occurs.

If one wanted to construct a "true" or "best" model of reality through which hypotheses would be tested and refined, as the modern project of escaping subjectivity and context has sought, one would perhaps set down rigorous criteria for the human evaluation of experience. Such a paradigm and corresponding process would be said to turn out the best knowledge available. A postmodern response claims that the criteria themselves assume the truthfulness of specific facts before the inquiry even begins—facts about causality, knowledge, history, language, and human ability. In this way, the paradigm concept allows us to understand that no knowledge may be produced, supported, or "discovered" without other knowledge (unspoken facts about reality and truth) being quietly assumed and concealed within the processes of knowing and representing.

Since postmodernists find the hegemony of a single paradigm and vocabulary of knowledge to be politically disturbing, one goal is pluralization. Knowledge claiming universal or generalizable status is reduced to the common status of subjective-contextual construction, just one situated voice among the many. On the other end of the power spectrum, nonscientific descriptions of "how it looks from here" (most often the words of students, parents, and teachers) are accorded new respect and practical legitimacy in educational dialogues (Danforth, 1995; Duplass & Smith, 1995).

Such a reorganization of the words and expressed knowledges of various actors within educational activities blurs the lines between professional and nonprofessional, between educator and citizen. Perhaps all implicated and invested persons may be invited to be "educators"—active and respected and diverse contributors to the daily business of schools. As educators (from our positions of relative power and control), we might organize and initiate more situations in which students, parents, and others are allowed roles of knowledge, ability, and value.

Every Person an Educator

One postmodern alternative with implications for special education, written by historian Carl Becker (1932/1968) long before the epistemological hubbub of recent decades, points to a gradual, back-burner simmering of postmodern concepts during what is usually called the modern era.

Becker, then-president of the American Historical Association, gave an address called "Everyman His Own Historian," claiming that history is not merely the hallowed realm of lettered and learned men but that the average "Everyman" (or Everyperson) makes and utilizes historical knowledge each day in the most mundane of tasks and situations. Becker contests the privileged subject position from which professional historians offered supposedly truthful accounts. He proposes a pragmatist argument that persons construct knowledge not in correspondence to some metaphysical truth but for limited human purposes. Unable to rise above the planet to conceptualize or represent through a supreme logarithm, each knower is humbled to producing truths within the constraints of immediate reasons and realities. In this way, Becker tells of the similar knowledge-making processes of pedestrian/citizen and scientific/historian.

Weaving the tale of Mr. Everyman sorting through the details and records necessary to pay his coal bill (a knowledge and a task situated for us in an era gone by), Becker explains how Mr. Everyman gathers evidence and pieces together an explanation necessary to his immediate situation. Mr. Everyman seeks and selects facts that are both relevant to his purpose and acceptable within the social limitations prescribed by his sociocultural community. He has images and vocabulary of both a task and a social group, each contributing to a normative grounding for his selection and utilization of facts.

Like many current postmodernists, Becker attends to the role of language in the making of facts. Historical facts, like educational facts, are as malleable and ambiguous as the words that project them. Becker (1932/1968) neatly explains:

> However "hard" or "cold" they may be, historical facts are after all not material substances which, like

bricks or scantlings, possess definite shape and clear, persistent outline. To set forth historical facts is not comparable to dumping a barrow of bricks. A brick retains its form and pressure wherever placed; but the form and substance of historical facts, having a negotiable existence only in literary discourse, vary with the words employed to convey them. (p. 19)

Scientist and coal-consumer alike elicit factuality from experience and evidence, neither of them understanding the implications or the rational basis for those tales beyond the realm of personal subject position, beyond what that individual comprehends, imagines, and assumes to be pertinent and useful in that multidimensional living context.

Since the value of knowledge products—facts, truths, supported hypotheses—remains uncertain and negotiable within discourse, postmodernists set aside the goal of privileging factual products in favor of the goal of arranging pluralistic, inclusive dialogue. Perhaps, with the reduction of the authority of the voices of scientific vocabulary, a more egalitarian roundtable of educational discussion may be devised within specific contexts (Danforth, 1995; see also Skrtic, 1991, on adhocracy).

If Everyman may be a historian, might not every person involved in education be an educator? By this, I mean that all persons and their many vocabularies, reasonings, knowledges, and cultural backgrounds might be accorded more equal and respectful footing in the many educational conversations (see Chapters 8 and 9). To do so, we may redefine *educator* in an ironically deprofessionalized manner, making space for parents, students, teachers, paraprofessionals, administrators, and invested others to participate in an ongoing, posthierarchical conversation. Such a conversation, fraught with the problems, conflicts, and hopes of any important discussion, would produce not universal truths but local truths, not generalizable facts but situated negotiations. A community

struggles to make and use the knowledge necessary for its specific purposes. As Rorty (1989) writes;

> *A liberal society is one which is content to call "true" whatever the upshot of such encounters* (openminded discussions) *turns out to be.* [italics original] (p. 52)

If the making of truths is a communal and intentional activity, perhaps we can begin to arrange for more respectful and inclusive forms of truth-constructing communities.

Currently, the creation of such posthierarchical communities is greatly limited by the dominance of the grand narrative of modernism and the related disability stories. The grand narrative elevates the words and logics of modernist social scientists to a position above other speakers. The disability stories simultaneously submerge the knowledges of special education students and their families, creating an asymmetrical conversational plane.

Disability Stories

Growing from the modern social science grand narrative like limbs from a tree are the disability stories, our common way of describing and devaluing children in terms of a duality of normality and abnormality. These stories are firmly ensconced in federal and state laws, university research, teacher education programs, and school district placement procedures. They are perhaps the most dominating form of modern special education knowledge, pervading the talk of special education teachers in explanations of daily classroom experiences to ourselves, our colleagues, and our students. The reasons explaining much of what happens in a given classroom may be quickly gathered and applied from the well-known constructs of "behavior disorder," "learning disability," and so on.

If the normality/abnormality distinction were merely a bothersome side effect or nagging corollary element within special education activity, we might ignore it as a necessary evil. We could say, "It is really too bad that we have to call some children abnormal." Or we might work to cleanse our programs of such a nagging negative, working like a vacuum cleaner removing unwanted dust. However, if the normality/abnormality register and the corresponding disability stories are described as central to our history, character, and purpose as professionals, then we have a problem of a more dramatic and haunting nature. A look at the history of psychology, often held to be the parent field of special education (Skrtic, 1991), may yield some insight.

In his study of the development of psychology as a scientific discipline during the 19th and early 20th centuries, Gross (1987) concludes that the very existence of the field depended on a psychology's usefulness as a tool of social administration and control. At the bottom of this political utilization was a uniting of two scales of normativity—one statistical and one sociopolitical, one "objective" and scientific and one politically constructed and driven.

The first was the bell curve and the assumed mathematics of a statistical normativity of the population. This foundation provided scientific legitimacy for the field, allowing psychology to become a form of human physics, an algebra of individual and social living. Thus, psychology established itself as a "real" science not so much through focusing on the mind, the psyche, or the individual, but through derivation from the statistical norms of variability.

The bell curve rests as an empty template, ready to variegate qualities and essences along a scale of normality/abnormality. Yet it lacks criteria of moral evaluation. In and of itself, it contains no ability to evaluate, to outline and promote standards of what is normal and what is abnormal, of what is better and what is worse. For guidance and standards of abnormality, psychology accepted definitions proscribed "in terms of a norm of functioning specified by particular social apparatuses. . . . It was the school, the courts, the police, and the army which provided the psychology of the individual with those *whom it would have to be able to construe as abnormal* " (Gross, 1987, p. 229, italics original).

Psychology combined two forces of assigning abnormality—the trusted mathematical structure of statistical variation and the socially produced populations of dropouts, deviants, criminals, and unemployed as identified by various institutions of governmental administration. To be abnormal meant to not "fit in" among the expectations and requirements of major institutions of the modern state.

If we view special education as a form of psychology introjected into the school for the similar purpose of dealing with those who do not seem to fit in, we can see our disability stories as narratives of social control. We often tell ourselves that such stories of disability are necessary to ensure that children receive services within bureaucratic systems. Yet even this story only further supports the notion that disability itself serves as a means to effectively administer and contain the educational lives of specific students who do not learn or behave as schools expect and demand. The widely held belief that these stories reflect "objective reality" contributes to the continuation of systems of social control.

Yet, if one were to take a postmodern stance and question the role of narrative, language, and mathematics as neutral, truth-bearing vehicles, one stumbles upon the perhaps empty realization that there may be no unbiased accounts, no "true" stories. That does not mean that "untrue" stories have no value to educators. Ironically, we may find that hearing and telling stories without an evaluative criterion of fact/fiction—specific, not-so-grand narratives creating meaning and identity for individuals and communities—may be the most hopeful development of all.

Untrue Stories: Rushdie's Postmodernism

In *Haroun and the Sea of Stories* (1991), noted author Salman Rushdie crafts an Arabian Nights tale for the postmodern era, bringing his characters to confront the irony of living a life full of crucial meanings that may not even be true. Rushdie dances playfully among a variety of current, international themes: freedom of speech, the reality of appearance and appearance as reality, multiculturalism, the meeting of Eastern and Western cultures, the dangers of fascism, and the hopeful power of democratic dialogue. Perhaps, above all, he makes a storied case for the need to not allow any single evaluative criterion to squelch out the voices that do not satisfy that criterion. To do so is to end discussion and invite silence. To Rushdie, this silence is equivalent to life without meaning. It is the end.

I'll note briefly, before I move on to discuss Rushdie's work in relation to various aspects of postmodernism, that it may seem odd that a special education professor produce scholarship imitative of literary studies. Writing in many academic fields, including anthropology (Rosaldo, 1993) and philosophy (Rorty, 1989), has begun to look more like literary theory as scholars view academic writing as description and redescription, as texts about texts about texts. With the uncertain relationship of any single text to an "objective reality," scholars are tending to reflect and inquire among the many textual accounts of human experience. Indeed, the very reasons for taking this approach are addressed in this section as I question the utility of stories that claim no truth value.

"What's the point of it? What's the use of stories that aren't even true?" Haroun shouted at his father, Rashid, the storyteller. The boy had phrased a question that ignites an adventure, a question that

brings about a story that demonstrates how useful such tales can be.

Haroun's mother had run off with their neighbor, boring, story-despising Mr. Sengupta, leaving Haroun and his father, Rashid, heartbroken. Soon thereafter, Rashid lost his ability to tell stories, the glorious, made-up stories that had always brought audiences to laugh, cry, and imagine. His supply of Story Water from the source of all the stories, the Ocean of the Streams of Story, had been cut off.

Haroun decided to somehow save his father's storytelling, to restore the Story Water, leading Haroun and Rashid into a wondrous, heroic adventure to the odd but jovial Land of Gup and the dark Land of Chup. The evil Khattam-Shud (Hindustani word meaning "completely finished," "over and done with") was gradually poisoning the Ocean of the Streams of Story, dulling the multicolored riverlets of story into cold gray, bringing silence to all. Haroun and Rashid join the people of Gup (Hindustani word meaning "gossip," "fib," or "nonsense") to battle Khattam-Shud and his dark warriors, the members of the Union of Zipped Lips, the Chupwalas (Hindustani word meaning "quiet fellows").

In a silly and serious tale that far exceeds my abilities to summarize, Khattam-Shud was finally defeated, and the Ocean of the Streams of Story restored to health. Dialogue and imagination triumph over silence and singlemindedness.

Pluralistic Conversation as Democratic Dialogue

As the Gup military, led by General Kitab and Prince Bolo, depart across the ocean to engage the Chupwala enemy, an odd debate breaks out among the troops. The Gups have two military goal options: to save the Ocean of the Streams of Story or to rescue Prince Bolo's betrothed, Princess Batcheat. Unlike most armed forces in which command decisions are made at the top and passed down through an obedient hierarchy, this military pauses to fully and intensely debate the goal of their mission. Standardized efficiency was sacrificed for the sake of participatory democracy.

> Haroun noticed that old General Kitab himself, mounted on a winged mechanical bird very like Bolo's, was flitting from Barge-Bird to Barge-Bird to keep in touch with the various discussions; and such was the freedom allowed to the Pages (soldiers) and the other citizens of Gup, that the old General seemed perfectly happy to listen to these tirades of insults and insubordination without batting an eyelid. In fact, it looked to Haroun as if the General was on many occasions actually provoking such disputes, and then joining in with enthusiastic glee, sometimes taking one side, and at other times (just for fun) expressing the opposite point of view. (Rushdie, 1991, p. 119)

Unlike the modern leader who wants a community's actions conforming to his words—effectively carrying out policy—the old General values each perspective, each situated interpretation of the issue. He not only takes joy in hearing these specific voices, but he revels in stretching himself beyond his own limited subjectivity to inhabit and dramatize other subject positions. His wisdom is not singular and fixed, not "principled" as we might say, but facile, fluid, and multifaceted.

Later, as the Gup army meets the enemy, Rushdie (1991) notes the benefits of their prebattle debate.

> The Pages of Gup, now that they had talked through everything so fully, fought hard, remained united, supported each other when required to do so, and in general looked like a force with a common purpose. All those arguments and debates, all that openness, had created powerful bonds of fellowship between them. (pp. 184–185)

The common ground and social unity was constructed in a polyvocal, open dialogue in which hi-

erarchy was set aside and the participation of all was invited and respected. The soldiers joined, not through an allegiance to a common truth or common philosophical principle, but through a process of democratic conversation.

At the end of the battle, when the Land of Gup has defeated the Land of Chup, the victory is not one in which one land gains dominion over another. Instead, it is the end of a silence as Chup Cultmaster Khattam-Shud is dethroned: "A great victory has been won. . . . A dialogue has been opened . . ." (Rushdie, 1991, p. 193).

Laminations and the Thing-in-Itself

The word *lamination* has gained favor among postmodern philosophers and educators for the purpose of expressing the representation of reality as a social, linguistic process of symbolic layering. From this way of talking, each description, explanation, or theory is an additional perspective in a multihued conversation. This understanding differs from the modernist concept of textual and oral representation as an illumination of otherwise hidden essences, a fairly direct transfer of deep factual matter from human living to language by means of observation, reason, and objectivity. For the modernist, the researcher's or professional's language carries the truth as it has been observed or measured. The postmodernist, in contrast, hears many voices chiming in sometimes conflicting, sometimes agreeing, and always situated portrayals of "the way it is." Each voice makes a contribution to the social world, layering the many accounts in a scrambled and uncertain patchwork. The postmodernist claims that it is "possible to juggle several descriptions of the same event (or child) without asking which one is right" (Rorty, 1989, p. 39).

Within educational discourse—written or conversational, formal or informal, university-based or school-based—a "lamination" may be viewed as a single version of the truth, a depiction of reality, a representation utilizing cultural symbols of language. It may come from any source and for any purpose. Each lamination is put forth among many, adding to a moving social hodgepodge of descriptions and redescriptions concerning the subject matter.

One of the most obvious examples of this multilayered collage of laminations is the daily describing, explaining, and storying about the individual child. *Who is this child really?* wonder the modernist professionals: the psychometrician, the researcher, and the teacher. To fasten upon the child's real abilities, intelligence, emotional constitution, and personality is to prepare a solid foundation from which to take action. It is to deal with the objectively real world, a valued activity among modernist educators.

In doing so, the modernist tries to produce a telling that accurately represents the essence of the object of focus, what Gergen (1991) calls "the Thing-in-Itself." Quantitative and qualitative research methodologists have long struggled to somehow capture the Thing-in-Itself, providing words or numbers to present a symbolized reproduction of what is intrinsic to the Thing, seeking a clarified representation lacking all nonfactual elements. The goal has been to pare away the intrusive, non-Thing aspects, leaving the Thing-in-Itself resting in clear symbolization on the textual page. As Rorty (1989) explains, the modernist goal has been to produce "The One Right Description" (p. 40) of a given phenomenon or situation. Modernism tries to capture the essence of the matter, the Thing-in-Itself. This essence is translated into linguistic symbols (words, numbers, and so on) as the best possible approximation, the One Right Description.

We can see that the modernist version of a "lamination" is a description that claims to illuminate precisely what the case is, an ostensibly transparent representation that allows a clear mental access to the qualities and characteristics of the Thing-in-Itself that rests in the background.

Returning again to our tale of Haroun and Rashid, we find Salman Rushdie at serious play, bringing the term *lamination* to life in a physical sense as a metaphor for the deceptive power of a single version of reality. The modernist's goal of the transparent representation is literally tried on for size in this jovial critique.

As the tale moves toward a triumphant climax, Haroun and his father, Rashid, join the Guppee armada to rush across the water to save the captured Princess Batcheat and the Ocean of Stories. As they zoom across the watertop toward the enemy, the father and son chillingly realize that they are wearing only the meager nightshirts they had worn to bed.

> "How stupid we were to not dress more sensibly!" Rashid lamented. "In these nightshirts, we'll freeze solid in a few hours."
>
> "Fortunately," said the Water Genie, "I brought along a supply of Laminations . . ."
>
> . . . Laminations turned out to be thin, transparent garments as shiny as dragonfly wings. Haroun and Rashid pulled the long shirts of this material over their nightshirts, and drew on the long leggings, too. To their amazement the Laminations stuck so tightly to their nightshirts and legs that they seemed to have vanished altogether. All Haroun could make out was a faint gleamy sheen on his clothes and skin that hadn't been their before.
>
> "You won't feel the cold now," Iff promised.
>
> (Rushdie, 1991, p. 116)

Rushdie plays critically with a number of the characteristic dangers of any one description. To the modernist who strives for a single best representation as a certified "fact" for broad acceptance, Rushdie's critique is sharp and disruptive. To the postmodernist who seeks not privileged knowledge products but a cultural process of pluralistic conversation, Rushdie provides both insight and leadership to a political cause.

In the scene just described, Haroun and Rashid wrap themselves in the Lamination to alleviate a physical discomfort brought about by not behaving "sensibly." The Lamination is an assertion of sense over nonsense, reason over unreason, a palliation of uneasiness through the powers of logic.

Bernstein (1983) would describe Haroun and Rashid's discomfort as "Cartesian anxiety," a state of dis-ease and uncertainty for which the modernist prescribes foundational knowledge. To know and represent in the modernist sense is to epistemologically salve the human insecurities of living in a chaotic, disordered, and painful world. The cold are bundled in the apparent warmth of reasoned prediction and control.

Additionally, we notice that once the two Rushdie characters put on the Laminations, they are visually lost, no longer observable beneath the shine and gleamy of the representation. In this storied gesture, Rushdie has hit on a crucial point concerning the relationship of reality and representations. As we create a representation of reality, we simultaneously transfer our attention and discussion from that reality to the new representation. The reality is murky, ambiguous, difficult to grasp, while the representation inevitably takes on our social science and narrative standards of internal coherence and logical consistency. Reality, in whatever sense it may have been available to us to observe and describe, retires behind the very description we construct. The symbols and signifiers of reality, which modernists take to be mirroring reality itself, rise to center stage as new realities in and of themselves.

Ironically, the transparent Lamination that submerges reality into the background seems to provide a clear lens through which one may easily observe the underlying reality. It oddly occludes as it appears to clarify. As Haroun looks through the transparent Lamination at himself, he sees not his body and clothes but a "faint, gleamy sheen," a newly contrived surface image. Likewise, we may reflect that when we are only *reading* a textual representation—whether in our reading of Rushdie or *Time* magazine or *Exceptional Children*—we may mistakenly take the "faint, gleamy sheen" of the text to be the Thing-in-Itself.

Stories and Solidarity

Rorty (1989) writes of the unity of a postmodern community as "solidarity," emphasizing the local and specific bonding of a group who share a common identity. He claims that "our sense of solidarity is strongest when those with whom the solidarity is expressed are thought of as 'one of us,' where 'us' means something smaller and more local than the human race" (p. 191). Such a moral connection may not occur because we believe we are essentially the same as all other persons. Rorty contends that humans are incapable of such a universal, decontextualized morality. He describes a morality and unity that is specific to one's sense of local connection to persons considered to be of the same group.

Local community identities are encouraged and maintained by the telling of stories, the invocation of cultural and personal narratives that allow a people to feel unified, to make livable sense of their past, to organize their present situation, and to feel hopeful about their future. Such stories are best understood as neither true nor false, but meaningful in making and continuing a community.

Haroun and Rashid learn this lesson as they leave behind the wondrous Lands of Gup and Chup and return to their home, the Sad City of K. In the Sad City of K, smokestacks billow out sadness all day long, and not one citizen wears a smile. The reason for the sadness? The city has forgotten its name. They know only that the name begins with K. They are a town without a name, a community without a sense of identity, a people without hope.

Upon arrival in K, Haroun and Rashid find the townspeople dancing in the rainy streets. Haroun is baffled. Such joy cannot be real. A policeman provides the answer.

> "I'll tell you what we're happy about," said a policeman who chanced to be floating by on an upturned umbrella. "We remembered the city's name."
>
> "Well, out with it, tell us quickly," Rashid insisted, feeling excited.
>
> "Kahani," said the policeman brightly as he floated off down the flooded street. "Isn't it a beautiful name for a city? It means 'story,' you know." (pp. 209–210)

A town that knows it is a story is a town of solidarity, a people of beauty, a community involved each day in constructing themselves and their commonalities. They have a lively process, the storying of local identity, that propels them toward a future that can be brighter than the present.

A Special Education Future: Local Stories and Solidarity

In this chapter, I have described the field of special education as embracing two forms of stories, the first serving as the source and justification for the second. The first form is the grand narrative of modernism, the philosophical foundation of modern social science. This is the belief that an external, objective reality may be apprehended and represented in text through specific rational operations. These operations are scientific methodologies and vocabularies. Supported by this grand narrative are the disability stories—the conditions of mental retardation, learning disabilities, and so on—which I believe to be our primary means of explaining the activities of students designated "exceptional."

If, as the postmodernists contend, our adherence to these two forms of narrative cannot be supported by claims to truthfulness or factuality, then special educators may begin to view these stories as

historical and bureaucratic artifacts, aspects of an international special education and professional science that may be questioned and contested on local levels. This may bring about opportunities for the making of new stories: nongeneralizable tales of identity generating meaning for individuals and small educational communities.

My concern at this point is not so much to answer the question, "What stories should special education tell?" I prefer to encourage an inclusive storying process whereby teachers, students, and parents may confront, unseat, and move beyond the hegemonic modern narratives to develop their own small-scale, communal meanings. Whereas social science and the disability constructs foster standardized meanings and identities, local explanations of "who we are" and "what is important to us" may allow for the development of greater personal freedom and a less hierarchical classroom or school community.

A supervisor and a group of special education teachers at a specific school may mentally bracket the modernist social science and disability understandings, acknowledging them as categories and vocabularies central within funding and legal considerations but unhelpful in the discussion of issues of student needs and possible paths of action. The conventional vocabularies of disability conditions, characteristics, and severity may be set aside in order to open up a dialogue among professionals, parents, and students. That dialogue might be called "open," roughly meaning that the opinion and contribution of each participant is accepted, valued, and respected. No perspective transcends others as the bearer of "scientific truth" because even that perspective is limited and humanly constructed. A flexible, ad hoc community then forms around the general goal of building ways of making meaning that are beneficial to the lives of the students and their families.

Such a process of relationship may develop what Rorty (1989) calls solidarity—"the ability to think of people wildly different from ourselves as included in the range of 'us.'" To be "in the range of us" is to be equal yet not the same. In solidarity, goals of valuing individual uniqueness and building group unity are interdependent.

The local construction of solidarity—whether it be among members of an entire school community or between one student and one teacher—rarely occurs in a political vacuum in which the standard bearers of modern social science and disability stories kindly step aside. These two modernist story forms are pervasive and powerful, often thriving as assumed, unassailable realities within the thoughts and words of administrators, practitioners, and students. Although, as Becker (1932/1968) noted, such "facts" do not have the physical consistency and strength of bricks, they may indeed stand up like a solid brick wall when opposed or questioned in classroom practice. Many aspects of our current special education systems hold these two modern stories to be pillars of progress and virtue, making the practitioner who doubts or opposes them seem unprofessional and misguided.

Recommendations?
Two Postmodern Examples

By convention, a chapter such as this often concludes with a series of recommendations, a fairly specific guide for how to bring the ideas to life in practices, programs, and policies. While my discussion of solidarity certainly suggests forms of community supported by postmodern philosophy, I must conclude that the same postmodern philosophy does not call for the usual recommendations for professional action. The convention of one university faculty member presenting a summary of research findings and theoretical stances in order to somewhat universally prescribe the actions of persons in specific local contexts seems to run counter to my stated hope of supporting prac-

tical conversations lacking hegemony and universality. A forum of open dialogue may not tolerate expert pronouncements.

Instead, I will conclude this chapter by providing two examples of what I consider to be postmodern pedagogy and scholarship, two small stories of hope in a new key. These examples demonstrate teaching performances of what Gergen (1994) calls "dislodgement," intentional action that "loosens the grip of the conventional" (p. 58). Dominant cultural constructs and vocabularies that have become objectified and assumed "truths" are opened up to critique and recontextualized as merely situated accounts lacking universal factual authority. In special education, this often means a teaching process in which teacher and student confront and overturn the disability stories in favor of narratives offering life conditions and possibilities not typically open to "disabled" persons.

Duplass and Smith (1995) demonstrate a form of "dislodgement" pedagogy and narrative research in their nurturing of a teacher-student relationship in which the student himself contests his diagnosed disability. Over the course of many months of journal writing and discussion, the middle-school student wonders what it means to be "emotionally disturbed" and what it might mean for him to regard himself as not falling within this disability story. Gradually, he pioneers a more personally meaningful and livable story of self, one that implies increased personal strength, ability, and self-direction. Both teacher and student view the student's redefinition of himself as "able" instead of "disabled" as central to the development of a hopeful self-image (see Wanswart, 1995). Although most modernist special education practice focuses on teaching "normal" behaviors to the child designated "abnormal,"—a procedure that often only serves to reinforce the power of the socially constructed normality/abnormality distinction—this form of critical pedagogy confronts "abnormality" both within the student's beliefs and within the school system, utilizing the fluid arena of human connection as the space of personal transformation.

In collaboration with a small group of "developmentally disabled" adolescents, Coelho de Amorim and Cavalcante (1992) construct a similar transformational arena in the context of creating a puppet play. Over the course of eleven months (meeting once a week for 2 hours), the group home residents write a script, construct scenery, and perform a puppet play for videotaping. Staff members remain nondirective, interacting with the participants through probing questions instead of supervisory orders or commands. Additionally, the staff sets no schedule of production, deadlines, or standards of quality for the project. The participants work out all such issues among themselves.

Coelho de Amorim and Cavalcante (1992) describe this process as one of play, imagination, and imagination within the realm of self-stories. Through the activity, participants gradually reconstruct "narratives of self . . . the stories of stigmatized individuals who encountered the myths of deficiency constructed and rooted in their own societies" (p. 149). The puppet play serves as a symbolic medium and climactic moment for confronting issues of personal and social identity. It is "both a spontaneous and indispensible rite of passage . . . through which disabled persons attempt to transcend their current disabling status which led them to social marginalization" (p. 153). To young adults occupying positions such as "institutionalized patient," "sick person," or "dangerous person" within society, the puppet play process allows an opportunity for the development of new roles of personal power and self-determination. These nondeficit roles are simultaneously lived within the participants' experiences of being in charge of their own play and "played out" symbolically within the puppet drama they create.

Toying with the phrase "What a mess!" the participants produce a play called "The Story of Walter A. Mess," the narrative of a young group home resident attempting to deal with the many, messy practicalities and decisions of his life. Walter listens to both a good angel and a bad angel in sorting out how to handle a variety of life responsibilities. In developing this story, the lead scriptwriter (Liz) struggles when facing the question of how to end the story. How does Walter deal with his messy life? There are three conclusions to consider:

1. Nothing will change. He will muddle on within a mess.
2. In time, Walter will sort out his priorities and take control of his life.
3. The answer is uncertain. A question mark.

After deciding to solve the dilemma through a democratic vote, the puppeteers choose the third alternative, leaving the play open-ended so that the audience must decide what happens to Walter. This decision demonstrates the group's sense that each individual, faced with the stigmatized roles and limited life possibilities of deficiency labels, must sort out his or her own identity. The individual may assert some power over the socially constructed self, accepting or tossing aside the marginalized status dictated by others. Still, despite this individual power over self-narration, the future remains uncertain. No one can say how it will go for any person.

Each of these examples of postmodern teaching involves the setting aside of a professional vocabulary, knowledge base, and power in order to support the struggle of "exceptional" individuals confronting their socially constructed positions. Such work leads to unified efforts between professionals and students in the coconstruction of meaning, in the practical and political struggle to create improved possibilities and choices. Perhaps within the contextual meanings, words, and knowledges of small groups and individuals struggling to make better lives, limited stories may be created in order to make provisional sense of things. Special educators might collaborate with persons defined as deficient under the grand narrative of modernism, working together to conceptually and socially redefine lives, constructing value and hope in stigmatized social spaces.

References

Anderson, G. L., & Barrera, I. (1995). Critical constructivist research and special education: Expanding our lens on social reality and exceptionality. *Remedial and Special Education, 16*(3), 142–149.

Becker, C. (1968). Everyman his own historian. In R. W. Winks (Ed.), *The historian as detective* (pp. 5–23). New York: Harper & Row. (Original work published 1932)

Bernstein, R. J. (1983). *Beyond objectivism and relativism: Science, hermeneutics, and praxis.* Philadelphia: University of Pennsylvania Press.

Clifford, J. (1986). Introduction: Partial truths. In J. Clifford & G. E. Marcus (Eds.), *Writing culture: The poetics and politics of ethnography* (pp. 1–26). Berkeley: University of California Press.

Coelho de Amorim, A., & Cavalcante, F. G. (1992). Narrations of the self: Video production in a marginalized subculture. In S. McNamee & K. Gergen (Eds.), *Therapy as social construction.* London: Sage.

Danforth, S. (1995). Toward a critical theory approach to lives considered emotionally disturbed. *Behavioral Disorders, 20*(2), 136–143.

Danforth, S., Rhodes, W. C., & Smith, T. (1995). Inventing the future: Postmodern challenges in educational reform. In J. L. Paul, H. Rosselli, & D. Evans (Eds.), *Integrating school restructuring and special education reform* (pp. 214–236). Orlando: Harcourt Brace Jovanovich.

Duplass, D., & Smith, T. (1995). Hearing Dennis through his own voice. *Behavioral Disorders, 20*(2), 144–148.

Gergen, K. J. (1991). *The saturated self.* New York: Basic Books.

Gergen, K. J. (1994). Exploring the postmodern: Perils or potentials? *American Psychologist, 49*(5), 412–416.

Gross, M. (1987). *The psychological society.* New York: Random House.

Guba, E. G. (1990). *The paradigm dialog.* Newbury Park, CA: Sage.

Howe, K. R. (1985). Two dogmas of educational research. *Educational Researcher, 14,* 10–18.

Kuhn, T. S. (1962). *The structure of scientific revolutions.* Chicago: University of Chicago Press.

Lyotard, J. F. (1984). *The postmodern condition: A report on knowledge.* Minneapolis: University of Minnesota Press.

McPhail, J. C. (1995). Phenomenology as philosophy and method: Application to ways of doing special education. *Remedial and Special Education, 16*(3), 159–165.

Reid, D. K., Robinson, S. J., & Bunsen, T. D. (1995). Empiricism and beyond: Expanding the boundaries of special education. *Remedial and Special Education, 16*(3), 131–141.

Rorty, R. (1979). *Philosophy and the mirror of nature.* Princeton, NJ: Princeton University Press.

Rorty, R. (1989). *Contingency, irony, and solidarity.* New York: Cambridge University Press.

Rosaldo, R. (1993). *Culture and truth: The remaking of social analysis.* Boston: Beacon Press.

Rosenau, P. M. (1992). *Postmodernism and the social sciences: Insights, inroads, and intrusions.* Princeton, NJ: Princeton University Press.

Rushdie, S. (1991). *Haroun and the sea of stories.* New York: Penguin.

Sailor, W., & Skrtic, T. (1995). American education in the postmodern era. In J. L. Paul, H. Rosselli, & D. Evans (Eds.), *Integrating school restructuring and special education Reform* (pp. 418–432). Orlando: Harcourt Brace Jovanovich.

Skrtic, T. (1991). *Behind special education: A critical analysis of professional culture and school organization.* Denver: Love Publishing.

Wanswart, W. L. (1995). Teaching as a way of knowing: Observing and responding to students' abilities. *Remedial and Special Education, 16*(3), 166–177.

NAME INDEX

SUBJECT INDEX

TO THE OWNER OF THIS BOOK:

We hope that you have found *Foundations of Special Education: Basic Knowledge Informing Research and Practice in Special Education* useful. So that this book can be improved in a future edition, would you take the time to complete this sheet and return it? Thank you.

School and address: _____

Department: _____

Instructor's name: _____

1. What I like most about this book is: _____

_____

_____

2. What I like least about this book is: _____

_____

_____

3. My general reaction to this book is: _____

_____

4. The name of the course in which I used this book is: _____

_____

5. Were all of the chapters of the book assigned for you to read? _____

   If not, which ones weren't? _____

6. In the space below, or on a separate sheet of paper, please write specific suggestions for improving this book and anything else you'd care to share about your experience in using the book.

_____

_____

_____

_____

_____

Optional:

Your name: _____ Date: _____

May Brooks/Cole quote you, either in promotion for *Foundations of Special Education* or in future publishing ventures?

Yes: _____ No: _____

Sincerely,

James L. Paul et al.

FOLD HERE

NO POSTAGE
NECESSARY
IF MAILED
IN THE
UNITED STATES

BUSINESS REPLY MAIL
FIRST CLASS   PERMIT NO. 358   PACIFIC GROVE, CA

POSTAGE WILL BE PAID BY ADDRESSEE

ATT: *James L. Paul et al.* _____

**Brooks/Cole Publishing Company
511 Forest Lodge Road
Pacific Grove, California 93950-9968**

FOLD HERE